Mika Colling

INSIDE STORIES III

SECOND EDITION

D0768187

Edited by
RICHARD DAVIES
JERRY WOWK

THOMSON
™
NELSON

071978

Copyright © Harcourt Canada Ltd.
Thomson Nelson
1120 Birchmount Road
Toronto, Ontario M1K 5G4
1-800-668-0671
www.nelson.com

About the Editors

Richard Davies

Richard has taught English in Alberta for 30 years, and has co-authored over 40 textbooks and guides. He teaches at Strathcona High School (Edmonton Public Schools), and is an established poet, musician, and film classification consultant for the province of Alberta.

Jerry Wowk

A teacher at Archbishop O'Leary High School in Edmonton Alberta, Jerry has taught junior high for most of his teaching career, with a brief stint as Edmonton Catholic Schools district consultant, focussing on Assessment in Language Arts.

National Library of Canada Cataloguing in Publication Data

Main entry under title:

    Inside stories III

2nd ed.
First ed. had title: Inside stories for senior students.
ISBN 0-7747-1514-6

1. Short stories, English. 2. English fiction—20th century.
3. Short stories, Canadian (English) 4. Canadian fiction (English)—20th century.
I. Davies, Richard II. Wowk, Jerry III. Title: Inside stories III.

PN6120.2.I59 2002   823'.01080914   C2002-900822-0

Project Manager: Ian Nussbaum
Developmental Editor: Sheila Barry
Production Editor: Gil Adamson
Production Coordinator: Cheri Westra
Permissions Coordinator: Karen Becker
Permissions Editor: Mary Rose MacLachlan
Photo Research: Maria DeCambra
Cover and Interior Design: Sonya V. Thursby/Opus House
Page Composition: Carolyn Sebestyen
Cover Illustration: Joyce Wieland; Detail from *Boat Tragedy*, 1964 (See back cover of book for full image and credit)
Printing and Binding: Transcontinental

Printed in Canada
 3 4 5   09 08 07 06

Remembering …
Lisa Renee MacDonnell
(friend, teacher, and remarkable person)

Table of Contents

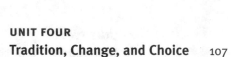

Acknowledgements

The editors and publisher gratefully acknowledge the teacher-reviewers listed below for their contribution to the development of this anthology.

Bryan Ellefson
Learning Team Facilitator
Palliser Regional Schools
Lethbridge, Alberta

Maureen Fazzari
Teacher, Notre Dame
Secondary School
Halton Catholic District
School Board
Burlington, Ontario

Carolyn Lewis-Shillington
Teacher, McNally High School
Edmonton Public Schools
Edmonton, Alberta

Carol Mayne
Teacher, Louis St. Laurent
Senior High School
Edmonton Catholic Schools
Edmonton, Alberta

Myron Moxley
Teacher, Kitsilano
Secondary School
Vancouver School Board
Vancouver, British Columbia

Margaret Stevens
Teacher, Oxford Regional
High School
Chignecto-Central Regional
School Board
Oxford, Nova Scotia

Shirley Turchet
Teacher, Middlefield
Collegiate Institute
York Region District
School Board
Markham, Ontario

To the Student

Welcome to *Inside Stories III*. This rich short story anthology contains 44 selections for you to think about, discuss, and enjoy. It contains many famous stories, including "The Rocking-Horse Winner," "The Painted Door," and "The Lottery." Half the writers are Canadian (including masters such as Alice Munro, Carol Shields, and Alistair MacLeod), and many of the stories are by writers from diverse cultural backgrounds, including Native-Canadian, French-Canadian, Chinese, Vietnamese, Japanese, East Indian, Arab, African, Caribbean, Brazilian, Colombian, and Russian.

The book is centred on eight common literary themes studied in grade 12: Individuals vs. Society; Outsiders and Isolation; Tradition, Change, and Choice; The Family; Relationships; Reality vs. Illusion; Ideals, Dreams, and Obsessions; Goals, Journeys, and Quests. It also includes examples of personal and critical responses to various stories, some of which are written by the authors and editors themselves.

Following each story are response questions and activities for you to explore in discussion, writing, and representation. At the end of this book you will find a section entitled "Responding to Story" that will help you organize your responses to the stories you read. As well, you will find information about the authors and a comprehensive glossary of fiction terms to review and use as you talk and write about the stories.

We wish you success in your studies of the short story this year. May the experiences and insights provided by *Inside Stories III* leave each of you with a deeper understanding of yourself, human nature, literature, and the world.

R.D.
J.W.

Critical Reading of Short Stories

Although this anthology supports a number of response approaches, it focuses mainly on the development of critical reading skills necessary for graduating students in their classroom and examination work. This section is a brief introduction to the questioning techniques and approaches often used by critical readers.

There are certain recurring elements to watch for and observe in the first reading of any story:

CHARACTER

- Who is the protagonist? (Note: terms used in this section are defined in the Glossary, which begins on p. 498.)
- What is the protagonist's goal, problem, or conflict?
- Is there an antagonist or character foil?
- When a character makes a choice, what might be her or his motivation?
- How and why is the protagonist changed or unchanged by the end of the story?

PLOT

- What happens in the story? What are its key moments or episodes?
- Is there a crisis or any foreshadowing of events to come?
- Where does the climax occur? How is it a turning point?
- How does the story end? Is there a resolution to its main conflict, or does it have an indeterminate (unresolved) ending?

CONFLICT

- Who or what is in conflict? What type of conflict is it? (External: protagonist vs. other characters, nature, or limiting circumstances; Internal: protagonist vs. self.)
- What causes the conflict? Is it resolved? Why or why not?

POINT OF VIEW

- From whose point of view is the story told?
- What does the choice of point of view (i.e., first person, limited omniscient, omniscient, or objective) contribute to the reader's experience of the story and knowledge about the characters and conflict?

SETTING, ATMOSPHERE, AND MOOD

- Where and when does the story take place? Is a particular historical, geographical, or cultural context used?
- Is the atmosphere of the story an important element? If suspense is an aspect of the story, how is it built up and maintained?
- What mood does the story create in the reader?
- How might setting and atmosphere affect or reflect the plot, characters, and conflict?

IRONY

- Does the writer use irony for presentation of plot, conflict, characterization, or theme?
- What types of irony are present—verbal, dramatic, or situational?

SYMBOLS

- Is symbolism (a pattern or sequence of symbols) used in the story?
- Are there any symbolic characters, actions, settings, or objects? How might these relate to characters, conflict, and theme?

THEME

- What main theme or idea is presented by the story?
- What other ideas or subthemes are presented by the story?
- What specific details support the theme?

PURPOSE

- Why did the writer write the story? What did the writer want to accomplish?
- Does the writer succeed in fulfilling her or his purpose? Why or why not?

STYLE

- What words could be used to describe the way in which the story is written?
- What is unique or original about the writer's use of story structure, methods, imagery, and diction?
- How does the style affect the reader's response to the story?

After a first reading, the critical reader typically returns to the story and focuses on some of its more fundamental aspects. Overall, she or he tries to

1. *identify basic fiction elements*—(e.g., protagonist, setting, point of view, etc.)
2. *understand motivation*—Why does the protagonist make certain choices? Does the protagonist have a goal, motivation, or internal conflict?
3. *respond to mood*—How does the reader's mood or the atmosphere of the story reflect and illuminate the protagonist's feelings and conflicts?
4. *recognize symbols and symbolism*—Symbols are often clues to conflicts and themes. Sometimes the symbols are arranged in a pattern (called symbolism) that invites extended or in-depth reader interpretation.
5. *consider different perspectives*—Often, a story contains more than one perspective or point of view. How might this fact influence conflict?
6. *reflect on the significance of the title*—Titles often help the reader to focus on a character, setting, symbol, conflict, or theme.

Considered together, all of the above help to "open up" a story's meanings and possibilities for the reader.

Sample Analysis of a Specific Text

Read the following story, "Identities" by W.D. Valgardson, by yourself. Write down questions or comments that occur to you as you read, and then compile as many as you can once you finish reading and before you proceed with the following guided question activity.

W.D. Valgardson
Identities

1   Normally, he goes clean-shaven into the world, but the promise of a Saturday liquid with sunshine draws him first from his study to the back yard, from there to his front lawn. The smell of burning leaves stirs the memories of childhood car rides, narrow lanes adrift with yellow leaves, girls on plodding horses, unattended stands piled high with pumpkins, onions, beets, so that each one was, in its own way, a still life. Always, there were salmon tins glinting with silver, set above hand-painted signs instructing purchasers to deposit twenty-five or fifty cents. This act of faith, containing all the stories he has read in childhood about the North—cabins left unlocked, filled with supplies for hapless wayfarers—wakes in him a desire to temporarily abandon the twice-cut yards and hundred-year-old oaks.

2   He does not hurry, for he has no destination. He meanders, instead, through the suburban labyrinth of cul-de-sacs, bays and circles, losing and finding himself endlessly. Becoming lost is made all the easier because the houses repeat themselves with superficial variations. There grows within him, however, a vague unease with symmetry, with nothing left to chance, no ragged edges, no unkempt vacant lots, no houses rendered unique by necessity and indifference.

3   The houses all face the sun. They have no artificial divisions. There is room enough for everyone. Now, as he passes grey stone gates, the yards are all proscribed by stiff picket fences, and quickly, a certain untidiness creeps in: a fragment of glass, a chocolate bar wrapper, a plastic horse, cracked sidewalks with ridges of stiff grass. Although he has on blue jeans—matching pants and jacket made in Paris—he is driving a grey Mercedes Benz. Gangs of young men follow the car with their unblinking eyes. The young men stand and lean in tired, watchful knots close to phone booths and seedy-looking grocery stores.

4   Their hair glistens as though shellacked. Their jackets gleam with studs. Eagles, tigers, wolves and serpents ride their backs.

5   He passes a ten-foot wire fence enclosing a playground bare of equipment and pounded flat. The gate is double locked, the fence cut and rolled into a cone. Three boys throw stones at pigeons. Paper clogs the fence like drifted snow. The school is sheathed in heavy screens. Its yellow brick is pockmarked, chipped.

6   The houses are squat, as though they were once taller and have, slowly, sunk into the ground. Each has a band of dirt around the bottom. The blue glow of television sets lights the windows. On the front steps of a red-roofed house, a man sits. He wears black pants, a tartan vest, a brown snap-brimmed hat. Beside him is a suitcase.

7   Fences here are little more than fragments. Cars jam the narrow streets, and he worries that he might strike the unkempt children who dart back and forth like startled fish. Street lights come on. He takes them as a signal to return the way he came, but it has been a reckless, haphazard path. Retracing it is impossible. He is overtaken by sudden guilt. He has left no message for his wife.

8   There have been no trees or drifting leaves, no stands covered in produce, no salmon tins, but time has run away with him. His wife, he realizes, will have returned from bridge, his children gathered for supper. He also knows that, at first, they have blamed his absence on a neighbour's hospitality and gin. However, by the time he can return, annoyance will have blossomed into alarm. His safe return will, he knows from childhood and years of being locked in domestic grief, degenerate to recriminations and apology.

9   Faced with this, he decides to call the next time he sees a store or phone booth. So intent is he upon the future that he dangerously ignores the present and does not notice the police car, concealed in the shadows of a side street, nose out and follow him.

10   Ahead, there is a small store with windows covered in hand-painted signs and vertical metal bars. On the edge of the light, three young men and a girl slouch. One of the men has a beard and, in spite of the advancing darkness, wears sunglasses. He has on a fringed leather vest. His companions wear leather jackets. Their peaked caps make their heads seem flat, their foreheads nonexistent. The girl is better looking than she should be for such companions. She is long-legged and wears a white turtleneck sweater that accentuates her breasts.

11   In spite of his car, he hopes his day-old beard, which he strokes upward with the heel of his hand, will, when combined with his clothes, provide immunity. He slips his wallet into his shirt pocket, does up the metal buttons on his jacket and slips a ten-dollar bill into his back pocket. Recalling a television show, he decides that if he is accosted, he will say that the ten is all he's got, that he stole the car and ask them if they know a buyer.

12   He eases out of the car, edges nervously along the fender and past the grille. The store window illuminates the sidewalk like a stage. Beyond the light, everything is obscured by darkness. He is so intent upon the three men and the girl that he does not notice the police car drift against the curb, nor the officer who advances with a pistol in his hand.

13   When the officer, who is inexperienced, who is nervous because of the neighbourhood, who is suspicious because of the car and because he has been trained to see an unshaven man in blue jeans as a potential thief and not as a probable owner, orders him to halt, he is surprised. When he turns part way around and recognizes the uniform, he does not feel fear but relief. Instinctively relaxing, certain of his safety, in the last voluntary movement of his life, he reaches his hand toward his wallet for his identity.

Now take a look at the story a second time and write down any further questions that occur to you.

Compare the following questions with those you raised in your first read-through. Are any of them similar? What new elements did you notice as you read and reread the story?

(Alternatively, you might try answering your questions and the following ones with a partner or in a small group. This will give you fresh perspectives on this particular story and on the process of critical reading—it may even answer some of the more difficult questions.)

Identities

- What does the title make the reader think of? What does it mean to have an identity?
- What are some ways in which people are "identified" in their lives?

1   Normally, he goes clean-shaven into the world, but the promise of a Saturday liquid with sunshine draws him first from his study to the back yard, from there to his front lawn. The smell of burning leaves stirs the memories of childhood car rides, narrow lanes adrift with yellow leaves, girls on plodding horses, unattended stands piled high with pumpkins, onions, beets, so that each one was, in its own way, a still life. Always, there were salmon tins glinting with silver, set above hand-painted signs instructing purchasers to deposit twenty-five or fifty cents. This act of faith, containing all the stories he has read in childhood about the North—cabins left unlocked, filled with supplies for hapless wayfarers—wakes in him a desire to temporarily abandon the twice-cut yards and hundred-year-old oaks.

- How is the first word in the story important?
- Who is the protagonist? What sort of neighbourhood does he live in?
- Why does he leave home? What is his motivation or goal?

2   He does not hurry, for he has no destination. He meanders, instead, through the suburban labyrinth of cul-de-sacs, bays and circles, losing and finding himself endlessly. Becoming lost is made all the easier because the houses repeat themselves with superficial variations. There grows within him, however, a vague unease with symmetry, with nothing left to chance, no ragged edges, no unkempt vacant lots, no houses rendered unique by necessity and indifference.

- Does he know where he is going? Why does he get lost?
- What note of tension is introduced in this paragraph? Which words create mood?

3   The houses all face the sun. They have no artificial divisions. There is room enough for everyone. Now, as he passes grey stone gates, the yards are all proscribed by stiff picket fences, and quickly, a certain untidiness creeps in: a fragment of glass, a chocolate bar wrapper, a plastic horse, cracked sidewalks with ridges of stiff grass. Although he has on blue jeans—matching pants and jacket made in Paris—he is driving a grey Mercedes Benz. Gangs of young men follow the car with their unblinking eyes. The young men stand and lean in tired, watchful knots close to phone booths and seedy-looking grocery stores.

- Describe the new setting. How do this neighbourhood and its people contrast with his own neighbourhood and himself?
- What does the reader learn about his social status? What are other people's reactions to him in this section?

4   Their hair glistens as though shellacked. Their jackets gleam with studs. Eagles, tigers, wolves and serpents ride their backs.

- Whose hair "glistens"? What is the reader's impression of the people described?
- What mood is created by the images in this paragraph? Are any of the images symbolic or stereotypical?

5   He passes a ten-foot wire fence enclosing a playground bare of equipment and pounded flat. The gate is double locked, the fence cut and rolled into a cone. Three boys throw stones at pigeons. Paper clogs the fence like drifted snow. The school is sheathed in heavy screens. Its yellow brick is pockmarked, chipped.

- What impressions are created by the writer's description of the playground and the school? So far in the story, what have all the reader's impressions been based on?

6   The houses are squat, as though they were once taller and have, slowly, sunk into the ground. Each has a band of dirt around the bottom. The blue glow of television sets lights the windows. On the front steps of a red-roofed house, a man sits. He wears black pants, a tartan vest, a brown snap-brimmed hat. Beside him is a suitcase.

- What does the first sentence suggest about the neighbourhood? Why is the man sitting on the step? Why might this man be mentioned?
- Make a list of the colours used so far in the story and speculate on possible associations.

7   Fences here are little more than fragments. Cars jam the narrow streets, and he worries that he might strike the unkempt children who dart back and forth like startled fish. Street lights come on. He takes them as a signal to return the way he came, but it has been a reckless, haphazard path. Retracing it is impossible. He is overtaken by sudden guilt. He has left no message for his wife.

- How does the protagonist feel at this point? Why is he nervous? Does he have any reason to be?

8   There have been no trees or drifting leaves, no stands covered in produce, no salmon tins, but time has run away with him. His wife, he realizes, will have returned from bridge, his children gathered for supper. He also knows that, at first, they have blamed his absence on a neighbour's hospitality and gin. However, by the time he can return, annoyance will have blossomed into alarm. His safe return will, he knows from childhood and years of being locked in domestic grief, degenerate to recriminations and apology.

- How does this paragraph tie in with an earlier one in the story? What is learned of the man's family's attitude toward him? Look up the word "recriminations," and then describe his marriage.

9   Faced with this, he decides to call the next time he sees a store or phone booth. So intent is he upon the future that he dangerously ignores the present and does not notice the police car, concealed in the shadows of a side street, nose out and follow him.

- In what sense is he unaware of the present? Why is he being followed by the police?

10   Ahead, there is a small store with windows covered in hand-painted signs and vertical metal bars. On the edge of the light, three young men and a girl slouch. One of the men has a beard and, in spite of the advancing darkness, wears sunglasses. He has on a fringed leather vest. His companions wear leather jackets. Their peaked caps make their heads seem flat, their foreheads nonexistent. The girl is better looking than she should be for such companions. She is long-legged and wears a white turtleneck sweater that accentuates her breasts.

- Why are there bars on the windows? What are the four people like? How can the reader tell? What is the protagonist's attitude toward the girl? How does this reveal his character?

11   In spite of his car, he hopes his day-old beard, which he strokes upward with the heel of his hand, will, when combined with his clothes, provide immunity. He slips his wallet into his shirt pocket, does up the metal buttons on his jacket and slips a ten-dollar bill into his back pocket. Recalling a television show, he decides that if he is accosted, he will say that the ten is all he's got, that he stole the car and ask them if they know a buyer.

- What kind of "immunity" is he thinking about? Why does he put his wallet in his shirt pocket? Why is he prepared to tell a false story?

12   He eases out of the car, edges nervously along the fender and past the grille. The store window illuminates the sidewalk like a stage. Beyond the light, everything is obscured by darkness. He is so intent upon the three men and the girl that he does not notice the police car drift against the curb, nor the officer who advances with a pistol in his hand.

- In what sense is the man on "a stage"? Why does the policeman have a gun in his hand?

13   When the officer, who is inexperienced, who is nervous because of the neighbourhood, who is suspicious because of the car and because he has been trained to see an unshaven man in blue jeans as a potential thief and not as a probable owner, orders him to halt, he is surprised. When he turns part way around and recognizes the uniform, he does not feel fear but relief. Instinctively relaxing, certain of his safety, in the last voluntary movement of his life, he reaches his hand toward his wallet for his identity.

- In this context, what is likely the policeman's view of the protagonist? Is there any foreshadowing that the officer would view the protagonist this way? What is ironic about the protagonist's reaction to seeing the policeman?
- What do the words "last voluntary movement of his life" suggest? What will probably happen next?
- What are some meanings of the last sentence?
- Why is the story written in the present tense? Was this a good choice on the writer's part?

On the surface, "Identities" seems to be about an urban man in search of an identity, perhaps one he lost (e.g., "memories of childhood car rides"). He is a well-to-do person who appears to be unhappy or unfulfilled by his relatively prosperous lifestyle.

As he drives, he moves away from a familiar neighbourhood to another, more mysterious one. For him, it is like experiencing a different world, one that identifies itself to him through its surface images. For instance, the images of the young men in paragraph three introduce a note of menace, later revived in paragraph ten.

Ironically, the man has temporarily lost his usual identity or left it behind him. His identity at home has possibly contributed to his leaving; his family assumes he is drinking somewhere, and there are details that suggest an unhappy marriage.

In paragraph eleven, he prepares to change his identity to fit in with his new environment, but he cannot change the look of his expensive car. Unfortunately for him, the policeman also judges him on the basis of *his* appearance. Just as *he* judges others, he in turn is (mis)judged by a police officer. Ironically, he is shot because his usual identity is not visible in this foreign context.

Putting all this information together, one can reasonably conclude that this story is an exploration of identity and, in part, an exploration of how people define themselves and are, in turn, defined by others.

The theme of the story might be stated in a number of different ways, as in the following sample thematic statements:

- Identity is something superficial that can be easily misunderstood, sometimes with tragic results.
- People identify both themselves and others on the basis of appearances that can often be deceptive and dangerous.

In critical reading, it is not unusual to discuss or write about literature this concisely. Composing thematic statements is one effective means of communicating the main idea of a story. The reader who is able to state a story's theme thoughtfully and accurately in her or his own words can feel confident that a reasonable understanding of the story has been attained and expressed.

To review, it is a good idea when reading critically to ask yourself many questions—especially of the who, what, why, and how variety—when beginning the initial study of a short story.

It also makes sense to look at the parts and fiction elements of the story and to pay close attention to the implications and meanings of words, images, and symbols. This approach gives any would-be critical reader a foothold for understanding that will eventually lead to paraphrasing, summarizing, and making concise statements about the story based on specific detail and evidence. ("Responding to Story," the final section of this book, describes the various kinds of responses—personal, creative, and so on—that readers can have to short stories.)

In the rest of this book, you will be reading stories with common literary themes. Along the way, you may be asked to analyze, write about, or present on stories. This introductory section is ultimately a handy reference, then, for illustrating the methods and types of questions that may be necessary to develop your own successful critical readings in the classes that lie ahead.

Individuals vs. Society

Every face is the other face.
The individual is the one illusion.
— *Marguerite Young*

Society is no comfort
To one not sociable.
— *William Shakespeare*

The theme of Individuals vs. Society is one of the most common themes in all of literature. All people are born into societies or social groupings that are organized for common purposes, such as defining standards for social behaviour or moral conduct.

There is an old cliché about "trying to put square pegs in round holes"—in other words, society trying to mould individuals for the sake of conformity. It is not surprising, then, given the average person's uniqueness, that individuals sometimes do not "fit" societal expectations and, therefore, come into conflict with their communities. In this unit, there are five such characters.

In Alice Munro's "The Shining Houses," we meet Mrs. Fullerton, an eccentric outsider who is introduced through the character of Mary, the protagonist. Mary is faced with a dilemma when she defends the old woman against her neighbour-friends, all the while understanding their arguments and foreseeing the likely success of their eviction plans.

In Winnipeg writer Carol Shields' "Invitations," a single woman is besieged with same-day invitations to a variety of social functions, each of which tries to win her over and persuade her to attend. Ultimately, she finds the invitations a threat to her personal life and makes a surprising, but entirely appropriate, decision.

"Black Walls" is a humorous story from China about a man in an apartment complex who does not play "the social game" and elects to paint his interior walls black, much to the annoyance and fear of his more conventional neighbours.

Shirley Jackson's classic story "The Lottery" is about an annual draw held in a small town that demands a great sacrifice for the community on the part of the winner. Jackson's story is a timeless social commentary that challenges readers' expectations and, simultaneously, exposes serious social flaws in the process.

All four stories contain individuals in conflict with their societies. All four stories ask us to side with either the individual or the dominant group. Inevitably, they get us to think vicariously about what *we* would do if we were in the protagonists' positions.

Alice Munro
The Shining Houses

PRE-READING

1. Define the word "dilemma" (then take a look at the Glossary in this book). Recount a situation in which you were presented with a dilemma. What choices were available to you? Which choice did you make? What convinced you to make that choice?

2. What is it that makes a community? With a partner, brainstorm a list of general rules or principles that would be important, perhaps necessary, for a group of individuals to adhere to if they were to consider themselves part of a community.

Mary sat on the back steps of Mrs. Fullerton's house, talking—or really listening—to Mrs. Fullerton, who sold her eggs. She had come in to pay the egg money, on her way to Edith's Debbie's birthday party.

Mrs. Fullerton did not pay calls herself and she did not invite them, but, once a business pretext was established, she liked to talk. And Mary found herself exploring her neighbour's life as she had once explored the lives of grandmothers and aunts—by pretending to know less than she did, asking for some story she had heard before; this way, remembered episodes emerged each time with slight differences of content, meaning, colour, yet with a pure reality that usually attaches to things which are at least part legend. She had almost forgotten that there are people whose lives can be seen like this. She did not talk to many old people any more. Most of the people she knew had lives like her own, in which things were not sorted out yet, and it is not certain if this thing, or that, should be taken seriously. Mrs. Fullerton had no doubts or questions of this kind. How was it possible, for instance, not to take seriously the broad blithe back of Mr. Fullerton, disappearing down the road on a summer day, not to return?

"I didn't know that," said Mary. "I always thought Mr. Fullerton was dead."

"He's no more dead than I am," said Mrs. Fullerton, sitting up straight. A bold Plymouth Rock walked across the bottom step and Mary's little boy, Danny, got up to give rather cautious chase. "He's just gone off on his travels, that's what he is. May of gone up north, may of gone to the States, I don't know. But he's not dead. I would of felt it. He's not old neither, you know, not old like I am. He was my second husband, he was younger. I never made any secret of it. I had this place and raised my children and buried my first husband, before ever Mr. Fullerton came upon the scene. Why, one time down in the post office we was standing together by the wicket and I went over to put a letter in the box and left my bag behind me, and Mr. Fullerton turns to go after me and the girl calls to him, she says, here, your mother's left her purse!"

Mary smiled, answering Mrs. Fullerton's high-pitched and not trustful laughter. Mrs. Fullerton was old, as she had said—older than you might think, seeing her hair still fuzzy and black, her clothes slatternly-gay, dime-store brooches pinned to her ravelling sweater. Her eyes showed it, black as plums, with a soft inanimate sheen; things sank into them and they never changed. The life in her face was all in the nose and mouth, which were always twitching, fluttering, drawing tight grimace-lines down her cheeks. When she came around every Friday on her egg deliveries her hair was curled, her blouse held together by a bunch of cotton flowers, her mouth painted, a spidery and ferocious line of red; she would not show herself to her new neighbours in any sad old-womanish disarray.

"Thought I was his mother," she said. "I didn't care. I had a good laugh. But what I was telling you," she said, "a day in summer, he was off work. He had the ladder up and he was picking me the cherries off of my black-cherry tree. I came out to hang my clothes and there was this man I never seen before in my life, taking the pail of cherries my husband hands down to him. Helping himself, too, not backward, he sat down and ate cherries out of my pail. Who's that, I said to my husband, and he says, just a fellow passing. If he's a friend of yours, I said, he's welcome to stay for supper. What are you talking about, he says, I never seen him before. So I never said another thing. Mr. Fullerton went and talked to him, eating my cherries I intended for a pie, but that man would talk to anybody, tramp, Jehovah's witness, anybody— that didn't need to mean anything."

"And half an hour after that fellow went off," she said, "Mr. Fullerton comes out in his brown jacket and his hat on. I have to meet a man downtown. How long will you be, I said. Oh, not long. So off he goes down the road, walking down to where the old tram went— we was all in the bush then—and something made me look after him. He must be hot in that coat, I said. And that's when I knew he wasn't coming back. Yet I couldn't've expected it, he liked it here. He was talking about putting chinchillas in the back yard. What's in a man's mind even when you're living with him you will never know."

"Was it long ago?" said Mary.

"Twelve years. My boys wanted me to sell then and go and live in rooms. But I said no. I had my hens and a nanny goat too at that time. More or less a pet. I had a pet coon too for a while, used to feed him chewing gum. Well, I said, husbands maybe come and go, but a place you've lived fifty years is something else. Making a joke of it with my family. Besides, I thought, if Mr. Fullerton was to come back, he'd come back here, not knowing where else to go. Of course he'd hardly know where to find me, the way it's changed now. But I always had the idea he might of suffered a loss of memory and it might come back. That has happened.

"I'm not complaining. Sometimes it seems to me about as reasonable a man should go as stay. I don't mind changes, either, that helps out my egg business. But this baby-sitting. All the time one or the other is asking me about baby-sitting. I tell them I got my own house to sit in and I raised my share of children."

Mary, remembering the birthday party, got up and called to her little boy. "I thought I might offer my black cherries for sale next summer," Mrs. Fullerton said. "Come and pick your own and they're fifty cents a box. I can't risk my old bones up a ladder no more."

"That's too much," Mary said, smiling. "They're cheaper than that at the supermarket." Mrs. Fullerton already hated the supermarket for lowering the price of eggs. Mary shook out her last cigarette and left it with her, saying she had another package in her purse. Mrs. Fullerton was fond of a cigarette but would not accept one unless you took her by surprise. Baby-sitting would pay for them, Mary thought. At the same time she was rather pleased with Mrs. Fullerton for being so unaccommodating. When Mary came out of this place, she always felt as if she were passing through barricades. The house and its surroundings were so self-sufficient, with their complicated and seemingly unalterable layout of vegetables and flower beds, apple and cherry trees, wired chicken-run, berry patch and wooden walks, woodpile, a great many roughly built dark little sheds, for hens or rabbits or a goat. Here was no open or straightforward plan, no order that an outsider could understand; yet what was haphazard time had made final. The place had become fixed, impregnable, all its accumulations necessary, until it seemed that even the washtubs, mops, couch springs and stacks of old police magazines on the back porch were there to stay.

Mary and Danny walked down the road that had been called, in Mrs. Fullerton's time, Wicks Road, but was now marked on the maps of the subdivision as Heather Drive. The name of the subdivision was Garden Place, and its streets were named for flowers. On either side of the road the earth was raw; the ditches were running full. Planks were laid across the open ditches, planks approached the doors of the newest houses. The new, white and shining houses, set side by side in long rows in the wound of the earth. She always thought of them as white houses, though of course they were not entirely white. They were stucco and siding, and only the stucco was white; the siding was painted in shades of blue, pink, green and yellow, all fresh and vivid colours. Last year, just at this time, in March, the bulldozers had come in to clear away the brush and second-growth and great trees of the mountain forest; in a little while the houses were going up among the boulders, the huge torn stumps, the unimaginable upheavals of that earth. The houses were frail at first, skeletons of new wood standing up in the dusk of the cold spring days. But the roofs went on, black and green, blue and red, and the stucco, the siding; the windows were put in, and plastered with signs that said, Murry's Glass, French's Hardwood Floors; it could be seen that the houses were real. People who would live in them came out and tramped around in the mud on Sundays. They were for people like Mary and her husband and their child, with not much money but expectations of more; Garden Place was already put down, in the minds of people who understood addresses, as less luxurious than Pine Hills but more desirable than Wellington Park. The bathrooms were beautiful, with three-part mirrors, ceramic tile, and coloured plumbing. The cupboards in the kitchen were light birch or mahogany, and there were copper lighting fixtures there and in the dining ells. Brick planters, matching the fireplaces, separated the living rooms and halls. The rooms were all large and light and the basements dry, and all this soundness and excellence seemed to be clearly, proudly indicated on the face of each house—those ingenuously similar houses that looked calmly out at each other, all the way down the street.

Today, since it was Saturday, all the men were out working around their houses. They were digging drainage ditches and making rockeries and clearing off and burning torn branches and brush. They worked with competitive violence and energy, all this being new to them; they were not men who made their livings by physical work. All day Saturday and Sunday they worked like this, so that in a year or two there should be green terraces, rock walls, shapely flower beds and ornamental shrubs. The earth must be heavy to dig now; it had been raining last night and this morning. But the day was brightening; the clouds had broken, revealing a long thin triangle of sky, its blue still cold and delicate, a winter colour. Behind the houses on one side of the road were pine trees, their ponderous symmetry not much stirred by any wind. These were to be cut down any day now, to make room for a shopping centre, which had been promised when the houses were sold.

And under the structure of this new subdivision, there was still something else to be seen; that was the old city, the old wilderness city that had lain on the side of the mountain. It had to be called a city because there were tramlines running into the woods, the houses had numbers and there were all the public buildings of a city, down by the water. But houses like Mrs. Fullerton's had been separated from each other by uncut forest and a jungle of wild blackberry and salmonberry bushes; these surviving houses, with thick smoke coming out of their chimneys, walls unpainted and patched and showing different degrees of age and darkening, rough sheds and stacked wood and compost heaps and grey board fences around them—these appeared every so often among the large new houses of Mimosa and Marigold and Heather Drive—dark, enclosed, expressing something like savagery in their disorder and the steep, unmatched angles of roofs and lean-tos; not possible on these streets, but there.

"What are they saying," said Edith, putting on more coffee. She was surrounded in her kitchen by the ruins of the birthday party—cake and molded jellies and cookies with animal faces. A balloon rolled underfoot. The children had been fed, had posed for flash cameras and endured the birthday games; now they were playing in the back bedrooms and the basement, while their parents had coffee. "What are they saying in there?" said Edith.

"I wasn't listening," Mary said, holding the empty cream pitcher in her hand. She went to the sink window. The rent in the clouds had been torn wide open and the sun was shining. The house seemed too hot.

"Mrs. Fullerton's house," said Edith, hurrying back to the living-room. Mary knew what they were talking about. Her neighbours' conversation, otherwise not troubling, might at any moment snag itself on this subject and eddy menacingly in familiar circles of complaint, causing her to look despairingly out of windows, or down into her lap, trying to find some wonderful explanatory word to bring it to a stop; she did not succeed. She had to go back; they were waiting for cream.

A dozen neighbourhood women sat around the living room, absently holding the balloons they had been given by their children. Because the children on the street were so young, and also because any gathering-together of the people who lived there was considered a healthy thing in itself, most birthday parties were attended by mothers as well as children. Women who saw each other every day met now in earrings, nylons and skirts, with their hair fixed and faces applied. Some of the men were there too—Steve, who was Edith's husband, and others he had invited in for beer; they were all in their work clothes. The subject just introduced was one of the few on which male and female interest came together.

"I tell you what I'd do if I was next door to it," Steve said, beaming good-naturedly in expectation of laughter. "I'd send my kids over there to play with matches."

"Oh, funny," Edith said. "It's past joking. You joke, I try to do something. I even phoned the Municipal Hall."

"What did they say?" said Mary Lou Ross.

"Well I said couldn't they get her to paint it, at least, or pull down some of the shacks, and they said no they couldn't. I said I thought there must be some kind of ordinance applied to people like that and they said they knew how I *felt* and they were very *sorry*—"

"But no?"

"But no."

"But what about the chickens, I thought—"

"Oh, they wouldn't let you or me keep chickens, but she has some special dispensation about that too, I forgot how it goes."

"I'm going to stop buying them," Janie Inger said. "The supermarket's cheaper and who cares that much about fresh? And my God, the smell. I said to Carl I knew we were coming to the sticks but I somehow didn't picture us next door to a barnyard."

"Across the street is worse than next door. It makes me wonder why we ever bothered with a picture window, whenever anybody comes to see us I want to draw the drapes so they won't see what's across from us."

"Okay, okay," Steve said, cutting heavily through these female voices. "What Carl and I started out to tell you was that, if we can work this lane deal, she has got to go. It's simple and it's legal. That's the beauty of it."

"What lane deal?"

"We are getting to that. Carl and I been cooking this for a couple of weeks, but we didn't like to say anything in case it didn't work out. Take it, Carl."

"Well she's on the lane allowance, that's all," Carl said. He was a real estate salesman, stocky, earnest, successful. "I had an idea it might be that way, so I went down to the Municipal Hall and looked it up."

"What does that mean, dear?" said Janie, casual, wifely.

"This is it," Carl said. "There's an allowance for a lane, there always has been, the idea being if the area ever got built up they would put a lane through. But they never thought that would happen, people just built where they liked. She's got part of her house and half a dozen shacks sitting right where the lane has to go through. So what we do now, we get the municipality to put through a lane. We need a lane anyway. Then she has to get out. It's the law."

"It's the law," said Steve, radiating admiration. "What a smart boy. These real estate operators are smart boys."

"Does she get anything?" said Mary Lou. "I'm sick of looking at it and all but I don't want to see anybody in the poorhouse."

"Oh, she'll get paid. More than it's worth. Look, it's to her advantage. She'll get paid for it, and she couldn't sell it, she couldn't give it away."

Mary set her coffee cup down before she spoke and hoped her voice would sound all right, not emotional or scared. "But remember she's been here a long time," she said. "She was here before most of us were born." She was trying desperately to think of other words, words more sound and reasonable than these; she could not expose to this positive tide any notion that they might think flimsy and romantic, or she would destroy her argument. But she had no argument. She could try all night and never find any words to stand up to their words, which came at her now invincibly from all sides; *shack, eyesore, filthy, property, value.*

"Do you honestly think that people who let their property get so rundown have that much claim to our consideration?" Janie said, feeling her husband's plan was being attacked.

"She's been here forty years, now we're here," Carl said. "So it goes. And whether you realize it or not, just standing there that house is bringing down the resale value of every house on this street. I'm in the business, I know."

And these were joined by other voices; it did not matter much what they said as long as they were full of self-assertion and anger. That was their strength, proof of their adulthood, of themselves and their seriousness. The spirit of anger rose among them, bearing up their young voices, sweeping them together as on a flood of intoxication, and they admired each other in this new behaviour as property-owners as people admire each other for being drunk.

"We might as well get everybody now," Steve said. "Save going around to so many places."

It was supper time, getting dark out. Everybody was preparing to go home, mothers buttoning their children's coats, children clutching, without much delight, their balloons and whistles and paper baskets full of jelly beans. They had stopped fighting, almost stopped noticing each other; the party had disintegrated. The adults too had grown calmer and felt tired.

"Edith! Edith, have you got a pen?"

Edith brought a pen and they spread the petition for the lane, which Carl had drawn up, on the dining-room table, clearing away the paper plates with smears of dried ice cream. People began to sign mechanically as they said goodbye. Steve was still scowling slightly; Carl stood with one hand on the paper, businesslike, but proud. Mary knelt on the floor and struggled with Danny's zipper. She got up and put on her own coat, smoothed her hair, put on her gloves and took them off again. When she could not think of anything else to do she walked past the dining-room table on her way to the door. Carl held out the pen.

"I can't sign that," she said. Her face flushed up, at once, her voice was trembling. Steve touched her shoulder.

"What's the matter, honey?"

"I don't think we have the right. We haven't the right."

"Mary, don't you care how things look? You live here too."

"No, I—I don't care." Oh, wasn't it strange, how in your imagination, when you stood up for something your voice rang, people started, abashed; but in real life they all smiled in rather a special way and you saw that what you had really done was serve yourself up as a conversational delight for the next office coffee party.

"Don't worry, Mary, she's got money in the bank," Janie said. "She must have. I asked her to baby-sit for me once and she practically spit in my face. She isn't exactly a charming old lady, you know."

"I know she isn't a charming old lady," Mary said.

Steve's hand still rested on her shoulder. "Hey what do you think we are, a bunch of ogres?"

"Nobody wants to turn her out just for the fun of it," Carl said. "It's unfortunate. We all know that. But we have to think of the community."

"Yes," said Mary. But she put her hands in the pockets of her coat and turned to say thank you to Edith, thank you for the birthday party. It occurred to her that they were right, for themselves, for whatever it was they had to be. And Mrs. Fullerton was old, she had dead eyes, nothing could touch her. Mary went out and walked with Danny up the street. She saw the curtains being drawn across living-room windows; cascades of flowers, of leaves, of geometrical designs, shut off these rooms from the night. Outside it was quite dark, the white houses were growing dim, the clouds breaking and breaking, and smoke blowing from Mrs. Fullerton's chimney. The pattern of Garden Place, so assertive in the daytime, seemed to shrink at night into the raw black mountainside.

The voices in the living room have blown away, Mary thought. If they would blow away and their plans be forgotten, if one thing could be left alone. But these are people who win, and they are good people;

they want homes for their children, they help each other when there is trouble, they plan a community—saying that word as if they found a modern and well-proportioned magic in it, and no possibility anywhere of a mistake.

There is nothing you can do at present but put your hands in your pockets and keep a disaffected heart.

NOTES

dispensation   official permission to disregard an ordinance

ordinance   regulation or law made by a city or town

tram   streetcar

RESPONDING PERSONALLY

3. The closing paragraphs of the story are written from the perspective of Mary's thoughts. But what if she had chosen differently? Write a revised closing to the story: Try to convey the same mood, maintain a similar tone, but let her thoughts clearly disclose the emotions she is feeling.

4. Think back and write about a time when you felt compelled to go along with a group decision with which you did not agree. In hindsight, did you make the "right" or the "wrong" decision? What were some of the factors that led you to your decision? What were the negative ramifications, if any, of your decision?

RESPONDING CRITICALLY/ANALYTICALLY

5. A theme the writer develops early and then carries throughout is that of the façade, the false front hiding some other reality. This theme of appearance masking truth is signalled very early in the story, initially through the use of the word "pretext." Numerous instances of "pretending"—environmental, societal, personal, emotional, and verbal pretence—occur during the story. Find examples of "pretending" as revealed in the words or actions of each of the following
   a) Mrs. Fullerton
   b) Mary
   c) the community of neighbours

6. Conflict in the story is established through a series of contrasts, most noticeably contrasting settings, both physical and social, and contrasting motivations and goals. Design a T-chart. Title one column "Mrs. Fullerton" and the other "her community." With a partner, identify as many varied examples of contrast as you are able. Share your results with classmates. What is the writer's purpose in setting up so many different contrasts?

7. Find the paragraph in which the word "barricade" is used by the protagonist to describe Mrs. Fullerton's home. Identify other words from the same paragraph whose connotations help to convey the impression of barricades.
   a) What are some of the physical barricades that Mrs. Fullerton has surrounded herself with?
   b) What are the social barricades?
   c) What are the emotional barricades?

   What appears to have been her purpose in erecting all these barricades?

8. The story is told from Mary's limited omniscient perspective. Identify some of her early observations of Mrs. Fullerton that hint at Mary's final decision at the conclusion of the birthday party. Has her character been consistently portrayed throughout the story, or do there appear to be inconsistencies? Provide support for your answer: What are some of the defining moments of her character portrayal?

9. In a sentence or two, write a thematic statement that you feel effectively identifies the controlling idea (or one of the controlling ideas) of the story. Be prepared to defend your statement in terms of the choices the writer appears to have made.

RESPONDING CREATIVELY

10. Extract the dialogue from the two scenes of the discussion among the adults at the birthday party
    a) as Mary initially objects mildly to the proposed plan to evict
    b) as the petition is placed on the table for all to sign

    Role-play the dialogue between Mary defending her neighbour on the one hand, and the others rationalizing their attack upon Mrs. Fullerton. Which characters will be standing and which sitting when Mary speaks? Where will Mary be placed relative to the others? How loudly will Mary speak relative to the others?

GROUP ASSESSMENT

Play out one scene first, with at least two different groups performing. Then play out the second. Assess the differences in the performances. Which do you feel most appropriately depicts the tone the writer attempted to convey?

PROBLEM SOLVING OR DECISION MAKING

11. Discuss the "flimsy" argument that Mary desperately considers presenting on Mrs. Fullerton's behalf. With a partner, write the argument that might have better appealed to such a group. What sorts of appeals might have moved them? What might have convinced them?

Carol Shields
Invitations

PRE-READING

1. a) Imagine the following: You have received an envelope in the mail. It appears to be a letter, rather than just business communication or junk mail, and it has been addressed to you personally, though you do not yet know who wrote it. Before you open the letter, what kinds of emotions are you feeling, generally? What causes you to feel these emotions?

   b) What does the expression "mixed emotions" mean to you? To a partner, describe a time when you were in a situation where you felt mixed emotions.

2. Tell about a time you had to make a difficult decision that involved possibly disappointing someone else. Did you resolve the predicament to your own satisfaction or to that of others? Explain.

On Monday she looked in her mailbox, although she had no reason to expect a letter so soon. But there it was, a small, square card. She held it in her two hands, testing its weight.

It was an invitation to an exhibition of drawings at a private gallery. The name of the artist was only faintly familiar to her, and she couldn't decide if she'd ever seen his work or not. She tried to imagine what kind of drawings she was being invited to view—would they be primitive or abstract or what was sometimes called "magic realism"? She summoned these categories to mind and then decided it didn't matter. What mattered was that she had been invited.

The invitation pleased her, though she wasn't such a fool as to think she'd been specifically singled out because of her aesthetic sensitivity or because of her knowledge of modern graphics or even because of the pleasure of her company. The address on the card had been typed; her name, in fact, was misspelled, the last two letters transposed. Somewhere, no doubt, she'd turned up on a mailing list—that was all.

She would wear a certain printed velvet skirt she had and with it a black turtleneck sweater. No one would expect her to buy a drawing or even to comment on the exhibition. It was necessary only to accept a glass of wine and a cube of orange cheese and stand for a minute or two in front of each drawing, nodding comprehendingly and perhaps murmuring something properly neutral into the air such as "nicely detailed" or "wonderful sense of space." There was a good chance no one would even speak to her, but it would be better than spending Saturday evening in her new apartment, sitting in an armchair with a book and feeling loneliness drink her drop by drop.

The previous tenant had left behind a single item, which was a paperback copy of Jane Austen's *Mansfield Park*, a book that, oddly enough, she had always intended to read. She couldn't help feeling there had been something deliberate—and something imperative, too—about this abandoned book, as though it had been specifically intended for her and that she was being enjoined to take it seriously. But how much better it would be to be going *out*; how much easier it would be to say, should anyone ask, that on Saturday evening she would be attending an opening of an interesting new exhibition.

On Tuesday she was again taken by surprise, for in her mailbox there was another invitation, this time for a cocktail party given by a distant friend of a friend, someone she'd never met but whose name she dimly remembered having heard. It was a disappointment that the party was being held on the same night as the gallery opening and that, furthermore, it was at the same hour. For a minute she entertained the possibility of attending both functions, galloping breathlessly from one to the other. But no, it was not feasible; the two parties were at opposite ends of the city. It was a great pity, she felt, since invitations are few and far between when one moves to a new address. She would have to make a choice.

Of course she would choose the cocktail party. The gallery opening, now that she stopped to think about it, was no more than a commercial venture, an enticement to buyers and patrons. It would be fraudulent of her to attend when she'd no intention of buying a picture, and besides, she was drawn to cocktail parties. She was attracted, in fact, to parties of all kinds, seeing them as an opportunity to possess, for a few hours at least, a life that was denser, more concentrated and more vigorous than the usual spun-out wastes of time that had to be scratched endlessly for substance. She could still wear her certain velvet skirt, but with a pretty red satin blouse she'd recently acquired.

On Wednesday, strangely, she received a third invitation—and it, too, was for Saturday evening. This time the invitation was hand-written, a rather charming note which she read through quickly three times. She was being invited to a small buffet supper. There would be only a dozen or so guests, it was explained. The author of a new biography would be there, and so would the subject of the biography who was, by chance, also a biographer. A particular balding computer scientist would be in attendance along with his wife, who was celebrated for her anti-nuclear stance and for her involvement in Navajo rugs. There would be a professor of history and also a professor of histology, as well as a person renowned for his love of Black Forest cakes and cheese pastries. There would be a famous character actor whose face was familiar, if not his name, and also the hairdresser who'd invented the Gidget cut and raised razor cuts to their present *haute* status.

Of course she could not say no. How much more congenial to go to a supper party than to peer at violent works of art and mutter, "Interesting, interesting," and how much more rewarding than standing about with a drink and a salty canapé and trying to make conversation with a room full of strangers. Her green silk dress would be suitable, if not precisely perfect, and she could gamble safely enough on the fact that no one would have seen it before.

Thursday's mail brought still another invitation, also unfortunately for Saturday evening. She smiled, remembered how her mother used to say, "It never rains but it pours." The invitation, which was for a formal dinner party, was printed on fine paper, and there was a handwritten note at the bottom. "We do hope you can make it," the note said. "Of course we know you by reputation and we've been looking forward to meeting you for years."

It had been some time since she'd attended a formal dinner party, and she was flattered to be sent an invitation with a handwritten note at the bottom. It pleased her to imagine a large, vaulted dining room and parade of courses elegantly served, each with a different wine. The gleam of light through cut glass would sparkle on polished linen and on the faces of the luminaries gathered around the table. Her green silk, with perhaps the double strand of pearls, would be festive enough, but at the same time subdued and formal.

She wasn't entirely surprised to look into her mailbox on Friday and see that she'd been sent yet another invitation. The paper was a heavy, creamy stock and came enclosed in a thick double envelope. There was to be a reception—a *gala* it was called—at the top of a large downtown hotel on Saturday evening. The guest of honor, she read, was to be herself.

She felt a lurch of happiness. Such an honor! But a moment later her euphoria gave way to panic, and when she sat down to collect herself, she discovered she was trembling not with excitement but with fear.

On Saturday she surveyed the five invitations which were arranged in a circle on her coffee table. These missives, so richly welcoming, persuading and honoring, had pleased her at first, then puzzled her. And now she felt for the first time directly threatened. Something or someone was conspiring to consume a portion of her life, of herself, in fact—entering her apartment and taking possession of her Saturday evening just as a thief might enter and carry off her stereo equipment or her lovely double rope of pearls or a deep slice of her dorsal flesh.

She decided to stay home instead with a cup of coffee and her adventitiously acquired copy of *Mansfield Park*. Already it was dark, and she switched on the small reading lamp by her chair. The shade of the lamp was made of a pale, ivory-yellow material, and the light that shone through it had the warm quality of very old gold.

It happened that people passing her window on their way to various parties and public gatherings that night were moved to see her, a woman sitting calmly in an arc of lamplight, turning over—one by one—the soft pages of a thick book. Clearly she was lost in what she was reading, for she never once glanced up. Her look of solitary containment and the oblique angle with which the light struck the left side of her face made her seem piercingly lovely. One of her hands, curved like a comma, lay on her lap; the other, slowly, thoughtfully, turned over the pages.

Those who passed by and saw her were seized by a twist of pain, which was really a kind of nostalgia for their childhood and for a simplified time when they, too, had been bonded to the books they read and to certain golden rooms which they remembered as being complete and as perfect as stage settings. They felt resentment, too, at the cold rain and the buffeting wind and the price of taxis and the hostility of their hosts. They felt embarrassed by their own small, proffered utterances and by the expanded social rubric they had come to inhabit.

As they moved to and fro in large, brightly-lit rooms, so high up in glittering towers that they felt they were clinging to the sides of cliffs, their feet began to ache and exhaustion overcame them. Soon it was past midnight, no longer the same day, but the next and the next. New widths of time clamored to be filled, though something it seemed, some image of possibility, begged to be remembered.

Outside, the wind blew and blew. The sky slipped sideways, turning first yellow, then a mournful, treasonous purple, as though time itself was drowning in a waterfall of shame.

NOTES

Gidget cut	trendy hairstyle made popular by movie star Sandra Dee; named after her teenage character Gidget
haute	fashionable
magic realism	term from the arts and literature referring to ordinary events being turned into something magical (unreal, strange); also relevant to this story is the idea that magic realism transcends "clock time"
Mansfield Park	1814 Jane Austen novel about male–female relationships and constancy

RESPONDING PERSONALLY

3. Are you pleased with the central character's final decision? Would you have taken the same action? Explain why or why not.

4. Write to the central character. As a friend from home, provide her with any advice or insights you feel would be appropriate. In your letter, describe a choice you once made that was similar to the one she made.

RESPONDING CRITICALLY/ANALYTICALLY

5. The central character rationalizes her initial acceptance and subsequent rejection of each invitation. In chart form, identify and plot her reasons for accepting each invitation, followed by her reasons for rejecting each. What generality can be drawn about the influences that appear to be the motivation for her decisions?

6. a) The plot of the story appears contrived. The daily delivery of invitations and the highly structured escalation in the kinds of invitations seem too coincidental to be realistic. Why might the writer have chosen to sacrifice realism for functionality? Could she have achieved a similar effect yet structured her story differently? Comment on her technique.

b) There is a turn in the story that occurs shortly after the final invitation is received: "She discovered she was trembling not with excitement but with fear." In the way it is presented, is this turn realistic? Has the writer adequately prepared the reader for what is to follow? Explain.

PEER ASSESSMENT

In small groups, share your responses to the question of plot credibility. Whose response to this question is the most convincing?

7. Discuss the effect of the writer's switch from a limited-omniscient point of view or perspective to one that might be described as "expanded omniscience." In what way is the continuity of the story affected by the change?

8. References to light figure prominently in the story. Contrast the writer's use of language that is suggestive of "bright" lights following the reception of Thursday's letter with the "muted" lights and language following her decision on Saturday not to attend. In terms of mood creation, what descriptive purpose does such contrast serve? Does the description in the second-to-last paragraph support your answer? Explain.

9. With a partner, search out a plot summary or a review of Jane Austen's novel *Mansfield Park*. Based on the information you are able to gather about the story, how does that book take on a symbolic importance in this story? In what way might the person who left the book behind have done so for a reason that was "deliberate ... imperative ... specifically intended for her"? In what way does the central character's initial decision to not pick the book up add to its symbolic impact?

RESPONDING CREATIVELY

10. The expression "life imitates art" often does ring true, as it may indeed for this story's central character. Has something similar ever happened to you? Think of an incident, however brief, from your own life experience in which life has imitated art. Write about that experience in narrative form. Write objectively, in the third person ("he" or "she") and in the past tense.

11. Write the "invitation" that the writer and the central character seem to be offering the reader.

PROBLEM SOLVING OR DECISION MAKING

12. Through most of the story, the central character responds rather predictably to what might be called the forces of society. Yet at the end, she responds to a force that is innate, that comes from within. Should one take precedence over the other? Is there a generalization that can be drawn? Discuss in a small group, and share the product of your discussion with the class.

Translated by Alice Childs

Liu Xin-Wu
Black Walls

PRE-READING

1. Alone or with a partner, define in the broadest possible terms the maximum and minimum limits of what you personally would consider to be a threat. What causes us to feel threatened?

2. English Romantic poet William Wordsworth wrote the line "The Child is father of the Man." What does this seemingly self-contradictory statement mean to you? Is there, as with all paradox, a hidden truth? Explain.

SUMMERTIME. Sunday.

A courtyard in an alley. Three fruit trees, five or six households. Early morning. 7:30 A.M.

The room at the eastern end of the courtyard is the Zhous'. Actually there is just one certain Mr. Zhou, about thirty years old, who lives there on his own. One might assume that he has never been married, though he uses a basin with a large, red double happiness design. One might also assume that he had been married and divorced but then why does he lower his head, study the ground and walk off in the other direction when he sees an unmarried woman in the court-yard? He only recently moved in and his work unit has a long and complicated name so his neighbours have not been able to work out exactly what he does for a living. By reckoning on their fingers they can work out that at his age, having been sent to the countryside for eight years, he can only have been working for about seven years at the most. Consequently, the amount of money in his monthly wage packet is not interesting enough to keep them guessing for long. Since he moved in he has never caused any trouble. He never drops in on anyone, nor does he receive any guests. When he meets neighbours in the courtyard they may first ask him: "How are you?" He will reply neither shyly nor arrogantly: "I'm very well, thank you"; or he may first ask the neighbour: "Finished for the day?", and the neighbour will reply: "Lord no! I'm just sitting in the cool breeze awhile." But he will not stop and chat. Sometimes when he goes to the communal tap in the courtyard to fetch water, wash his clothes, or wash some rice and he bumps into a neighbour, of course they have to say something to each other. He only speaks when forced to reply to a question. If he answers, he will not follow it with another question. The other families who have lived in the courtyard a long time cannot say that they like him, nor that they dislike him.

He was busy very early one morning. First he moved everything out of his room, then he mixed some sort of liquid in a large wash basin. He must have borrowed a foot operated spray gun yesterday. Clearly, he was going to paint his room.

This began as nothing out of the ordinary. When the neighbours bumped into him at the communal tap, they asked him: "Are you painting your room today?" "Yes, yes I am." Then they asked him politely, "Do you need some help?" He thanked them: "I've got a spray gun so it should be an easy job! Thank you anyway." After collecting the water he calmly walked away. A calling cicada was hiding in the umbrella-like crown of a scholar tree whose trunk was only as wide as the mouth of a bowl. The noise was getting louder, but they had all grown accustomed to it and so did not find it annoying anymore.

7:46 A.M.

"Chi — chi — chi ..."

It was a new sound but it was clear what it was. Zhou had started spraying his room.

7:55 A.M.

Several of the young people from the courtyard had the day off and went out one by one. Naturally they were all dressed up in the latest fashions, each one different from the next. One girl, a meat cutter during the week, was wearing imitation jewel earrings and cream coloured high-heels. As she left the courtyard, she opened a blue-flowered, nylon, automatic umbrella. There was also a young man who worked in the foundry's workshop. On his upper half, he was wearing an Indiana State University T-shirt, printed in English. On his legs, he wore grey corduroy hunting trousers originally made for export. He put on a pair of large-framed, purple sunglasses as he walked out, pushing a small-wheeled bicycle. A second girl hurried out of the courtyard. She studied business management at the local branch of the university. She was wearing a pale green dress, loose at the waist, which she had made herself, and was carrying a round, rattan handbag. The events which followed may have occurred because they all went out, but it is hard to say if things would have been different if they had not done so, as there was still one young person who remained behind the entire time. This young man sold glassware in the local market and was enjoying a day off. After breakfast, he lay on his bed, reading *The Lamp Without Light*. When his mother called him to join in the following events, he smiled, lay back down and continued to read his book.

8:15 A.M.

The atmosphere in the courtyard was heating up. It is not quite correct to say "in the courtyard"; it would be better to say "in the room." It was not in every room, but it was in the north room in the middle of the courtyard. That was where the Zhao family lived. Mr. Zhao was fifty-six years old. He had retired early so his second daughter could take over his job. Soon after his retirement, he went to another work unit to "fill in" for a time. Recently, that unit began making cutbacks, leaving Mr. Zhao out of work. Currently, he was trying to arrange another job in a different work unit.

Several of the neighbours gathered at his house. They told Mr. Zhao the news: Mr. Zhou was not spraying his walls white but black! He was actually spraying his walls black! They did not know what kind of paint he was using but it was black as ink! Pitch black!

Mr. Zhao was both astounded and strangely pleased at the same time. Ten years before, he had been the deputy-in-charge of the Workers' Propaganda Team in a song and dance troupe. At that time when some "activists" came to inform him about some "new trends," his manner and tone were just as they were now. Mrs. Zhao felt much as her husband did. Eight years before she had been the head of a "socialist neighbourhood committee." Once when some people told her about the remains of a reactionary slogan written at the base of the wall behind the date tree, the atmosphere was much as it was now. Who could guess that something would happen to bring the dead issues of a decade or so ago back to life again?

"That's just not right," Mr. Zhao proclaimed.

"How dreadful," said Mrs. Zhao indignantly.

8:25 A.M.

"Chi — chi — chi ..."

Mr. Zhou was still spraying his room.

Newsflash: He had sprayed the ceiling black, too!

Mr. Zhao asked them all to sit down, giving the room the feeling of a meeting hall. Meetings can take on all forms: at some, everyone is bored; at others, only you are interested; at still others, it is you who is bored. Mr. Zhao enjoyed the present meeting. He put forward the motion: "In this sort of situation we should inform the police as soon as possible."

If this were eight or ten years ago, this would not have been a mere proposal but a conclusive decision; not just a man giving his own opinion, but a leader's directive.

But, this was the present, not the past. Tall, thin Mr. Qian went so far as to immediately oppose him, saying, "As I see it, we shouldn't go to the authorities ... that is, we have no basis. What can we tell the police?"

Mr. and Mrs. Zhao both stared hard at him. They were both thinking: Damn tailor! Years ago when he was an entrepreneur he never dared to open his mouth, much less oppose our suggestions, but now he does some private business at home, buys a colour television and his whole tone of voice changes.

Mr. Qian sat up straight and began fervently expressing his opinion: "Brother Zhou may be suffering from a recurring illness. There are such diseases; I've read about them in the paper. Sufferers have been known to behave strangely under stressful conditions ... Young Zhou was airing his quilt outside his front door last Sunday. Perhaps no one noticed but the quilt cover was made of bright red silk while the underside was duller red. Really, very odd! So I say we should not go to the police but fetch a doctor instead. Although I have heard that traditional medicines don't work on these kinds of illnesses, it would not hurt to consult him."

Not many people responded to Mr. Qian's words because as he talked they could not help gazing out of the window, through the shade of the scholar tree, to where they could see "Brother Zhou." Perfectly calm and collected, he continued to spray his walls. Faintly, they could hear him humming a song. Was this the manner of a sick person?

Mr. Sun, who was sitting by the door, passed his little finger through his thinning hair and suggested: "Shouldn't we just go and ask him why he is spraying his walls black? If he can't give a good reason, we can just forbid him—no, advise him not to—yes, advise him not to do it any more."

Another neighbour, Mrs. Li, who was sitting in the middle of the crowd, took the opportunity to say, "Why don't you go and ask him for us?"

Everyone agreed to this suggestion.

8:36 A.M.

When Mr. Sun made his suggestion he thought it would naturally be Mr. and Mrs. Zhao who would confront Mr. Zhou. He never imagined it would be he who would be sent to ask. He regretted sitting by the door. For the past thirty years, he had worked in a primary school in charge of general affairs. He had not taught a class in his life. Consequently, he had picked up many of the mannerisms of a teacher but, now faced with a situation where he had to straighten his back and go to investigate a "strange phenomenon," he felt as though he had been forced to the front of a podium to deliver a speech. His hands and knees shook uncontrollably and he was completely tongue tied.

8:37 A.M.

"Chi — chi — chi ..." The spraying continued.

"Bzzzzzzzz ..." Inside the room, they continued talking in hushed voices.

Mr. Sun flicked the long nail of the little finger on his left hand and stared at the tips of his shoes. He was not willing to go to question "Brother Zhou." How could he ever face them again if he received a brash refusal? How could he explain such a failure? What if the idiot said something incriminating? Should he report it directly and be responsible for the unknown consequences, or should he keep the information to himself and risk being accused of protecting Mr. Zhou? And what if some evidence came to light in the future ...

He gave it tremendous thought. Beads of sweat broke out on his forehead as he said, "Maybe ... maybe Mr. Zhao could go and ask instead?"

As no one else wanted the job, everyone agreed and said in chorus, "Yes! Let Mr. Zhao go!"

Mr. Zhao did not make any immediate move, but waited for them to stop urging and start pleading with him. Only then did he abruptly stand and declare, "I'll go and ask!" He turned and left the room.

Everyone gazed out the window and watched the receding figure of Mr. Zhao walking straight towards Mr. Zhou's front door. They all listened attentively, hoping to catch a part of the conversation. All they could hear was the incessant call of the cicadas, high in the scholar tree.

8:41 A.M.

Ashen-faced, Mr. Zhao returned to the room and reported, "That rascal says he will come and explain to me when he has finished. I knew he would pull some trick. He doesn't respect us, his neighbours."

Mrs. Zhao pointed out of the window and said, "That's the man come to read the water meter, isn't it? He'll go and look in Mr. Zhou's room! He'll probably spread all kinds of rumours about black paint and our courtyard, and give us all a bad name!"

Mrs. Li, whose job was fluffing cotton into quilts, had a very placid nature and so put forward an explanation to make them all feel better, "Perhaps the black paint is just the undercoat. When it's dry he'll spray a top coat of white paint."

8:43 A.M.

"Chi—chi—chi ..." The noise from the spray gun continued. Looking towards the room all they could see was blackness. No one really believed Mrs. Li's explanation. The more Mrs. Li looked, the more she could not help despairing.

What could one say? Black walls! In this very courtyard! Mr. Zhou is not afraid of doing evil things himself, but he should not get others involved.

8:45 A.M.

Everyone in the room agreed about one thing: he should not spray his walls black! How could anyone spray his walls and ceiling black? Most people would not dare even think of such a thing. He did not just think about it, he actually did it! Extraordinary! Weird! Half-mad! Reactionary!

Mr. Zhao still thought the police should be informed. Just as he was about to go and do so, he had second thoughts. The police station is not the same as it was eight or ten years ago (at that time there was not a police station but a "group to smash the leaders of the judicial and public security institutions." It was in the same courtyard as the present-day police station). Today the police are not as extreme nor do they think themselves as important as in the past. They always talk about "going by the book" but once you start doing things "by the book" then problems like the black wall dilemma will drag on and possibly never be resolved. Mr. Zhao hesitated. He felt strongly about it and really did want to report it. It was a responsibility he could not shirk, a duty he had to take quick action to deal with. Could he be doing it for his own good? But what possible benefit could come of reporting it?

Mrs. Zhao realized what her husband must be feeling and felt very bitter. How different it was eight or ten years ago! Her husband was actually suffering now because he lacked any real skills, and could only work as an assistant or warehouse watchman. Was it because he had not tried to learn a trade? Certainly not. For the past thirty odd years he had been transferred to work in various campaigns. The campaigns had come and gone, so now he had no way of earning a living. Formerly all his pride had come from his political sensitivity. Now he had a chance to display this talent, but his eyes, wrinkled face and the corners of his mouth showed hesitancy. Why was it? What was all this exertion for today? Could it be just for the good of his own family?

More and more, Mr. Zhao believed that "Brother Zhou" was suffering from a recurring illness. He admitted that what he had just been thinking was wrong. Traditional doctors were unable to treat this sort of illness. Could he not just let the doctor take his pulse? Not really. He would still have to get a Western doctor. But doctors didn't make house calls nowadays. It would be extremely difficult. Who could persuade him to go to the out-patient's department?

Mrs. Li wanted to go home and get her lump of a son to stop reading his novels and think of what to do. Perhaps he could bring Mr. Zhou to his senses, and even help spray the walls white again. White is so nice! Why should anyone want anything different?

Mr. Sun wanted to go home but was too embarrassed to make the move. In this sort of situation a person ought to make clear his position on the matter, so in the future he could not be accused of "sitting on the fence." Of course a person should not leave it so that in any future situation he could not be accused of having played a part in a "misjudged case." Ideally one would avoid any sort of criticism in the past, present or future. He had already shown enough "intention" to go to Mr. Zhou's, so he should now make an early retreat. But it would be hard to slip out without being noticed....

8:48 A.M.

Mr. Zhao had a grandson affectionately known as "Little Button" who was not much more than ten years old. At the start of all this he had been painting in the back room. At length, he came and leaned on the doorway between the two rooms, curiously listening to the adults' discussion. He thought the room crowded, muggy, hot and disordered. Why did adults have to torment themselves like this?

Once again they began to discuss the matter and once again the atmosphere heated up. Little Button stood before his grandfather, turned his head and asked: "Grandpa, what are you all doing?"

Mr. Zhao said to him firmly, "Off with you! Go and play! There's nothing for you here!"

Little Button was not convinced and thought to himself: Are you angry with Uncle Zhou for spraying his walls? Uncle Zhou is a very nice man. He's such fun. Once he called me to his room. He took some pieces of card from a drawer. The pieces were of every colour under the sun and were as big as the *Evening News*. He kept changing them and pressed them up to my eyes so that all I could see was that colour. Then he asked: "Do you like it or not? Does it feel hot or cold? Dry or wet? Pleasant or nasty to smell? Does it make you want to go to sleep or go out and play? What does it make you think of? Or does it make you think nothing at all? Does it make you feel frightened or calm? Does it make you thirsty or not? Do you want to go on looking at it or not?" He jotted down every reply that I made. See how much fun he is! If you don't believe me, go over to his place and see for yourselves!

Little Button thought this far, then raised his head and said loudly, "Grandpa, you still haven't finished your discussion. You must be awfully tired. Can I say something now?"

There was nothing for it but for everyone to stop talking. They all looked at him.

Mr. Zhao waved his hands as if he had been wronged and said, "Right, right! Go ahead!"

Little Button asked: "When Uncle Zhou has finished his room, will he go from door to door spraying everyone else's rooms as well?"

8:49 A.M.

Everyone went blank.

8:50 A.M.

Mr. Zhao blurted out: "I'm sure he'd dare!" Mrs. Zhao echoed, "He'll try!" Mrs. Li and Mr. Sun said at once, "He wouldn't, he'd never ..." Mr. Qian thought carefully before saying, "He doesn't look like a troublemaker. His illness only seems to recur in his own home ..."

8:51 A.M.

Little Button turned round, blinked his round, black eyes, blacker even than the walls, shining black. He smiled innocently and said in a shrill voice: "So that's settled! Uncle Zhou is spraying the walls of his own room, and it has nothing to do with us, so what are you all going on about?"

8:52 A.M.

Everyone went silent.

The "chi—chi—chi ..." of the wall spraying drifted over, mingling with the sound of the cicadas, becoming even more pronounced.

RESPONDING PERSONALLY

3. a) Share your own reaction to Little Button's rhetorical question at the conclusion of the story.
   b) Imagine and write down the thoughts of one of the adult characters in response to Little Button's question.
   c) What was the author's purpose in having a ten-year-old pose that question?

4. Evaluate Little Button's closing statement—"... it has nothing to do with us, so what are you all going on about?"—in relation to your own life. Write about an incident when you told somebody to mind their own business.

RESPONDING CRITICALLY/ANALYTICALLY

5. Even in translation, the story is very simply told, almost childlike in the simplicity of its diction and sentence structure, especially in the dialogue. Might the story have been written this way for a purpose? In what ways is the style of writing suited to the ideas in the story?

SELF-ASSESSMENT

Do you enjoy this manner of storytelling? Would the style be better suited to a class of younger students? Explain.

6. Examine the first long paragraph of the story. The description provides an initial glimpse of Mr. Zhou's personality, as well as of the perception others have of him. In what way does the description prepare the way for the conflict that will be played out? Why is it significant that this description, in contrast to the rest of the story, is written in the present tense?

7. The story generally moves quite slowly, right up until the end. Then it speeds up, and the ending happens very quickly. How has the writer succeeded in creating such a contrast in the story's speed of movement? Is the shift appropriate? What purpose does it serve?

8. One word in the story's title—black—appears often throughout. Following a brief splash of colours following the 7:55 A.M. description of young people leaving to go out, all colour disappears from the story. The reader is left only with the black paint of Mr. Zhou's walls contrasted occasionally with the neighbours' preference for "white." What is the significance of such a stark contrast? Does the writer attach a symbolic significance to the contrast, or is the purpose something different?

Responding Creatively

9. Using stick-men with round heads that reveal the expressions on their faces, draw two pictures:
   a) Show the expressions on the neighbours' faces following Little Button's question at 8:49 A.M.
   b) Show the identical characters in the same relative positions but with changed facial expressions immediately following his final question at 8:52 A.M.

Share with a partner. Support the intent of your drawing.

Peer Assessment

Pass your drawings around the room. Without being critical of one another's artistic endeavours, select the one or two drawings that you feel most appropriately capture the contrast of expressions between the two settings. Provide reasons for your choices.

Problem Solving or Decision Making

10. The neighbours all seem tentative about approaching Mr. Zhou—who "only recently moved in"—with their concerns. What might be their reasons for acting this way? Why aren't they more forthright, more confrontational about expressing their concerns? What might have been the result had they approached him more directly?

Shirley Jackson
The Lottery

PRE-READING

1. Lotteries are generally established to serve some community purpose. Describe a particular lottery that you know of and explain the way in which the greater community benefits from the running of this lottery.

2. What is the purpose of tradition and ritual in people's lives, and in the life of a community? Why are traditions maintained? For what reasons might they be changed, or abandoned? What is the difference between ritual and tradition?

The morning of June 27th was clear and sunny, with the fresh warmth of a full-summer day; the flowers were blossoming profusely and the grass was richly green. The people of the village began to gather in the square, between the post office and the bank, around ten o'clock; in some towns there were so many people that the lottery took two days and had to be started on June 26th, but in this village, where there were only about three hundred people, the whole lottery took less than two hours, so it could begin at ten o'clock in the morning and still be through in time to allow the villagers to get home for noon dinner.

The children assembled first, of course. School was recently over for the summer, and the feeling of liberty sat uneasily on most of them; they tended to gather together quietly for a while before they broke into boisterous play, and their talk was still of the classroom and the teacher, of books and reprimands. Bobby Martin had already stuffed his pockets full of stones, and the other boys soon followed his example, selecting the smoothest and roundest stones; Bobby and Harry Jones and Dickie Delacroix—the villagers pronounced this name "Dellacroy"—eventually made a great pile of stones in one corner of the square and guarded it against the raids of the other boys. The girls stood aside, talking among themselves, looking over their shoulders at the boys, and the very small children rolled in the dust or clung to the hands of their older brothers or sisters.

Soon the men began to gather, surveying their own children, speaking of planting and rain, tractors and taxes. They stood together, away from the pile of stones in the corner, and their jokes were quiet and they smiled rather than laughed. The women, wearing faded house dresses and sweaters, came shortly after their menfolk. They greeted one another and exchanged bits of gossip as they went to join their husbands. Soon the women, standing by their husbands, began to call to their children, and the children came reluctantly, having to be called four or five times. Bobby Martin ducked under his mother's grasping hand and ran, laughing, back to the pile of stones. His father spoke up sharply, and Bobby came quickly and took his place between his father and his oldest brother.

The lottery was conducted—as were the square dances, the teenage club, the Halloween program—by Mr. Summers, who had time and energy to devote to civic activities. He was a round-faced, jovial man and he ran the coal business, and people were sorry for him, because he had no children and his wife was a scold. When he arrived in the square, carrying the black wooden box, there was a murmur of conversation among the villagers, and he waved and called, "Little late today, folks." The postmaster, Mr. Graves, followed him, carrying a three-legged stool, and the stool was put in the center of the square and Mr. Summers set the black box down on it. The villagers kept their distance, leaving a space between themselves and the stool, and when Mr. Summers said, "Some of you fellows want to give me a hand?" there was a hesitation before two men, Mr. Martin and his oldest son, Baxter, came forward to hold the box steady on the stool while Mr. Summers stirred up the papers inside it.

The original paraphernalia for the lottery had been lost long ago, and the black box now resting on the stool had been put into use even before Old Man Warner, the oldest man in town, was born. Mr. Summers spoke frequently to the villagers about making a new box, but no one liked to upset even as much tradition as was represented by the black box. There was a story that the present box had been made with some pieces of the box that had preceded it, the one that had been constructed when the first people settled down to make a village here. Every year, after the lottery, Mr. Summers began talking again about a new box, but every year the subject was allowed to fade off without anything being done. The black box grew shabbier each year; by now it was no longer completely black but splintered badly along one side to show the original wood colour, and in some places faded or stained.

Mr. Martin and his oldest son, Baxter, held the black box securely on the stool until Mr. Summers had stirred the papers thoroughly with his hand. Because so much of the ritual had been forgotten or discarded, Mr. Summers had been successful in having slips of paper substituted for the chips of wood that had been used for generations. Chips of wood, Mr. Summers had argued, had been very well when the village was tiny, but now that the population was more than three hundred and likely to keep on growing, it was necessary to use something that would fit more easily into the black box. The night before the lottery, Mr. Summers and Mr. Graves made up the slips of paper and put them in the box, and it was then taken to the safe of Mr. Summers' coal company and locked up until Mr. Summers was ready to take it to the square next morning. The rest of the year, the box was put away, sometimes one place, sometimes another; it had spent one year in Mr. Graves' barn and another year underfoot in the post office, and sometimes it was set on a shelf in the Martin grocery and left there.

There was a great deal of fussing to be done before Mr. Summers declared the lottery open. There were the lists to make up—of heads of families, heads of households in each family, members of each household in each family. There was the proper swearing-in of Mr. Summers by the postmaster, as the official of the lottery; at one time, some people remembered, there had been a recital of some sort, performed by the official of the lottery, a perfunctory, tuneless chant that had been rattled off duly each year; some people believed that the official of the lottery used to stand just so when he said or sang it, others believed that he was supposed to walk among the people, but years and years ago this part of the ritual had been allowed to lapse. There had been, also, a ritual salute, which the official of the lottery had had to use in addressing each person who came up to draw from the box, but this also had changed with time, until now it was felt necessary only for the official to speak to each person approaching. Mr. Summers was very good at all this; in his clean white shirt and blue jeans, with one hand resting carelessly on the black box, he seemed very proper and important as he talked interminably to Mr. Graves and the Martins.

Just as Mr. Summers finally left off talking and turned to the assembled villagers, Mrs. Hutchinson came hurriedly along the path to the square, her sweater thrown over her shoulders, and slid into place in the back of the crowd. "Clean forgot what day it was," she said to Mrs. Delacroix, who stood next to her, and they both laughed softly.

"Thought my old man was out back stacking wood," Mrs. Hutchinson went on, "and then I looked out the window and the kids were gone, and then I remembered it was the twenty-seventh and came a-running." She dried her hands on her apron, and Mrs. Delacroix said, "You're in time, though. They're still talking away up there."

Mrs. Hutchinson craned her neck to see through the crowd and found her husband and children standing near the front. She tapped Mrs. Delacroix on the arm as a farewell and began to make her way through the crowd. The people separated good-humoredly to let her through; two or three people said, in voices just loud enough to be heard across the crowd, "Here comes your Missus, Hutchinson," and "Bill, she made it after all." Mrs. Hutchinson reached her husband, and Mr. Summers, who had been waiting, said cheerfully, "Thought we were going to have to get on without you, Tessie." Mrs. Hutchinson said, grinning, "Wouldn't have me leave m'dishes in the sink, now, would you, Joe?" and soft laughter ran through the crowd as the people stirred back into position after Mrs. Hutchinson's arrival.

"Well, now," Mr. Summers said soberly, "guess we better get started, get this over with, so's we can go back to work. Anybody ain't here?"

"Dunbar," several people said. "Dunbar, Dunbar."

Mr. Summers consulted his list. "Clyde Dunbar," he said. "That's right. He's broke his leg, hasn't he? Who's drawing for him?"

"Me, I guess," a woman said, and Mr. Summers turned to look at her. "Wife draws for her husband," Mr. Summers said. "Don't you have a grown boy to do it for you, Janey?" Although Mr. Summers and everyone else in the village knew the answer perfectly well, it was the business of the official of the lottery to ask such questions formally. Mr. Summers waited with an expression of polite interest while Mrs. Dunbar answered.

"Horace's not but sixteen yet," Mrs. Dunbar said regretfully. "Guess I gotta fill in for the old man this year."

"Right," Mr. Summers said. He made a note on the list he was holding. Then he asked, "Watson boy drawing this year?"

A tall boy in the crowd raised his hand. "Here," he said. "I'm drawing for m'mother and me." He blinked his eyes nervously and ducked his head as several voices in the crowd said things like "Good fellow, Jack," and "Glad to see your mother's got a man to do it."

"Well," Mr. Summers said, "guess that's everyone. Old Man Warner make it?"

"Here," a voice said, and Mr. Summers nodded.

A sudden hush fell on the crowd as Mr. Summers cleared his throat and looked at the list. "All ready?" he called. "Now, I'll read the names—heads of families first—and the men come up and take a paper out of the box. Keep the paper folded in your hand without looking at it until everyone has had a turn. Everything clear?"

The people had done it so many times that they only half-listened to the directions; most of them were quiet, wetting their lips, not looking around. Then Mr. Summers raised one hand high and said, "Adams." A man disengaged himself from the crowd and came forward. "Hi, Steve," Mr. Summers said, and Mr. Adams said, "Hi, Joe." They grinned at one another humorously and nervously. Then Mr. Adams reached into the black box and took out a folded paper. He held it firmly by one corner as he turned and went hastily back to his place in the crowd, where he stood a little apart from his family, not looking down at his hand.

"Allen," Mr. Summers said. "Anderson.... Bentham."

"Seems like there's no time at all between lotteries any more," Mrs. Delacroix said to Mrs. Graves in the back row. "Seems like we got through with the last one only last week."

"Time sure goes fast," Mrs. Graves said.

"Clark.... Delacroix."

"There goes my old man," Mrs. Delacroix said. She held her breath while her husband went forward.

"Dunbar," Mr. Summers said, and Mrs. Dunbar went steadily to the box while one of the women said, "Go on, Janey," and another said, "There she goes."

"We're next," Mrs. Graves said. She watched while Mr. Graves came around from the side of the box, greeted Mr. Summers gravely, and selected a slip of paper from the box. By now, all through the crowd there were men holding the small folded papers in their large hands, turning them over and over nervously. Mrs. Dunbar and her two sons stood together, Mrs. Dunbar holding the slip of paper.

"Harburt.... Hutchinson."

"Get up there, Bill," Mrs. Hutchinson said, and the people near her laughed.

"Jones."

"They do say," Mr. Adams said to Old Man Warner, who stood next to him, "that over in the north village they're talking of giving up the lottery."

Old Man Warner snorted. "Pack of crazy fools," he said. "Listening to the young folks, nothing's good enough for *them*. Next thing you know, they'll be wanting to go back to living in caves, nobody work any more, live *that* way for a while. Used to be a saying about 'Lottery in June, corn be heavy soon.' First thing you know, we'd all be eating stewed chickweed and acorns. There's *always* been a lottery," he added petulantly. "Bad enough to see young Joe Summers up there joking with everybody."

"Some places have already quit lotteries," Mrs. Adams said.

"Nothing but trouble in *that*," Old Man Warner said stoutly. "Pack of young fools."

"Martin." And Bobby Martin watched his father go forward. "Overdyke.... Percy."

"I wish they'd hurry," Mrs. Dunbar said to her older son. "I wish they'd hurry."

"They're almost through," her son said.

"You get ready to run tell Dad," Mrs. Dunbar said.

Mr. Summers called his own name and then stepped forward precisely and selected a slip from the box. Then he called, "Warner."

"Seventy-seventh year I been in the lottery," Old Man Warner said as he went through the crowd. "Seventy-seventh time."

"Watson." The tall boy came awkwardly through the crowd. Someone said, "Don't be nervous, Jack," and Mr. Summers said, "Take your time, son."

"Zanini."

After that, there was a long pause, a breathless pause, until Mr. Summers, holding his slip of paper in the air, said, "All right, fellows." For a minute, no one moved, and then all the slips of paper were opened. Suddenly, all the women began to speak at once, saying, "Who is it?" "Who's got it?" "Is it the Dunbars?" "Is it the Watsons?" Then the voices began to say, "It's Hutchinson. It's Bill," "Bill Hutchinson's got it."

"Go tell your father," Mrs. Dunbar said to her older son.

People began to look around to see the Hutchinsons. Bill Hutchinson was standing quiet, staring down at the paper in his hand. Suddenly, Tessie Hutchinson shouted to Mr. Summers, "You didn't give him time enough to take any paper he wanted. I saw you. It wasn't fair."

"Be a good sport, Tessie," Mrs. Delacroix called, and Mrs. Graves said, "All of us took the same chance."

"Shut up, Tessie," Bill Hutchinson said.

"Well, everyone," Mr. Summers said, "that was done pretty fast, and now we've got to be hurrying a little more to get done in time." He consulted his next list. "Bill," he said, "you draw for the Hutchinson family. You got any other households in the Hutchinsons?"

"There's Don and Eva," Mrs. Hutchinson yelled. "Make *them* take their chance!"

"Daughters draw with their husbands' families, Tessie," Mr. Summers said gently. "You know that as well as anyone else."

"It wasn't *fair*," Tessie said.

"I guess not, Joe," Bill Hutchinson said regretfully. "My daughter draws with her husband's family, that's only fair. And I've got no other family except the kids."

"Then, as far as drawing for families is concerned, it's you," Mr. Summers said in explanation, "and as far as drawing for households is concerned, that's you, too. Right?"

"Right," Bill Hutchinson said.

"How many kids, Bill?" Mr. Summers asked formally.

"Three," Bill Hutchinson said. "There's Bill, Jr., and Nancy, and little Dave. And Tessie and me."

"All right, then," Mr. Summers said. "Harry, you got their tickets back?"

Mr. Graves nodded and held up the slips of paper. "Put them in the box, then," Mr. Summers directed. "Take Bill's and put it in."

"I think we ought to start over," Mrs. Hutchinson said, as quietly as she could. "I tell you it wasn't *fair*. You didn't give him time enough to choose. *Everybody* saw that."

Mr. Graves had selected the five slips and put them in the box, and he dropped all the papers but those onto the ground, where the breeze caught them and lifted them off.

"Listen, everybody," Mrs. Hutchinson was saying to the people around her.

"Ready, Bill?" Mr. Summers asked, and Bill Hutchinson, with one quick glance around at his wife and children, nodded.

"Remember," Mr. Summers said, "take the slips and keep them folded until each person has taken one. Harry, you help little Dave." Mr. Graves took the hand of the little boy, who came willingly with him up to the box. "Take a paper out of the box, Davy," Mr. Summers said. Davy put his hand into the box and laughed. "Take just *one* paper," Mr. Summers said. "Harry, you hold it for him." Mr. Graves took the child's hand and removed the folded paper from the tight fist and held it while little Dave stood next to him and looked up at him wonderingly.

"Nancy next," Mr. Summers said. Nancy was twelve, and her school friends breathed heavily as she went forward, switching her skirt, and took a slip daintily from the box. "Bill, Jr.," Mr. Summers said, and Billy, his face red and his feet over-large, nearly knocked the box over as he got a paper out. "Tessie," Mr. Summers said. She hesitated for a minute, looking around defiantly, and then set her lips and went up to the box. She snatched a paper out and held it behind her.

"Bill," Mr. Summers said, and Bill Hutchinson reached into the box and felt around, bringing his hand out at last with the slip of paper in it.

The crowd was quiet. A girl whispered, "I hope it's not Nancy," and the sound of the whisper reached the edges of the crowd.

"It's not the way it used to be," Old Man Warner said clearly. "People ain't the way they used to be."

"All right," Mr. Summers said. "Open the papers. Harry, you open little Dave's."

Mr. Graves opened the slip of paper and there was a general sigh through the crowd as he held it up and everyone could see that it was blank. Nancy and Bill, Jr., opened theirs at the same time, and both beamed and laughed, turning around to the crowd and holding their slips of paper above their heads.

"Tessie," Mr. Summers said. There was a pause, and then Mr. Summers looked at Bill Hutchinson, and Bill unfolded his paper and showed it. It was blank.

"It's Tessie," Mr. Summers said, and his voice was hushed. "Show us her paper, Bill."

Bill Hutchinson went over to his wife and forced the slip of paper out of her hand. It had a black spot on it, the black spot Mr. Summers had made the night before with the heavy pencil in the coal-company office. Bill Hutchinson held it up, and there was a stir in the crowd.

"All right, folks," Mr. Summers said. "Let's finish quickly."

Although the villagers had forgotten the ritual and lost the original black box, they still remembered to use stones. The pile of stones the boys had made earlier was ready; there were stones on the ground with the blowing scraps of paper that had come out of the box. Mrs. Delacroix selected a stone so large she had to pick it up with both hands and turned to Mrs. Dunbar. "Come on," she said. "Hurry up."

Mrs. Dunbar had small stones in both hands, and she said, gasping for breath, "I can't run at all. You'll have to go ahead and I'll catch up with you."

The children had stones already, and someone gave little Davy Hutchinson a few pebbles.

Tessie Hutchinson was in the center of a cleared space by now, and she held her hands out desperately as the villagers moved in on her. "It isn't fair," she said. A stone hit her on the side of the head.

Old Man Warner was saying, "Come on, come on, everyone." Steve Adams was in the front of the crowd of villagers, with Mrs. Graves beside him.

"It isn't fair, it isn't right," Mrs. Hutchinson screamed, and then they were upon her.

RESPONDING PERSONALLY

3. With a partner, describe your feelings about the ending. How is it shocking and different from what you expected?

4. Write about a personal experience or another work of literature in which an individual came into serious conflict with her or his society.

RESPONDING CRITICALLY/ANALYTICALLY

5. a) What is the first point in the story at which you sense something is not quite right? What specifically generates that feeling?

   b) Make a list of the clues that foreshadow the outcome of the lottery.

   c) The writer makes an initial mention of stones — "Bobby Martin had already stuffed his pockets full of stones ..." — but then not again until the end of the story. What might have been her purpose in doing this? How effective is this?

6. a) Find examples of description and dialogue that create a congenial mood in the reader. Why does the writer start the story this way?

   b) At what point does the story's atmosphere change? Which details or comments begin to make the reader more nervous or uncertain?

7. In a small group, discuss the following:
   - Tessie's initial opinions about the lottery and how these later changed
   - Old Man Warner's view and his reasons
   - the views implicit in the choices of the other villages

   Then write a paragraph summarizing the conflicts raised by the various viewpoints.

8. Examine the symbolism in the story. Comment on the significance of each of the following:
   a) the lottery date
   b) the children's attitudes
   c) the names and roles of Summers and Graves
   d) the purposeful mispronunciation of Delacroix
   e) the shabbiness of the black box
   f) the treatment of the box the rest of the year
   g) the substitution of paper for wood chips
   h) the change to the ritual chant and salute
   i) the way in which the winner is determined
   j) the stoning finale

   How do these symbols reflect the main theme of the story?

9. The story uses what has been called an objective narrative point of view. Based on how the story is written, how would you define such a narrative point of view? How does it affect the way a reader experiences the story? What would have been the effect of using another point of view? Discuss the writer's choice.

RESPONDING CREATIVELY

10. Imagine and write a letter from a citizen of another village to one of the minor characters in the story, explaining why your village has abolished the lottery. The justification given in the letter should be within the bounds of the context of the story.

11. Create a visual collage based on the idea of scape-goating.

Problem Solving or Decision Making

12. Given the violent ending of the story, should it be dropped from grade 12 literature studies? If not, would the story be appropriate for, say, grade 8 or 9 classes? Discuss in a group and try to establish a group position. Then present your position to the class.

Group Assessment

- How did other groups' views compare with yours?
- Was there general agreement or consensus from the groups on the questions?
- What did some groups agree to disagree on?

Outsiders and Isolation

Society decides which of its segments are going to be outside its borders.
— *Kristin Hunter*

We are all of us sentenced to solitary confinement inside our own skins.
— *Tennessee Williams*

As we've seen in the previous unit, individuals often find that their desires or preferences do not line up with those of the communities in which they live. This unit focuses on characters who are obvious outsiders, or those who experience a profound sense of isolation or separation from the group.

Katherine Mansfield's "Miss Brill" is about one such outsider who fancies that she is very connected to her society and is a central character in the "play of life" she imagines. Ironically, her point of view comes into conflict with two young lovers who reveal the pathetic nature of her own fundamentally lonely existence.

"The Man Who Followed His Hand" by Regina's Connie Gault is a story about a strange man who "crashes" a neighbourhood barbecue and alters the host couple's relationship as well as a party's sociable atmosphere. At a deeper level, this selection is an honest but compassionate exploration of how outsiders are viewed by others who are very different from them.

Janette Turner Hospital is another Canadian writer who has written thoughtfully and sensitively on this unit's theme. Her heavily symbolic story "Here and Now" is about how isolated we can be in a time of crisis—even from those most sympathetic and best known to us.

Ontario writer Timothy Findley's "Foxes" closes the unit with a tongue-in-cheek piece about a compulsive communications expert who goes to the Royal Ontario Museum to investigate ancient fox masks. What he finds instead is an exotic community that "speaks" logically to his isolation more than anything else in his empty, reclusive life.

Each of the four stories explores what it means to be an outsider and isolated from society. Their protagonists experience loneliness, alienation, and even discrimination. But all these characters also gain self-knowledge, new insights, and epiphanies about the range of human experience.

Katherine Mansfield
Miss Brill

PRE-READING

1. Which aspects of your personality do you share with others, or even allow others to see? In a written paragraph, describe yourself—the part of you that is made visible to others. Write the description from the perspective of one of your more casual acquaintances.

2. "All the world's a stage,
   And all the men and women merely players:
   They have their exits and their entrances."

   The above is a passage from William Shakespeare's *As You Like It*. Paraphrase the passage. Do you agree with the thinking behind the words? Explain.

Although it was so brilliantly fine—the blue sky powdered with gold and great spots of light like white wine splashed over the Jardins Publiques—Miss Brill was glad that she had decided on her fur. The air was motionless, but when you opened your mouth there was just a faint chill, like a chill from a glass of iced water before you sip, and now and again a leaf came drifting—from nowhere, from the sky. Miss Brill put up her hand and touched her fur. Dear little thing! It was nice to feel it again. She had taken it out of its box that afternoon, shaken out the moth powder, given it a good brush, and rubbed the life back into the dim little eyes. "What has been happening to me?" said the sad little eyes. Oh, how sweet it was to see them snap at her again from the red eiderdown! ... But the nose, which was of some black composition, wasn't at all firm. It must have had a knock, somehow. Never mind—a little dab of black sealing-wax when the time came—when it was absolutely necessary.... Little rogue! Yes, she really felt like that about it. Little rogue biting its tail just by her left ear. She could have taken it off and laid it on her lap and stroked it. She felt a tingling in her hands and arms, but that came from walking, she supposed. And when she breathed, something light and sad—no, not sad, exactly—something gentle seemed to move in her bosom.

There were a number of people out this afternoon, far more than last Sunday. And the band sounded louder and gayer. That was because the Season had begun. For although the band played all the year round on Sundays, out of season it was never the same. It was like some one playing with only the family to listen; it didn't care how it played if there weren't any strangers present. Wasn't the conductor wearing a new coat, too? She was sure it was new. He scraped with his foot and flapped his arms like a rooster about to crow, and the bandsmen sitting in the green rotunda blew out their cheeks and glared at the music. Now there came a little "flutey" bit—very pretty!—a little chain of bright drops. She was sure it would be repeated. It was; she lifted her head and smiled.

Only two people shared her "special" seat: a fine old man in a velvet coat, his hands clasped over a huge carved walking-stick, and a big old woman, sitting upright, with a roll of knitting on her embroidered apron. They did not speak. This was disappointing, for Miss Brill always looked forward to the conversation. She had become really quite expert, she thought, at listening as though she didn't listen, at sitting in other people's lives just for a minute while they talked round her.

She glanced, sideways, at the old couple. Perhaps they would go soon. Last Sunday, too, hadn't been as interesting as usual. An Englishman and his wife, he wearing a dreadful Panama hat and she button boots. And she'd gone on the whole time about how she ought to wear spectacles; she knew she needed them; but that it was no good getting any; they'd be sure to break and they'd never keep on. And he'd been so patient. He'd suggested everything—gold rims, the kind that curved round your ears, little pads inside the bridge. No, nothing would please her. "They'll always be sliding down my nose!" Miss Brill had wanted to shake her.

The old people sat on the bench, still as statues. Never mind, there was always the crowd to watch. To and fro, in front of the flower beds and the band rotunda, the couples and groups paraded, stopped to talk, to greet, to buy a handful of flowers from the old beggar who had his tray fixed to the railings. Little children ran among them, swooping and laughing; little boys with big white silk bows under their chins, little girls, little French dolls, dressed up in velvet and lace. And sometimes a tiny staggerer came suddenly rocking into the open from under the trees, stopped, stared, as suddenly sat down "flop," until its small high-stepping mother, like a young hen, rushed scolding to its rescue. Other people sat on the benches and green chairs, but they were nearly always the same, Sunday after Sunday, and—Miss Brill had often noticed—there was something funny about nearly all of them. They were odd, silent, nearly all old, and from the way they stared they looked as though they'd just come from dark little rooms or even—even cupboards!

Behind the rotunda the slender trees with yellow leaves down drooping, and through them just a line of sea, and beyond the blue sky with gold-veined clouds.

Tum-tum-tum tiddle-um! tiddle-um! tum tiddley-um tum ta! blew the band.

Two young girls in red came by and two young soldiers in blue met them, and they laughed and paired and went off arm-in-arm. Two peasant women with funny straw hats passed, gravely, leading beautiful smoke-colored donkeys. A cold, pale nun hurried by. A beautiful woman came along and dropped her bunch of violets, and a little boy ran after to hand them to her, and she took them and threw them away as if they'd been poisoned. Dear me! Miss Brill didn't know whether to admire that or not! And now an ermine toque and a gentleman in gray met just in front of her. He was tall, still, dignified, and she was wearing the ermine toque she'd bought when her hair was yellow. Now everything, her hair, her face, even her eyes, was the same color as the shabby ermine, and her hand, in its cleaned glove, lifted to dab her lips, was a tiny yellowish paw. Oh, she was so pleased to see him—delighted! She rather thought they were going to meet that afternoon. She described where she'd been—everywhere, here, there, along by the sea. The day was so charming—didn't he agree? And wouldn't he, perhaps? ... But he shook his head, lighted a cigarette, slowly breathed a great deep puff into her face, and, even while she was still talking and laughing, flicked the match away and walked on. The ermine toque was alone; she smiled more brightly than ever. But even the band seemed to know what she was feeling and played more softly, played tenderly, and the drum beat, "The Brute! The Brute!" over and over. What would she do? What was going to happen now? But as Miss Brill wondered, the ermine toque turned, raised her hand as though she'd seen some one else, much nicer, just over there, and pattered away. And the band changed again and played more quickly, more gayly than ever, and the old couple on Miss Brill's seat got up and marched away, and such a funny old man with long whiskers hobbled along in time to the music and was nearly knocked over by four girls walking abreast.

Oh, how fascinating it was! How she enjoyed it! How she loved sitting here, watching it all! It was like a play. It was exactly like a play. Who could believe the sky at the back wasn't painted? But it wasn't till a little brown dog trotted on solemn and then slowly trotted off, like a little "theater" dog, a little dog that had been drugged, that Miss Brill discovered what it was that made it so exciting. They were all on the stage. They weren't only the audience, not only looking on; they were acting. Even she had a part and came every Sunday. No doubt somebody would have noticed if she hadn't been there; she was part of the performance after all. How strange she'd never thought of it like that before! And yet it explained why she made such a point of starting from home at just the same time each week— so as not to be late for the performance—and it also explained why she had quite a queer, shy feeling at telling her English pupils how she spent her Sunday afternoons. No wonder! Miss Brill nearly laughed out loud. She was on the stage. She thought of the old invalid gentleman to whom she read the newspaper four afternoons a week while he slept in the garden. She had got quite used to the frail head on the cotton pillow, the hollowed eyes, the open mouth and the high pinched nose. If he'd been dead she mightn't have noticed for weeks; she wouldn't have minded. But suddenly he knew he was having the paper read to him by an actress! "An actress!" The old head lifted; two points of light quivered in the old eyes. "An actress— are ye?" And Miss Brill smoothed the newspaper as though it were the manuscript of her part and said gently: "Yes, I have been an actress for a long time."

The band had been having a rest. Now they started again. And what they played was warm, sunny, yet there was just a faint chill—a something, what was it?—not sadness—no, not sadness—a something that made you want to sing. The tune lifted, lifted, the light shone; and it seemed to Miss Brill that in another moment all of them, all the whole company, would begin singing. The young ones, the laughing ones who were moving together, they would begin, and the men's voices, very resolute and brave, would join them. And then she too, she too, and the others on the benches—they would come in with a kind of accompaniment—something low, that scarcely rose or fell, something so beautiful—moving.... And Miss Brill's eyes filled with tears and she looked smiling at all the other members of the company. Yes, we understand, we understand, she thought—though what they understood she didn't know.

Just at that moment a boy and a girl came and sat down where the old couple had been. They were beautifully dressed; they were in love. The hero and heroine, of course, just arrived from his father's yacht. And still soundlessly singing, still with that trembling smile, Miss Brill prepared to listen.

"No, not now," said the girl. "Not here, I can't."

"But why? Because of that stupid old thing at the end there?" asked the boy. "Why does she come here at all—who wants her? Why doesn't she keep her silly old mug at home?"

"It's her fu-fur which is so funny," giggled the girl. "It's exactly like a fried whiting."

"Ah, be off with you!" said the boy in an angry whisper. Then: "Tell me, ma petite chère—"

"No, not here," said the girl. "Not yet."

On her way home she usually bought a slice of honeycake at the baker's. It was her Sunday treat. Sometimes there was an almond in her slice, sometimes not. It made a great difference. If there was an almond it was like carrying home a tiny present—a surprise—something that might very well not have been there. She hurried on the almond Sundays and struck the match for the kettle in quite a dashing way.

But today she passed the baker's by, climbed the stairs, went into the little dark room—her room like a cupboard—and sat down on the red eiderdown. She sat there for a long time. The box that the fur came out of was on the bed. She unclasped the necklet quickly; quickly, without looking, laid it inside. But when she put the lid on she thought she heard something crying.

NOTE

Jardins Publiques   French for public gardens

RESPONDING PERSONALLY

3. Generally, readers tend to identify with characters in stories, usually the protagonist. Do you, at any point, find yourself identifying with Miss Brill? With one of the "other people"? At what point in the story did this occur? If you did not identify with one of the characters, why might that be?

4. Have you ever used your imagination to embellish the significance of your own role in an incident or event in which you were involved? Describe your memory of the incident as it actually occurred. What has your imagination done to modify that memory, however slightly? Is it natural that people's memories act selectively? What purpose does a "selective memory" serve?

RESPONDING CRITICALLY/ANALYTICALLY

5. Is the relative sparseness of dialogue in the story thematically appropriate? What purpose does such a stylistic choice serve? What is ironic about the little bit of dialogue—the overheard conversation—that does take place?

6. a) Review the protagonist's observations about some of the elderly "other people" in the park:
   - Those who "sat on the benches and green chairs"
   - The "ermine toque"
   - The "funny old man"
   How does she regard these people in general?
   b) As a point of comparison, how do the boy and the girl at the end regard Miss Brill?
   c) What does the writer appear to be suggesting?

7. What motivates the protagonist's interpretations of the people and the events that she encounters? Can the story's resolution, then, and the pathos that accompanies it, be expected? Is there a tragic dignity of any kind in Miss Brill's closing actions? Explain.

8. Examine the symbolism in the story. Comment on the significance of each of the following:
   - The name of the title character (look up "brill" in the dictionary)
   - The season of the year
   - Her fur (look up "whiting" in the dictionary)
   - The box in which the fur is kept
   - The park setting

   How do these symbols develop the meaning of the main theme of the story?

RESPONDING CREATIVELY

9. With a small group, prepare and present a tableau representing Miss Brill in the park along with some of the "other people." The scene should be clear about which of the "other people" are represented.

SELF-ASSESSMENT

What did you and your group decide should be the facial and body expressions of Miss Brill? What is her state of mind at the time the scene is enacted? In what way do her mannerisms depict this?

10. Write Miss Brill's thoughts near the end of the story as she "passed the baker's by." Do her thoughts maintain the sense of gentility and decorum of the earlier part of the story, or have they changed? Explain your rationale.

PROBLEM SOLVING OR DECISION MAKING

11. If you, as either the boy or the girl at the end of the story, had noticed that Miss Brill had overheard you,
   a) What likely expression, if any, would you have perceived in either her face or her manner?
   b) What, if anything, might you have said to her to ease the feelings she was showing?
   c) What would have been your reason for either speaking or not speaking to her?

   In what way are your responses to these questions a reflection of society today?

Kate Fullbrook
On "Miss Brill"

If Katherine Mansfield's stories about women psychologically alone in the smart sets of London and New Zealand are painful, those written about women left outside the protective screens of men, money and class are often devastating in their emotional impact. Along with her contemporary, Jean Rhys, Katherine Mansfield has a reputation for her stories of the *femme seule*, and many of her late stories fit into this category. This sub-genre is in many ways a continuation of the nineteenth-century "governess" novel—we are close to the conventions of *Jane Eyre* here—with the change that there is no hope for a happy ending, no matter how qualified, no chance that the excluded woman will be fitted back, on any terms, into the relationships that are meant to define and enclose her life.

Katherine Mansfield's "Miss Brill," written in 1920, is probably her most famous sketch of a woman alone. As she explained in a letter, she worked to put the story together in terms of "a musical composition—trying to get it nearer and nearer to the expression of Miss Brill—until it fitted her." Once again, Katherine Mansfield's mature narrative method operates in the story as the writing strives to convey the experience of Miss Brill through the presentation of events in the vocabulary and cadences of her mind.

"Miss Brill" is the loneliest of all of Katherine Mansfield's stories about lonely women. It is sometimes compared with James Joyce's "Clay," but is different in tone, in its ultimate significance, and in its impression of participation in the miseries of the woman's consciousness which is portrayed. Like Joyce's little laundress, so extravagantly willing to be pleased by a world that gives her little but hard knocks, Miss Brill is eager to be part of a scene that ruthlessly excludes her. But whereas in the *Dubliners* story we are asked to pity Maria, and we are not sure of the extent to which she absorbs the humiliation we so painfully see, in "Miss Brill" the reader is more closely implicated, both with the character and with the world, as we are made to watch the character take the full force of the transformation of her consciousness of herself from participant to exile. It is a cruel process, and Katherine Mansfield refuses to temper any detail of its typicality.

Miss Brill lives alone in France, patching together an income from scraps of English teaching and from reading the newspaper to an invalid. She keeps herself going by reining her expectations in tightly with a chirpy inconsequentiality of mind and with her conformity to a tattered notion of gentility. Her surroundings smack of the deprivation of a lone woman—a dark little room, her meagre treat of a honey-cake which she looks forward to each week as her only self-indulgence. She most significantly identifies herself with her fur-piece, a decayed thing she keeps in a box under her bed, and which represents to her all the luxury and adventure in life that she convinces herself she shares. She values, too, the sensuality and flirtatiousness of the fur, itself an emblem of the traditional man-fascinating ways out of poverty for a woman that she still obliquely believes apply to herself. But the fur, her only friend, is not what it used to be; even Miss Brill can see that.

> *Dear little thing! It was nice to feel it again. She had taken it out of its box that afternoon, shaken out the moth powder, given it a good brush, and rubbed the life back into the dim little eyes.... But the nose, which was of some black composition, wasn't at all firm.... Little rogue! Yes, she really felt like that about it. Little rogue biting its tail just by her left ear.* (page 57)

The lonely woman feels herself as roguish as her fur as she slips out to the public concert which is her Sunday entertainment. For her, the afternoon in the park is concert and theatre combined, for she feels herself part of a complex drama as she watches the other concert-goers from her bench. She prides herself on her understanding of life and her ability to interpret strangers' affairs from a distance. But her keenest pleasure is in eavesdropping, and at first she is disappointed, as a woman starved for words, with the silent old couple sharing the bench. When a pair of young lovers replaces them she is delighted; she loves lovers, they are an unexpected treat. She sees them as the hero and heroine in a thrilling drama she directs and in which she participates. Smiling, she listens to their conversation:

"No, not now," said the girl. "Not here, I can't."
"But why? Because of that stupid old thing at the end there?" asked the boy.
"Why does she come here at all—who wants her? Why doesn't she keep her silly old mug at home?"
   "It's her fu-fur which is so funny," giggled the girl. "It's exactly like a fried whiting." (page 61)

Miss Brill drags herself back to "her room like a cupboard" and, without looking, puts the fur into its box. "But when she put the lid on she thought she heard something crying" (page 61). The extraordinary pathos of the story and of Miss Brill herself derives from the depth of the central character's courage and self-control which is nevertheless expended in acquiescence to a view of a woman's function that is bound to abase her. The story portrays a consciousness distancing itself from its own suffering isolation with a tremendous degree of pain and yet with a dignity that is in itself a kind of virtue. Miss Brill is written off as a horror by a code that condemns her on the grounds of sex, age, beauty, poverty and singleness, the same code that Miss Brill herself uses to explain her disappointment with the old couple on the bench and which now comes full circle to indict her as less than human. This is a portrait of a woman caught by the contradictions of social preconceptions that she herself has internalised. What Miss Brill stuffs into the box under the lonely bed of the *femme seule* is, according to the logic of the image, herself.

Connie Gault
The Man Who Followed His Hand

PRE-READING

1. Have you ever experienced a time in your life when you felt completely disconnected from those around you? Do you remember what caused those feelings? What, if anything, did you do to actively overcome those feelings?

2. What is it that makes a story realistic? Is it the setting? The conflict? The characters? The characters' motivations? Or is it something else entirely? Give your own definition of what makes a story realistic.

About the time the guests were saying it was the nicest part of the evening, the last hour of light, the man arrived at Sandra's back yard. The guests were sitting in a circle of chairs on the lawn. The man stepped into the shade at the corner of the house and waited. Children were playing. He listened to them calling to one another as if great distances separated them. He saw their freckles and flushed cheeks and the sunburnt rims of their ears. He thought: on a summer evening when the last light runs like a river through the suburbs, the voices of children sound lonely. The children stopped their game when they saw him. The adults gradually noticed the quiet and looked up. Just then Sandra walked out of the house onto the deck.

The man knew nothing about her. He didn't know her name. She was simply a woman he'd followed home the day before, an easy enough accomplishment though she'd been in her car and he'd been on foot. She'd had to drive slowly through the neighbourhood because of the children playing on the streets. A couple of times she'd stopped while they'd pulled their goalie nets aside or wobbled ahead of her on their bikes. He'd seen her eyes through the windshield while she waited at a stop sign longer than she needed to wait. She had watched him walk down the sidewalk. He always knew when people were watching. She turned and looked again when she passed him.

Funny how people didn't realize they could be seen through car windows. He'd often wondered at it. He didn't drive, himself. He didn't follow women to their homes either, usually.

She hugged a salad bowl to her chest, breathing in the smell of garlic. At first she didn't see him. She thought the guests were looking at her and wondering when they'd get to eat. She hadn't been ready when they'd arrived. She'd forgotten to put the wine into the fridge and to take the steaks out. Her hair was still wet from the shower. So David was just beginning to slide the steaks onto the barbeques.

She had a habit of answering her own questions before she knew she'd asked them. This is why we have these parties, she thought. The women toss the salads. The men tend the barbeques. Three men were helping her husband prod the steaks. The men all had beers in their hands. David knew how to make the others feel at home. She used to know how, but it seemed she had lost the knack. She had already offended the women by refusing to allow them into her kitchen. She hadn't offended her neighbour from across the street, though, to be fair. Nothing much bothered her beautiful, bleached-blonde neighbour. Without so much as a hello, Emily had set a tray of brownies from Safeways on the picnic table and made her way cheerfully to the cooler full of beer. An admirable woman, a good-natured soul, with no great affinity for kitchens.

Sandra had chased the other women from her house. She'd been rude to Lou, her husband's boss's wife, who'd tried to make her write down the recipe of her vegetable pizza. But Lou was already drunk by then, so it really hadn't mattered.

One of the men at the barbeques called to the man in the shade by the corner of the house. "Grab a lawn chair," he said, "and come on over." Harry was one of the older men who had lived in the subdivision for years, which meant that he could take over the host's role when the host was busy, in this case telling a joke, one all of them swore they hadn't heard. The man didn't respond. He stood staring at them all, but the other guests smiled and shifted their chairs, repeating the welcome. Sandra was not impressed. She thought their benevolence was easy. But she was not in the mood to give them credit. She was tired of them, without knowing why, before she'd even begun with them, tired of their golf games and their house renovations and the many accomplishments of their ever-active offspring.

She recognized the man, of course. He remained by the corner of the house, refusing the others' invitation, as she had known he would. He gazed at them, seriously, as if estimating their goodwill or taking the temperature of the party. His right arm was a little raised, his hand tentatively forward. The children stared at him. The adults looked embarrassed.

"What a lovely yard," they'd said when they'd arrived, the ones who hadn't visited before. "Your trees are huge," they'd said. "Isn't it nice to sit out here under the trees on an evening like this." Sandra had always thought of herself as a woman who had no conversation, but perhaps none was better than this. Every time someone new had arrived, the others had nodded and looked up into these trees, which were nothing but straggly American elms, as if they'd been given to them to sit under, as if something depended on the scrawny branches bobbing in the breeze. This is what we share, they seemed to be telling one another, the shade, the breeze, the trembling leaves. David understood. He wanted them to be happy. He offered them wine and beer as soon as they sat down.

Many of the guests didn't know one another, even some of those who were neighbours hadn't met, but they were all used to meeting strangers. David had made the introductions. "I don't think you know everyone," was his standard line. One of the women said, "No, but how nice to see new faces." These words buzzed in Sandra's mind over and over, whenever her husband introduced someone new.

"How nice to see new faces," she whispered, hugging her salad bowl, standing on the deck above them. They all knew so well what was expected of them, but they didn't know what to do about the man standing in the shade of the house with his hand outstretched.

He'd been walking down the sidewalk in a very distinctive way. She'd stayed at the stop sign longer than she needed to, watching him. She hadn't meant to stare and she hoped he hadn't noticed. At the time, she was almost sure he hadn't, he was so involved with making his way down the sidewalk, following his erratic hand. And he did follow his hand, she saw that immediately. Wherever his hand pointed, like an insane rudder, his body was pulled. But the intriguing thing about him was that he'd devised a way of directing the course he had to follow. With his free hand, the one he could control, he guided, from time to time, the other hand, which seemed to have a mind of its own. So he made his way, slowly and awkwardly, but effectively, and she admired him greatly. She was, in fact, fascinated by him and felt as if the rest of the world had fallen away and only he remained. He might have been the last man of earth, that's how alone he was on that sidewalk, dependent only on himself, his one commitment the carving out of his own path. He followed his hand, nothing else, so he could survive, she told herself, when all around him had perished.

Except for the odd bird's chatter, the yard was quiet. The only movement was in the trees. The branches swayed in the breeze. The slanting light caught the undersides of the leaves and Sandra imagined the yard submerged in water. The time between birds' calls and the sighing of the branches had an underwater sound. She saw that the guests had become tense and David was deciding what he should do. He was holding a barbeque fork uselessly in both hands. Soon he would have to put it down and do something.

"Where's Albert?" Sandra asked him, before he could make a move. She knew that the dog was tied at the side of the house where he couldn't see strangers and bark at them. David didn't bother even to look up. He didn't answer questions she asked for her own purposes. After eighteen years of marriage, he knew what to ignore. But their son Jamie was sitting on the grass below the deck and heard his mother. He didn't like the silence between them. He didn't want his parents to embarrass him. Now that he was twelve, he often found he hated adults and their ways, especially the silences that meant so much. He answered his mother's question.

Sandra felt ashamed, looking at her son. At least for him, she should be sociable. She should help David get rid of the strange man and make their invited guests comfortable again. She looked very seriously at Jamie to focus her better intentions. His face was getting longer, the bones more prominent. He was not her little boy any more, he would never again sit on her knee. She wasn't a particularly wise mother. She'd have detained him if she could have thought of a way to keep him by her side. She would have run her hand over his hair, but he took off as she reached out.

Before David could decide what to do about the situation, the man advanced into the yard, hand first. He walked between the children and their parents. A few of the parents stood up. One of the smallest boys jumped to his feet and ran blindly towards the adults, cutting through the man's path. The man showed no inclination to stop, if he noticed the boy at all. He was so intent on following his hand, it was doubtful he saw anything but the circle of lawn chairs, which was where he seemed to be headed. The little boy missed crashing into him by about two seconds. When he got to the circle, the child searched out his mother and burrowed his head into her lap.

Sandra set the salad bowl on the deck and took hold of the railing. The man continued in his own way and she watched him, once again fascinated by his ability to single-mindedly pursue his own path. Often he was pulled off course when his hand swung outward in a right angle to his body. With a sudden jerk each time, his body followed and he struck off towards the side yard. When that happened, he took his left hand and deliberately, sharply slapped at his right until he'd turned it back in front of him again. In this way he reeled towards the guests, who could do nothing but watch while their host, at last, tried to intercept him. Unfortunately, and farcically, the man kept veering off, so David was continually left stranded. Feeling foolish, he found himself opposite Sandra. His face and neck had turned red. She, in contrast, was pale. He thought she was thinking he deserved this fuss because it was his idea to have the party. He was sure she telegraphed this information to him, standing calmly erect above him, her hands resting lightly on the railing.

For an instant he wanted to kill her. She saw it in his face. It was the most hopeful thing she'd seen in months.

The guests were embarrassed, with the exception of Lou, the boss's wife, who was much too loaded to care, and Emily, the beautiful bleached-blonde neighbour, who liked a good fight. The host and hostess were behaving badly. And they were doing nothing to stop the man who was taking forever to work his way towards them, diligently prodding his right arm when it swung inward, slapping it back when it flew out, with every step following its direction.

When he finally reached the circle, Harry, the neighbour who'd invited him to join them, stood up and said, "Hey, hey now," in his most authoritarian bank manager's voice. Several of the guests stood and stepped back from their chairs. David grabbed the man's arm and swung him around.

Some of the guests looked as though they were afraid of a fight, but the man himself was not surprised by David's anger. He was doing what he thought Sandra wanted, invading the party. It was only right that her husband would be upset.

Sandra wished the man would say something to the guests, something no one else could tell them. They would have to believe such an artless man. But then she chided herself; it was she who should change rather than trying to change everyone else. She was always wanting people to be more than they possibly could be.

"What can we do for you?" David asked the man. He might have been talking to any one of the guests, he accorded the man that much dignity. He spoke quietly, his anger gone.

Sandra loved her husband. He didn't ask anything of anyone that he wouldn't expect of himself. She tried to hold that moment, when he forgot her and the guests and himself, and cared only about this man.

But it was soon over. While she was telling herself she wouldn't forget it, would keep it separate somehow in her mind for future use, it was being transmuted by what happened next. Jamie had slipped around the house to the side yard and untied the dog. He was afraid of the strange man, unsure of his father's gentle methods, and he thought the dog would strengthen David's authority over their yard. Albert bounded up barking just because he was free. He frightened the stranger. The man stood paralyzed while the dog leapt into the circle and lunged for his master's legs.

"Get down," David yelled. He yelled at Jamie too. "Tie Albert up," he ordered. "Get him out of here and tie him up."

The man was shaking. He didn't know what to do next, where to go. The guests, too, didn't know what might be expected of them.

Jamie took the dog away. Sandra saw his face, the knowledge that he'd done the wrong thing. His long face, with the changing bones.

They would all be bones one day. Again she imagined the yard submerged in water, their bones floating along the grass like the leaves floating on the breeze. They would all be bones one day so the square footage of their houses and the scores of the golf games and the trophies their children brought home should not matter to them. They should concern themselves with bigger things. Sandra knew it was wrong to judge them on their dinner party conversation, but she was sick of never hearing anything else. She would rather be alone than be with them.

In Toronto, where she visited now and then, the art gallery has a room filled with Henry Moore sculptures. Once Sandra found herself

there alone, surrounded by the strange, sad forms that reminded her of human bones and human dinosaurs. Among them, she felt she was among the relics of the human race and mourning her own kind. Yet they were the bones of people who had been strong and good and had for a time endured. They were huge and their largeness made her bigger. With them, she was one with all those in the history of the world who had lived before her and with all those who would come after. But now she stood in the midst of a party in her own back yard, hating everyone in sight.

They were all talking, suddenly they all had something to say. One of the women was sure she'd seen the man before, in the library downtown, where the derelicts hang out when it's too hot or too cold outside. Nobody would admit to thinking he was dangerous, but a few of them went so far as to say they were uneasy in his presence. He stood in the centre of the circle with David, and the guests talked about him as if he wasn't there. He seemed to be staring at nothing, but Sandra thought he heard them. She came down from the deck and joined her husband and the man. "How about some supper?" she asked of them both. David ignored her and asked the man, again, "What can we do for you?" The man peered up into the trees as if the answer might be there. Someone suggested they call the police who'd come and pick him up. "Nonsense," Sandra said. "Aren't you all hungry? I'm starved. I guess the steaks will be well done."

"About medium right now, if you get a move on," replied Jack, their next door neighbour, who had remained at the barbeques.

The man understood that he was still needed at the party, but he had been frightened by the dog and he didn't know what he should do next.

Sandra ushered the guests over to the picnic table where the plates were piled. Some of them dragged their feet a bit, but they were hungry, they soon followed the others. The children had already eaten their supper. Sandra called to Jamie to bring over the salad and to get a ball or something new for the others to play with. He gave her a look that said her behaviour was only barely acceptable and wouldn't much longer be tolerated. Even so, she asked the children what they would like to do next as she walked towards them, her arms flapping as if she was shooing chickens. They were about as dear to her right then as a flock of chickens in her yard. What they wanted to do, of course, at least the older ones, was watch to see what would happen next between the adults and this strange man. When Jamie came down with the salad, she insisted that he take the children to the front of the garage where they could shoot baskets. He said it was getting too dark to shoot baskets. He glared at her, but she wouldn't respond so he turned and followed her bidding, and the others reluctantly followed him.

Next she advanced on the adults. "Eat, eat," she ordered the few who were still without plates. "Here's the salad," she called to the others. She took a plate herself over to the man, who was still standing beside David, gazing into the trees. "What would you like?" she asked him. "Would you like a steak? Some salad?" She took his arm and began to lead him to the barbeques. David stared after her; she felt his disgust on her back. Suddenly, the man pulled away and began walking very quickly about the yard. He didn't bump into anyone, but he came close a few times.

"He's marching," someone said as he strode by, his arm held high like a drum major, his head high too, even his feet lifting high off the ground and coming smartly down.

"He's marching, all right," someone else said quietly.

The yard was getting darker; the sun was almost set. David was deciding to call the police. Sandra was deciding she wouldn't let him. She blocked his way onto the deck, knowing he wouldn't want to embarrass the guests by arguing with her. "I'll put on some more music," she said. "Something quiet. He'll calm down." Because she knew her husband deserved more, she added that she couldn't bear to think of the man being taken away. Then she got back to her duties, completely forgetting the music. She interrupted two women who were talking about taking their children home. "Come on," she said, linking her arms into theirs and steering them back to the lawn chairs.

"This is supposed to be a party. Now, where are your glasses? I'll get some more wine."

On her way back with the wine bottle, she dragged a few more people into the circle. "Relax," she told them. Music tripped out across the yard and Sandra stopped short. The guests looked at one another. It was Beethoven's Sixth, the *Pastoral Symphony*.

"What is this?" someone asked.

Sandra said, "I think it's the sound of my husband mocking me."

Some of the guests giggled nervously. The music was so out of place and yet so apt, or perhaps it was the time that was wrong and the place that was so right. The man who followed his hand loved it. He adapted immediately. He danced over the grass among the trees. Sandra had a silly wish that she could join him, that all of them could rise up off their cheap plastic lawn chairs and dance in the twilight under the trees, sway with the music and cry. She would have liked to cry very hard while she danced.

A little girl was standing where the man first appeared at the corner of the house. She was crying. Sandra saw her and went to her. She knelt beside her. "I feel like crying, too," she said. This information did nothing to soothe the child. She sobbed all the harder. Her father came along and asked what was wrong. She said she wanted to go home. "No, no," Sandra said. "Don't go. It's all right to cry." The child's father beckoned to the mother and before Sandra could rise to her feet, they were leaving. "The music's too loud," she said to herself, but she did nothing to change it.

The man who followed his hand stopped under the tree nearest to the circle of lawn chairs, his arm upraised, his eyes again on the leaves as they fluttered and floated as if to the music. "Don't go," Sandra said, seeing another couple get to their feet. "Please," she said, and they sat again. "Have some more wine," she said. "It's a party. It's early." David came over with two plates, loaded. He handed one to her and kept the other for himself. They sat on opposite sides of the circle. "I'm starving," she said, digging in.

The music began to storm. Even when it was quiet, it held the threat of more storm. The sky was suddenly as dark as it would get all night. The man followed his hand up the tree. He climbed as high as he could and sat huddled against the trunk, pointing down at the guests. The music punched at them, then fondled them, over and over, alternately, and all the time the man in the tree pointed at them and Sandra wanted to cry hard and David ignored everything and all the guests wanted to leave. The music seemed to know more than they did about their own lives and they found it unbearable to sit under such knowledge, such insistent, repetitive knowledge of themselves, and the more tender the music got, the harder it was for them to listen, and finally they just all got up and left. Neither the host nor the hostess bothered to say goodbye.

Sandra decided the music was telling her that all our bones are fragile, all our thoughts are weak, our passions puny, and our souls scrabble on the ground in the dust and dead leaves under the trees. Or we are too light, we rise too easily to the surface. We should be heavier, stronger. We should work harder, climb steadily, and not look back.

David rose to his feet and began to gather plates and napkins and empty beer bottles. We should have passions, Sandra was thinking. We should dare something, risk something, strive for something. We should try to be bigger than we are. We should want to leave something behind for others to see. None of her thoughts stopped him from his cleaning up. Back and forth he went, from the yard to the house, carting food and garbage, and she raged because everyone had left, they'd followed one another and left because they were people who wanted only to follow one another. They had no passion, no greatness, no anger or real love. They wanted only to do what the others did and not be embarrassed, not be revealed for what they were. They wanted to live their lives undisturbed by strangers. They wanted to meet only the strangers who could not disturb, only those who were not really strangers at all because they were just like them, more followers after the same followers. So they had gone. And she was left with her husband, who cleaned up the mess in silence.

She was angry about the silence too, because the music had died too soon and not strongly enough for her. There was too much village festival and shepherd's song and not enough storm. How could she say to David while he hosed down the barbeques, making the coals hiss and steam, that she hated his cleaning up and shutting down, that she wanted to fight. He knew she wanted to fight, he'd known it all evening, and he wasn't going to let her. Please, she would have said to him if there were any way of saying it, please just let's fight. Their son had gone to bed or at least he'd gone to his room or to watch TV. Only the man in the tree would hear them and he wouldn't care. It was time to quit being host, she wanted to tell her husband. It was time to stand up and fight. He pulled the lids down over the barbeques and turned to face her. She couldn't say a thing.

She watched him walk steadily across the lawn and up the steps to the house and she knew he wasn't going to turn around. She went and sat on a chair under the tree where the man still huddled, though she could no longer see him for the darkness, and his hand no longer pointed at anyone. Now that David was gone, she tried to remember the moment when he was good to the man, that moment she'd remembered she loved him. But she couldn't really imagine it. She kept thinking, instead, of him walking away from her and both of them knowing he wasn't going to turn around. Both of them knowing the door would not open, he would not come down those steps, he wasn't going to fight or even talk. Over and over again, her memory took him across the lawn, up the steps, away from her.

All night the man waited in the tree, thinking he'd been forgotten.

When the light came up in the morning, she heard a movement in the branches. A hand reached down hesitantly, as if testing the water. It was a frail, thin hand, the skin almost translucent in the rosy light. Inside it, the bones trembled.

NOTES

Henry Moore sculptures	large, abstract sculptures by the famous twentieth-century English sculptor
Pastoral Symphony	romantic composition by Beethoven idealizing country living

RESPONDING PERSONALLY

3. Following your reading of the story, list any words or expressions that come immediately to mind that might indicate your sense of the story.

   a) Select one of those words or phrases, the one that most completely captures or summarizes the effect of the story on you. Beginning with that word, freewrite for the next six minutes. Do not lift your pen from the paper: simply write as quickly as you can, without stopping, capturing every thought that enters your mind.

   b) In small groups of three or four, exchange your freewrite with classmates. Select one of your group's members' freewrites to share with the rest of your class.

4. With a partner, share your thoughts about the ending of the story. Was it an ending you might have anticipated? If so, explain what led you to expect the story to end as it did. If not, what were you expecting to happen, and why? Were you disappointed with the ending?

RESPONDING CRITICALLY/ANALYTICALLY

5. Notice that the writer begins the story with a form of suspense that "hooks" the reader's attention almost immediately, certainly within the first two paragraphs. With a partner, identify several different strategies that the writer seems to have employed specifically for this purpose. Share your findings with the rest of the class.

6. Very quickly, the writer establishes a connection of sorts, an affinity, between Sandra and the man.

   a) How does the writer achieve this so quickly? Examine in particular the quickly shifting narrative perspectives of the second paragraph of the story. Are these shifts warranted? What purpose do they serve?

   b) Identify another section of the story where narrative points of view shift. Why does this occur? In what way does the unity of the narrative remain undisturbed?

7. a) How is Sandra isolated by others in her "community"? How does she isolate herself? Are her motivations adequately identified and explained?

   b) The man's hand seems to nearly take on the role of a character in the story. Write a brief character sketch of the man's hand.

   c) Compare the above two character sketches (one of Sandra and the other of the hand). What are the differences? What are the similarities?

   d) Whose hand is described in the closing paragraph of the story?

8. Select one of the following passages from the story. In writing, explore the meaning the passage holds for you. Share with classmates. Respond to one another's explanations:

   • "... she watched him, once again fascinated by his ability to single-mindedly pursue his own path" (p. 71).

- "For an instant he wanted to kill her. She saw it in his face. It was the most hopeful thing she'd seen in months" (p. 71).
- "Sandra wished the man would say something to the guests, something no one else could tell them" (p. 72).
- "The man understood that he was still needed at the party ..." (p. 74).
- "The music seemed to know more than they did about their own lives and they found it unbearable to sit under such knowledge, such insistent, repetitive knowledge of themselves ..." (p. 76).

SELF/PEER ASSESSMENT

Evaluate the interpretations provided by your classmates. Is there consistency of interpretation among all of you? Or are there conflicting readings and interpretations of ideas in the story?

RESPONDING CREATIVELY

9. With a partner, script the conversation that Sandra and David will have the morning following their yard party. You may wish to prepare by building each character's motivational setting, and then role-playing an improvised version of the conversation before setting pen to paper. Explore the characters orally first, and then follow up in written form.
   a) Share your duologue with your classmates.
   b) Be prepared to justify the characters you have just "sketched."

PROBLEM SOLVING OR DECISION MAKING

10. For group discussion: An unspoken but palpable anger, perhaps even a form of reciprocal violence, exists between Sandra and David. How does one begin to break through the walls that have been erected between people?

Janette Turner Hospital
Here and Now

Pre-Reading

1. When do you typically share your innermost emotions? With whom? In what physical or social environments? In what emotional frame of mind? What generalizations can you draw?

2. Everyone has heard the expression "opposites attract." What does the expression mean to you? Do you agree with the expression, or do you find the converse to be more often true? Share your thinking with your classmates; listen to their thoughts. Is there some degree of consensus?

As it happened, Alison was wearing black when the phone call came; black velvet, cut low in front, with a thin silver chain at her throat. Only minutes before, she had been under the shower. Before that, she had been shovelling snow from the driveway. She had got the car out before the surface slicked over again, and before the city ploughs came through to toss a fresh barricade across the top of the drive. She had showered and put on the black dress. Car keys in hand, she was just pulling the front door shut behind her.

Damn, she thought. Will I answer it or not?

Afterwards it seemed to her that she had known from the first microsecond of the first ring. Four o'clock on a winter's Sunday afternoon, Lake Ontario veined with early ice, darkness already closing in: this is when such phone calls come. In Brisbane it was tomorrow already, it was dawn on Monday morning. Such phone calls are made at dawn.

At the Faculty Club, Alison's car slewed a little on the ice, nudged a parked Toyota, hesitated, then slid obediently into the neighbouring space. She sat trembling slightly, her hands on the wheel, the engine still running, and stared through the windshield at the Brisbane River. Here, on the lip of the campus, a membrane of ice already stretched across the water for as far as she could see. The membrane was thinner than a fingernail, milky white.

(High in the mango tree, hidden from the other children, frightened, she sucks comfort from the milk iceblocks her mother makes.)

"Metro Toronto engineers," the car radio announced, "are mystified by this morning's explosions in the city's sewer system. Throughout the streets in the downtown core, sewer caps have been popping like champagne corks, an extraordinary sight on a quiet Sunday morning in Toronto."

It is still Sunday here, Alison thought. It is not Monday yet.

It is still now, she thinks.

She turns off radio and ignition and gets out of the car, stepping with infinite care so as not to fracture the thin membranes of ice and time. The air, several degrees below zero, turns into crystal splinters in her lashes and nostrils. Something hurts. It is important to breathe very carefully.

Inside the Faculty Club, champagne corks are popping like pistol shots; a Christmas party, a retirement celebration for a distinguished colleague, two sabbatical farewells, all rolled into one elegant festive affair. Soon Alison will play her public part, make her speech. Then the small talk that rises like wisps of fog will engulf her and drift up river with her, past Kenmore, past the westernmost suburbs of Brisbane, up into the Great Dividing Range. She will be able to make her escape. She is desperate for solitude and rainforest.

"Wonderfully done," someone enthuses, handing her another drink. "A fitting tribute."

She has skated through it then, on thin ice and champagne. Soon it will be possible to leave. She smiles and talks and laughs and talks and smiles. In her glass, the ice in the champagne punch twists and dwindles. She holds the glass up to the light. The icecubes are as thin as the wafers of capiz shell that wash up on Queensland beaches.

"Alison," someone says. "Congratulations. I just heard the news."

Alison holds herself very still. "Yes?" she says faintly. She will not be able to speak of it yet. They will have to excuse her.

"Your invitation to Sydney, I mean, for next year. You must be thrilled. When do you go?"

"Ah," she says. Her voice comes from a long way off. "Nothing can be done on a Sunday. I'll have to make arrangements in the morning."

Her colleague raises a quizzical eyebrow as she slides away, nodding, nodding, smiling. Discreetly heading for the cloakroom, head lowered, she collides with Walter who has propped himself against a shadowy window niche. She mumbles an apology and lurches on.

"Alison," he calls in his frail and elderly voice.

"Walter. Oh, Walter, I'm sorry." She turns back and hugs him.

"Please join me," he begs.

"Oh Walter, I'm not fit company."

"You're my favourite company," he says. "These things, these things ..." He waves vaguely at the room with his knobbed walking stick. "I find these things difficult. I only come because I'm perverse." Walter's own retirement party is twenty-five years behind him, though he has just recently published yet another scholarly book. "I'm the loneliest man in the world," he says. "Do you know how old I am?"

She knows of course, everyone knows, that he's ninety. The acuity of his mind and speech is a local wonder. Only time gets muddled for him. He gets the First and Second World Wars confused; he fought in both.

"I'm as old as Methuselah," he says, "and as fond of Australians as ever. Have I told you why?"

He has of course. Many times. He has spoken of the Australian and New Zealand regiments stationed near him in Italy. That was during the Second World War. Or was it the first? In one of those wars, an Australian saved his life, dragging his wounded body through enemy fire.

"That was partly why," he says. "That was the beginning. But even more than that it's the whales."

"The whales?" she asks, politely. She has not heard about the whales.

"Dying on the beaches. All the way from Tasmania to Queensland, a shocking thing."

"When was this, Walter?"

"Now," he says, agitated, a little annoyed with her. "Here and now!" He is tapping on his forehead with his walking stick, a semaphore of distress. "Beached and gasping and dying by the hundreds."

"Walter, I hadn't..." She is confused. She is guilty of something. "I've heard nothing. Was this on the news?"

"Yes," he says. "And in the National Geographic. Stranded high and dry, out of their element, the loneliest, most awful..." There are tears in his eyes. "But the people of the coast are forming water lines, passing buckets, keeping them wet and alive. One by one, they are being dragged back to the water and towed out to sea. Wonderful people, the Australians. I walk along the beaches, you know, and watch. You hear a lot of rough talk out there, and some people think Australians are crude, but I know what I see."

He hunches into the window seat and stares out at the freezing lake. "It was because of the whales that I sent my son out there, after the war. He never came back."

"I didn't know you had a son in Australia, Walter."

"School was never the place for him. It happens often, doesn't it, with the children of scholars? And after that trouble, after the penitentiary. I couldn't think of a better place to give him a fresh start. I thought: Australians will make a man of him. Look at the way they fight and the way they are with whales."

"Walter," she murmurs, leaning her forehead momentarily against his. She is afraid of this confluence of griefs. She is afraid the sewer caps will not hold.

"What I'm sorry about," Walter says, "is that I never told him ... I mean, I should have said to him: I *am* proud of your racing car driving. There have been all these other things, all these ... We go on and on, you know, fathers do, about the disappointments. But I should have told him: I do admire your courage and speed behind that wheel!"

In the window seat, he seems to fold himself up into nothing.

"I visited the place. I visit. I go there often, more and more often now. It's a very steep and winding road, you can see how dangerous. From Cairns up to the Atherton Tableland, do you know it?"

She nods, unable to speak. The roads of Queensland, north and south, are imprinted in her veins. She stares at the map of her forearm and sees the hairpin turns on the way from Cairns to Kuranda.

"You can see it was an accident, can't you?" he says. "He had everything to live for, a young wife and a little boy. We stay in touch. My grandson still sends me Christmas cards from Australia."

"Sometimes," he says, "I think I may have told him I was proud of the driving. Sometimes I think I remember saying it."

"Walter," she says shakily, embracing him. "Merry Christmas, dear Walter. Forgive me. I have to go."

She manages, somehow to get out to her car. She sits in the darkness, holding herself very still. She turns on the car radio in time for the hourly news bulletin. "Sewer caps popping like corks," she hears. She turns it off and leans on the wheel and begins to shiver. She shivers violently, her teeth chattering, her body possessed by the shakes. Her bones clatter, even her skin is noisy, the din of her thoughts drowns out the tapping at her window. It is not until Walter leans across the front of her car and signals through the windshield that she can make him out, dimly, through the thin tough cataract of Sunday. She blinks several times. He taps on the window again.

"Walter," she says shocked, opening the door. "God, Walter, get in the car. You *mustn't* stand out in this cold, you'll catch your..."

"I would like to think so," he says quietly. "It's been a terribly long and lonely wait. Alison, you can tell an old man anything. What is it, dear child?"

"My mother," she begins to say. She puts her head against Walter's weathered shoulder and sobs. Orphaned at fifty: it sounds faintly embarrassing and comic, it's not supposed to be a major shock, it's not even listed in the register of traumas. "My mother," she begins again, quietly, "died in Brisbane at 4:40 A.M. this Monday morning."

She looks out at the frozen loop of a Queensland river. "My mother," she says, frowning a little, "died in the early hours of tomorrow morning."

Walter feels the car come plummeting off the Kuranda road, turning cartwheels through ferns and bougainvillea. It twists and twists and goes on falling through the gaping hole that opens somewhere behind his ribs. He hears the explosion that is now and always taking place.

"There is such gentleness," he says, stroking Alison's cheek, "in the most unexpected people, the roughest people. The way those men pass the buckets of water from hand to hand, the way they stroke the whales with wet cloths. I have never forgotten it."

Tomorrow, Alison thinks, I will fly all the way back to the beginning.

NOTES

cataract	downpour of rain
Methuselah	very old man in Bible who lived 969 years
semaphore	system of signals using flags, hands, and arms

RESPONDING PERSONALLY

3. If you have ever experienced the death of a person close to you, take a few moments now to recollect your memories of when you first learned of the person's passing.
   a) Where were you? Who was with you? What were you doing? What were you thinking? What were you feeling?
   b) In what way were you left with a sense of aloneness?

   Explain your recollections in writing.

4. "Orphaned at fifty" is a statement that expresses a literal truth. Yet at the same time, the metaphor that envelops the expression is perhaps more accurate than the statement of fact. Explore this idea in writing: Put yourself into the position of an adult who has just recently become an orphan. Are the emotions so very different from those of a child? What might be some differences? Some similarities? Share your thoughts in discussion.

RESPONDING CRITICALLY/ANALYTICALLY

5. What is the irony of the Faculty Club setting of the story? What are some of the descriptive details that fill out this irony?

6. a) The story seems full of little duplications of detail, some more obvious, some less. For example, the outdoor "popping" of sewer caps and the indoor popping of champagne corks; Alison's car nudging a parked Toyota and Alison colliding with Walter. Brainstorm with a partner: What other such parallels of detail can you find?
   b) Alison's and Walter's stories are revealed in a series of parallel unfoldings.
      • Using a T-chart, identify the similarities in the details of the two characters' stories of personal loss.
      • In a second T-chart, identify any parallels between the manner in which those details are gradually revealed to the reader.

7. a) The title expression "Here and Now" occurs twice in the story. The first time it is used, the words are split between two sentences. That point in the story serves as the division between the past and present tense of the story's narration. Why has the writer chosen to make such a change? Does the tense shift parallel a story or plot shift? Discuss.
   b) How does the closing sentence provide yet another shift? How does the closing sentence give the story a sense of completion?

c) Comment on the effectiveness of the writer's use of shifting time throughout the story and how it affects Alison and Walter.

SELF-ASSESSMENT

Have your classmates' responses to this question altered your opinion of the writer's technique? How do you personally determine the quality of a writer's work? What criteria do you employ?

8. Walter recounts two poignant stories to Alison. The first is his story of the Australians and the whales. The second is his story of his son. What are the similarities between the central "characters" of those two stories? What are the emotional parallels with his confidante that Walter appears to be experiencing, that result in his need to recount these stories? What suggestion is being made about Alison's needs?

RESPONDING CREATIVELY

9. As a group project, create a visual poem-collage that captures as completely as possible the prevailing mood of the story. Cut photographs out of magazines that will be placed onto a background in such a way that the appropriate mood is evoked. Some decisions will need to be made:
   - What colour of background will be used?
   - Will coloured photographs, or black-and-white, be used? If colours, what tones?
   - Which is the dominant image? Where will it be placed?
   - How might the Juxtapositioning of various images help to create the intended effect?
   - How might the placement of the images influence the direction of movement of the viewer's eye as the "poem" is "read"?

GROUP ASSESSMENT

In what way did group collaboration influence the "writing" of your "poem"? Were you comfortably able to reach consensus? Which collaborative processes most assisted you in the completion of this project?

PROBLEM SOLVING OR DECISION MAKING

10. How do you approach a friend or acquaintance who is emotionally distressed? How do you yourself wish to be approached in a similar situation? Is it difficult to discern the fine line between helping and imposing? What rule of thumb might serve people in similar circumstances?

Timothy Findley
Foxes

PRE-READING

1. As preparation for reading the story,
   a) Research the use of masks in theatrical dramatic presentations. What purpose do masks serve? When are they worn? How are they physically handled by the wearer? What are some of the theatrical protocols regarding the use of masks? If possible, research some of the history behind the use of masks in theatre. What are some connotative meanings that accompany the word "mask"?
   b) Research the history of the use of animal totems in various cultures and religions. What is the connection between animals and humans?
   c) Explore your understanding of the imagery of the fox. Draw up a list of words that come to mind when you think of "the fox." Can any kind of suggestion or generalization be drawn?

The face is only the thing to write.

— *Roland Barthes*

All the appropriate people had been forewarned: Morris Glendenning would be coming to the Royal Ontario Museum to do some private research in the Far Eastern Department. He was not to be approached; he was not to be disturbed.

Glendenning's reclusiveness was legendary, made doubly curious by the fact he was the world's best-known communications expert—a man whose public stances and pronouncements had put him at centre stage as long ago as 1965. The thing was, Morris Glendenning could not bear to be seen.

But, as with most eccentric beings, part of what was eccentric in him seemed determined to thwart whatever else was eccentric. In Morris Glendenning's case, his passion for privacy was undone by his need for warmth—which led to a passion for things made of wool and, as well, to what some considered to be the most eccentric habit of dress in the whole community of North American intellectuals.

He wore old-fashioned galoshes—the kind made of sailcloth and rubber, sporting metal fasteners shaped like little ladders lying on their sides. He was also given to wearing a multiplicity of woollen garments layered across his chest: scarves, sweaters, undervests—each of a prescribed colour. He wore, as well, a navy blue beret, pulled down over the tops of his prominent ears. He was six feet, six inches tall and was made, it seemed, almost entirely of bone. His skin was pale, translucent and shining—as if he polished it at night with a chamois cloth. Glendenning's over-coat was blue and had a military cut—naval, perhaps. It was pinched at the waist and almost reached his ankles. In magazine photographs—taken always on the run—Morris Glendenning had the look of Greta Garbo, heading for doorways and ducking into elevators:

"COMMUNICATIONS EXPERT ESCAPES YET AGAIN!"

Mrs. Elston, in charge of secretarial work for the Far Eastern Department at the Royal Ontario Museum, had been told by her boss that Glendenning would be turning up on the Friday morning, last week in February. She was quite looking forward to meeting the famous man. Dr. Dime, the curator, had instructed her to offer all available assistance without stint and without question. On no account, she was told, was he to be approached by staff. "Whatever help he requires, he will solicit: probably by note...." By mid-afternoon, however, on the day of the visit, Mrs. Elston said: "it doesn't take much to guarantee the privacy of someone who doesn't even bother to show up."

At which point Myrna Stovich, her assistant, said: "but he *is* here, Mrs. Elston. Or—*someone* is. His overcoat and galoshes are sitting right there...." And she pointed out a huddled, navy blue shape on a chair and a pair of sailcloth overshoes squatting in a large brown puddle.

"For heaven's sake," said Mrs. Elston. "How can that have happened when I've been sitting here all day?"

"You haven't been sitting here all day," said Myrna Stovich. "You took a coffee break and you went to lunch."

The night before, and all that morning, it had snowed. The clouds were a shade of charcoal flannel peculiar to clouds that lower above Toronto at the dirty end of winter. Merely looking at them made you cough. Morris Glendenning had supplemented his already over-protective array of woollen garments with one more scarf, which he pulled down crossways over his radiator ribs and tied against the small of his back. Even before he departed his Rosedale home, he pulled his beret over his ears and bowed his head beneath the elements.

Walking across the Sherbourne Street bridge, Morris set his mind on his destination and, thereby, shut out the presence of his fellow pedestrians. His destination at large was the Royal Ontario Museum but his absolute destination was its collection of Japanese theatre masks.

Long after midnight, Morris Glendenning had sat up watching the snow eradicate the garden and the trees beyond his windows. Now, he was tired. And reflective. Progress with his current work had stalled, partly due to the residue of sorrow over his wife's midsummer death and partly due to the fact he had published a book two

months later, in September. The work itself—the massing of materials, the culling of ideas—had been passing through an arid stage and it was only in the last few days that he'd begun to feel remotely creative again. Not that he hadn't traversed this particular desert before. Far from it. After every piece of exploration—after every publication of his findings—after every attempt at articulating the theories rising from his findings, Morris Glendenning—not unlike every other kind of writer—found himself, as if by some sinister miracle of transportation, not at the edge but at the very centre of a wasteland from which he could extract not a single living thought. For days—sometimes for weeks—his mind had all the symptoms of dehydration and starvation: desiccated and paralyzed almost to the point of catatonia. Five days ago it had been in that state. But, now, it was reviving—feeding again, but gently. And all because of a chance encounter with a photograph.

The photograph had appeared in a magazine called *Rotunda*, published by the Royal Ontario Museum; and it showed a Japanese theatre mask recently purchased and brought from the Orient. "Fox," the caption read. But it wasn't quite a fox. It was a *human fox*, alarming in its subtle implications. Reading about it, Morris Glendenning discovered it was one of three or four others—a series of masks created for a seventeenth-century Japanese drama in which a fox becomes a man. Each of the masks, so the article informed him, displayed a separate stage in the transformation of a quintessential fox into a quintessential human being. Glendenning's curiosity was piqued—and more than piqued; a trigger was pulled in the deeps of his consciousness. Something had been recognized, he realized, and he felt the reverberations rising like bubbles to the surface: signals, perhaps—or warnings.

He very well remembered reading David Garnett's horror story *Lady Into Fox*—that masterful, witty morality tale in which the English "hunting class" is put in its place when one of its wives becomes a fox. But here, in these Japanese masks, the process had been reversed. It was the fox who took on human form. On the other hand, this was more or less standard procedure when it came to balancing the myths and customs of the Orient against the myths and customs of the West. Almost inevitably, the icons and symbols employed by custom and by myth were opposites: white in the

Orient, black in the West for mourning; respect for, not the arroga-
tion of nature; death, not birth as access to immortality.

Whose fate, Glendenning had written in the margin next to the
provocative photograph, *is being fulfilled within this mask? The fox's?
Or the man's?*

Clipping the whole page out of the magazine, he slipped it into
a file marked *Personae*, and five minutes later, he retrieved it—held
it up in the snow-white light from the windows and stared at it,
mesmerized. The question became an obsession. Looking into the
lacquered face of the mask he imagined stripping off the layers of
the human face. Not to the bone, but to the being.

The blooming of this image took its time. It occurred to him
slowly that under the weight of all his personal masks, there was
a being he had never seen. Not a creature hidden by design—but
something buried alive that wanted to live and that had a right
to life.

"Foxes into humans," he said out loud as he watched the photograph. *Their choice, not ours.*

Standing in the bathroom, later that afternoon, something sent a shudder through his shoulders and down his back when, in the very instant
of switching on the light, he caught the image of his unmasked self in
the mirror. And he noted, in that prodding, ever-observant part of his
brain—where even the death of his wife had been observed with the
keenest objectivity—that what had been unmasked had not been
human. What he had seen—and all he had seen—was a pair of pale gold
eyes that stared from a surround of darkness he could not identify.

Half an hour later, Morris picked up the telephone and placed a call
to the Curator of the Far Eastern Collection at the Royal Ontario
Museum, who happened to be his old acquaintance, Harry Dime.
What privileges could Harry Dime afford him? Could he inspect the
Japanese masks alone?

Privately, Harry Dime would later conclude he should have said
no. For all his own awareness of intellectual curiosity, he had no
sense at all of the dangerous threshold at which Glendenning
stood. Dime had forgotten that, when he returned with these treasures from another time, he brought them with all their magic

intact. Not with ancient spells, of course, since all such things are nonsense—but the magic they released in others: in those who beheld them without the impediment of superstition.

On the snowy Friday morning, Morris Glendenning debated whether to walk or to chance the subway. Chancing the subway might mean recognition, and given the loss of time that recognition inevitably produced, he decided to walk. Walking, he was certain no one would see him—let alone recognize him. *How many eyes*, he once had said to Nora, his wife, *meet yours on a crowded avenue?*

Bloor Street on a Friday is always massed with shoppers, most of whom, Glendenning noted, like to give the appearance of worldly indifference. *I could go in and buy that coat if I wanted to,* they seemed to be telling themselves. *But I won't do that today, I'll do that on Monday. Maybe Tuesday ...* Their impassivity was almost eerie and it troubled Morris Glendenning.

The street, for all its people and all its motor traffic, was silent beneath the falling snow. Morris could see his own and everyone else's breath. If he paused, he could count the breaths and he could take the pulse of where he stood—each breath embracing so many heart beats—all the heart beats racing, lagging—all the secret rhythms of all the people visible in the frosted air. Even the motor traffic gave the appearance of being alive; as much an appearance of life as the people gave with their wisps and plumes of vapours. In behind the windows of these vehicles, the faces peering out of the silence were reflected in the clouds of glass that fronted Harry Rosen's; Cartier's; Bemelmans; Eddie Bauer's. Holt Renfrew ... moon phases; passing on Bloor Street.

Morris Glendenning could feel the subway tumbling beneath him, not like an earthquake—merely an indication that something was there, alive and at work, whose underground voice made no more sound than voices make in dreams. Morris paused at the corner of Bellair Street and watched a man he had intimately known in boyhood wander past him with his eyes averted. Later on, both of them would say: *I saw old so-and-so out on Bloor Street, today. He looked appalling; dead ...*

I saw old so-and-so today. We passed.

Here, Morris thought, was a kind of debilitating apartness—an apartness that once had been entirely foreign to all these people: the ones who were perfect strangers and the ones who were intimate friends.

We needed each other. That was why we looked each other in the eye. We needed each other. Morris clenched his jaw, afraid that perhaps his lips had been moving over the words. *We've always shared this dreadful place—these awful storms—this appalling climate—and we knew we couldn't afford to be alone. But now ...*

Now he was approaching the final stretch of Bloor Street before the stop at Avenue Road, where he would wait for the light to change, the way he had waited there for over forty years.

Beyond the veils of snow he could see the vaguest hint of neon, red in the air above him: *Park Plaza Hotel*—though all he could see was part of the *z* and part of the final *a*.

A small crowd of people formed near the curb and Morris Glendenning was aware, all at once, how many of them wore fur hats. A dozen fur hats and fifteen heads.

Not one person was looking at any other; only Morris Glendenning, counting. Why were they so unconcerned with one another? When had they all become collectively impassive?

Probably last Tuesday.

Morris smiled. Rhetorical questions formed the backbone of his profession, but he delighted in providing stupid, banal and irritating answers. It was a form of private entertainment.

Still, it affected everything they did—this intractable indifference. It affected the way they walked, he observed—the speed with which they walked—their gait, as they made their way along the street. They moved, Morris thought—gazing at them through the falling snow—with the kind of apathy acquired by those whom something—bitterness?—has taught that nothing waits for those who hurry home. It came to him slowly, standing on the curb at Avenue Road and Bloor, that, when he rode on the subway and was recognized, it was not their recognition of him that mattered: but their hope that he—in all his ballyhooed wisdom and fame—might recognize them and tell them who they were. *I know you from somewhere:* that's what they yearned for him to say. *I know—I recognize who you are.*

In the cellars at the ROM, there is a labyrinth of halls and passage-ways that leads, through various degrees of light and temperature, to various sequestered rooms where various treasures lie in wait for someone to come and give them back their meaning. Bits and pieces, shards and corners of time—numbered, catalogued, guessed at.

Morris Glendenning stood in one of these rooms—perspiring, it so happened—holding in his fingers, his fingers encased in white cotton gloves—the very mask he had encountered first in its photo-graphed image.

The door behind him was closed.

The room—effectively—was sound-proofed by its very depth in the cellars and its distance from the active centre of the building. A dread, white light was all he had to see by: "daylight" shining from computered bulbs.

The mask's companions—three in number—were set out, sterile on a sterile tray: the fox on its way to becoming a man.

He thought of surgery.

He thought of layers.

How small, he thought, *the face is.*

Looking down at the others, beyond the mask he held, he counted over the variations and degrees of change—the fox in his hands at one extreme and the trio of variations, lying on their tray, bur-geoning feature by feature into a close proximity of Oriental human beauty. The widely tilted, oval eyes of the fox became the evenly centered, almond eyes of a man. Of *a priest*, so the collection's catalogue had told him.

A priest. So apt a designation, it could only be amusing. Though amusing, of course, in a sinister way.

Morris felt like a marauding and possibly destructive child bent on mischief. A vandal, perhaps. Most certainly, he knew he was trespassing here, the victim of an irresistible impulse: *put it on....*

He had spent over three hours standing there, touching—lift-ing—contemplating the masks. Around him, resting on shelves and laid out, numbered in other sterile trays was the department's whole collection of Japanese theatre masks. Each mask was hidden: slung in a silk and sometimes quite elaborate bag, the drawstrings tied in neat, fastidious bows.

Heads, he thought. *The victims of some revolution.*

The truth was—he dared not open the bags to look.

Some of the bags were darkly stained. And, even though he fully recognized the stains were merely of time and of mildew, he could not bring himself to touch them.

Put it on. Don't be afraid.

Go on.

He held the mask up gently before his face.

He could smell its ... what? Its mustiness?

Or was it muskiness?

He closed his eyes and fitted the moulded inner surface over the contours of his bones.

He waited fully fifteen seconds before he dared to open his eyes.

The masks below him, sitting on their tray, were smiling.

Had they smiled before?

He waited, knowing he must not give up until the whole sensation of the mask had been experienced—no matter how long it took.

He thought he heard a noise somewhere out in the corridor. The voice of someone calling.

He held his breath, in order to hear.

Nothing.

And then, as he began to breathe again, he felt the vibrations of a sound between his face and the mask.

Another voice. But whose?

He was a long way off inside himself and standing in another light. A pattern of leaves threw shadows over what he saw: perhaps the verge of a clearing somewhere.

Creatures—not human—moved before him.

Foxes.

How elegant they were. How delicate: precise and knowing.

Why was he so unconcerned and unafraid?

He began to receive the scent of earth as he had never smelled the earth before: a safe, green, sun-warmed scent.

He looked at his hands. He held them out as far as he could. Human hands—in white gloves. Whose were they?

He tried to speak, but could not.

What emerged, instead of speech, was an inarticulate and strangled sound he had never heard before.

Down below him, where the earth replaced the floor, one of the foxes came and sat at his feet and stared up into his face. It seemed, almost, to know who he was.

Never in all of Morris's life had he been so close to anything wild. He was mesmerized.

Other foxes came, as if to greet him, and they leaned so close against his legs that he could feel their bones against his shins.

The fox that had been the first to come and sit before him narrowed its gaze. It stared so intently, Morris felt that something must be going to happen.

Say something to us, the fox appeared to be saying. Tell us something. Speak to us....

Yes—but how?

Morris was bereft of words. But the impulse to speak was overwhelming. He could feel the sound of something rising through his bowels—and the force of the sound was so alarming that Morris pulled the mask away from his face and thrust it from him—down into the tray from which he had lifted it. When?

How much time had passed. An hour? A day? How far away had he been? Who was he, now? Or what?

He looked—afraid—at the backs of his hands, but they were covered still with the gloves.

The creatures in the tray appeared to stir.

Morris closed his eyes against the notion he was not alone. He did not want to see the floor—for fear the floor was still the sun-warmed ground it had been a moment before.

And yet ...

He wanted them back. Their breath and their eyes already haunted him. He waited for their voices—but no voices came.

Morris removed the white cotton gloves. He took a long, deep breath and let it very slowly out between his teeth.

His fingers dipped towards the tray and even before they reached the mask, he smiled—because he could feel the head rising up as sure and real as the sun itself. And when the mask he had chosen was in place, he paused only for seconds before he dared to breathe again; one deep breath, and he found his voice—which was not his human voice but another voice from another time.

Now—at last—he was not alone.

Just before five that afternoon, Mrs. Elston was putting the cover on her IBM Selectric and preparing to leave, when she became aware all at once of someone standing behind her.

"Oh," she said—recovering as best she could. "We thought you were not here, Professor Glendenning."

She smiled—but he did not reply.

His enormous height was bending to the task of pulling on his galoshes.

"Shall we be seeing you tomorrow?" Mrs. Elston asked.

With his back to her, he shook his head.

"Monday, perhaps?"

But he was buckling his galoshes; silent.

He drew his many scarves about him, buttoned his greatcoat, took up his leather bag and started away.

"Professor Glendenning ... It was such a great pleasure ..."

But Mrs. Elston could not reach him. He was gone and the door swung to and fro.

Mrs. Elston sniffed the air.

"Myrna?" she said. "Do you smell something?"

Myrna Stovich needed no prompting.

"Sure," she said. "Dog."

"But there *can't* be a dog!" said Mrs. Elston.

"Yeah, well," said Myrna. "We also thought there wasn't no Professor Glendenning, didn't we."

"True," Mrs. Elston laughed. "You're quite right, my dear. But ... goodness! What a day!" she said. "And now we have to go out into all that snow."

"Yeah," said Myrna Stovich. "Sure. But I like the snow."

"Yes," said Mrs. Elston, and she sighed. "I like it, too, I guess." And then she gave a smile. "I suppose I have to, don't I—seeing it's what we've got."

NOTES

catatonia	state associated with schizophrenia, featuring rigid muscles and stupor
Greta Garbo	famous Swedish movie star, renowned for her reclusiveness
Roland Barthes	French social and literary critic and theorist, an important twentieth-century thinker

RESPONDING PERSONALLY

2. Do you feel that the writer has provided a sense of conclusion to the end of the story? Are you satisfied with the conclusion? What is it about the ending that leaves you feeling as you do?

3. Reflect on and write about an experience you have had that is similar to Morris Glendenning's in the story, where you felt powerfully drawn to something.

RESPONDING CRITICALLY/ANALYTICALLY

4. Except for the opening, the closing, and one brief passage in the middle, the story focuses entirely on Morris Glendenning's thoughts and actions. What has been the writer's purpose in beginning and ending the story as he has? Would the story have been as effective had it been written from only a limited omniscient point of view?

5. The writer establishes a series of contrasts and juxtapositions:
   - Morris Glendenning, a communications expert with a passion for privacy who, except for one very brief phrase, never speaks.
   - The stories and symbols, and interpretations of symbols, of Japanese and Western cultures.
   - The feelings of "alone"ness that extend throughout the story, and the occasional brief passages describing people's need for one another.
   - The less pleasant "muskiness" of the mask's initial smell, and the warmly satisfying "scent of earth."
   - The pervasive "danger" that Morris Glendenning seems to suffer, and the feeling of "safety" that arises when, near the end, the masks seem to begin to smile.
   - The long italicized passage that contrasts with Morris Glendenning's thoughts leading up to his climactic interaction with the masks.
     a) In a small group, select one of the above contrasts. Focusing especially on the irony it contains, explore the contrast in depth. With your partners, arrive at a conclusion as to the purpose and the effect of that contrast. Present a discussion of your findings to the rest of the class.

b) Following all class presentations, have a general discussion of the conflict at the heart of the story. What universal life statement suggested by the story can you formulate?

PEER ASSESSMENT

Assess the other groups' presentations. Were their presentations clear? Did you agree with their comments? Did their understandings of the writer's use of contrasts mesh with yours? Were there clear thematic similarities? Explain.

6. Much is made of Morris Glendenning's need for layers of clothing, and the sense of "protectiveness" it offers him. In what way does the mask also offer him "protection"? Why does he remove the white gloves at such a key moment?

RESPONDING CREATIVELY

7. About midway through the story, Harry Dime reflects about the favour he granted his friend and concludes that "he should have said no. For all his own awareness of intellectual curiosity, he had no sense at all of the dangerous threshold at which Glendenning stood." With a partner, speculate as to the life direction to which Morris Glendenning will turn. What would be a reasonable expectation about his future? Craft a one-page epilogue to Findley's story.

8. It might be said that everyone, at one time or other, escapes into an alternative persona. In a free verse poem, write about a situation in which you might have worn a "mask."

PROBLEM SOLVING OR DECISION MAKING

9. Morris Glendenning arrives "a long way off inside himself." In your opinion, has he trespassed? Has he gone where he should not have? Can one trespass upon her/himself? Are there times or situations when one should not? Discuss your thoughts with others. Are there differing viewpoints? If so, why might people's viewpoints differ?

Glen Kirkland
An Interview with Timothy Findley

Glen Kirkland [GK]: The first question that does emerge is about the epigraph: "The face is only the thing to write." Would you like to comment on its function?

Timothy Findley [TF]: This is a quote that is taken from Roland Barthes' book, *Empire of Signs*, about the iconography that he explored when he was in Japan. It was because of my own interest in Japan and Japanese culture that I got this book. And, as you can see, that plays into the hands of the story itself. There is about Japanese culture a wonderful sense of presentation and ceremony and face, and "The face is only the thing to write" comes from the section in Barthes' book about Japanese theatre. When an actor makes up to play in *kabuki*—and all the young performers in *kabuki* are male—the first thing they do is to completely whiten their face; in other words, they completely remove their own face. Then they write upon that face the mode of expression that is the most telling aspect of the character they're going to play. So they are not just writing but making a statement in a single expression or a single line. And that's what that epigraph is about for me; it's literally the wiping away of self and the placing of the most telling aspect of the character.

GK: It certainly reverberates through the story, thank you. That brings up the story's main character, Morris Glendenning. Would you like to comment on what he emerged from in terms of your own experience, in terms of imagination? What brought him to light for you?

TF: Well, let's go to the end of that question. I have argued that you conceive of the character versus the situation. When I'm writing, most of what I write starts with a person. The person always comes first— they and the story attached to them—*by necessity* because my first encounter with characters in my mind as they loom up is that they have something they want to tell me *or* something they don't want to tell me, and their silence is so extraordinary that I figure that I gotta get it out of them.

So, it *usually* does start with the person. I want to say that right off the top: that is the normal procedure. But, in this one instance, I had been invited to write a story for *Rotunda*. At the Royal Ontario Museum [or ROM, the publisher of *Rotunda*], they said "Is there a story in your mind that might emerge from the museum?" and, of course, I went straight in my mind to Japanese masks. I had already encountered some of these masks at the museum. Morris zapped into my mind on his own and I thought: "My goodness, I do have a story and the story has to do with the masks and this man who encounters them." The character himself has very large elements in him emerging from Marshall McLuhan [Canadian theorist whose ideas about communication focused on the influence of electronic media on the popular culture].

GK: I was wondering about the communications expert.

TF: Yes. The whole impetus in Morris Glendenning to think about how we communicate comes from McLuhan. But the recluse, the genius, the artist aspect comes from [Canadian classical pianist] Glenn Gould. My encounter with Gould involved his making music for the film based on *The Wars*. I found him a very fascinating and very moving person.

GK: There's so much of the artist in the character. His experiences, I'm sure, reflect some of the writer's, generally speaking. Certainly, the tension between the privacy and the need to communicate is there.

TF: And the precision. So it's a kind of blend, I guess.... I can only speak for myself, but I can't believe it would be otherwise for other authors, given some conversations I've had with other writers. There is *always* some autobiographical element, if in this sense only: It is *you* who's putting it on the page. So, you're drawing not only from a field of imagery and knowledge that you've acquired but also from the stuff of your own daily life, so that the views from the window, the sense of being in that building or walking along Bloor Street are very much reflections of my own presence in those places. But I don't think that there's much of my personal character in Morris; I was really trying much more to capture someone like Gould or McLuhan.

GK: The link to the foxes certainly becomes something of a metaphor for Morris' predicament or the tension I mentioned between his need to avoid contact and his need for communication. I'm curious why perhaps it felt so right to use foxes. Had you considered any other animal?

TF: That idea stemmed from the fact that that sequence of masks tells the story as it's told in Japan. They were created to be used in a play that exists, I think a "Noh" play, about a fox that becomes a priest, which is interesting because priests, too, are aesthetically inclined to view the world from a kind of silence. They are observers, in the Buddhist sense of priests, and they're very deeply involved with nature.

GK: I was wondering if there was a Japanese cultural view of the fox as a creature that might be part of this as well, or if the concept of the wildness and the community with nature is the important dimension there.

TF: My own sense is that nature is very much a part of life in Japan as reflected in classical writing, as reflected in all the paintings, as reflected in the necessity of that huge mass of people living in that tiny little place. They can't get away from it. But also I think there's a great respect for animals and animal characteristics that North American culture has ignored. The fox is a greatly respected figure, however, in the culture that produced these masks.

GK: That accounts even more for the link to the priest, who would also be a figure of respect.

TF: Yes. I'm fascinated, too, by the whole aspect of opposites in things Japanese, which is a constant reflection that occurs over and over again. The opposite is the opposite is the opposite: black for joy and white for mourning, et cetera; and, in this instance, that the fox becomes a man—but, in our culture, the man becomes a fox. You know the British story "The Lady and the Fox," and the whole thing of hunting the fox, the fox as a wily enemy we must outwit. Whereas, in Japan, the fox is a wily *companion* living in nature with us and we must understand it, rather than outwit it.

GK: Certainly, the camaraderie Morris feels more when he dons the mask, the sense of peacefulness, as such, is part of what you're saying there.

Now, I'll invite you to comment on whether there is something further about Timothy Findley's writing that emerges in the experiences of the story "Foxes."

TF: I think so. I very often find that I'm trying to write my way out of despair. And I don't mean that is *why* I write. I'm a writer and that's why I write. My motto is taken from Samuel Johnson [English writer], who wrote just before he died and as he was preparing to die: "Make prayers against despair." Isn't that incredible? That is my motto. So, the story is yet one more way to find my way past despair; the thoughts that Morris has walking on Bloor Street are very much the same thoughts that I have there.

GK: In a sense I felt the ending of the story moved from despair to the positive or to some strengthening. In the end Morris returns— through his need to communicate—to being with people again.

TF: Absolutely. Because he gets back to where he came from. Because he gets back to looking down through the mask. I found I was moved by this, because that image conjured itself in my own mind as I was writing of this golden circle, the smell of the earth and this circle of beasts which is the circle we have lost. And when he goes out smelling like a dog, he's found it again.

GK: Yes. Indeed. There's a real feeling of affirmation for him that he would carry on and he would get past this depth of despair he was in. I found, too, the closing scene suggested to me that inside of him there was an acceptance of the world because of what we have in us; though it may not give him everything, it still is part of him.

TF: Oh, indeed. He cannot utterly walk away from it because that's where we have to do our living—in the real world. That is something that I share as well; that's the way I think.

GK: That brings me to my following question. "Foxes" is a "large" story in some ways in that there are many dimensions to it. When we speak of the masks of Morris', perhaps, near obsession or madness or despair, so much is going on in the story. The richness is all centred around Morris' own consciousness and the tension I've referred to earlier between his need to avoid and his need to communicate. Morris' is a positive story in spite of that and I'd like to leave it open for any kind of comment. You mentioned that the character is the heart of the story, and character is that which tells you what doesn't belong in the story and what does belong.

TF: Yes, absolutely. But I think that there's one more step to go with that in reference to this question, and that is: because Morris *is* Morris, that's one thing, and that generates certain elements; but because Morris *as* Morris is at this moment looking from a *particular* perspective in terms of his own moment in crisis, what he is *looking* at is form and face and mask. That was for me the joy in making this story: that *that* matched the thing from which it sprung, which was the mask itself. And that means looking at the faces and the encounter with the mask. Morris and his boyhood friend don't speak but then go away and each one says, "I saw old so and so out on Bloor Street today...." Everything is an encounter that is struck through the appearance of the mask worn by the person on the street.

Tradition, Change, and Choice

Traditions are the signposts driven deep into our subconscious minds.
— *Ellen Goodman*

I am not now
That which I have been.
— *Lord Byron*

Every act is an act of self sacrifice. When you choose anything, you reject everything else.
— *G.K. Chesterton*

This unit looks at three interconnected themes—tradition, change, and choice. Our desire for order and permanence leads us to maintain and preserve tradition. However, tradition and order are at best transitory in today's rapidly changing world. Some philosophers have said that the only constant is change itself. Regardless of the relative amount of tradition, order, and change in our own lives, we often must make significant personal choices in favour of one or more of these three recurring values.

Wayson Choy's "The Jade Peony" is about a Chinese grandmother and grandson who find themselves at odds with the rest of their more modern-minded Vancouver family. But the impressionable Sek-Lung is greatly influenced by his grandmother's traditional beliefs and learns much from his preferred role model, who clings to the "old ways" and her memory of a former lover.

"Totem" is a witty, satirical piece by one of Canada's best Aboriginal writers, Thomas King. It is about an unusual traditional totem pole that threatens the safe, predictable order and peaceful façade of a museum as well as the conventional expectations of its employees.

Jane Urquhart is the latest in a continuing line of excellent Canadian fiction writers. Her symbolic story "Storm Glass" is about an unexpected, momentous change in the relationship and lives of a couple who have previously avoided the symbolic storm glass of harsh personal experience.

"Behind the Headlines" by Vidyut Aklujkar is about an East Indian Canadian housewife who is packing her husband's things for a business trip. As she reviews the predictability of her life, she makes a sudden, unexpected personal choice that will change the order of her traditional lifestyle dramatically.

In each of these stories, we see characters trying to hang on to the past and the familiar. But change proves to be insidious, and with change will come the challenge of choices that will affect these characters beyond the scope of each of their stories' conflicts.

Wayson Choy
The Jade Peony

PRE-READING

1. You may have known one or more of your grandparents well. If that is
   the case, tell about her or him. Relate an incident from this
   grandparent's life that is indicative of either the kind of person she or he
   is or was, or of the special relationship the two of you have had, or both.
   Share your grandparent's "story."

2. Family superstitions are relatively common, though not often shared in
   public. Does your family now, or has it in the past, observed any
   superstitious beliefs or customs? If so, and if possible, research their
   origins, and share the information with classmates.

When Grandmama died at 83 our whole household held its breath.
She had promised us a sign of her leaving, final proof that her present
life had ended well. My parents knew that without any clear sign, our
own family fortunes could be altered, threatened. My stepmother
looked endlessly into the small cluttered room the ancient lady had
occupied. Nothing was touched; nothing changed. My father, thinking that a sign should appear in Grandmama's garden, looked at the
frost-killed shoots and cringed: *no, that could not be it.*

My two older teenage brothers and my sister, Liang, age 14, were
embarrassed by my parents' behaviour. What would all the white
people in Vancouver think of us? We were Canadians now, *Chinese-
Canadians*, a hyphenated reality that my parents could never accept.
So it seemed, for different reasons, we all held our breath waiting for
something.

I was eight when she died. For days she had resisted going into
the hospital ... *a cold, just a cold* ... and instead gave constant
instructions to my stepmother and sister on the boiling of ginseng
roots mixed with bitter extract. At night, between wracking coughs
and deadly silences, Grandmama had her back and chest rubbed

with heated camphor oil and sipped a bluish decoction of an herb called Peacock's Tail. When all these failed to abate her fever, she began to arrange the details of her will. This she did with my father, confessing finally, "I am too stubborn. The only cure for old age is to die."

My father wept to hear this. I stood beside her bed; she turned to me. Her round face looked darker, and the gentleness of her eyes, the thin, arching eyebrows, seemed weary. I brushed a few strands of gray, brittle hair from her face; she managed to smile at me. Being the youngest, I had spent nearly all my time with her and could not imagine that we would ever be parted. Yet when she spoke, and her voice hesitated, cracked, the somber shadows of her room chilled me. Her wrinkled brow grew wet with fever, and her small body seemed even more diminutive.

"I—I am going to the hospital, Grandson." Her hand reached out for mine. "You know, Little Son, whatever happens I will never leave you." Her palm felt plush and warm, the slender, old fingers boney and firm, so magically strong was her grip that I could not imagine how she could ever part from me. Ever.

Her hands *were* magical. My most vivid memories are of her hands: long, elegant fingers, with impeccable nails, a skein of fine, barely-seen veins, and wrinkled skin like light pine. Those hands were quick when she taught me, at six, simple tricks of juggling, learnt when she was a village girl in Southern Canton; a troupe of actors had stayed on her father's farm. One of them, "tall and pale as the whiteness of petals," fell in love with her, promising to return. In her last years his image came back like a third being in our two lives. He had been a magician, acrobat, juggler, and some of the things he taught her she had absorbed and passed on to me through her stories and games. But above all, without realizing it then, her hands conveyed to me the quality of their love.

Most marvelous for me was the quick-witted skill her hands revealed in making windchimes for our birthdays: windchimes in the likeness of her lost friend's only present to her, made of bits of string and scraps, in the center of which once hung a precious jade peony. This wondrous gift to her broke apart years ago, in China, but Grandmama kept the jade pendant in a tiny red silk envelope, and kept it always in her pocket, until her death.

These were not ordinary, carelessly made chimes, such as those you now find in our Chinatown stores, whose rattling noises drive you mad. But making her special ones caused dissension in our family, and some shame. Each one that she made was created from a treasure trove of glass fragments and castaway costume jewellery, in the same way that her first windchime had been made. The problem for the rest of the family was in the fact that Grandmama looked for these treasures wandering the back alleys of Keefer and Pender Streets, peering into neighbours' garbage cans, chasing away hungry, nervous cats and shouting curses at them.

"All our friends are laughing at us!" Older Brother Jung said at last to my father, when Grandmama was away having tea at Mrs. Lim's.

"We are not poor," Oldest Brother Kiam declared, "yet she and Sek-Lung poke through those awful things as if—" he shoved me in frustration and I stumbled against my sister, "—they were beggars!"

"She will make Little Brother crazy!" Sister Liang said. Without warning, she punched me sharply in the back; I jumped. "You see, look how *nervous* he is!"

I lifted my foot slightly, enough to swing it back and kick Liang in the shin. She yelled and pulled back her fist to punch me again. Jung made a menacing move towards me.

"Stop this, all of you!" My father shook his head in exasperation. How could he dare tell the Grand Old One, his aging mother, that what was somehow appropriate in a poor village in China, was an abomination here. How could he prevent me, his youngest, from accompanying her? If she went walking into those alley-ways alone she could be attacked by hoodlums. "She is not a beggar looking for food. She is searching for—for...."

My stepmother attempted to speak, then fell silent. She too, seemed perplexed and somewhat ashamed. They all loved Grandmama, but she was *inconvenient*, unsettling.

As for our neighbours, most understood Grandmama to be harmlessly crazy, others that she did indeed make lovely toys but for what purpose? Why? they asked, and the stories she told me, of the juggler who smiled at her, flashed in my head.

Finally, by their cutting remarks, the family did exert enough pressure so that Grandmama and I no longer openly announced our expeditions. Instead, she took me with her on "shopping trips," ostensibly for clothes or groceries, while in fact we spent most of our time exploring stranger and more distant neighbourhoods, searching for splendid junk: jangling pieces of a vase, cranberry glass fragments embossed with leaves, discarded glass beads from Woolworth necklaces.... We would sneak them all home in brown rice sacks, folded into small parcels, and put them under her bed. During the day when the family was away at school or work, we brought them out and washed every item in a large black pot of boiling lye and water, dried them quickly, carefully, and returned them, sparkling, under her bed.

Our greatest excitement occurred when a fire gutted the large Chinese Presbyterian Church, three blocks from our house. Over the still-smoking ruins the next day, Grandmama and I rushed precariously over the blackened beams to pick out the stained glass that glittered in the sunlight. Small figure bent over, wrapped against the autumn cold in a dark blue quilted coat, happily gathering each piece like gold, she became my spiritual playmate: "There's a good one! *There!*"

Hours later, soot-covered and smelling of smoke, we came home with a Safeway carton full of delicate fragments, still early enough to steal them all into the house and put the small box under her bed. "These are special pieces," she said, giving the box a last push, "because they come from a sacred place." She slowly got up and I saw, for the first time, her hand begin to shake. But then, in her joy, she embraced me. Both of our hearts were racing, as if we were two dreamers. I buried my face in her blue quilt, and for a moment, the whole world seemed silent.

"My juggler," she said, "He never came back to me from Honan ... perhaps the famine...." Her voice began to quake. "But I shall have my sacred windchime ... I shall have it again."

One evening, when the family was gathered in their usual places in the parlour, Grandmama gave me her secret nod: a slight wink of her eye and a flaring of her nostrils. There was *trouble* in the air. Supper had gone badly, school examinations were due, Father had failed to meet an editorial deadline at the *Vancouver Chinese Times*. A huge sigh came from Sister Liang.

"But it is useless this Chinese they teach you!" she lamented, turning to Stepmother for support. Silence. Liang frowned, dejected, and went back to her Chinese book, bending the covers back.

"Father," Oldest Brother Kiam began, waving his bamboo brush in the air, "you must realize this Mandarin only confuses us. We are Cantonese speakers...."

"And you do not complain about Latin, French or German in your English school?" Father rattled his newspaper, signal that his patience was ending.

"But, Father, those languages are *scientific*," Kiam jabbed his brush in the air. "We are in a scientific, logical world."

Father was silent. We could all hear Grandmama's rocker.

"What about Sek-Lung?" Older Brother Jung pointed angrily at me. "He was sick last year, but this year he should have at least started Chinese school, instead of picking over garbage cans!"

"He starts next year," Father said, in a hard tone that immediately warned everybody to be silent. Liang slammed her book.

Grandmama went on rocking quietly in her chair. She complimented my mother on her knitting, made a remark about the "strong beauty" of Kiam's brushstrokes which, in spite of himself, immensely pleased him. All this babbling noise was her family torn and confused in a strange land: everything here was so very foreign and scientific.

The truth was, I was sorry not to have started school the year before. In my innocence I had imagined going to school meant certain privileges worthy of all my brothers' and sister's complaints. The fact that my lung infection in my fifth and sixth years, mistakenly diagnosed as TB, earned me some reprieve, only made me long for school the more. Each member of the family took turns on Sunday, teaching me or annoying me. But it was the countless hours I spent with Grandmama that were my real education. Tapping me on my head she would say, "Come Sek-Lung, we have *our* work," and we would.walk up the stairs to her small crowded room. There in the midst of her antique shawls, the old ancestral calligraphy and multi-coloured embroidered hangings, beneath the mysterious shelves of sweet herbs and bitter potions, we would continue doing what we had started that morning: the elaborate windchime for her death.

"I can't last forever," she declared, when she let me in on the secret of this one. "It will sing and dance and glitter," her long fingers stretched into the air, pantomiming the waving motion of her ghost chimes; "My spirit will hear its sounds and see its light and return to this house and say goodbye to you."

Deftly she reached into the Safeway carton she had placed on the chair beside me. She picked out a fish-shape amber piece, and with a long needle-like tool and a steel ruler, she scored it. Pressing the blade of a cleaver against the line, with the fingers of her other hand, she lifted up the glass until it cleanly snapped into the exact shape she required. Her hand began to tremble, the tips of her fingers to shiver, like rippling water.

"You see that, Little One?" She held her hand up. "That is my body fighting with Death. He is in the room now."

My eyes darted in panic, but Grandmama remained calm, undisturbed, and went on with her work. Then I remembered the glue and uncorked the jar for her. Soon the graceful ritual movements of her hand returned to her, and I became lost in the magic of her task: she dabbed a cabalistic mixture of glue on one end and skillfully dropped the braided end of a silk thread into it. This part always amazed me: the braiding would slowly, *very* slowly, *unknot*, fanning out like a prized fishtail. In a few seconds the clear homemade glue began to harden as I blew lightly over it, welding to itself each separate silk strand.

Each jam-sized pot of glue was precious; each large cork had been wrapped with a fragment of pink silk. I remember this part vividly, because each cork was treated to a special rite. First we went shopping in the best silk stores in Chinatown for the perfect square of silk she required. It had to be a deep pink, a shade of colour blushing toward red. And the tone had to match—as closely as possible—her precious jade carving, the small peony of white and light-red jade, her most lucky possession. In the center of this semi-translucent carving, no more than an inch wide, was a pool of pink light, its veins swirling out into the petals of the flower.

"This colour is the colour of my spirit," she said, holding it up to the window so I could see the delicate pastel against the broad strokes of sunlight. She dropped her voice, and I held my breath at the wonder of the colour. "This was given to me by the young actor who taught me how to juggle. He had four of them, and each one had a center of this rare colour, the colour of Good Fortune." The pendant seemed to pulse as she turned it: "Oh, Sek-Lung! He had white hair and white skin to *his toes! It's true*, I saw him bathing." She laughed and blushed; her eyes softened at the memory. The silk had to match the pink heart of her pendant: the colour was magical for her, to hold the unravelling strands of her memory....

It was just six months before she died that we really began to work on her windchime. Three thin bamboo sticks were steamed and bent into circlets; 30 exact lengths of silk thread, the strongest kind, were cut and braided at both ends and glued to stained glass. Her hands worked on their own command, each hand racing with a life of its own: cutting, snapping, braiding, knotting.... Sometimes she breathed heavily and her small body, growing thinner, sagged against me. *Death*, I thought, *He is in the room*, and I would work harder alongside her. For months Grandmama and I did this every other evening, a half a dozen pieces each time. The shaking in her hand grew worse, but we said nothing. Finally, after discarding hundreds, she told me she had the necessary 30 pieces. But this time, because it was a sacred chime, I would not be permitted to help her tie it up or have the joy of raising it. "Once tied," she said, holding me against my disappointment, "not even I can raise it. Not a sound must it make until I have died."

"What will happen?"

"Your father will then take the center braided strand and raise it. He will hang it against my bedroom window so that my ghost may see it, and hear it, and return. I must say goodbye to this world properly or wander in this foreign devil's land forever."

"You can take the streetcar!" I blurted out, suddenly shocked that she actually meant to leave me. I thought I could hear the clear-chromatic chimes, see the shimmering colours on the wall: I fell against her and cried, and there in my crying I knew that she would die. I can still remember the touch of her hand on my head, and the smell of her thick woolen sweater pressed against my face. "I will always be with you, Little Sek-Lung, but in a different way ... you'll see."

Months went by, and nothing happened. Then late one September evening, when I had come home from Chinese school, Grandmama was preparing supper when she looked out our kitchen window and saw a cat—a long, lean white cat—jump into our garbage pail and knock it over. She ran out to chase it away, shouting curses at it. She did not have her thick sweater on and when she came back into the house, a chill gripped her. She leaned against the door: "That was not a cat," she said, and the odd tone of her voice caused my father to look with alarm at her. "I cannot take back my curses. It is too late." She took hold of my father's arm: "It was all white and had pink eyes like sacred fire."

My father started at this, and they both looked pale. My brothers and sister, clearing the table, froze in their gestures.

"The fog has confused you," Stepmother said. "It was just a cat."

But Grandmama shook her head, for she knew it was a sign. "I will not live forever," she said. "I am prepared."

The next morning she was confined to her bed with a severe cold. Sitting by her, playing with some of my toys, I asked her about the cat.

"Why did father jump at the cat with the pink eyes? He didn't see it, you did."

"But he and your mother know what it means."

"What?"

"My friend, the juggler, the magician, was as pale as white jade, and he had pink eyes." I thought she would begin to tell me one of her stories, a tale of enchantment or of a wondrous adventure, but she only paused to swallow; her eyes glittered, lost in memory. She took my hand, gently opening and closing her fingers over it. "Sek-Lung," she sighed, "*he* has come back to get me."

Then Grandmama sank back into her pillow and the embroidered flowers lifted to frame her wrinkled face. I saw her hand over my own and my own began to tremble. I fell fitfully asleep by her side. When I woke up it was dark and her bed was empty. She had been taken to the hospital and I was not permitted to visit.

A few days after that she died of the complications of pneumonia. Immediately after her death my father came home and said nothing to us, but walked up the stairs to her room, pulled aside the drawn lace curtains of her window and lifted the windchimes to the sky.

I began to cry and quickly put my hand in my pocket for a handkerchief. Instead, caught between my fingers, was the small, round firmness of the jade peony. In my mind's eye I saw Grandmama smile and heard, softly, the pink center beat like a beautiful, cramped heart.

NOTES

Cantonese   Chinese language spoken in Canton and Hong Kong

decoction   extract made by boiling something

Mandarin   main language used in China, especially Beijing

Woolworth   older department store known for its cheap prices

RESPONDING PERSONALLY

3. This story opens with several statements that express the embarrassment and the shame felt by the family due to the grandmother's somewhat unusual behaviour, and the resulting "dissension ... frustration ... exasperation" that grips the rest of the family. Can you recall ever experiencing a feeling of public embarrassment because of the behaviour of a family member? Describe the situation in writing. If you are willing, share it with your classmates.

4. What is it between the young narrator and his grandmother that makes this relationship special? Is it only that he, at his age, is a "captive audience"? Or is there something more? What does each offer that the other needs?

RESPONDING CRITICALLY/ANALYTICALLY

5. The "marvellous" world of the grandmother's past is presented in juxtaposition to the "scientific, logical world" of the younger generation.
   a) Identify the family's feelings as it is caught between the burden of cultural tradition and the demands of societal assimilation.
   b) Identify some of the particular words and images used by the young Sek-Lung that clearly identify him as a narrator sympathetic to the grandmother's situation.
   c) Why does the writer employ such dramatic contrast in words and images?

6. The story begins and ends with the grandmother's death. As well, death references recur throughout the story.
   a) In which situations do the most abundant references to death appear? What seems to be the writer's purpose?
   b) What is the significance of the grandmother's references to her mysterious "juggler"? What is the impact of his "presence" on the young Sek-Lung?

7. Like the jade peony of the title, the writer's use of language is both delicate and beautiful. Examine the words and images the writer uses to describe the materials the grandmother selects from which to fabricate her windchimes. Compile a list of the varied nouns and adjectives used in these descriptions. What is the writer attempting to do through his use of such language?

8. Consider the many and varied references to colour in the story. What observations can you make about the writer's use of colour symbolism?

9. The writer inserts mild humour into the story. Find one or two such examples. Why is gentle humour appropriate in a story such as this?

Responding Creatively

10. Review the description of the pendant the grandmother owns and of the windchime that she makes before her death. Taking direction from these descriptions, draw and colour the "peony of white and light-red jade" with its centre "pool of pink light." Share your interpretation with your classmates.

Self/Peer Assessment

Devise an evaluation guide, perhaps a rubric, that would enable your teacher to fairly evaluate an assignment such as the above. Remember that this is an English literature rather than an art assignment: What are two or three criteria by which such an assignment might be graded? What kinds of things would your teacher look for in your assignment that would reflect your understanding of the story?

11. If his grandmother had not died, do you think Sek-Lung's relationship with his "spiritual playmate" would have changed with time? What does the story say or suggest that lends support to your position? Script the conversation between the two as they discuss the now 18-year-old Sek-Lung's post–high school plans.

Problem Solving or Decision Making

12. A cliché of today's world is that change is the only constant. It is said that all the knowledge of the known world doubles approximately every 18 months. Additionally, in an increasingly global community, linguistic and cultural "sharing" is rapidly becoming the norm. With all this in mind, is there a way in which to help people, especially those older and more set in their ways, to cope with change, especially the kinds of change that they may not particularly desire? How can society better honour those who have contributed willingly all their lives, but can no longer continue to contribute in ways that society still finds useful?

Thomas King
Totem

PRE-READING

1. In class discussion, share your collective understandings of both the fact
   and the idea of "totem"
   - as an animal or other natural object
   - as a guardian spirit
   - in its relationship to a Native clan, family, or individual
2. What is the meaning of the term "satire"? (See also the Glossary for
   more on the term.) Why is satire so often used as a form of social
   criticism?

Beebe Hill stood at the reception desk of the Southwest Alberta Art
Gallery and Prairie Museum and drummed her fingers on the counter
until Walter Hooton came out of the director's office. She was annoyed, she told Walter, and she thought other people were annoyed,
too, but were too polite to complain about the noises the totem pole
in the far corner of the room was making.

"It sounds like gargling."

Walter assured her that there wasn't a totem pole in the entire place
including the basement and the storage room. The current show, he
explained, featured contemporary Canadian art from the Atlantic
provinces.

"It's called 'Seaviews,'" Walter said, smiling with all his teeth showing. There had been, he admitted, a show on Northwest Coast carving at the gallery some nine years back, and, as he recalled, there
might have been a totem pole in that exhibit.

Mrs. Hill, who was fifty-eight and quite used to men who smiled
with all their teeth showing, took his hand and walked him to the
back of the gallery. "Gargling," said Beebe. "It sounds like gargling."

Mrs. Hill and Mr. Hooton stood and looked at the corner for a very
long time. "Well," said the director finally, "it certainly *looks* like a

totem pole. But it doesn't sound at all like gargling. It sounds more like chuckling."

Mrs. Hill snorted and tossed her head over her shoulder. And what, she wanted to know, would a totem pole have to chuckle about. "In any case," said Mrs. Hill, "it is quite annoying, and I think the museum should do something about the problem." It would be a fine world, she pointed out, if paintings or photographs or abstract sculptures began carrying on like that.

Walter Hooton spent much of the afternoon going over the museum's records in an attempt to find out who owned the totem pole or where it had come from. At four o'clock, he gave up and called Larue Denny in the storeroom and asked him to grab Jimmy and a hand cart and meet him in the gallery.

"The problem," Walter explained to the two men, "is that this totem pole is not part of the show, and we need to move it someplace else."

"Where do you want us to take it," Larue wanted to know. "Storeroom is full."

"Find some temporary place, I suppose. I'm sure it's all a mistake, and when the secretary comes back on Monday, we'll have the whole thing straightened out."

"What's that sound?" asked Larue.

"We're not sure," said the director.

"Kinda loud," said Jimmy.

"Yes, it was bothering some of the patrons."

"Sort of like laughing," said Larue. "What do you think Jimmy?"

Jimmy put his ear against the totem pole and listened. "It's sort of like a chant. Maybe it's Druidic."

"Druidic!"

"There was this movie about the Druids on a flight from England to New York ... they did a lot of chanting ... the Druids ..."

Larue told Jimmy to tip the totem pole back so they could get the dolly under the base. But the totem pole didn't move. "Hey," he said, "it's stuck."

Larue pushed on the front, and Jimmy pulled on the top, and nothing happened. "It's really stuck."

Walter got on his hands and knees and looked at the bottom. Then he took his glasses out of their case and put them on. "It appears," he said, "that it goes right through the floor."

Both Larue and Jimmy got down with the director. Larue shook his head. "It doesn't make any sense," he said, "because the floor's concrete. I was here when they built this building, and I don't remember them pouring the floor around a totem pole."

"We could get a chainsaw and cut it off close to the floor," Jimmy volunteered.

"Well, we can't have it making noises in the middle of a show on seascapes," said Walter. "Do what you have to do, but do it quietly."

After the gallery closed for the evening, Larue and Jimmy took the chainsaw out of its case and put on their safety goggles. Larue held the totem pole and Jimmy cut through the base, the chain screaming, the wood chips flying all around the gallery. Some of the larger chips bounced off the paintings and left small dents in the swirling waves and the glistening rocks and the seabirds floating on the wind. Then they loaded the totem pole on a dolly and put it in the basement near the boiler.

"Listen to that," said Jimmy, knocking the sawdust off his pants. "It's still making that noise."

When Walter arrived at the gallery on Monday morning, the secretary was waiting for him. "We have a problem, Mr. Hooton," she said. "There is a totem pole in the corner, and it's grunting."

"Damn!" said Hooton, and he called Larue and Jimmy.

"You're right," said Larue, after he and Jimmy had looked at the totem pole. "It does sound like grunting. Doesn't sound a thing like the other one. What do you want us to do with this one?"

"Get rid of it," said Walter. "And watch the paintings this time."

Larue and Jimmy got the chainsaw and the safety goggles and the dolly, and moved the totem pole into the basement alongside the first one.

"That wasn't hard," said the director.

"Those grunts were pretty disgusting," said the secretary.

"Yes, they were," agreed Walter.

After lunch, the totem pole in the corner of the gallery started shouting, loud, explosive shouts that echoed through the collection of sea scenes and made the paintings on the wall tremble ever so slightly. When Walter returned, the secretary was sitting at her desk with her hands over her ears.

"My God!" said Walter. "How did this happen?"

That evening, Walter and Larue and Jimmy sat in Walter's office and talked about the problem. "The trick I think," said Larue, "is to cut the pole down and then cover the stump with pruning paste. That way it won't grow back."

"What about the shouting?"

"Well, you can't hear it much from the basement."

"Alright," said Walter. "We'll give that a try. How many poles are in storage?"

"Three with this one, and we haven't got room for any more."

The next day, the totem pole in the corner was singing. It started with a high, wailing, nasal sound and then fell back into a patient, rhythmic drone that gave Walter a huge headache just above his eyes and made him sweat.

"This is getting to be a real problem," he told Larue and Jimmy. "If we can't solve it, we may have to get some government assistance."

"Provincial?"

"It could be more serious than that," said Walter.

"Maybe we should just leave it," said Jimmy.

"We can't just leave it there," said the director. "We need the space for our other shows, and we can't have it singing all the time, either."

"Maybe if we ignore it, it will stop singing," said Jimmy. "It might even go away or disappear or something. Besides, we don't have any place to put it. Maybe, after a while, you wouldn't even notice it ... like living next to the train tracks or by a highway."

"Sure," said Larue, who was tired of cutting down totem poles and trying to find space for them. "Couldn't hurt to give that a try."

The totem pole stayed in the corner, but Jimmy and Larue were right. After the first week, the singing didn't bother Walter nearly as much, and, by the end of the month, he hardly noticed it at all.

Nonetheless, Walter remained mildly annoyed that the totem pole continued to take up space and inexplicably irritated by the low, measured pulse that rose out of the basement and settled like fine dust on the floor.

NOTES

Druidic   referring to a tribe of ancient Celtic holy men who worshipped
           trees

totem   animal, plant, or other natural object believed to be related to, or the guardian spirit of, a tribe, clan, or individual

RESPONDING PERSONALLY

3. At which point in the story did you first begin to sense that the narrative was not as factually realistic as you might have at first believed? Recall what you did at that point in your reading: Did you actually stop reading? Did you look back, or reread? Did you pause and then continue? As clearly as you can recall, share your thoughts at that point in your reading.

4. Who is the intended audience of this story? How seriously is this story meant to be taken? Discuss these questions in a small group, exploring the greater implications of the surface story. Share the product of your discussion with the class.

   ### GROUP ASSESSMENT

   a) Was there consensus within your small group? If so, was it difficult to reach consensus in discussion? Is it always necessary to reach consensus? What, if any, might be the advantages of not reaching consensus?

   b) When you shared in class, how did classmates respond to your group's thinking? Was there general agreement?

RESPONDING CRITICALLY/ANALYTICALLY

5. What is understatement? Find and examine the writer's use of understatement in the story. How does his use of understatement evoke humour from the narrative situation? Is understatement an effective form of criticism? Explain why or why not. In what kinds of situations would it be most effective?

6. a) Besides understatement, what has the writer used to create humour? Identify an example of that technique.
   b) Does the humour surface in a single incident or is it used as part of a pattern?
   c) Share your findings with your classmates. Together, compile a comprehensive list of the various techniques the writer has used.

7. Identify the series of noises the totems produce. Search for a pattern: what is the progression that is established? In what way are human emotions a part of that pattern? What, if any, might be the writer's purpose here?

8. Is it the writer's intention that the story's main conflict be resolved? In terms of the conflict, what is the significance of the final two paragraphs?

9. In a sentence or two, write a thematic statement that you feel effectively identifies the controlling idea (or one of the controlling ideas) of the story. Be prepared to defend your statement in terms of the choices the writer appears to have made.

RESPONDING CREATIVELY

10. Working with a partner or in a small group, and using the story "Totem" as a model, outline the plot sequence of a similar story where satire is used to criticize the recognized folly of some societal action or endeavour.
    a) Begin the story realistically.
    b) Gradually, but without yet becoming obvious, unfold the real reason for your story.
    c) Compose small bits of dialogue or description with embedded irony.
    d) Plan an ending that emphasizes the emotional genuineness of your criticism.

    Time permitting, and with the help of your teacher or peers, expand the outline into full story form.

PROBLEM SOLVING OR DECISION MAKING

11. a) Why is humour an effective form of criticism? Are there times, however, when humour, as mild as it may be, is clearly inappropriate? In what instances?
    b) The writer of the story is dealing with issues of stereotyping and of race. Is he perhaps in danger of crossing the bounds of propriety? Is there a specific point in the story where he goes too far?

    With your teacher as moderator, share your views with your classmates in the venue of a panel discussion.

Jerry Wowk
Personal Response to "Totem"

I have just completed reading Thomas King's "Totem" for the first time ever. My thoughts are all over the place. There are all kinds of poems in my head.

A quick explanation of the meaning of "poems." A well-respected teacher of English teachers put forth a rather unusual explanation for what she termed "poem": Whenever a reader's personal background of experiences interacts with a literary text, a "poem" of meaning emerges. While a given text remains the same no matter who reads it, each reader's poem is inevitably different because each reader's experiences and understandings are unique. In fact, the same reader, upon reading the same text a second time, will generate a new and different poem still, because that reader's current understandings will have been influenced by her or his earlier reading.

So, back to the poems in my head. Three such poems seem to be taking shape. The first takes me back to my teen years. In my last year of high school and first two years of university, I worked part-time weekends and summers at a municipal art gallery. My summer job—the midnight shift—required frequent inspection tours of the building, among other things checking that the temperature and humidity of the viewing galleries remained constant. Through these duties came the opportunity to view the paintings in the galleries many times every night, allowing me to become more and more familiar with them. Over time, a number of personal favourites emerged. One such favourite was a painting by Emily Carr depicting trees dancing in a pine forest. Enjoyment of the painting propelled me to search out other works by the same painter, and this brought me into contact with her wonderful depictions of Aboriginal totems from the west coast of Canada. Whether the wonder and power and majesty of the totems came from the totems themselves or from her representation of the totems, I don't know. But wonderful and powerful and majestic they certainly were. They remain with me as a vivid memory today, many years later.

A second, related poem. Near the end of my second year of university coursework, while contemplating a change in fields of study from chemistry to English literature, I would spend hours between labs in the university library, in the literature section, reading. At one point my interests centred on various writers' memoirs and personal journals, and it was then that I stumbled onto one such journal by Emily Carr. An entry of hers caught and held my interest: it was a description of her own experience with one totem in particular, and of how she continued in her travels to chance upon the totem, encountering it repeatedly in different locations. She wrote of how she first felt terrified by the ferocity of the totem's expression, but that upon repeated contact with it she seemed to gain a new understanding, not of the terror it evoked, but instead of a sense of its strength, of its power. Over time, however, even her newfound understanding was altered, and she came to discern a power that was more *protective* than merely strong, even feminine and motherly, in its nature. Carr, it seems, learned to understand more completely and to appreciate the elemental essense of this particular totem.

The third poem. Since first reading him, I've always enjoyed Thomas King. His novels, short stories, even his sometimes provocative radio drama series, "The Dead Dog Café Comedy Hour," are in degrees hokey, funny, witty, sensitively intelligent. Often dealing with issues of contemporary Canadian interculturalism, they seem to stand on the edge of satire, sometimes venturing in, sometimes holding back, but always ready to make you reflect on your own perceptions of a societal reality that is not always pleasant, and certainly not always politically correct. But funny. King regularly pokes fun at himself, and, by association, at his Aboriginal ancestry. I laugh at him, yet I laugh with him, because he exposes the foibles of not just one person or one group of people, but of all people. While preferring to associate myself with his heroes, such as they are, I find myself just as clearly represented in his foils, in the characters and environments that obtusely stand in the way of plain common sense. I understand *what* he says, and I can feel the frustration behind the *why* of his saying it, yet at the same time I enjoy the *how* of his manners and words. He lets me appreciate that I am in all ways a member of a global society, a "human" being.

Now it's time to go back and reread his story. I sense a fourth poem.

Jane Urquhart
Storm Glass

PRE-READING

1. Is the expression of the story's title a part of your experience? What do the words suggest to you; to what might they refer? Where or how might the expression have originated?

2. Can you remember a time in your life when, even for only a short while, you felt completely at peace with yourself and with those around you? Try to recall that feeling. Close your eyes and visualize the setting.
   - Describe the setting.
   - What brought the feeling about?
   - How long did it last?
   - Why did it end?

From where she lay she could see the lake. It seemed to her to be heading east, as if it had a definite destination in mind and would someday be gone altogether from the place where it was now. In fact, however, she knew that it was going nowhere; just staying in one place and changing internally. It was diminished by sun, replenished by rain and pushed around by strong winds, but it was always a lake. And always there. God knows it had its twentieth-century problems; its illness, its weaknesses. Some had even said it was dying. But she knew better. She was dying, and although she felt as close as a cousin to the lake, she did not sense that it shared with her this strong, this irreversible dilemma. It would always be a lake, always there, long after she had gone somewhere else. Alone.

She was alone in the room now. As alone as she would be a few months later when the brightness of the last breath closed on the dark, forever. She had imagined the voyage in that dark—her thoughts speaking in an alien tongue—textural black landscape— non visual—swimming towards the change. And then she had hoped that she would be blessed with some profound last words, some small

amount of theater to verify the end of things. But somehow she sensed it would be more of a letting go, slipping right through the center of the concentric circles that are the world and into a private and inarticulate focus and then...

The shore had changed again and again since her first summers there. One year there had been unexpected sand for her babies to play in. She remembered fine grains clinging to their soggy diapers and their flat sturdy footprints which had existed for seconds only before the lake gathered them up. But a storm in the following winter had altered the patterns of the water and the next year her small children had staggered over beach stones to the edge. In subsequent weeks their bare feet had toughened, allowing them to run over rocks and pebbles without pain. Her own feet had resisted the beach stones summer after summer, forcing her to wear some kind of shoes until she left the land for the smooth soft surface of the water.

Her husband, larger, more stubborn, less willing to admit to weaknesses than she, would brave the distance of the beach, like the children, barefoot. But his feet had never toughened, and standing, as she sometimes had, on the screened verandah, she had watched the pain move through his stiffened legs and up his back until, like a large performing animal, he had fallen, backwards and laughing, into the lake.

He was not there now, unwilling to admit to this, her last, most impossible weakness.

Yet he came and went, mostly at mealtimes, when a hired woman came to cook for them. He came in heavy with the smell of the farm where he had worked and worked making things come to be; a field of corn, a litter of pigs, or even a basket of smooth, brown eggs. The farm took all of his time now, as if, as she moved down this isolated tunnel towards that change, it was even more important that he make things come to be. And though this small summer cottage was only minutes away from the earth that he worked, the fact of her lying there had made it a distance too great for him to travel except for the uncontrollable and predictable responses of hunger and of sleep.

The beach was smaller this year, and higher. Strong spring winds had urged the lake to push the stones into several banks, like large steps, up to the grass. These elevations curved in a regular way around the shoreline as if a natural amphitheater had been mysteriously provided so that audiences of pilgrims might come and sit and watch the miracle of the lake. They never arrived, of course, but she sometimes found it fun to conjure the image of the beach filled with spectators, row on row, cheering on the glide of a wave, the leap of a fish, the flash of a white sail on the horizon. In her imagination she could see their backs, an array of colourful shirts, covering the usual solid grey of the stones.

And yet, even without the imaginary spectators, the grey was not entirely solid. Here and there a white stone shone amongst the others, the result of some pre-cambrian magic. In other years the children had collected these and still old honey pails full of them lined the sills of the windows on the porch. The children had changed, had left, had disappeared into adulthood, lost to cities and success. And yet they too came and went with smiles and gifts and offers of obscure and indefinite forms of help. She remembered mending things for them; a toy, a scratch of the skin, a piece of clothing, and she understood their helpless, inarticulate desire to pretend that now they could somehow mend her.

In her room there are two windows. One faced the lake, the other the weather which always seemed to come in from the east. In the mornings when the sun shone a golden rectangle appeared like an extra blanket placed on the bed by some anonymous benevolent hand. On those days her eyes moved from the small flame of her opal ring to the millions of diamonds scattered on the lake and she wished that she could lie out there among them, rolling slightly with the current until the sun moved to the other side of the sky. During the heat of all those summers she had never strayed far from the water, teaching her children to swim or swimming herself in long graceful strokes, covering the distance from one point of land to another, until she knew by heart the shoreline and the horizon visible from the small bay where the cottage was situated. And many times she had laughed and called until at last, with a certain reluctance, her husband had stumbled over the stones to join her.

He seldom swam now, and if he did it was early in the morning before she was awake. Perhaps he did not wish to illustrate to her his mobility, and her lack of it. Or perhaps, growing older, he wished his battle with the lake to be entirely private. In other times she had laughed at him for his method of attacking the lake, back bent, shoulders drawn forward, like a determined prize fighter, while she slipped effortlessly by, as fluid as the water, and as relaxed. His moments in the lake were tense, and quickly finished; a kind of enforced pleasure, containing more comedy than surrender.

But sometimes lately she had awakened to see him, shivering and bent, scrambling into his overalls in some far corner of the room and knowing he had been swimming she would ask the customary questions about the lake. "Was it cold? Was there much of an undertow?" And he had replied with the customary answers. "Not bad, not really, once you are in, once you are used to it."

That morning he had left her early, without swimming. The woman had made her bed, bathed her and abandoned her to the warm wind that drifted in one window and the vision of the beach and the lake which occupied the other. Her eyes scanned the stones beyond the glass trying to remember the objects that, in the past, she had found among them. Trying to remember, for instance, the look and then the texture of the clean dry bones of seagulls; more delicate than the dried stems of crysanthemums and more pleasing to her than that flower in full bloom. These precise working parts of once animate things were so whole in themselves that they left no evidence of the final breakdown of flesh and feather. They were suspended somewhere between being and non being like the documentation of an important event and their presence somehow justified the absence of all that had gone before.

But then, instead of bone, she caught sight of a miniscule edge of colour, blue green, a dusty shine, an irregular shape surrounded by rounded rocks—so small she ought not to have seen it, she ought to have overlooked it altogether.

"Storm glass," she whispered to herself, and then she laughed realizing that she had made use of her husband's words without thinking, without allowing the pause of reason to interrupt her response as it so often did. When they spoke together she sometimes tried expressly to avoid his words; to be in possession of her own, hard thoughts. Those words and thoughts, she believed, were entirely her own. They were among the few things he had no ability to control with either his force or his tenderness.

It must have been at least fifteen summers before when the children, bored and sullen in the clutches of early adolescence, had sat day after day like ominous boulders on the beach, until she, remembering the honey pails on the windowsills, had suggested they collect the small pieces of worn glass which were sometimes scattered throughout the stones. Perhaps, she had remarked, they could do something with them; build a small patio or path, or fill glass mason jars to decorate their bedrooms. It would be better, at least, than sitting at the water's edge wondering what to do with the endless summer days that stretched before them.

The three children had begun their search almost immediately; their thin backs brown and shining in the hot sun. The majority of pieces that they found were of dark ochre colour, beer bottles no doubt, thrown into the lake by campers from the provincial park fifteen miles down the road. But occasionally they would come across a rarer commodity, a kind of soft turquoise glass similar to the colour of bottles they had seen in antique shops with their mother. These fragments sometimes caused disputes with respect to who had spotted them first but, as often as not, there were enough pieces to go fairly around. Still rarer and smaller, were particles of emerald green and navy blue which were to be found among the tiny damp pebbles at the very edge of the shore, and which were remnants of bottles even more advanced in age than those which were available in shops. But the children had seen these intact as well, locked behind the glass of display cases in the county museum. Often the word POISON or a skull and crossbones would be visible in raised relief across the surface of this older, darker glassware. Their mother knew that the bottles had held cleaning fluid which was as toxic now in its cheerful, tin and plastic containers as it was then housed in dark glass, but the children associated it with dire and passionate plots, perhaps involving pirates, and they held it up to their parents as the most important prize of all.

The combing of the beach had lasted two days, maybe three, and had become, for awhile, the topic of family conversations. But one evening, she remembered, when they were all seated at the table, her husband had argued with her, insisting, as he often did on his own personal form of definition—even in the realm of activities of children.

"It's really storm glass," he had announced to the children who had been calling it by a variety of different names, "that's what I always called it."

"But," she had responded, "I remember a storm glass from high school, from physics, something to do with predicting weather, I don't know just what. But that's what it is, not the glass out there on the beach."

"No," he had continued, "storms make it with waves and stones. That wears down the edges. You can't take the edge off a piece of glass that lies at the bottom of a bird bath. Storms make it, it's storm glass."

"Well, we always called it beach glass, or sometimes water glass when we were children, and the storm glass came later when we were in high school."

"It is storm glass," he said, with the kind of grave finality she had come to know; a statement you don't retract, a place you don't return from.

It was after all these small, really insignificant, disputes that they would turn silently away from each other for awhile; each one holding fiercely, quietly, to their own privacy, their own person. To him it seemed she simply would not accept his simplified sense of order of things, that she wished to confuse him by leaning towards the complexities of alternatives. He was not a man of great intellect. Almost every issue that he had questioned had settled into fact and belief in early manhood. He clung to the predictability of these preordained facts with such tenacity that when she became ill the very enormity of the impending disorder frightened him beyond words and into the privacy of his own belief that it was not so, could not be happening to her, or, perhaps more importantly, to him. They did not speak of it but turned instead quietly from each other, she not wishing to defend her own tragedy, and he not wishing to submit to any reference to such monumental change.

But fifteen years before in the small matter of the glass the children had submitted easily, as children will, to the sound of authority and storm glass it had become. Within a week, however, their project had been abandoned in favour of boredom and neither path nor patio had appeared. Nevertheless, the glass itself appeared year after year among the stones on the beach and, try as she might, she could never quite control the impulse to pick it up. The desire to collect it was with her even now, creating an invisible tension, like a slim, taut wire, from her eyes to her hands to the beach as she lay confined within her room. It was, after all, a small treasure, an enigma; broken glass robbed by time of one of its more important qualities, the ability to cut. And though she could no longer rub it between her palms she knew it would be as firm and as strong as ever. And as gentle.

From where she lay she could see the lake and she knew that this was good; to be able to see the land and the end of the land, to be able to see the vast indefinite bowl of the lake. And she was pleased that she had seen the storm glass. She felt she understood the evolution of its story. What had once been a shattered dangerous substance now lay upon the beach harmless, inert and beautiful after being tossed and rubbed by the real weather of the world. It had, with time, become a pastel memory of a useful vessel, to be carried, perhaps in a back pocket and brought out and examined now and then. It was a relic of that special moment when the memory and the edge of the break softened and combined in order to allow preservation.

How long, she wondered, did it take, from the break on the rocks, through the storms of different seasons, to the change? When did the edges cease to cut?

That night he came in tired and heavy, followed by the smell of making things come to be. He spoke of problems with the farm; of obstinate machinery that refused to function or of crops with inexplicable malformations—events that, even in the power of his stubbornness, he could never hope to control. And when he turned to look at her his eyes were like fresh broken glass; sharp, dangerous, alive. She answered him with kindness, though, knowing the storm ahead and then the softening of edges yet to come.

"There's storm glass on the beach," she said.

RESPONDING PERSONALLY

3. The speaker of the story appears to be searching to regain some kind of order and ultimate harmony from an increasingly disordered state of existence. Control is now literally out of her hands. Recall an elderly person in your lifetime, real or fictional, who also needed to regain some semblance of order before dying. Write about her or his attempts.

4. Is the ending of the story satisfactory to you?
   • Did you expect something different?
   • Were you left wanting more? Or does the ending deliver to you all it should?

Share your thoughts about the ending of the story. Discuss your reaction in light of what has gone before: Is the ending in keeping with the rest of the story? Explain.

RESPONDING CRITICALLY/ANALYTICALLY

5. The opening mood of the story is very "dark": it is focused on the speaker's thoughts of aloneness and impending death. Identify examples of effective imagery in the first three paragraphs that the writer has used successfully to evoke this mood.

6. As the story proceeds, there occurs a very gradual uncovering of the speaker's personality, layer by layer, until by the end of the story, the final core, the essence of who she is now, is revealed. Describe the person you find at the core of her personality.

7. While taking place in the present, the story seems to float back and forth between past and present time—the transitions are not clear and precise, and the reader may experience occasional uncertainty. Find an example in the story where this occurs. What is the effect on the reader? In what way is this effect suited to the content of the story?

8. a) The word "change" and the related imagery of change are used repeatedly in the first three paragraphs. Identify as many separate instances of change imagery in that section as you can.

   b) The references to storm glass throughout the story are so prevalent and so emphatic that the object clearly takes on symbolic value. Find one example in the writer's description of the storm glass that articulates particularly well the symbolic overtones of the object.

   c) The speaker of the story clearly sees herself in the storm glass. Locate and identify specific references to the storm glass that serve also as parallel references to the speaker. Share your examples with the rest of the class.

   d) It is significant that in a narrative virtually devoid of dialogue the writer ends her story with spoken words. What seems to be the writer's intent? What resolution does the protagonist attempt to bring to her own conflict when she speaks the closing words of the story?

   e) In a story that is largely monochromatic—white and black and grey are the colours most mentioned—there appears a brief passage of vividly descriptive colour. The woman reminisces about her children of 15 years ago gathering the storm glass. What is the irony of the colourfulness of this one isolated passage?

RESPONDING CREATIVELY

9. At one point in the story, the speaker is reminded of her adult children's "helpless, inarticulate desire to pretend that now they could somehow mend her." Compose the monologue that one of her children might

attempt to articulate, about the difficulty of both of them knowing but not speaking of the inevitability of what is to come.

10. At the conclusion of the story, the husband looks at the speaker with eyes "like fresh broken glass; sharp, dangerous, alive." She answers his look "with kindness." Along with your classmates, search out magazine photographs of people's eyes. Purposely look for eyes that appear either "sharp, dangerous" or filled "with kindness." Collect all the photographs and prepare a display with a visual layout that suggests the contrast that is present in the closing scene.

GROUP ASSESSMENT

Examine the process that resulted from this assignment.
- Did everyone contribute? Equitably?
- Did conflicts occur? At which point(s) in the process?
- Did someone attempt to "take charge"? Was the person successful? Why or why not?
- How might a similar process be made more successful next time?

PROBLEM SOLVING OR DECISION MAKING

11. What are some of the moral implications involved in living with a close friend or family member who is terminally ill? When does one "pretend," and when does one not? Who makes that determination? While everyone's situation is different, are there still some absolute boundaries of communication that must be maintained? Discuss this in a full-class setting.

Vidyut Aklujkar
Behind the Headlines

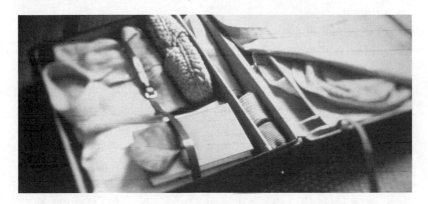

PRE-READING

1. A dilemma is a situation in which a person must make a choice between two mutually unsatisfactory alternatives. Have you ever found yourself facing a dilemma? Write about your dilemma.
   - In what difficult position did you find yourself?
   - What were your choices?
   - Which did you choose? Why?
   - Did it turn out to be the better choice? Explain.

2. How should a person react when dealing with others whose behaviours are clearly unbefitting the sense of human dignity that one individual is expected to show another? Would your response change if the circumstances of the interaction were between immediate family members? In what way?

The phone rang as Lakshmi was taking the weekender out from the closet. Lakshmi expected it to be from Hariharan's secretary, but it was from the Vancouver Crisis Centre. Old Mrs. Mierhoff from the centre was on the phone asking whether Lakshmi would be able to fill in today from two o'clock onwards. They were rather short on volunteers that afternoon. Lakshmi looked at her watch, and consented right away. Hariharan's flight to Toronto was at eleven this morning, and after he left, Lakshmi's time was her own. Mrs. Mierhoff thanked her heartily for coming to their aid on such short notice, and Lakshmi could hear a distinct sigh of relief in her aged voice. Somebody was going to be happy because of her being close by. Her mere presence was going to warm some hearts, heal some wounds. That was a rewarding thought.

Lakshmi placed the weekender on the bed and opened it. She had already laid out Hariharan's clothes beside the suitcase. Just as she was about to start packing, the phone rang again. This time it *was* Hariharan's secretary from the University. Lakshmi knew by heart what she was going to say. She did not have to hear it. She had taken identical phone calls for the last twelve years. She held the receiver to her ear and twisted her lips to mime the words of the secretary, while she watched her own reflection in the mirror of her bedroom. But today, she did not feel like laughing over the call as she used to do all these years. After the call was over, she turned back to the empty suit-case lying open on the bed, and stood staring at it for a while. She saw her own life yawning in front of her in the form of that empty suit-case. Lakshmi shuddered at that thought. She closed the lid of the suitcase and looked away.

Hariharan's secretary had conveyed the usual message. "Dr. Hariharan has asked me to remind you to pack the morning news-papers. He will be home to pick up his suitcase on his way to the airport." Lakshmi should have been used to all this executive neatness by now. After all, she was married for twelve years. Wasn't one supposed to be reconciled to all such quirks in that much time? Her mother had seemed to be all her life. Somehow, they still bothered Lakshmi. She thought of the many times she had packed such week-enders for Hariharan's conferences. Not a single mistake ever. And still he kept on sending these unnecessary messages via his secretary. Such a lack of trust. But try as she would, she had not been able to convince Hariharan that there was a lack of trust in his sending these reminders to her through his secretary. He did not feel he was insulting her intelligence in any sense. This was routine for him. He was a born executive. Memos, reminders, double-checking, all these predictable details of executive life were bread and butter to him. He never made any distinction between his home and his office. "Everything in its place, and a place for every little thing," he would say. Lakshmi had a place in his home just as his computer had a place on his desk. She had a specific job, specific duties. When those were taken care of, he had no complaint against her. She was free to do whatever she wanted with her time, as long as his needs and his routine were looked after scrupulously. What more freedom did a woman want?

In Tamil, her language, a twelve-year period was called a "tapas," a penance. Did I really serve a term of penance in Hariharan's company? Lakshmi wondered. What did I achieve in these twelve years? She was going over the balance sheet. There was not much to show on the side of profit. The daily routine was set here. She did not have to spend as much time on cooking or cleaning as her mother in Chidambaram. There were only two of them in her house, so once Hariharan went to work, she had nothing much to do. Even when he was at home, he did not have a lot to say to her. What was there to talk about? Every once in a while, Lakshmi would start a conversation, but she would soon begin to sense the futility of it all. Her talk would invariably be about the people nearby, in the neighbourhood, or in her family, or in her life. She had nothing of international importance to convey to her husband. And Hariharan was interested in news of international importance. The dinner table was the only place where there was any occasion for conversation between the two, but even there, Hariharan would have a newspaper in his left hand and his ears would be tuned to the news on the radio. His hands would be busy putting in his mouth the delicacies prepared by Lakshmi, but that was by sheer force of habit. His mind was preoccupied with the World. So Lakshmi had learned to be quiet while he was around.

Hariharan had no complaints about Lakshmi. An onlooker would not have been able to accuse him of mistreating her. He was a prominent professor of economics in a respectable Canadian university. Over the years he had served on many executive committees on campus, and so had acquired a reputation for being a conscientious administrator as well. He was fulfilling his academic duties by attending and participating in a few conferences each year. She had a nice house, a respectable bank balance, and a car for her use as well. She had no children, but Hariharan had never harassed her about that. She could not be considered one of those abused or mistreated wives. Even though Hariharan would spend most of his time on campus, he never forgot to call his wife from his office. As soon as he came to his office at twelve thirty-five after his class, he would ring her up. Of course, there would not be anything other than the two predictable questions in his call, "Any phone calls for me? Any letters? All right then, see you later."

Lakshmi could recite Hariharan's routine by heart even in her sleep. There was not much change in it in the last twelve years. He did not ever fall sick. Jogging was in the morning, breakfast with the morning newspaper, and "The World at Eight" on CBC. Then the morning classes at the University and office hours. The nap after two-thirty for exactly fifteen minutes on the divan in his office, coffee at the Faculty Club exactly at three, then the correspondence and committee work. Home by seven. Dinner at seven-thirty. Again the evening newspapers to read over dinner, research papers on the computer after dinner, and the national news at ten on the television. Everything was laid out just so for all these years. The dentist's appointments would be every six months apart, and the medical check-up every year. Lakshmi got tired just thinking about the predictability of her life and she sat down on the bed. The bed. Yes, even that was predictable. The only time that routine would be disturbed would be just before he went to such a conference.

She looked at the things she had laid out on the bed to pack in his suitcase. White shirts for two days, night clothes, a suit, the little shaving kit with its lotion and after-shave, the file of conference papers that Hariharan had packed himself, and the morning newspaper that he did not get to finish. Hariharan would forget his own name perhaps, but never the newspaper. There would be newspapers on the plane, but what if fellow passengers grabbed them all before him and never let go? Anticipating such adversities he would make sure he had the paper with him from home. Even at home, his newspapers and news hours covered Lakshmi's life like a shroud.

When Lakshmi was growing up in India, she would wake up to the sound of her grandmother singing the Venkatesha stotra from her temple room. Then there would be the shehnai of Bismillah at the end of the morning radio program. And devotional songs, bhajans, to warm one's heart with a warm cup of coffee. Mornings begun thus with Sanskrit and Sangeet would make one feel warm and pure. When she got married to Hariharan and followed him to Canada, of course, she had to forget all about that. As soon as he woke up,

Hariharan would stretch his hand towards the headboard, and turn the clock radio on. The world would rush into her bedroom before she even had a chance to wash her mouth. When he went to jog, he had his walkman stuck to his ears. Breakfast would be in the company of the provincial and national news. She did not mind the sound of English so much, she liked English literature. But she hated to listen to news about how many died in the floods and how many were raped, the first thing in the morning. These news items would make her morning coffee all the more bitter. Not a single day passed when the morning news did not have either wars, fights, strikes, firing squads, or earthquakes, floods, robberies, drought, starvation, child abuse, and rapes. Let alone the shehnai, she would have settled for a little conversation just between the two of them before actually facing the world. She had talked about this to him in their early days of togetherness. But he did not think much of it. He was in the habit of carrying out as many little tasks as he could all at once. "This is economy of time, my dear," he had answered her in earnest. When Lakshmi had seen that the radio was not going to be turned off, she had acquired the habit of turning off her own ears.

It was not that Lakshmi was not interested in other people's lives. She liked to hear about the lives of people in a smaller circle, people in whose lives she had a certain say, where she could make a little difference. She would feel terribly helpless, utterly inconsequential when she had to listen to the akhandpaath, the constant chanting, of news items about places and people to which she had nothing to contribute.

Since she had come to the west coast, she had tried to get to know her neighbours, but everyone in her neighbourhood had young children and their lives revolved around the schools, kindergartens, carpools, and schedules checkered with swimming lessons and sports activities. Lakshmi had the whole day in front of her. Of course, Hariharan had no objection to her spending her time whichever way pleased her. Lakshmi used to go to the public library and borrow a heap of books to read, but then there was no one to discuss those books with. Hariharan used to declare with pride that he had not been able to read a single novel over the past several years. "No time for light reading," was his favourite sentence at the departmental parties. Some of his colleagues used to praise him when they heard that remark at the parties. Lakshmi was used to hearing praise for her husband's singlemindedness and his academic productivity, but she could feel the emptiness in that praise. She was quite thrilled when she read Rushdie's *The Satanic Verses* long before it became known to the world, and wanted to share her thrill with Hariharan, but could not due to his being so preoccupied. Then almost a year later when Hariharan heard about the book and the fatwa in the news, he had exclaimed to her, "How can anyone get so excited about a mere naavel?" She had only smiled and let it pass. Their tracks ran parallel, without any hope of intersection. What could she do about it?

She was pausing again and again while packing that little suitcase today. She was thinking about the earlier phone call from the Crisis Centre. She had started to go there regularly as a volunteer for over a year now. Hariharan did not even know that. He never asked her what she did all day long. In the early days of their married life, she used to offer that information to him but as she sensed his utter lack of interest in the activities that seemed significant to her, she had developed a habit of not communicating anything about herself. His daily schedule was not altered in the least by her visits to the centre. After his midday call, she would go there, and even after a four-hour shift she would have enough time to come home and prepare his dinner. Her own life, however, was thoroughly altered due to this work. She was getting to know about the lives of people totally different from herself. She had entered into many lives that were down in the pits, due to childhood abuse, adult frustrations, and the miseries and loneliness of old age. However, she also was beginning to realize how strong a person's resilience could be in spite of all kinds of unimaginable adversities. There was something else. She was amazed at how effective she could be in someone's life by simply talking over the phone. She had found the strength in her own voice. She could actually communicate over the phone to the person at the end of the line, and share her caring feelings, her warmth with them. Some calls would be interrupted, and then she would feel frustrated, but most callers would simply want someone to listen to their plight. She was a sympathetic voice-companion in their lonely battles. Many injured minds were getting a breeze of concern blown on their sore spots thanks to her soft and soothing voice. Many were hanging on to that slender thread for support in total darkness.

She looked at her watch again. In a short while, Hariharan would start from his office and on his way to the airport, stop home to pick up his weekender. She had almost finished packing it. Only the newspaper to be placed on top now. She glanced at the front page. The headlines were of the Iraqi occupation of Kuwait along with pictures of wailing Kuwaiti women. Pity for the plight of that little nation that was about to lose its identity welled in her heart. On an impulse, she unpacked everything that she had packed in Hariharan's weekender. She emptied it altogether. She ran downstairs to the garage and brought up a pile of old newspapers. She filled the week-ender with all those papers, unfolded and placed the latest one on top, closed it, brought it down and kept it ready by the door. "Prominent economist stranded due to wife's mischief," she imagined the headlines that might appear in some newspaper. She wondered which would be more hilarious, to see his face when he opened the weekender, or when he read about it in the local newspaper if it made the headlines.

Then she took out another suitcase from the closet, filled it with her own clothes and some of her favourite books, locked it, and placed it on the bed. She heard the sound of the garage door being opened downstairs. Hariharan must be at the cul-de-sac. Lakshmi took his newly filled weekender in her hand and stood by the garage door. She felt a strange affinity to that garage door which opened and shut automatically by a sheer flick of his fingers as and when he needed it so. The thought shook her to the core. Hariharan's car eased into the garage. He remained seated, waiting. As she opened the side door, he said, "Hope you didn't forget the papers." She nodded without a word and placed the weekender on the seat beside him. As she closed the car door, he backed out and turned to go to the airport.

She ran upstairs, picked up her suitcase, put it in her car, and was about to turn the key. She stopped, opened her purse, and took out the house keys. She got down, went to the front door, and carefully dropped the keys into the mail slot. She then went back to the car and set off towards the Crisis Centre.

NOTE

fatwa   in Islamic countries, an authoritative ruling on a religious matter

RESPONDING PERSONALLY

3. At what point in your reading did you first begin to feel uncomfortable? What made you feel that way? Why do you believe you had that feeling?

4. At one point the speaker says, "An onlooker would not have been able to accuse him of mistreating her." The implication is that someone with knowledge of her home situation *would* have been able. Relate a situation from your past when you were mistreated by another, but in a way that was not made obvious to others, and therefore went largely unnoticed. How was your situation similar to Lakshmi's? Why would frustration, and eventually even anger, be an expected outcome of such a situation?

RESPONDING CRITICALLY/ANALYTICALLY

5. The story begins by providing the reader with only sketchy information, and then gradually filling in the gaps with additional bits as required.
   a) What is the resulting effect on the reader? How does such a narrative process suit the writer's purpose?
   b) What is your very initial impression of Lakshmi? Who, or what, does she appear to be?

6. The story reveals the motivation that lies behind a major life decision the protagonist will be making. It does so by focusing in large measure on a description of the actions of the secondary character, her husband. Identify several different passages that, taken together, present those traits of the husband's personality that will ultimately become the protagonist's motivation to leave.

   In a small group, combine your found passages. Add to these your interpretations and analysis of the husband's personality. Prepare a short but telling character sketch.

7. The imagery the writer chooses is highly visual in its simplicity.
   a) Explain, for example, why the following simile is effective: "Even at home, his newspaper and news hours covered Lakshmi's life like a shroud."
   b) Find a second such visual metaphor. Share both it and your understanding of it with the class.
   c) Notice the images that blend together a figurative with a literal description: "The world would rush into her bedroom before she even had a chance to wash her mouth." What makes the blending of the figurative with the literal effective?
   d) Find a second such blended description. Share it with the class.

8. The final few paragraphs of the story contain a series of ironies. Lakshmi thinks of the people she assists at the Crisis Centre: "She had entered into many lives that were down in the pits, due to childhood abuse, adult frustrations, and the miseries and loneliness of old age." Explain the irony of her situation. Find another, similar, example of such irony.

Identify a specific sentence or phrase from elsewhere in the story that points to the irony.

9. Lakshmi's decision that concludes the story occurs somewhat abruptly. Is it too abrupt?

   a) Is the surprise achieved fairly? Has the writer foreshadowed her actions in such a way that, while perhaps unexpected, they are still in keeping with her character? With a partner, locate several passages that you feel have tried to prepare the reader for what transpires.

   b) What is the symbolic significance of her parting indignity of simply dropping the house keys in the mailbox? Discuss, and share your thoughts with your classmates.

RESPONDING CREATIVELY

10. The reader has heard a great deal about the character of Hariharan but has not directly met him. Do that now. Write a brief sequel to the story, an epilogue of sorts, in which Hariharan arrives in Toronto and finds the newspapers. Write his thoughts using stream-of-consciousness technique. Be certain that the character description you are creating is predicated on the information about him that the story has provided. Share your sequel with your classmates.

PEER ASSESSMENT

- Evaluate the presentations of your classmates. Have the student-writers remained true to the characters as presented in the story?

- If possible, as a class, design the assessment rubric by which you will complete your evaluations. What are the necessary content criteria for a strong presentation?

PROBLEM SOLVING OR DECISION MAKING

11. Most readers will likely support, on an emotional level, Lakshmi's decision to leave. But is it the right decision? For whom? If you were a marriage counsellor, what advice would you give her? What would you tell her husband?

The Family

Call it a clan, call it a network, call it a tribe, call it a family. Whatever you call it, whoever you are, you need one.
— *Jane Howard*

Wherever there is lasting love, there is a family.
— *Shere Hite*

Many stories have been written about the longest-standing institution of all time—the family. Lately, though, the notion of what a family means has become quite different from the 1950s, "Father Knows Best," television ideal of father-mother-daughter-son.

"The Harness" by Nova Scotia's Ernest Buckler is a classic about Art, a frustrated single parent trying to raise David, his difficult young son, as best he can. When a couple of crises occur, Art is forced to learn how to become a more understanding, empathic father, and this changes his awkward relationship with David for the better.

From Africa comes "The Setting Sun and the Rolling World" by Charles Mungoshi. This story is about an older father and his grown-up son, who has decided to break with the traditional rural lifestyle of their family. The ideas of the "generation gap" and moving out as a rite of passage are familiar ones associated with family life.

"Voices from Near and Far" is about an Arab mother whose son has not yet written her while he is away doing military service. The story is about the poignant suffering and love of all parents for absent children, regardless of culture and circumstance.

The last story, "The Day They Set Out," involves a member of an extended family who is not understood or appreciated by others in the family. In response to different crises, he and the sympathetic protagonist dramatically break out of their routine existences and start a new life with only one another.

The selections in this unit show that family is still an important reference point and context by which changes and challenges can be assessed. Despite the threats posed by change and circumstance, family can still be seen as meaningful in the lives of individuals.

Ernest Buckler
The Harness

1. The "harness" of the title is of some significance to the story. Describe a young child's harness: What does it look like? How is it used? Why is it used?

2. Have you ever felt the need to live up to someone else's expectations? Would you think of that as a positive experience or as a negative one, or perhaps some of both? What made it that for you? Could you understand and accept the perspective of someone who saw it as otherwise? Explain why or why not.

There are times when you can only look at your son and say his name over and over in your mind.

I would say, "David, David ..." nights when he was asleep—the involuntary way you pass your hand across your eyes when your head aches, though there is no way for your hand to get inside. It seemed as if it must all have been my fault.

I suppose any seven year old has a look of accusing innocence when he is asleep, an assaulting grudgelessness. But it seemed to me that he had it especially. It seemed incredible that when I'd told him to undress he'd said, "You make me!" his eyes dark and stormy. It seemed incredible that those same legs and hands, absolutely pliant now, would ever be party to that isolating violence of his again.

His visible flesh was still; yet he was always moving in a dream. Maybe he'd cry, "Wait.... Wait up, Art." Where was I going in the dream, what was I doing, that even as I held him in my arms he was falling behind?

He called me "Art," not "Dad." The idea was: we were pals.

I had never whipped him. The thought of my wife—who died when David was born—had something to do with that, I guess. And a curious suggestion of vulnerability about his wire-thin body, his perceptive face, so contrasted with its actual belligerence that the thought of laying a hand on him—well, I just couldn't do it. We were supposed to *reason* things out.

Sometimes that worked. Sometimes it didn't.

He *could* reason, as well as I. His body would seem to vibrate with obedience. His friendship would be absolutely unwithholding. "You stepped on my hand," he'd say, laughing, though his face was pinched with the pain of it, "but that doesn't matter, does it, Art? Sometimes you can't see people's hands when they stick them in the way." Or if we were fishing, he'd say, "You tell me when to pull on the line, won't you, Art ... just right *when*."

Then, without any warning whatever, he'd become possessed by this automatic inaccessible mutiny.

I'd get the awful feeling then that we were both lost. That whatever I'd done wrong had not only failed, but that he'd never know I'd been *trying* to do it right for him. Worse still, that his mind was rocked by some blind contradiction he'd never understand himself.

Maybe I'd be helping him with a reading lesson. I tried to make a game of it, totalling the words he named right against words he named wrong. He'd look at me, squinting up his face into a contortion of deliberate ingratiation. He'd say "Seventeen right and only one wrong ... wouldn't that make you *laugh*, Art?" Then maybe the very next word I'd ask him, he'd slump against the table in a pretended indolence, or flop the book shut while the smile was still on my face.

Or maybe we'd be playing with his new baseball bat and catcher's mitt.

His hands were too small to grasp the bat properly and his fingers were lost in the mitt. But he couldn't have seemed more obliteratingly happy when he did connect with the ball. ("Boy, that was a solid hit, wasn't it, Art? You throw them to me *just* right, Art, just *right*.") He'd improvise rules of his own for the game. His face would twist with the delight of communicating them to me.

Then, suddenly, when he'd throw the ball, he'd throw it so hard that the physical smart of it on my bare fingers would sting me to exasperation.

"All right," I'd say coolly, "if you don't want to play, I'll go hoe the garden."

I'd go over to the garden, watching him out of the corner of my eye. He'd wander forlornly about the yard. Then I'd see him coming slowly toward the garden (where his tracks still showed along the top of a row of carrots he'd raced through yesterday). He'd come up behind me and say, "I have to walk right between the rows, don't I? Gardens are hard *work*, aren't they, Art ... you don't want anyone stepping on the rows."

David, David....

The strange part, it wasn't that discipline had no effect because it made no impression.

One evening he said out of a blue sky, "*You're* so smart, Art ... I haven't got a brain in my head, not one. You've got so many *brains*, Art, *brains*...." I was completely puzzled.

Then I remembered: I had countered with complete silence when he'd called me "dumb" that morning. I'd forgotten the incident entirely. But he hadn't. Though he'd been less rather than more tractable since then, he'd been carrying the snub around with him all day.

Or take the afternoon there was only one nickel in his small black purse. I saw him take it out and put it back again several times before he came and asked me for another. He never asked me for money unless he wanted it terribly. I gave him another nickel. He went to the store and came back with two Cokes. For some reason he had to treat me.

My face must have shown my gratification. He said, with his devastating candour, "You look happier with me than you did this morning, don't you, Art?"

I couldn't even recall the offence that time. *He* had felt my displeasure, though on my part it must have been quite unconscious.

What had I done wrong? I didn't know.

Unless it was that, when he was small, I'd kept a harness on him in the yard. He rebelled, instinctively, at any kind of bond. But what else could I do? Our house was on a blind corner. What else could I do, when I had the picture of the strength of his slight headlong body falling against the impersonal strength of a truck, or the depth of a well?

David, David....

I said, "David, David ..." out loud, that particular afternoon he lay so still on the ground; because this is the way it had happened.

I had taken him fencing with me that morning. It was one of those perfect spring mornings when even the woods seem to breathe out a clean water-smell. He was very excited. He'd never been to the back of the pasture before.

I carried the axe and the mall. He carried the staple-box and the two hammers. Sometimes he walked beside me, sometimes ahead.

There was something about him that always affected me when I watched him moving *back to*. I'd made him wear his rubber boots because there was a swamp to cross. Now the sun was getting hot. I wished I'd let him wear his sneakers and carried him across the swamp. There was something about the heavy boots *not* slowing up his eager movement and the thought that they must be tiring him without his consciousness of it.

I asked him if his legs weren't tired. "Noooooo," he scoffed. As if that were the kind of absurd question people kid each other with to clinch the absolute perfection of the day. Then he added, "If your legs do get a little tired when you're going some place, that doesn't hurt, does it, Art?"

His unpredictable twist of comment made him good company, in an adult way. Yet there was no unnatural shadow of precocity about him. His face had a kind of feature-smalling brightness that gave him a peaked look when he was tired or disappointed, and when his face was washed and the water on his hair, for town, a kind of shining. But it was as childlike and unwithholding as the clasp of his hand. (Or maybe he didn't look much different from any other child. Maybe I couldn't see him straight because I loved him.)

This was one of his days of intense, jubilant, communicativeness. One of his "How come?" days. As if by his questions and my answers we (and we alone) could find out about everything.

If I said anything mildly funny he worked himself up into quite a glee. I knew his laughter was a little louder than natural. His face would twitch a little, renewing it, each time I glanced at him. But that didn't mean that his amusement was false. I knew that his intense willingness to think anything funny I said was as funny as anything could possibly be, tickled him more than the joke itself. "You always say such funny things, Art!"

We came to the place where I had buried the horse. Dogs had dug away the earth. The brackets of its ribs and the chalky grimace of its jaws stared whitely in the bright sun.

He looked at it with a sudden quietness beyond mere attention; as if something invisible were threatening to come too close. I thought he was a little pale. He had never seen a skeleton before.

"Those bones can't move, *can* they, Art?" he said.

"No," I said.

"How can bones move?"

"Oh, they have to have flesh on them, and muscles, and...."

"Well, could he move when he was just dead? I mean right then, when he was right just dead?"

"No."

"How come?"

I was searching for a reply when he moved very close to me. "Could *you* carry the hammers, Art, please?" he said.

I put the hammers in my back overalls pocket.

"Could you carry an axe and a mall both in one hand?" he said.

I took the axe in my left hand, with the mall, so that now we each had a hand free. He took my hand and tugged me along the road. He was quiet for a few minutes, then he said, "Art? What goes away out of your muscles when you're dead?"

He was a good boy all morning. He was really a help. If you fence alone you can't carry the tools through the brush at once. You have to replace a stretch of rotted posts with the axe and mall; then return to where you've left the staple-box and hammers and go over the same ground again, tightening the wire.

He carried the staple-box and hammers and we could complete the operation as we went. He held the wire taut while I drove the staples. He'd get his voice down very low. "The way you do it, Art, see, you get the claw of your hammer right behind a barb so it won't slip ... so it won't *slip*, Art, see?" As if he'd discovered some trick that would now be a conspiratorial secret between just us two. The obbligato of manual labour was like a quiet stitching together of our presences.

We started at the far end of the pasture and worked toward home. It was five minutes past eleven when we came within sight of the skeleton again. The spot where my section of the fence ended. That was fine. We could finish the job before noon and not have to walk all the way back again after dinner. It was aggravating when I struck three rotten posts in a row; but we could still finish, if we hurried. I thought David looked a little pale again.

"You take off those heavy boots and rest, while I go down to the intervale and cut some posts," I said. There were no trees growing near the fence.

"All right, Art." He was very quiet. There was that look of suspension in his flesh he'd get sometimes when his mind was working on something it couldn't quite manoeuvre.

It took me no more than twenty minutes to cut the posts, but when I carried them back to the fence he wasn't there.

"Bring the staples, chum," I shouted. He didn't pop out from behind any bush.

"David! David!" I called, louder. There was only that hollow stillness of the wind rustling the leaves when you call to someone in the woods and there is no answer. He had completely disappeared.

I felt a sudden irritation. Of all the damn times to beat it home without telling me!

I started to stretch the wire alone. But an uneasiness began to insinuate itself. Anyone could follow that wide road home. But what if ... I didn't know just what ... but what if something ...? Oh dammit, I'd have to go find him.

I kept calling him all the way along the road. There was no answer. How could he get out of sound so quickly, unless he ran? He must have run all the way. But why? I began to run, myself.

My first reaction when I saw him standing by the house, looking toward the pasture, was intense relief. Then, suddenly my irritation was compounded.

He seemed to sense my annoyance, even from a distance. He began to wave, as if in propitiation. He had a funny way of waving, holding his arm out still and moving his hand up and down very slowly. I didn't wave back. When I came close enough that he could see my face he stopped waving.

"I thought you'd come home without me, Art," he said.

"Why should you think that?" I said, very calmly.

He wasn't defiant as I'd expected him to be. He looked as if he were relieved to see me; but as if at the sight of me coming from that direction he knew he'd done something wrong. Now he was trying to pass the thing off as an amusing quirk in the way things had turned out. Though half-suspecting that this wouldn't go over. His tentative over-smiling brushed at my irritation, but didn't dislodge it.

"I called to you, Art," he said.

I just looked at him, as much as to say, do you think I'm deaf?

"Yes, I called. I thought you'd come home some other way."

"Now I've got to traipse all the way back there this afternoon to finish one rod of fence," I said.

"I thought you'd gone and left me," he said.

I ignored him, and walked past him into the house.

He didn't eat much dinner, but he wasn't defiant about that, either, as he was, sometimes, when he refused to eat. And after dinner he went out and sat down on the banking, by himself. He didn't know that his hair was sticking up through the heart-shaped holes in the skullcap with all the buttons pinned on it.

When it was time to go back to the woods again he hung around me with his new bat and ball. Tossing the ball up himself and trying to hit out flies.

"Boy, you picked out the very best bat there was, didn't you, Art?" he said. I knew he thought I'd toss him a few. I didn't pay any attention to what he was doing.

When I started across the yard, he said, "Do you want me to carry the axe this afternoon? That makes it *easier* for you, doesn't it, Art?"

"I'll be back in an hour or so," I said. "You play with Max."

He went as far as the gate with me. Then he stopped. I didn't turn around. It sounds foolish, but everything between us was on such an adult basis that it wasn't until I bent over to crawl through the barbed wire fence that I stole a glance at him, covertly. He was tossing the ball up again and trying to hit it. It always fell to the ground, because the bat was so unwieldy and because he had one eye on me.

I noticed he still had on his hot rubber boots. I had intended to change them for his sneakers. He was the sort of child who seems unconsciously to invest his clothes with his own mood. The thought of his clothes, when he was forlorn, struck me as hard as the thought of his face.

Do you know the kind of thoughts you have when you go back alone to a job which you have been working at happily with another?

When that work together has ended in a quarrel ... with your accusations unprotested, and, after that, your rejection of his overtures unprotested too?

I picked up my tools and began to work. But I couldn't seem to work quickly.

I'd catch myself, with the hammer slack in my hands, thinking about crazy things like his secret pride in the new tie (which he left outside his pullover until he saw that the other children had theirs inside) singling him so abatedly from the town children, the Saturday I took him to the matinee, that I felt an unreasonable rush of protectiveness toward him.... Of him laughing dutifully at the violence in the comedy, but crouching a little toward me, while the other children, who were not nearly so violent as he, shrieked together in a seizure of delight.

I thought of his scribblers, with the fixity there of the letters which his small hand had formed earnestly, but awry.

I thought of those times when the freak would come upon him to recount all his transgressions of the day, insisting on his guilt with phrases of my own I had never expected him to remember.

I thought of him playing ball with the other children.

At first they'd go along with the outlandish variations he'd introduce into the game, because it was his equipment. Then, somehow, *they'd* be playing with the bat and glove and he'd be out of it, watching.

I thought now of him standing there, saying, "Boy, I hope my friends come to play with me *early* tomorrow, early, Art"—though I knew that if they came at all their first question would be, "Can we use your bat and glove?"

I thought of him asleep. I thought, if anything should ever happen to him that's the way he would look.

I laughed; to kid myself for being such a soft and sentimental fool. But it was no use. The feeling came over me, immediate as the sound of a voice, that something *was* happening to him right now.

It was coincidence, of course, but I don't believe that ... because I had started to run even before I came over the crest of the knoll by the barn. Before I saw the cluster of excited children by the horse stable.

I couldn't see David among them, but I saw the ladder against the roof. I saw Max running toward the stable, with my neighbour running behind him. I knew, by the way the children looked at me—with that half-discomfited awe that was always in their faces whenever any recklessness of David's was involved—what had happened.

"He fell off the roof," one of them said.

I held him, and I said, "David, David...."

He stirred. "Wait," he said drowsily, "Wait up, Art...."

I suppose it's foolish to think that if I hadn't been right there, right then, to call his name, he would never have come back. Because he was only stunned. The doctor could scarcely find a bruise on him. (I don't know just why my eyes stung when the doctor patted his head in admiration of his patience, when the exhaustive examination was over. He was always so darned quiet and brave at the doctor's and dentist's.)

I read to him the rest of the afternoon. He'd sit quiet all day, with the erasure on his face as smooth as the erasure of sleep, if you read to him.

After supper, I decided to finish the fence. It was the season of long days.

"Do you want to help me finish the fence?" I said. I thought he'd be delighted.

"No," he said. "You go on. I'll wait right here. Right here, Art."

"Who's going to help me stretch the wire?" I said.

"All right," he said.

He scarcely spoke until we got almost back to the spot where the skeleton was. Then he stopped and said, "We better go back, Art. It's going to be dark."

"G'way with ya," I said. "It won't be dark for hours." It wouldn't be although the light *was* an eerie after-supper light.

"I'm going home," he said. His voice and his face were suddenly defiant.

"You're not going home," I said sharply. "Now come on, hurry up."

I was carrying an extra pound of staples I had picked up in town that afternoon. He snatched the package from my hand. Before I could stop him he broke the string and strewed them far and wide.

I suppose I was keyed up after the day, for I did then what I had never done before. I took him and held him and I put it onto him, hard and thoroughly.

He didn't try to escape. For the first few seconds he didn't make a sound. The only retraction of his defiance was a kind of crouching in his eyes when he first realized what I was going to do. Then he began to cry. He cried and cried.

"You're *going* home," I said, "and you're going right to *bed*."

I could see the marks of my fingers on his bare legs, when I undressed him. He went to sleep almost immediately. But though it was perfectly quiet downstairs for reading, the words of my book might have been any others.

When I got him up to the toilet, he had something to say, as usual. But this time he was wide awake. I sat down on the side of his bed for a minute.

"Bones make you feel funny, don't they, Art?" was what he said.

I remembered then.

I remembered that the skeleton was opposite the place where he sat down to rest. I remembered how he had shrunk from it on the way back. I remembered then that the wind had been blowing *away* from me, when I was cutting the posts. That's why I hadn't heard him call. I thought of him calling, and then running along the road alone, in the heavy, hot, rubber boots.

David, David, I thought, do I always fail you like that? ... the awful misinterpretation a child has to endure! I couldn't answer him.

"I thought you'd gone home, Art," he said.

"I'm sorry," I said. I couldn't seem to find any words to go on with.

"I'm sorry too I threw the staples," he said eagerly.

"I'm sorry I spanked you."

"No, no," he said. "You spank me every time I do that, won't you, Dad? ... *spank* me, Dad."

His night-face seemed happier than I had ever seen it. As if the trigger-spring of his driving restlessness had been finally cut.

I won't say it came in a flash. It wasn't such a simple thing as that. But could that be what I had done wrong?

He had called me "Dad." Could it be that a child would rather have a father than a pal? ("Wait.... Wait up, Art.") By spanking him I had abrogated the adult partnership between us and set him free. He could cry. His guilt could be paid for all at once and absolved.

It wasn't the spanking that had been cruel. What had been cruel were all the times I had snubbed him as you might an adult—with implication of shame. There was no way he could get over that. The unexpiable residue of blame piled up in him. Shutting him out, spreading (who can tell what unlikely symptoms a child's mind will translate it into?), blocking his access to me, to other children, even to himself. His reaction was violence, deviation. Any guilt a sensitive child can't be absolved of at once he blindly adds to, whenever he thinks of it, in a kind of desperation.

I had worried about failing him. That hadn't bothered him. What had bothered him was an adult shame I had taught him, I saw now, for failing *me*.

I kissed him good-night. "Okay, son," I said, "I'll spank you sometimes."

He nodded, smiling. "Dad," he said then, "how come you knew I jumped off the roof?"

That should have brought me up short—how much farther apart we must be than I'd imagined if he was driven to jump off a roof to shock me back into contact. "Jumped," he said, not "fell."

But somehow it didn't. It gave me the most liberating kind of hope. Because it hadn't been a question, really. It had been a statement. "How come you *knew* ...?" He hadn't the slightest doubt that no matter what he did, wherever I was I would know it, and that wherever I was I would come.

Anyhow, it is a fine day today, and we have just finished the fence. He is playing ball with the other children as I put this down. Their way.

Notes

absolved   declared free of sin or guilt

precocity   state of being mature for one's age

unexpiable   not able to make amends for one's errors

Responding Personally

3. Near the beginning of the story, the speaker says of his relationship with his son, "The idea was: we were pals."
   a) Is it possible for a parent to be at the same time a "pal"? Is it right to attempt to be both? Or should parenting be an either/or proposition?
   b) In the story, whose "idea" was it that they be pals?

4. The critical part of the story is the scene near the end of the reconciliation between the two:

"I'm sorry...."

"I'm sorry...."

"I'm sorry...."

a) Describe an experience when you reconciled with someone close to you, be it a sibling, a parent, a relative, or a friend. What happened? Who initiated the act of reconciliation? How did it turn out?

b) Who in this short story first demonstrates conciliatory behaviour? Support your answer with reference to the story. Share your response with your classmates. Are you in agreement with the others?

c) Can you arrive at a generalization regarding which of the persons involved in a misunderstanding or quarrel is usually the one to initiate the reconciliation?

Responding Critically/Analytically

5. The story is written from the first-person point of view. It assumes the tone of an apologia, a justification for the father's actions. Who might be the audience for the story? Identify some examples of the language the father uses—the expressions that give the story its apologetic tone.

6. At one point in the story, when the father returns to the fence for the second time, he is unable to work. He is distracted by a series of different memories of his son. Which are the incidents he remembers? In what way are these particular thoughts indicative of a father's natural empathy for his child? Find at least one other instance of the father's strongly empathic behaviour.

7. "I'd kept a harness on him in the yard." While this is the only mention of it in the entire story, this child's restraining device is given such symbolic significance that the writer has chosen it for the title of his story.

a) The boy is a very perceptive child. He seems to understand the "harness" he is presently forced to wear. What is his harness? What are some things he says or does that suggest he understands his harness?

b) Near the end of the story, the speaker says, "It gave me the most liberating kind of hope." The father has also been freed from a harness of sorts: What has been his harness? When does he first understand that he, too, is wearing one? What is the relationship between his wife, "who died when David was born," and the harness he wears?

8. The father, on numerous occasions and in various ways, suggests that he is often inarticulate in his ability to fully communicate with his son:
   • "There are times when you can only look at your son."
   • "I couldn't seem to find any words to go on with."

Find at least one additional example of such an admission. What is the irony of the father's statements?

RESPONDING CREATIVELY

9. The story lends itself to a mind-map interpretation; it is rich in visual imagery. Create a mind-map. Place images of the father, the son, and three or four additional images from the story on the page. How will you depict the father? The son? Which images did you choose? When you have determined the content, consider the placement: let relative proximity represent the closeness of relationship between characters as well as between character and physical object. Which character or object will you place at the centre of your paper?

SELF-ASSESSMENT

Examine the mind-maps of your classmates. Consider yours in light of theirs. Having seen their interpretations, would you make revisions to your thinking? What revisions? Why?

PROBLEM SOLVING OR DECISION MAKING

10. "... I had snubbed him as you might an adult—with implication of shame." The speaker's words imply that an adult can understand and can deal with being shamed, while a child cannot. Does this mean that it *is* appropriate behaviour to shame an adult as punishment for a transgression? Debate the issue with your classmates.

Charles Mungoshi
The Setting Sun and the Rolling World

Old Musoni raised his dusty eyes from his hoe and the unchanging stony earth he had been tilling and peered into the sky. The white speck whose sound had disturbed his work and thoughts was far out at the edge of the yellow sky, near the horizon. Then it disappeared quickly over the southern rim of the sky and he shook his head. He looked to the west. Soon the sun would go down. He looked over the sunblasted land and saw the shadows creeping east, clearer and taller with every moment that the sun shed each of its rays. Unconsciously wishing for rain and relief, he bent down again to his work and did not see his son, Nhamo, approaching.

Nhamo crouched in the dust near his father and greeted him. The old man half raised his back, leaning against his hoe, and said what had been bothering him all day long.

"You haven't changed your mind?"

"No, father."

There was a moment of silence. Old Musoni scraped earth off his hoe.

"Have you thought about this, son?"

"For weeks, father."

162

"And you think that's the only way?"

"There is no other way."

The old man felt himself getting angry again. But this would be the last day he would talk to his son. If his son was going away, he must not be angry. It would be equal to a curse. He himself had taken chances before, in his own time, but he felt too much of a father. He had worked and slaved for his family and the land had not betrayed him. He saw nothing now but disaster and death for his son out there in the world. Lions had long since vanished but he knew of worse animals of prey, animals that wore redder claws than the lion's, beasts that would not leave an unprotected homeless boy alone. He thought of the white metal bird and he felt remorse.

"Think again. You will end dead. Think again, of us, of your family. We have a home, poor though it is, but can you think of a day you have gone without?"

"I have thought everything over, father, I am convinced this is the only way out."

"There is no only way out in the world. Except the way of the land, the way of the family."

"The land is overworked and gives nothing now, father. And the family is almost broken up."

The old man got angry. Yes, the land is useless. True, the family tree is uprooted and it dries in the sun. True, many things are happening that haven't happened before, that we did not think would happen, ever. But nothing is more certain to hold you together than the land and a home, a family. And where do you think you are going, a mere beardless kid with the milk not yet dry on your baby nose? What do you think you will do in the great treacherous world where men twice your age have gone and returned with their backs broken—if they returned at all? What do you know of life? What do you know of the false honey bird that leads you the whole day through the forest to a snake's nest? But all he said was: "Look. What have you asked me and I have denied you? What, that I have, have I not given you for the asking?"

"All. You have given me all, father." And here, too, the son felt hampered, patronized, and his pent-up fury rolled through him. It showed on his face but stayed under control. You have given me damn all and nothing. You have sent me to school and told me the importance of education, and now you ask me to throw it on the rubbish heap and scrape for a living on this tired cold shell of the moon. You ask me to forget it and muck around in this slow dance of death with you. I have this one chance of making my own life, once in all eternity, and now you are jealous. You are afraid of your own death. It is, after all, your own death. I shall be around a while yet. I will make my way home if a home is what I need. I am armed more than you think and wiser than you can dream of. But all he said, too, was:

"Really, father, have no fear for me. I will be all right. Give me this chance. Release me from all obligations and pray for me."

There was a spark in the old man's eyes at these words of his son. But just as dust quickly settles over a glittering pebble revealed by the hoe, so a murkiness hid the gleam in the old man's eye. Words are handles made to the smith's fancy and are liable to break under stress. They are too much fat on the hard unbreaking sinews of life.

"Do you know what you are doing, son?"

"Yes."

"Do you know what you will be a day after you leave home?"

"Yes, father."

"A homeless, nameless vagabond living on dust and rat's droppings, living on thank-yous, sleeping up a tree or down a ditch, in the rain, in the sun, in the cold, with nobody to see you, nobody to talk to, nobody at all to tell your dreams to. Do you know what it is to see your hopes come crashing down like an old house out of season and your dreams turning to ash and dung without a tang of salt in your skull? Do you know what it is to live without a single hope of ever seeing good in your own lifetime?" And to himself: Do you know, young bright ambitious son of my loins, the ruins of time and the pains of old age? Do you know how to live beyond a dream, a hope, a faith? Have you seen black despair, my son?

"I know it, father. I know enough to start on. The rest I shall learn as I go on. Maybe I shall learn to come back."

The old man looked at him and felt: Come back where? Nobody comes back to ruins. You will go on, son. Something you don't know will drive you on along deserted plains, past ruins and more ruins, on and on until there is only one ruin left: yourself. You will break down, without tears, son. You are human, too. Listen to the *haya*—the rain bird—and heed its warning of coming storm: plough no more, it says.

And what happens if the storm catches you far, far out on the treeless plain? What then, my son?

But he was tired. They had taken over two months discussing all this. Going over the same ground like animals at a drinking place until, like animals, they had driven the water far deep into the stony earth, until they had sapped all the blood out of life and turned it into a grim skeleton, and now they were creating a stampede on the dust, grovelling for water. Mere thoughts. Mere words. And what are words? Trying to grow a fruit tree in the wilderness.

"Go son, with my blessings. I give you nothing. And when you remember what I am saying you will come back. The land is still yours. As long as I am alive you will find a home waiting for you."

"Thank you, father."

"Before you go, see Chiremba. You are going out into the world. You need something to strengthen yourself. Tell him I shall pay him. Have a good journey, son."

"Thank you, father."

Nhamo smiled and felt a great love for his father. But there were things that belonged to his old world that were just lots of humbug on the mind, empty load, useless scrap. He would go to Chiremba but he would burn the charms as soon as he was away from home and its sickening environment. A man stands on his feet and guts. Charms were for you—so was God, though much later. But for us now the world is godless, no charms will work. All that is just the opium you take in the dark in the hope of a light. You don't need that now. You strike a match for a light. Nhamo laughed.

He could be so easily lighthearted. Now his brain worked with a fury only known to visionaries. The psychological ties were now broken, only the biological tied him to his father. He was free. He too remembered the aeroplane which his father had seen just before their talk. Space had no bounds and no ties. Floating laws rule the darkness and he would float with the fiery balls. He was the sun, burning itself out every second and shedding tons of energy which it held in its power, giving it the thrust to drag its brood wherever it wanted to. This was the law that held him: the mystery that his father and ancestors had failed to grasp and which had caused their being wiped off the face of the earth. This thinking reached such a pitch that he began to sing, imitating as intimately as he could Satchmo's voice:

"What a wonderful world." It was Satchmo's voice that he turned to when he felt buoyant.

Old Musoni did not look at his son as he left him. Already, his mind was trying to focus at some point in the dark unforeseeable future. Many things could happen and while he still breathed he would see that nothing terribly painful happened to his family, especially to his stubborn last-born, Nhamo. Tomorrow, before sunrise, he would go to see Chiremba and ask him to throw bones over the future of his son. And if there were a couple of ancestors who needed appeasement, he would do it while he was still around.

He noticed that the sun was going down and he scraped the earth off his hoe.

The sun was sinking slowly, bloody red, blunting and blurring all the objects that had looked sharp in the light of day. Soon a chilly wind would blow over the land and the cold cloudless sky would send down beads of frost like white ants over the unprotected land.

NOTE

Satchmo   nickname for American jazz trumpet player Louis Armstrong; one of his most famous songs is "What a Wonderful World"

RESPONDING PERSONALLY

3. All families experience a "setting sun" and a "rolling world."
   a) In writing, share some of the "rolling world" of your family, be it your own, personal world, or that of one or both of your parents, or even your grandparents. Has your family's experience more closely resembled Old Musoni's fears, or Nhamo's expectations? If you wish, share your personal connection to the story with your classmates.
   b) While there is a certain sadness in the metaphor of the title, there is also hope. In what way is the metaphor of the title a hopeful one?

4. Can you appreciate Old Musoni's perspective? Why does he fear for Nhamo? What might be some of the very specific fears he harbours?

RESPONDING CRITICALLY/ANALYTICALLY

5. The narrative point of view switches back and forth several times in "blocks" of story narrated alternately by Old Musoni and by Nhamo.
   a) What is the advantage of using this alternating kind of structure? Why does it particularly suit this story?

b) Identify precisely where each change in point of view occurs. Why does the writer give Old Musoni the greater amount of story to tell?

c) How does the decision to let Old Musoni tell most of the story add to the development of the story's theme?

6. Compare and contrast the belief systems of Old Musoni and Nhamo. Construct a three-column T-chart. In the first column, identify passages that contain statements showing Old Musoni's beliefs. In the second column, across from the corresponding statements of the first, identify statements made by Nhamo that support his father's views. In the third column, across from the corresponding statements of the first, identify statements that oppose his father's views. What pattern evolves?

Self-Assessment

What can you learn that might give you direction from your examination of the way belief systems evolve from one generation to the next? Have you ever thought to critically examine the difference(s) between your own and your parents'/guardians' beliefs?

7. Comment on the unity of imagery between the opening and closing paragraphs—the "bookends"—of the story.

a) In what way does the final paragraph bring closure to the imagery of the first?

b) Comment on the feeling of negativity implicit in the final paragraph. In what way does it bring thematic closure to the story as a whole?

c) Does the "setting sun" of the title and the opening and closing paragraphs achieve symbolic status? Support your response.

8. In a sentence or two, write a thematic statement that you feel effectively identifies the controlling idea (or one of the controlling ideas) of the story. Be prepared to defend your statement in terms of the choices the writer appears to have made.

Responding Creatively

9. Search out the lyrics to "What a Wonderful World."

a) In a small group, examine the appropriateness of the lyrics to the story as a whole, as well as to the situations of the two characters.

- Which line of the song would Nhamo deem most "buoyant"? Which line best supports his perspective?
- Which lines might Old Musoni be willing to accept? To which would he most vehemently object?
- Discuss the irony in the song that Nhamo has obviously not picked up on.

b) Rewrite the lyrics to the song so they express Old Musoni's view. You may wish to retain some of the original. In what way does your revision of the song affect its tone?

If possible, perform Old Musoni's song.

10. If you were to make a drawing or painting that represented the idea at the heart of the story, what would that drawing look like?
    a) What person(s) and/or physical object(s) would comprise your picture?
    b) What colours would your representation employ?

    Share your "picture" with the class. Explain the reasons for your choices.

PROBLEM SOLVING OR DECISION MAKING

11. Life is a series of stages through which people pass; some are more necessary, others less so. Consider the event central to the story—a child leaving the family home. Is leaving the family home a necessary stage in growing up? Recognizing that all people and all situations are not the same, can you nonetheless arrive at a generalization? Discuss this question openly in class. Use examples from your own life.

Translated by Denys Johnson-Davies

Abdul Ilah Abdul Razzak
Voices from Near and Far

Pre-Reading

1. Most parents will say that the love of a parent for a child is the strongest love that one will ever experience. If this is true, why might that be so? What elements must motivate this love that other loving relationships do not have?

2. Can you ever remember being frightened by something, yet being unable to fully articulate your fear? What was it that made you frIghtened? Why do you believe that you were unable to express your fear?

Squatting down on the ground, he took out a rectangular pad with a torn cover from a low shelf alongside him. He then rummaged in his pockets and produced a pale-coloured pencil. Without waiting for her to say anything he pressed the tip of the pencil against the top of the piece of paper and began to write slowly. Certain slight signs of concentration marked his narrow forehead that jutted out from the fold of his head-dress. Then she saw him turning his face towards her with a sort of enquiring movement.

"Is there anything else?"

"What have you written?"

His head moved in a semblance of irritation. Without looking at the paper he said:

"A long time has passed and I haven't ..."

"Three months."

He wasn't there and there was no news of him. She found herself facing a real fear that continued to spread through her furiously, a fear that would not come to terms with her, would not give way to the boldness of hope.

Again he moved the pen, adding:

"No letter's come to you from him. I've said to him: 'Write as soon as you get this letter,' also that you're disturbed about him and that you're always wondering how he is."

She raised her hand in front of her as though wishing to say something, but then she froze. Lowering her head, she said slowly:

"Tell him I'm worried."

Lifting up a torn shred from the remains of the cover of the pad that jogged about in his hands, he answered:

"I've written that."

Wringing her hands nervously, she said:

"Write: A letter arrived from Isma'il to his family, while I, while I ..."

She swallowed her spittle.

At the time, before the incident had upset her, they said to her that Isma'il sent her son's greetings to her and that like him he was well ... Why hadn't he done like Isma'il? ... We're telling you? We're far away, very far away and two letters posted in the same box, it wouldn't be long before they got separated. The smallest mistake was liable to make one of them go astray and it could make its way here or go off somewhere else. A long time might go by till it found its way to you. Just be patient a little.

He looked into her face, moved the pencil over the paper slowly, then stopped a while to think and continued writing rather fast. Again he raised his head:

"Anything else?"

She was silent. She stared up at the ceiling which was open to the empty space ablaze with the sun's rays. Before she closed her eyelids a small, scattered flock of birds moved across the narrow space coming from the direction of the distant marshes. She rubbed at her nose, then shook her head as she said with a sigh:

"Can he come back on leave? Others do ... Write ..."

The man continued to write. She bent over slightly and said:

"And write to him also that I ... that I no longer believe ..."

It was on just such a day. He was looking into her eyes and the suitcase was swaying in his hand and the door giving out on to the sun. When he turned away from her to leave he lingered for a while. Certainly something was troubling him at the time. Certainly he had heard something.... She herself was not in a mood that allowed her to be in a state of such complete awareness that she could observe both herself and him. When he had arrived closer to the door she had stretched out her hand automatically and had said nothing. He, though, acting like someone who had anticipated such a movement from her, had inclined his head to one side in an attempt to turn around. However, he came to a stop in the empty doorway where his figure was blocking the sun's light and there was a dark patch touching his shoulders. When she had looked long at him her eyes clouded over because of the mingling of light with the shadows, and when she opened them again the door was slowly closing on him and a high-pitched whistling was reverberating in her ears in a way that hurt her.

He darted an enquiring glance at her:

"What do you mean?"

She coughed hard, then added in a tense tone:

"No. It's not that, it's just ... tell him I'm frightened."

It was real fear. The fear brought about by inner apprehensions never misses. Even the simple and good things are changed by it into an arid sadness. Prayers and hopes and striving, all are impotent in the face of inner apprehensions.

Turning the paper over, he said:

"I've said something similar to that. What more?"

She rested her hand on her bosom and said:

"It doesn't matter—write it again. Write it."

Then, nervously, she pulled at her apron.

Coming back to the sheet of paper without interest, he added:

"And you are of course in good health?"

"Me?" she answered immediately.

He regarded her with concentration, in semi-astonishment. Moving his head back and forth, he said, as though talking to himself:

"Such things must be written."

She gave a slight shudder, and as though she had recollected something, said quickly:

"Because of you I bought a radio and every night I listen to the soldiers' voices. Why don't you do the same as them? When will your turn come?"

Every night a furious joy would enwrap her, a feeling of joy that something must come about, something that is interwoven in the soldiers' voices and that shines despite the gloom of fear. The thing that occurs leaves within the area of itself some sort of an ending which may be now or tomorrow or the day after that, or during the days that are yet to come, so long as he exists and he continues to be. Therefore his voice will come with theirs, for nothing is stopping its continuance.

These voices, though, when she heard them, appeared the same because of the speed with which they talked. This required her to listen ever so carefully to every name that was given out, for it seemed to her that, if she were to be inattentive when listening to the names, the voices would scatter and coagulate, become like the voice of a single man, at times disjointed, at others flowing on, and between the flowing and the disjointedness was created this conformity or this strange similarity between them. More than once she asked herself: What is it that gives their voices this similar tone? Is it the love that binds them together? Or is it that great shared thing that unites them?

They are pleasant moments when they talk. Why, then, are they so frugal with their words? Is it the sensation of love for all the beautiful things that causes them to unite into a single voice, a single tone?

His hand wrote quickly then came to a stop. He stared at her with a blank gaze. She whispered to herself: I love them ... those are my sons.

"What is it?"

But why do their voices seem so quick despite their strength, as though, like them, they were travelling as far away from being identified as they are far away from their families. Names that are of a kind and names that are dissimilar. Despite everything they unite in the intoxication of that one voice that proceeds from across remote distances.

He looked at her in astonishment. She averted her face slightly, then again whispered to herself:

"I think I forgot."

"What?"

As she looked at him she gave a slight sigh, then said:

"I forgot to turn it off."

She made a small gesture with her hand and a sort of smile came to her lips.

The palm of her hand climbed up the cold frame of the transistor radio and the voice of a soldier was held back in her hand.

"Not that one either," she whispered, shaking her head.

A song comes to her from afar; it seems as though it is emanating from outside, from across the lonely waters in the thickets of reeds sleeping in the silent depths. The transistor radio was over there, broadcasting softly, its front turned aside.

Stretching his leg a little, the man said:

"I don't think there's anything else."

She made not a sound. Her eyes were closed as she breathed in the freshness of a light breeze that stroked her gaunt forehead; she couldn't help but give herself up to it.

She heard the sound of the sheet of paper being torn from the pad.

When she looked up she saw that it alone was in his hands and that the pad was resting under a corner of the mat.

"Now read it out to me," she said in a quavering voice as she drew slightly closer to him.

RESPONDING PERSONALLY

3. Write down all the questions you have immediately following your reading of the story.
   a) Of all the questions, select three that you believe, if answered well for you, will best help you to gain a deeper, more complete understanding of the story.
   b) Pair up with another student. Share your six questions with each other. Spend some time suggesting possible answers to your questions. At the end of your discussion time, identify which two or three questions still require further probing.
   c) Pair up again, this time with another pair. In your group of four, share your final questions. Again, spend time in discussion. At the end of your time, identify which one or two questions require further probing.
   d) Present your final questions to the class. In discussion, ask other students to respond to your question(s). Do the same for your classmates.

GROUP ASSESSMENT

Were you and your classroom colleagues able to help one another make meaning of the text? Did their input change your understanding of the text, or did it merely direct and focus your thinking?

RESPONDING CRITICALLY/ANALYTICALLY

4. One common definition of a short story is that it represents just a "slice of life."

    a) What does this phrase mean? Discuss the implications of the definition.

    b) How does the definition suit this story?

5. Identify the roles of the two principal characters in the story. Describe the relationship between them. Examine the woman's body mannerisms as the two interact: do her mannerisms indicate anything about their relationship? What is the purpose of her interruptions? Does their relationship change in any way during the story? Why is this?

6. Twice, the writer speaks of the woman's fear, and she herself says, "Tell him I'm frightened." What is it that she so fears? What has she said or remembered elsewhere in the story that supports your response?

7. There are three extended passages of antecedent information interspersed among the dialogue.

    a) What purpose do these passages serve?

    b) The third passage gives rise to the title of the story. What are the voices she hears? What is the relevance of the voices to her life? What is the significance of the voices sounding the same? Why does it concern her so deeply?

8. Explain the significance to the story of each of the following:
   - The "torn cover" and pages of the rectangular pad of writing paper.
   - The "small, scattered flock of birds" that moves across the sky.
   - The song that "comes to her from afar."

RESPONDING CREATIVELY

9. Suggest a context for this story. What is happening around these two characters? Create a collage of visual images placed around the two characters in the centre, images that suggest the mother's turmoil. Support your choices with references from the story itself.

10. Complete one or more of the following sentences that she herself begins, but leaves unfinished:
    - "A letter arrived from Isma'il to his family, while I, while I...."
    - "And write to him also that I ... that I no longer believe...."
    - "No. It's not that, it's just...."

    Share your sentences in a small-group setting. Has anyone else in the group ended one of their sentences with something similar?
    If so, inquire what prompted their response. Is there a similarity of reasons?

Problem Solving or Decision Making

11. The woman acts almost as if her son's well-being is tied to her *will*. Is such a thing possible? Are there unseen but perceptible forces that do bind people this strongly? In small groups, share what you might do if a member of your family, perhaps while travelling on vacation, were not heard from for a long period of time, well beyond the date of the return ticket home.

Beverly Harris
The Day They Set Out

PRE-READING

1. When the word "unusual" is used to describe a person, what kinds of character traits come to mind? Describe an immediate- or extended-family member for whom the term "unusual" might be appropriate.

2. To be called a "giving" person is a compliment. It is a term used normally with appreciation and with respect.
   a) What does the expression mean to you? What kind of person would it be used to describe? Do you know any such person? Describe her or him.
   b) Why is it that some people act so freely in a giving capacity? What personal benefits, of any kind, might they derive from their actions?

Even before her eyes were open in the morning, Jean could see the whole day ahead very clearly. It appeared before her as an expanse of water which reared up and became a frothing, threatening figure, often a male figure. It was a vertical stretch of water which was fraught with dangers of many kinds. *Fraught* was the perfect word, for to Jean it meant *jagged*. It represented sharp peaks and treacherous, seething rapids, or a waterfall which shot upwards instead of down.

The light from the ceiling fixture was a needle thrust into her half-open eye. There was the splash of the cold water on her hands because the warm took so long to rise to the ground floor after a night in the basement pipes. There was that terrible moment when Jean must take off her nightgown in the drafty bedroom and she felt too bare for all she must do. There were a hundred decisions and a hundred more humiliations. They began for her in the instant that she drew the night cover from her body.

Jean had a brother-in-law, Hugh, who, thirty years ago at the age of twenty-eight, decided to keep his covers on. Hugh thought of his bed as an unsinkable old houseboat. Except to go to the bathroom, he hadn't been out of it in all that time. He was content (although he knew they whispered and even cajoled) to let Life dash around it and occasionally to splash up a little along the sides. He put a toe down when he felt like it, just enough to test, to see if anything had changed. But nothing did, for as Jean herself knew, Life was too fraught. So Hugh thought it was better to stay put. His mother, Geraldine, was a widow and Hugh's needs filled her days. They lived together in an upper duplex in an area of the city that was slowly going downhill. "It's the renters, Jean. You know, this was once a very handsome street," Geraldine always told her when Jean forgot and mentioned weeds or crumbling brick or motorcycles parked in groups along the curb.

Jean's children were all grown up now and two of them were married and out, so she had taken it upon herself to go over to Hugh's and "Mother's" on Wednesdays to do their washing for them. While she was changing sheets and gathering up soiled linen to take down to the basement, she could overhear what they said to one another. It was never very different; their rituals protected them.

Geraldine would rap lightly on Hugh's door and say diffidently, "It's me, dear."

"Come in." Hugh was always weary.

Geraldine first put her head around the door. "Do you feel up to some tea now, dear?"

"Thank you, Mother, I'll try some of that tuna now, if I'm able."

Geraldine would shuffle into Hugh's room with the meal covered with a warm plate. "Try your best with it, will you, dear?" She paused. "The door, dear?"

"Closed, Mother."

Geraldine always closed the door reluctantly, and would go out to the kitchen to make a custard. For there would be no going back in.

Once the door was closed, she would have to wait until a suitable length of time had elapsed. Sometimes the door remained closed most of the day and into the evening and she just sat in the front room, staring out the window to the street, watching a bit of television now and then. Geraldine Shields was a fleshy old woman who filled a chair completely. She sat in the one with the stiff wooden arms so that she could heave herself out of it whenever she heard the door to Hugh's room stay open on one of his trips back from the bathroom.

Sometimes she said to Jean, "Today I think he seems a little better. I know he's going to like this custard for supper if I can manage to put it together. I'm not feeling too good myself. But custards are so feeding." And wasn't that an interesting word too? *Feeding* was Geraldine's word, but Jean agreed that in a fraught time, food was the best antidote, to make of your body a swollen shield.

Geraldine would haul the stool from the sink to the edge of the kitchen table and sit down to stir the milk into the eggs. She poured the custard mixture into the cups, set them in a tray of water, and placed the whole thing into the oven. She would wipe her hands on her apron and glance at the clock above the sink. Then she hobbled to the refrigerator to go over in her mind all the details of the evening meal. "Fine," she would say, and then she went and got her deck of cards from her bureau drawer. She plunked herself down on the kitchen stool to play Solitaire until the custard was done.

Jean's mother-in-law wanted only to win occasionally. "If the game's too easy, what's the use in playing it, eh, dear?" she would ask Jean, making a point. Once she had the cards set out in a row at the top, she proceeded to turn up the remaining, one at a time. She looked at each one very closely because she needed to place it correctly. Black over red. Red over black. She took a great deal of time to scrutinize the "board." If she had a chance of winning, she never wanted to lose it through an oversight. And if she was meant to lose, well, she always wanted to have done her best.

When the custard was done and cooling, Geraldine would knock on Hugh's door, the same way as before and say, "Were you able to have any, dear? I fixed the sauce the way you like it."

"Yes, I know, Mother, but I wasn't feeling up to it just now. Save it for later, will you?"

"All right, dear. I'll put it back in the warming drawer. Anything else I can get you, dear? More tea?"

"All right, Mother."

"A biscuit to go with it, dear? I bought those wafer ones you like."

"Not just now, Mother."

"The door, dear?"

"You can leave it open for awhile."

When Hugh finished his tea, he would try to read, but often he felt too tired and depressed. Perhaps he wished he had asked his mother to close the door after all. Instead, he would close his eyes against the grey-green light that was in his room even on sunny days. The narrow window was covered up more each year by a spreading maple, the only vegetation in the back yard. In the beginning, it gave just the perfect amount of shade so he could rest comfortably in the daytime. But each year the wide leaves came closer to the window, so that if he looked out, he was hardly able to see what kind of day it was. The leaves pressed so close to the glass, it seemed their weight might break it. When it stormed, Hugh was forced to witness every lashing the leaves took from the wind and the rain against the pane until he seemed tired out from the experience.

Sometimes, if Jean saw the door open, she also knocked timidly and let herself into the room. "Hi, Bozo," she said cheerfully. "Are you alive?"

"Hi, Beautiful," he called to her. "Come on in."

Then Hugh showed Jean what he had been working on with his wires and batteries or his little pen and pencil projects. All the time she could hear Geraldine out in the kitchen making loud noises with pots and cutlery to get attention. Once in a while she put her head in to ask if Hugh needed anything. She acted like a mother bird who smells a fox around the bottom of the tree. Geraldine looked and sniffed and left. She would go back into the kitchen to bang around some more.

Sometimes Hugh told Jean about his dreams. Jean remembered one he told her about his mother's custard getting mixed up with his homemade radio. "The radio was all in pieces, Jean—tubes, dials, wires all over the card-table. I knew where they all belonged but every time I put them back in, the radio still wouldn't work. Finally I held

the empty case up to the light and discovered a big glob of oven custard inside, dotted with nutmeg. I thought I gave the radio a hard rap
on the edge of the table, but it was only Mother knocking on the door,
coming in to take my tray away."

"I don't know what to say to that one," Jean always said to him.

But one Monday morning Geraldine had a stroke. Hugh found her
on his way to the bathroom heaped up by the stove. He managed to
get to the phone in the front hall, call for an ambulance, get a small
valise out of the bedroom cupboard, and fill it with his mother's things.
The ambulance attendants came and lifted the pale heavy woman onto
the stretcher and carried her out of the brick duplex. Then Hugh called
Jean to tell her and she went over and made him some tea.

Since then Jean had been driving over with Hugh's meals on a tray.
She didn't mind doing this because she wasn't very busy at home anyway. She had had the occasional part-time job before. Once she
worked in the jewellery department at Birks, once for a little while at
Eaton's, and once as a pharmacist's assistant at the corner. But she got
tired of standing so much. A few years ago, Jean went down to the
Royal Bank and wrote an employment test. She loved banks; everything seemed so cheerful there, and organized, someone behind the
counter and someone in front of the counter, and the someone behind
the counter knew what the one in front needed. She would have been
able to sit down a lot of the time, if she'd got the job. But she didn't
make it. They phoned and told her, "We're very sorry, perhaps you'd
like to try Eaton's." And that was that. So she was quite happy to have
something to take her mind off herself.

After his mother was hospitalized, Hugh seemed more lonely and
depressed than Jean had ever seen him. He had depended on her for
so long. And the worst part of it was that Jean thought that Hugh
realized that Geraldine probably wasn't coming back.

Hugh had his radio and his books and an occasional visitor. But
most of those visitors were like Mrs. Medford, the Red Feather woman
who talked so loudly, always telling him about her trips to Calgary to
see her niece, thinking it might goad him into getting out. She made
Hugh nervous.

The kind of people he found the most relaxing were the people
having a tough time just staying afloat, people who had been ill

themselves, or poor, or just cast aside, and knew what Life was all about. They had the time to talk slowly and carefully the way his mother always did. They didn't have the energy to flap around his room like birds gone berserk. He found young people the worst. They laughed too much and hardly sat down. If they did, they moved the chair as far from his bed as possible and then sat perched on the corner of it, ready for take-off. And Jean knew that it was the human hand that Hugh would always need; it was the human hand that we all needed, to get through Life.

Even Hugh's own brother, Jean's husband, Ross, did not seem to understand this, the simplest of all human behaviors. Several days after Geraldine was gone, Jean suggested to Ross that it might be a good day to go over and pay Hugh a visit, so he did. Jean was getting tea ready to take in to Hugh when Ross arrived.

"Is he asleep?" Ross asked her.

"No, I don't think so. Knock and see."

Ross's voice could really boom. "Hi, Hugh!" Jean heard him bellow. Hugh might have been weak, but he wasn't deaf. When Jean went in with the tray, she saw that Ross was sitting on the edge of the stiff chair and had moved it back with his body until he could sit with the back of his head resting on the wall. As Jean left, she heard him say, "How are you keeping, Hugh? What are you up to? Got the radio working?"

"I haven't had much time to try it yet."

Hugh had made his radio with every conceivable spare part. The plastic case was cracked. The dial was made from a lid of some kind. There was no back on it, just wires and more wires. The on-off switch was an old caster. Ross always had a good laugh about it. But it was Hugh's project, and Jean always defended it.

"I'll try it out for you, okay?" Ross asked. "Let's see if it works." Ross snapped on the radio and the old thing just crackled and spit. Ross wrenched the dial from side to side producing more crackles and then some louder noises like small explosions.

"Needs some more work on it, Hugh. Maybe the tuner is too old. Or maybe the dial is too loose. Still needs some work on it," said Ross and it sounded as though he gave the top of the radio a thump with his fist before switching it off. And he must have caught his foot on one splayed leg of the card table as he was on his way back to his chair, because Jean heard the table lurch noisily across the bare floor and then resettle.

"Can I get you anything, Hugh?" Ross's voice reverberated through the house. "I'm going back to the house. Do you need anything at the store? Batteries? Razor blades? I'll pick it up for you on my way."

"Not just now," Jean heard Hugh reply.

"Great, then! See you tomorrow, Hugh. Nothing I can get you, eh?"

"Not right now," said Hugh.

Ross shut the door with a bang.

When Jean went in to take Hugh's tray away, he just smiled at her weakly. He reached a long bony arm over to the radio dial. His fingers shook a bit but he steadied them with his other hand. Then he was able to click the on-off switch carefully and then to glide the dial gently back and forth until, as they listened closely, they could hear violin music behind the static. Then Hugh moved the dial in a little, towards the radio face, and suddenly the static disappeared and the clear sound of a violin went up in a sweet spiral from the radio speaker. Hugh put his head back and stared, it seemed to Jean, to Heaven.

The following day at about one o'clock Jean came up the dark inside stairs of the old duplex as usual. She was carrying a large enamelled dish drainer she used as a tray to carry Hugh's meals on. It was covered with a limp cloth and she was holding on to the cloth and the tray at the same time so that the food stayed protected from the air.

She closed the top door behind her with a slight click and went quietly down the long hallway to Hugh's room at the back. She tapped at his door and put her mouth up to the crack.

"Hi, Bozo," she said softly. "Are you alive?"

Jean heard Hugh stir in his bed. She heard some pretty instrumental music from his radio. She waited until she heard him say slowly, "Hi, Beautiful, come on in." Then she went in and said to him over the tray, "Got some nice things for you today. Blueberry muffins." Jean lifted up a corner of the cloth. "Homemade marmalade. New kind of meat loaf. Buns. Fresh broccoli."

Hugh nodded and smiled at her. Jean went out and set the tray on the kitchen table. She took off the cloth and folded it. She put some food in the refrigerator and made tea for them both. Then she picked up the tray again and went back into Hugh's room. She arranged it for him on top of his blanket and sat down on the edge of the bed with her cup of tea. Jean waited until he had eaten a bun and then she said to him, "The marmalade's good, isn't it, Hugh?" It wasn't so much that she wanted to know, as she wanted to comfort him, to ready him for her news.

"It's lovely."

"I just baked the buns this morning."

"They're good."

"How's your tea?"

"Just fine, thanks."

"You know," Jean said carefully, "that Barbara and Tim and Lorraine are coming from Halifax later today. They'll be here this afternoon." They sat looking at each other.

"I got that radio working perfectly now, Jean. Sounds pretty good," was what Hugh replied.

Jean looked fondly at the pieces of junk held together on the card table. "It sounds fine," she said. She rose and smoothed the blankets where she had been. "I've got to go down to the car and get a few things I've made for our little reunion. I'll be back in a minute."

Barbara and Tim and Lorraine were the children of another of Hugh's brothers, Bob, who was dead. Living in the Maritimes, they had lost touch with the rest of the family. They hadn't been to Montreal for years, but told Jean on the phone that they needed to come to say goodbye to their grandmother. Jean was very afraid that Hugh knew why they were coming. She was worried how he would react when he realized just how ill his mother was.

When the visitors arrived several hours later, Jean and Ross were there to greet them. So were Jean's two sons, Peter and Kevin, and her daughter and husband. Barbara and Tim and Lorraine made a big show of going in to see Hugh, to make him think that they wanted to visit him too, but Jean knew he wasn't fooled. When she went in to bring him some tea and cake, he lay with his head back on the pillow, looking very old and lost. He said to her, "Like a bad jug band, they sound like a jug band, Jean." He was referring to the cousins and their racket. And as he tried to talk to her, through the crack under the door squeezed the shouts and tinny laughter from the front room. The family reunion was in full swing. Blaring and popping up and down and sideways, the voices jangled as they hit the walls and came back to jangle with the others coming at them. Hugh faced the other way and Jean just left the room.

The next morning Jean awoke, glanced up and down at the day ahead, gave it her most defiant look, and eased her legs to the floor. She grabbed for her dressing gown and went into the bathroom to get things underway.

Her husband, Ross, was out in the kitchen arguing with Kevin, their youngest son. It was about Linda, the pretty waitress he'd been going fairly steady with in the past year. They'd been at loggerheads over that girl for quite a while, Kevin accusing Ross of paying precious little attention to him while he was growing up and then all of a sudden jumping in with such fatherly concern. Ross didn't like Linda. Jean hated to admit it, but she thought it might have been because Linda didn't return his little looks.

Kevin was saying, "Look, it's not my age, is it? I'm twenty. I'm working. I'm making okay money. You just don't like her or something."

"Now you look!" shouted Ross. "You haven't been around enough. Never mind you're twenty. You haven't been out on your own. I'd been fighting with the Navy for two years at your age and I still didn't know what I wanted."

There was a pause, a silence. Jean and Ross had been married at that time. Jean put her hand on the cold white edge of the sink in the bathroom for support. "Well, you did okay," she heard Kevin say, though he had lowered his voice. "And I'll do okay too. Just let me alone."

"I don't want you to marry beneath you," said Ross, speaking very deliberately, making his meaning clear. "You can see for yourself what happens."

"Dad!" said Kevin. And that was all Jean heard. She felt dizzy. The area under her feet seemed too small to hold her upright. She stayed in the bathroom until everyone had left for the day and then mechanically she got things ready to take over to Hugh's.

Jean pushed open the door of the duplex with the edge of the tray and she saw that the place needed a good dusting and vacuuming. Most of the things from yesterday's party were cleared away, but she could see that they had missed some beer bottles on the telephone table and a couple of ashtrays were full enough to give the house an unaired smell. When she rapped on Hugh's door, he didn't answer.

Jean went into the kitchen, put down the tray and tried again. Still he didn't answer her knock. Jean opened the door a little and poked her head into the room. The room was dark and the bed was empty. Hugh was gone. Jean was astounded at first and then she was very worried. She checked around and found that his slippers were missing and so was his old brown cardigan and the pants he kept in the closet. Then what? She didn't know who to phone or what to do.

Jean went to the phone and sat down. She started dialling. She phoned Mrs. Medford from Red Feather, but she was out on a call. She phoned the hospital, but he wasn't there. Jean just couldn't believe he was gone so she walked back to his room and rechecked. Then she got into her car and drove home. There didn't seem to be anything else to do.

Jean sat at home in her own plaid chair beside the phone in the bedroom going over in her mind the events of the past week, going over in her mind the events of the day so far, and saw the rest of the day glowering at her with frothy, treacherous, watery teeth bared, daring her. To do what? She didn't know. To go, or to stop? To keep going, or give up? And then she saw Life, a larger, more menacing entity, poised to strike her down. She was tired suddenly and wished to go back to bed, to pull the covers around her and to float, just float.

But the phone rang. It frightened her. There was a stranger on the line. It was the owner of The Yellow Submarine on Sherbrooke Street West. "There's a gentleman here wants you to come and pick him up," he said.

Jean grabbed her car keys and she was out the door. She parked right in front of the restaurant with the large circular bubble window and the sign in bright yellow inflated letters.

The restaurant was surprisingly cool and quiet. There was just one young couple sitting very close together at the very back, sharing a tall drink. The booth seats looked deep and comfortable. They, too, were yellow. There were windows like portholes, smaller versions of the one in front, beside each booth. Hugh was there looking out one of them. He was wearing an old tie over his pyjama top, and he was munching on a thick, toasted sandwich piled with lettuce and tomatoes and bacon and mayonnaise, and orange cheese.

"Hi, Bozo," Jean said to him. "Are you still alive?"

"Hi, Beautiful," Hugh replied. "What'll we do now?"

"I don't know," she said, "but we're going to do something."

NOTES

diffidently	shyly
fraught	filled

RESPONDING PERSONALLY

3. a) Which of the two characters, Jean or Hugh, do you initially find more agreeable? Why is this? What has the writer done to determine your preference?

   b) Do your views change in any way by the end of the story? Your views of one character, or of both? What is the change? What has the writer done to bring about the change?

4. At which point in the story are you first sure of the identity of the "they" of the title? What is the prediction that the title seems to be making?

RESPONDING CRITICALLY/ANALYTICALLY

5. Identify all the words in the opening paragraph that might have a negative connotation. What has been the writer's purpose in using such an abundance of charged language? If there is an element of foreshadowing in the use of the word "male," which character is it preparing the reader for? Explain.

6. Jean's husband, Ross, is introduced well into the story. He is not sympathetically presented. While his demeanour in some of the story's situations is understandable and perhaps even acceptable to a degree, his words or actions in other situations are far from acceptable.

   a) Are his words and treatment of Jean and Hugh more similar to each other, or different? What does his manner tell of the way he regards each of them?

   b) A strong contrast is drawn between the description of Ross's attempts to play the radio and Hugh's. What is the writer suggesting regarding the difference between the two?

   c) Jean's "humiliations" are mentioned at the very beginning of the story, but then seemingly ignored for most of the rest. What might have been the writer's purpose in doing this? Has the writer adequately prepared the reader for the scene of Jean's humiliation, or does it appear too much out of nowhere? Comment on the choice the writer has made with her story—does it enhance the telling?

7. The story depicts a strong empathy, perhaps even a correlation, between the lives of its two principal characters.

a) When in the story does the writer *first* indicate some sort of affinity between Jean and Hugh? Through which image does the writer accomplish this? In what way is the imagery appropriate?

b) When do you first sense an affection of sorts, a comfort, between the two? Does seeing such affection alter your attitude toward Hugh in any way? If so, in what way? Why do you think this happens?

c) At which point—which specific sentence—in the story does the writer most clearly reveal a bond of understanding between Jean and Hugh? Share your thoughts with your classmates.

PEER ASSESSMENT

Listen closely to the responses of your classmates. Has their reading of the story been the same as yours? If not, can you accept their reading? Does the text of the story allow for other readings? Discuss.

RESPONDING CREATIVELY

8. With a partner, improvise the dialogue between Jean and Hugh in the restaurant. Begin with their words, and continue. Within the context of the story as it has so far been told, what is the "something" they will do? Share your improvisation with the rest of the class.

9. Imagine that, during the restaurant discussion, Jean notices a jukebox in one corner of The Yellow Submarine. What song might she select to play? Justify your choice. If possible, play the song during your improvised scene.

PROBLEM SOLVING OR DECISION MAKING

10. When we see that others are in difficulty, are we always under a moral obligation to help? Should who the person is enter into the question? Respond individually in writing first. Then share your responses with classmates. Is this a "slippery slope" kind of issue?

Relationships

Do we really know anybody? Who does not wear one face to hide another?
— *Frances Marion*

We didn't have a relationship, we had a personality clash.
— *Alice Molloy*

Most people define themselves by the relationships in their lives. This unit reveals some of the problems and concerns that typically arise in the course of relationships such as those involving couples or friends.

"Small Potatoes" is about a female friendship that continues despite the relocation of one of the friends. The narrator continues to value and remember the special relationship, however, revealing how feelings never change when friendship is true.

"Holding Things Together" by Anne Tyler is a humorous story about a woman whose symbolic car troubles resemble her own unhappy marriage and unfulfilled desires. Ironically, what she finds through her dealings with Joel, her mechanic, is that others are no happier than she is, and that she must accept her husband for what he is.

From Vietnam comes "Reflections of Spring," a romance about a man whose routine life is interrupted by the memory of a young girl he once loved in his distant past. This unexpected, unsought reverie greatly changes him as well as his attitude toward his own life, marriage, and spouse.

Sinclair Ross's classic story "The Painted Door" is about an isolated farm couple whose marriage is tested by adversity and desire during the Depression. This popular, complex story features a love triangle, contrasting characters, guilt, true love, sacrifice, and a completely avoidable tragedy.

As these stories show, relationships can be very complicated and affect people's lives greatly for better or worse. All four selections reveal the kinds of challenges posed by relationships, old and new, and the adjustments people must make to accommodate or maintain them.

Nancy Lord
Small Potatoes

PRE-READING

1. In a small group, discuss the qualities you associate most with friendship. Use examples supported by your personal experience. Make a list of the three or four most important qualities. Compile a composite class list.

2. Write a profile of a special friend or special person in your life.
   a) Use evocative images and descriptions to tell about the person.
   b) Select perhaps five or six of the most vivid images, and reduce each into several short, single-line "thought units."
   c) Reorganize them into a portion of a short, free verse poem.

I make my own trail, not because it's quicker but because there's more to see. I don't do it enough anymore, traipsing through with an eye for rose hips or for the spider's snare with its lump of fluttering, tormented moth. As I bend branches, I'm comforted that there is still so much unfenced and untrammeled space. It hasn't come to that yet, that people here feel the need to mark it off and use it up.

Even as a little girl in Boston, I was looking for this. The day I learned about the Westward Movement—settlers trundling along in covered wagons, as it was presented—I raced around after school, drunk with the concept of first steps into unknown territory, stamping my feet into any unblemished patch of snow, shouting "Pioneer! Pioneer! Pioneer!"

When I came to Alaska, it was with the sure knowledge that here were places that, truly, no one had stepped. And it mattered, the sense of putting a foot down and knowing I was the first to look upon the world from exactly that vantage point. Every sight—of mountain or mouse hole—was a discovery.

You said it was the same for you, growing up in the Midwest. When we met, it was as though we'd once been members of the same backyard club, sisters who shared a coded language. When you spoke, it was as though you were saying my own thoughts. I felt we were resuming a friendship instead of beginning one.

That first summer, working together in the cannery, I lived in my tent and you lived in your van. Days off, we mucked about in the bay after clams, caking ourselves with mud that dried to a ghost-gray skin. Other times we hiked into the hills to fields of chamomile we picked for tea. I wonder if you still think about the day we walked the bluff's edge, weaving back around the ravines and then on out to the points of land where fireweed rippled in the sea breeze. Eagles rode the thermals above us, and we watched two at play, diving at each other and once locking talons as they tumbled above us. We agreed we both wanted to be birds in our next lives.

Now that the cold has come, causing the country to lie down and curl up around itself, it's easier to get through here. Only a couple of weeks ago, the trees and bushes were still lunging around, frothing with fevered leaves and seed, stretching, the grasses dizzy over my head. Now the exuberance is gone, leaving jaundiced alders, berries fallen or pinched to skin, grasses pale and brittle as though the frost has sucked the green resilience out of them. Yesterday's wind has turned the remaining leaves to bare their undersides like submissive bellies; it's flattened the grasses so they all lie in one direction. I bully my way through, kicking loose the snarls that catch my feet. The morning's frost flakes off and sprinkles down.

It's only when I reach the highway that the sun clears the trees. It's warmer, instantly, and I pause to unzip my jacket at the throat. It's early and a Saturday; there's no traffic this far out the road. Most people are still waking up, drinking coffee beside stoked stoves and staring out windows at reminders of chores to be done before freezeup:

gardens to be turned, skirting to be nailed, wood to be split and stacked. The first hard frost, no matter how late, always comes before any of us is ready. In homes up and down the road, lists—the must-dos of fall—are being assembled.

You, too, will have your list, that you've brought from Anchorage: weatherstripping to stick to the bottom of the door, mousetraps to set, a load of firewood to arrange for delivery. Your list is different from the rest of ours, now that you come only on an occasional weekend. It's not the list of buttoning-up, of drawing shelter close like a wrap of sweater. Instead, it's a list of absentee fixes, of purchases. The mousetraps will bang shut in the silence after you, catless, have closed the door behind you; the wood will arrive one day, heaved from the back of a pickup to lie in a pile at your doorstep like a yardful of stumps.

Walking along the empty road, I think again of the eagles that tumbled with locked talons, the day we discovered the old log cabin. It stood just at the edge of the bluff, ramshackle, the roof partly fallen in and the windows broken out. I poked my head through an opening and smelled the damp rot that was somehow satisfying in its earthiness. "Move," you said in your eager way and slung a leg over the splintered sill. We pawed through the debris, and you dug out an old spoon, tarnished green. Later, we sat outside, chewing on chives we found clumped against a wall, trailing them from our mouths like strings of licorice. We wondered who had lived there and where they had gone, and what it must have been like to have settled this land before the roads came through. Just as we wanted to be birds the next time around, we decided we'd been Indians, or explorers, or calicoed prairie wives before; we felt that much affinity for the open country.

This trip, besides your list of to-dos, you'll bring other things—groceries, cleaning supplies, new candles. You'll also have a second list—items you've decided you need in Anchorage and want to remember to take back. I've watched this ebb and flow between your two households. In comes the sack of groceries, out goes the smaller bag of garbage you'll drop in the dumpster as you pass through town. In comes the new broom. Out go the favorite chamois shirt, the binoculars, the game of Scrabble, the bread knife, and the vegetarian cookbook.

When you made the decision to work in Anchorage, that's just how you put it—you would work there, but it was temporary, a job away from home. Home would remain here, and you'd get back to it on weekends, as often as you could. You'd only be "camping out" in your furnished apartment, drinking out of jelly jars and browning toast in the oven. Your real, complete, household would be here, waiting.

I've watched it happen, though, the ebb of possessions. It's not like tides anymore, a wash in and out; it's like the flood of a river now. Every trip you take away more, emptying the house of those things that make it most yours. Load by load, you're moving away.

When I turn off to your place, I study the ruts, wondering if you're really here. You said you would be, when we talked. "This weekend for sure," you said, sounding guilty, regretful. "I want to spend some time with you. We'll pick cranberries. Plan on it."

It's funny in a way, how we've stayed so close through everything. Always, our friendship endured. We both looked for men to share our lives with, and expected that someday we would. I suppose I was jealous when you began spending so much time with Ron. And for me there was Patrick, and Mike, and Galen. They were all good men—yours and mine—but then you and I would always find ourselves together again, across one of our kitchen tables, drinking tea and talking. Every time it was as though we were finally able to communicate in the same language again, after having tried to get by with foreigners. I remember telling you about Galen and football and fishing. I had told him, while he was watching football on television, that I was going to hike down to the river to fish. He told me to wait—he would drive me down when the game was over. I didn't need to tell you that what I really wanted was the walk, that fishing was an excuse to carry a rod down and back through the woods, that I had to feel guilty because he offered a ride I didn't want, and then that he accused me of trying to rush him away from his game. You were already nodding; you knew exactly what I'd meant to begin with and what he would say, and even that the last three minutes of the game would go on and on.

The men came and went, for each of us, but neither of us ever found one that was a friend in the way we were to each other, someone with whom we could talk, saying everything without insult or doubt or misunderstanding and knowing what the other meant.

And now, each of us is by herself.

The ruts don't tell me much. The mud's frozen hard, tire tracks printed in it. Where it was wettest, it's crystallized like quartz, pointed spears of brown ice radiating from each pit. They crunch under my feet, shattering. It's clear that no one has driven in or out this morning.

The low light has that luminescent quality, as though it were slipping under the sides of things, filling them from within. The bent grasses along the road glow yellow; frost melting to dew magnifies in beads along the edges. You always used to remark on it, summer evenings when the light slanted in from the north, washing the trees and fields with an underwater greenness.

When I reach the top of the rise, I can see the roof of your house. The shakes catch the sunlight the same as the grass, the cedar burnished like gold. But it's the chimney I watch. Straining my sight against the wall of spruce that rises behind, I look for the wavy distortion the heat from a dampered, smokeless fire causes. The trees stand still as a painted backdrop, and I know that you're not here after all.

You're busy, I know. Things come up. It's hard to get away. You would be here if you could, pulling muffins from the oven and pouring springwater into your kettle.

I keep walking toward your house. As it materializes, top to bottom, I think how systematically it went the other way, the summer you built it. When you started you didn't even know the names of what you needed—joists or studs, rafters or siding. They were all just boards to you. The times I came to help, it was "Cut all those boards to look like this" and "Use those big nails over there." You knew exactly what you wanted, as if by instinct. And when it was done, one board nailed to the next, it was one solid piece—no holes, nothing extra sticking out.

Seven years later, there it is—still standing, still surprising me. With time, the rough-cut spruce, once so banana blond, has grayed to distinction. It reminds me of a Wyeth painting, with its patina of fog and seclusion.

In the beginning, when we moved to the hill, the places we found were simple and rough. Yours was a homestead cabin, with an uneven floor that sloped downhill. A pencil dropped in the kitchen rolled to the door, and in wet weather water seeped up through the floorboards. My place was less historically pleasing—plywood, its walls lined with cardboard from cases of beer. I tightened it up with some ceiling insulation, installed a barrel stove, and spent winter nights reading by a kerosene lamp. Later, when you built your own place, I settled into my rental in the trees. We joked about my electricity and your sheetrock. "It's real uptown," we said. "We better watch out that we don't get citified."

Your top storey stares at me first, the two south windows like eyes flashing, the smaller one caught in a wink. Beneath it more windows, none matching, line either side of the L. The short leg thrusts forward, throwing a small shadow like a wedge of night against the longer. You did right with the angles, capturing the best of the winter sun and avoiding the flat, spiritless faces common to new construction. The porch, along the side, adds an air of leisure and comfort, as though it might be hung with an old-fashioned wicker swing.

As I get closer, the look of desertion looms larger. The road cuts away, with the spur into your yard crowded from both sides by grass. The center strip of weeds stands firm; months have passed since it's been pushed over by the belly of a cat. The yard, too, grows wild: nettles collapsed over the splitting block, a dry pushki stalk parting the legs of a sawhorse.

I climb the steps, the sound of my boots a thudding of arrival. The door is padlocked. I tug on the lock, testing. When it holds, I move down the porch, nudging with my foot at a coffee can along the way. It's empty except for a stiff paintbrush.

Framing my gloved hands around my eyes, I press against the window to see inside. Plates and cups are stacked on a dish towel beside the sink, ready to be put away. There's a fancy cookie tin and a stick of margarine on the counter. Beyond the wood stove I can see the edge of a chair and some magazines—*New Yorkers*—scattered on the floor; their covers are like fall leaves—one mostly orange, another green and yellow. Ragg socks lie where they were pulled heel over toe.

My breath—I've tried to hold it in—finally steams up my space in the window. The interior pulls away as though masked by a cloud.

It's part of your plan, I know, to leave it every time like this—odds and ends of food and clothing lying around—so that when you return it feels like coming home, as though you've never really left.

"I can't eat the scenery." It's what you said when you took the job in Anchorage. You were joking, sort of—parodying what the business people said when they argued for more, faster growth. We both knew what the choice was—money and some professional achievement instead of the space and self-sufficiency and, yes, scenery that was ours here. Now you dress in suits and nylons and sit at a desk, reviewing plans and writing up reports. You told me that you don't even have a window in your office, and that the traffic after work is hell.

There's sacrifice either way, of course. Living here, I'll never be rich or influential. I'll never be quoted in the newspaper twice in a week; in fact, I may not even manage to read the paper twice in a week. Waking to knead bread and collect eggs from the henhouse, my days fill with mundane essentials. Instead of waiting in a traffic jam, I may spend an entire winter day chaining up my car and winching it through snowdrifts to the road. My words fall into cliché, howdy-do, and the sluggish thought that goes with chatter in the post office line or reporting to the cats at home. Work is what I can find, always strictly for money as I support a lifestyle the way others support too many children.

Sitting on the edge of your porch, I let my legs dangle. I look back the way I came, across to the mountains. Snowfields divided the pale sky from the water below as though bleeding off the color, draining it down the cracked and broken glaciers to the concentrate, undiluted blue of bay. There's never a time watching the mountains that I don't marvel at where I live, and I cannot imagine living where I couldn't watch the snowline rise and fall with the seasons.

And when I look around me again, I see the fenceposts of your garden. There it is, the old plot, looking small and indistinguishable from the rest of the field except for the gray posts that tilt like lightning-struck trees above the grass. Its chicken wire sags from one post to the next; moose, walking through, have pulled it free. In one corner, where it's still strung high, weeds—some climbing vines—have laced it together.

That's all that's left of the garden you turned by hand, layering in truckloads of horse manure and seaweed. You were so proud of what you grew—the early radishes, the chard, the heads of cabbage soft and leathery as medicine balls. I helped you dig potatoes when the plants lay limp over the hills and the soil was cold in our hands; they were small that year, the season short. Perfect for boiling, you said, content with what you had.

When was that, that all that happened—that the fireweed sneaked back across the fenceline as though it had never been spaded under, that the chicken wire loosened and the posts were heaved out by frost? All that's left looks so *old*, I can't believe it has anything to do with us. Somehow, we've become the ones who came before, as much a part of the past as the early homesteaders at the edge of the bluff or the later ones with sunken floors and cardboard walls.

Although you've left and I'm still here, the time when our lives were new and as brilliant as bright nails and fresh-sawn lumber is behind us both. Our first steps through—finding our ways along trails we parted, past rows we planted, up steps we hammered together— are history. I go on, holding to the vision, but I know now that you'll never be so satisfied again with small potatoes.

I drop down off the edge of the porch, landing harder than I expect. I've sat too long, stiffening. I walk over to the garden and around one side. The vine, I think, may be some surviving peas, but it's not; it's nothing I recognize, the leaves scalloped and tinted red, as though they've rusted over. I step across the fence and kick through the grass, searching for some sign. It's all weeds, as far as I can tell, the same as beyond the fence. I step out again and start back toward your house, wondering where I can find something to write a note with—charcoal, wax, anything—but there's nothing here, in this yard grayed out, gone to seed.

Instead, halfway back, I stop and pick some weeds: stalks of fireweed still stuck with wisps of fluff; brittle mare's tail; a handful of grasses fringed with seed cases; the paperlike shell of some cupshaped flower; a spiky pushki head, each pod spread like a parasol. I place them, inelegant and unarranged, in the paintbrush's can and set the whole bouquet against your door. When you come—whenever you come—they'll be waiting, frozen in time. Although snow may have buried the country, smoothing this morning's rugged beauty into flat, forgetful obliteration, these will stay as now, a reminder to you of what came before.

NOTES

affinity	natural attraction
The New Yorker	popular literary magazine
small potatoes	ironic reference to something not being important or worth very much

Wyeth painting   reference to the work of American painter Andrew Wyeth
                     (b. 1917), who painted rough-looking farmhouses

RESPONDING PERSONALLY

3. If this story were a letter that *you* had received from your friend, what
would be your response?

4. Friendships evolve: just as they are born, they may grow, they will almost
certainly change, and they may in time die. Describe a friendship in your
life that evolved over time. Did anything specific occur that changed the
relationship, or was it simply the natural passage of time?

RESPONDING CRITICALLY/ANALYTICALLY

5. This selection might be called an "interior story" rather than an "exterior
story." Identify the features that distinguish this as an interior story.

6. Examine the imagery of the story.
   a) The narrator's images for the friend's moving of items shift from a
   tidal "ebb and flow" to just an "ebb" to finally a "river now." In what
   way is this also a metaphor of their friendship?
   b) Explore the narrator's personification of the house. Suggest why the
   writer has developed this particular image so thoroughly. Why does
   she personify the house?
   c) Early in the story, the narrator speaks of the coming of winter. Discuss
   the appropriateness of the writer's choice of season as the setting for
   the story.
   d) Identify at least one more particularly apt use of imagery. Explain
   what it is about the image that you appreciate.

7. The story moves from a description of two friends whose characters
initially appear astonishingly similar to two people whose views and
needs in life have become quite different. Using a T-chart, identify two
clear areas of difference. Identify the actual passages that speak first of
the one character, and then of the other.
   a) What has the writer done to heighten the contrast between the two,
   to demonstrate that "now, each of us is by herself."
   b) Will the friend return? Support your answer with story detail.

8. "Tone" refers to the attitude of a writer toward her or his subject.
Describe the narrator's tone. What choices has the writer made that have
resulted in the development of this tone?

RESPONDING CREATIVELY

9. Reread the closing paragraph of the story. Why does the narrator leave
the bouquet by her friend's door? Is it done in friendship, or is the action
motivated by some other emotion? As the returning friend who arrives to
find the bouquet "waiting, frozen in time," respond to your friend's
memento. Do so using a similar "interior monologue" technique.

10. Create a short "found poem" of one of the very descriptive passages in the story.
    a) Select a variety of individual words or short phrases taken verbatim from the story. Phrases should be short, typically five or six words maximum.
    b) Place them into a suitable free verse sequence. They need not be in the same sequence as the original story.
    c) Have the final line bring some form of closure.
    d) Create a class display of "Small Potatoes" found poetry.

GROUP ASSESSMENT

    a) Have all others contributed fully and equitably to this display?
    b) Does the range of found poems cover the whole of the original story? Were parts of the story omitted? If so, why might that be?
    c) Does the "tone" of the display parallel the tone of the original story? If not, how might that be remedied?

PROBLEM SOLVING OR DECISION MAKING

11. How does one deal with a friendship that once was strong but now is waning? Does one attempt to "talk things through" with the friend, or is it better to just let it go, to let nature take its course? Support your response with reference to your own experience.

Anne Tyler
Holding Things Together

PRE-READING

1. Jot down a list of brainstormed words that would most suitably describe the person you believe you will eventually wish to marry. The words may describe character traits, talents, interests, or any other personal considerations you deem significant.
2. Tell about a time you were unnecessarily worried about something minor. What caused the worry? What resolved the situation? What "lessons," if any, did you learn?

He says that when he was ten, a family invited him to the movies and he got all dressed up in a new suit and tie and a blue striped shirt. But he didn't know how to tie the tie, and his father had died the year before and no one else in that household of women—mother, aunt, two sisters—knew how, either. They experimented most of Sunday afternoon, knotting and unknotting it until it was limp and crumpled. Finally, his aunt put it in her purse and caught a bus downtown. Standing in front of the show window at Patterson Brothers Menswear, she tied the tie so that it looked like the one on the mannequin. Then she took the bus home again and fastened the knot to his shirt with two straight pins. All through the movie he held his head at an angle, his hands hovering over his chest, protecting his long, clumsy tie as people squeezed past him to their seats.

There are a lot of questions I would like to ask about this. Couldn't he have gone to a neighbor? Didn't he have a male friend? Why wear a tie to a movie anyhow? At age *ten*?

You'd think at least he would have used a safety pin.

But I don't want to make too much of it. We've been married two years and I know by now: he doesn't like to talk about himself. In fact, I'm surprised he told me that story at all. I'm surprised he even remembered it.

He is forty years old, fifteen years my senior. A high-school principal. A large, pale, tired-looking man going bald. He always dresses formally, even for casual events—a home football game, a picnic—but generally there's something off kilter about his clothing. His lapels are spotted; his trousers are rumpled; his shirt is pricked with cigarette burns. His suit jacket always hangs lower in front, and the points of his collar curl up.

Of course, he knows how to tie a tie by now, but there are other things he's never learned. He can't fix a leaky faucet, for instance. He can't change the storm windows or put on tire chains. Is it because he lost his father so young? I was reared to believe that men take charge; I feel cheated. I do it myself, grumpily, or I call in a professional. I tell him I don't know where he'd be without me to hold things together. This always bothers him, and he walks away from me with his hands jammed into his pockets and his jacket sleeves rucked up to his elbows. Then I feel sorry; I never meant to sound so overbearing.

My car developed a shriek in the brakes and I had to take it to Exxon. This was last April, a beautiful, leafy April morning, but I was too upset to enjoy it. I can't stand to have something go wrong with my car. At the slightest symptom, I despair; I picture being stranded on the roadside, hood raised and white handkerchief fluttering, no one to stop for me but a couple of escaping convicts. Now here I was on my way to work and I heard this long, high shriek as I braked for a stoplight. I turned right around and drove to Exxon, where they know me. The mechanic on duty was Victor—a red-headed man with a carrot tattooed on his forearm. "Oh, Victor, just listen," I told him, and I had him stand out front while I drove back and forth, stopping every few feet. The brakes shrilled, though maybe not quite as loudly as before. I cut the motor and stepped out of the car. "What do you think it might be?" I asked.

He pulled at his nose. I waited. (My husband would have pressured him, supplied too much information, pushed for an immediate answer, but I knew enough to let him take his time.) Finally he said, "Just now start up?"

"Five minutes back," I told him.

"Little as *you* drive, chances are it's nothing at all."

"Yes, but what if I try to stop and can't? When it's the brakes, I get worried, Victor."

"Well, no, just calm down. You go in and have a seat. I'll give her a look."

I went into the office, with its two vinyl chairs and the coffee table stacked with *Popular Mechanics*. Tins of motor oil and bottles of windshield detergent were lined up neatly on the shelves. The tall blond boy named Joel was thumbing through an auto-parts catalogue. "Morning, Mrs. S.," he said. (He's fonder of me than Victor is; I think he likes the way I look. One time he asked where I bought my clothes, so that he could tell his wife.) He said, "Something gone wrong with the car again?"

"Victor's out checking my brakes," I told him. "Every time I slow down, they make this squeaky sound."

"Never mind. Lots of times brakes'll do that," he said.

"Really?"

"Sure. I wouldn't give it a thought."

"Oh, Joel, I hope you're right," I said.

Then I sank onto one of the chairs, and fluffed my skirt around my knees. I felt better already. Smaller boned. Joel was standing in a shaft of sunlight with lazy dust specks drifting around his head, and the chair was warm and smooth, and something gave off a nice leathery smell. When Victor came to get me (it was nothing, after all), I really was sorry to leave. I believe I could have sat there all morning.

My husband drives a Plymouth with a dented left fender, a smashed tail-light, and a BB scar like a little rayed sun on its right rear window. He seems determined just to use his car up—run it into the ground and walk away from it, as if it were something to be beaten into submission. Like his battered suits, or his shoes with the heels worn to lopsided slivers. What is it about him? I myself drive a Ford; I believe it's easiest to get parts for a Ford. It's five years old but it looks brand-new. Even the engine looks new; last year I had it steam-cleaned. Some people don't know you can do that, but you can.

If the weather has been dry, you can see the names of a couple of dozen high-school students written in the dust on my husband's fenders. Not to mention four-letter words, smiling faces, valentines. Inside, there are tattered files and magazines strewn across the seats, and squashed cigarette packs on the floor. The gearshift snaps in an alarming way when he goes into "Drive," and the engine tends to diesel long after he's cut the ignition. Also, his fan belt is loose; every time he makes a sharp turn you can hear a sound like a puppy's whimper. I tell him he ought to get it seen to. "You have to stay on top of these things," I tell him. "A machine is only worth the care you give it."

I feel ridiculous. I feel I'm turning into my father, a thorough, methodical man who wouldn't let me get my driver's license till I'd learned how to change a spare tire. Still, I know I'm right. "What if we're stranded somewhere?" I ask. "What if we're taking a very long trip and the car drops dead in the middle of an eight-lane highway?"

"Why, this is a *fine* car," my husband says.

He's offended, I can tell. He slumps in his seat, steering with only one wrist propped across the top of the wheel. He always drives abysmally—dashing start-ups, sudden swerves, jerky stops. At red lights, he refuses to shift to neutral. I tell him he ought to, but he says it's pointless. "Why get a car that's automatic and then spend your life shifting gears?" he asks.

"To save wear and tear on your transmission, of course."

He groans, and starts off again with a screech. I promise myself I won't say another word. But I can't resist a silent comment: as the car heads toward a curve at sixty miles an hour, I raise a hand deliberately and brace myself against the dashboard.

Last June, my old college roommate came to town and I took her out to lunch. Just the two of us; my husband doesn't like her. (He says she's brassy, loud, opinionated, but I believe he's jealous. Men imagine women are closer than they really are.) I picked her up at her sister-in-law's and drove her to Nardulli's, a little Italian restaurant I hardly ever get to go to. Bee looked wonderful. She wore tight white pants and a loose top, and ropes and ropes of branch coral. During the meal, we had all sorts of things to talk about—our jobs, our husbands, old friends—but by the time our coffee came we had more or less petered out. We drove back in near silence, the comfortable kind. Bee hummed "Star Dust" and let her arm hang loose out the window. I coasted down St. Johns Street, timing the lights perfectly.

Then on Delmore, where I had to turn left, the engine died. For no earthly reason. "Now, what ...?" I said. I shifted gears and started up again. We rode smoothly till the stop sign on Furgan Street; then the engine died again. After that, it died every time I slowed down. Red and green warning signals flashed on the instrument panel; horns kept honking behind me. My accelerator foot started shaking. "Oh, Lord, something has gone wrong," I told Bee.

"Maybe you're out of gas," she said.

"Gas? How could it be the gas? It keeps on starting up again, doesn't it? That's ridiculous," I said.

Bee glanced at me but said nothing. I was too frantic to apologize. "Listen, I've got to get to Exxon," I said.

"There's a Texaco station just ahead."

"But Exxon is where they know my car, and it's only two more blocks."

The engine died again. "Thank God we're not out on some highway," I said, and I wiped my eyes on my sleeve. I could feel Bee's sideways stare.

Then just as we rolled into Exxon the car gave a final shudder, like a desert wanderer staggering into an oasis. I jumped out, leaving the door swinging open behind me. I ran into the garage, where Joel was standing under an elevated Volkswagen, whistling and squinting upward with his thumbs hitched through his belt loops. "Joel?" I said. "My car's developed this terrible problem."

He stopped whistling. "Why, hello, Mrs. S.," he said.

"Can't you take a look for me?"

He followed me into the sunlight. I felt better already; he was so slow and peaceful. All the while I was telling him the symptoms, he was just coolly raising the hood, poking around, humming whatever he'd been whistling. "Turn her on," he told me. I slid behind the wheel, started the engine, and stopped it when he signalled. Then I got out and went to look under the hood again. I watched his long, bony fingers, which seemed to have more texture than other people's because of the grime in the creases. He jiggled a little black wire.

"Is it the fuel pump?" I asked him. I'd had a terrible experience once with a fuel pump. (I'm learning auto parts the hard way, the same way soldiers learn geography.)

But Joel said, "Can't tell for sure. Going to bring her on inside. It won't take long."

I told Bee. She got out and we went to the office to wait. In the summer, the leathery smell was stronger than ever. I collapsed on one of the chairs, closed my eyes, and tipped my head back. "I'm sorry," I told Bee. "I just get so upset when my car doesn't work."

"You know what I would do?" said Bee. "Take a course in auto mechanics."

I opened my eyes and looked at her.

"Sure," she said. "That's what I did when our lawn started getting me down. I went over to the college and studied landscape architecture. I got up at six every morning for this course on television. I bought a machine to spread lime on the—"

"Yes," I said, "but I already have so much to—"

"Be adventurous! There aren't any *roles* anymore. Just jump in and do what you feel like."

I thought a minute.

"Bee," I said finally, "tell me the truth. Did you do that because you felt like it? Or because you saw that no one else was going to do it?"

"Hmm?" she said. But by then she had picked up one of the magazines, and was idly flipping pages. It was plain she didn't think the question was important.

After a while, Joel came in, wiping his hands on a rag. "It's the filter," he told me. "You've got to get your filter changed."

"Is that serious?"

"No, we can have her ready by five this afternoon."

Bee said, "I'll call my sister-in-law. She can come pick us up."

"But the car," I said. "I mean, after this will it be as good as ever? Will it run without stalling?"

"No reason why it shouldn't," Joel said.

He wrote my name on a printed form: Mrs. Simmons, in large, competent capitals. At the second line, his pencil paused. "Address? Phone?" he said.

"Four four four four Nelson Road. Eight four four, two two four four."

"Four must be your lucky number," he said.

"No, nine."

He looked up. Then he laughed.

"Well, you asked," I told him. Then I laughed too, ignoring Bee's blank stare. I felt young and scatterbrained, but in a pleasant way. It was wonderful to know that by five o'clock everything would be all right again.

Bee's sister-in-law came to get us in a great big lavender Cadillac, and she drove me home. Before I got out, I apologized again to Bee.

"Oh, listen," she said, "forget it. But how about later, will you need a ride back to the station?"

"Oh, no. I'm sure Alfred will be home by then," I said.

"Well, if he isn't, now ..."

"I'll call you," I promised.

But I was right. My husband was home in time to take me. Just barely, though: I had to rush him right back out the door. He seemed befuddled, out of step. He drove more sloppily than ever. "*What* did you say went wrong? Last week, your car looked fine," he said. He turned right, bouncing over the curb. He went through a yellow light that was changing to red. At Exxon, he slowed and gazed dimly out the window. "Don't leave till I make sure it's fixed," I said. (You have to tell him these things.) I hopped out and went into the garage, where Joel was spinning a tire on a turntable. He smiled when he saw me. "All set," he said. "Feel better now?"

"I certainly do," I said. Then I turned and waved to my husband, telling him he was free to go. He waved back. His sleeve looked like a used lunch bag. For some reason, it made me sad to see his dusty little car go puttering off into traffic again.

I first met my husband while I was student-teaching at his school. I didn't like teaching at all, as it turned out (now I work in a library), but I thought I should go ahead and get my certificate anyway. Just in case, was how I put it—meaning in case I never married, or was widowed young, or something like that.

Alfred when I met him was exactly the way he is now—shabby, shambling, absentminded. The only difference was that he seemed so authoritative. I heard the teachers talking about him: he was "Mr. Simmons" and he didn't like undisciplined classrooms. When he came to a room to observe, some electricity seemed to pass through the students. They acted more alert. The teacher grew crisper. Now I sit across from him at the supper table and I try and try to see him again in that shine of unquestioned assurance. I squint, giving him distance. He becomes so distraught that he drops his fork. "What's the matter?" he asks. "Have I done something wrong?"

Yet at school, the few times I've been back, I notice that the teachers still make improvements in their posture when they see him coming down the hall.

While we were courting, it never occurred to me to ask what he knew how to do. Could he change the oil? Hang a screen door? Well, of course he could; all men could. And even if he couldn't, what difference did it make? I loved him. I would go weak with love just watching his cuff button spin dizzily from one frayed thread. If he got lost while driving me to a restaurant, I was glad; I hadn't wanted to eat anyhow. I was only waiting for the moment when he would park the car in front of my apartment and take me in his arms. His hands (with their spatulate nails, their pink, uncalloused palms that should have been a warning) seemed to mold me; I curved within them and grew taller, slimmer, prettier. It was hardly the moment to ask if he knew how to replace a wall switch.

Then we married and went to live in a middle-aged house on Coker Street. It was a hard time; my parents thought Alfred was disappointing, and they more or less withdrew themselves. I felt orphaned. I started work in the library, and every evening when I came home (dead tired, feet aching) I had to fix supper, take out the garbage, vacuum, dust. On weekends, I mowed the lawn and pruned the shrubs, and then I washed the woodwork, painted rooms, varnished floors. My husband only watched, from various doorways. I don't mean to imply that he was lazy. It's just that he didn't know how to help. He would gladly take out the garbage for me but forgot to replace the trash-can lid, so dogs would tip the can over and spread the garbage everywhere. He dripped paint, stepped in the varnish, broke a window trying to open it. It turned out that he had never learned how to handle money, and had therefore been assigned one of those special bank tellers who balance checkbooks for rich, helpless widows. Also, he had a cubbyhole in his desk at home that contained nothing but unpaid parking tickets.

Well, I paid the tickets, I took over the checkbook, I drew up a yearly budget. Quizzing him on deductible expenses (my father's task, in my childhood), I felt I was becoming angular, wider shouldered. I developed my father's habit of offering forth one flat, spread hand, palm upward, inviting others to be reasonable. "Well, think, Alfred. Did you buy any stamps? Office supplies? Any books that had to do with your profession?"

"Books?" he would say. "Why, yes, I believe I did."

"How much were they? Do you have the receipts?"

"Oh, no. I must have lost them."

"Five dollars? Ten?"

"I'm not quite sure."

"Think of the titles. Maybe that will help. Fifteen dollars? Twenty? Was it under twenty-five?"

"I just don't *know* Lucy. Please, does it matter all that much?"

At night, I began to have insomnia. I lay in bed with my hands curled tight, no matter how often I told myself to open them. I felt I was clutching all the strings of the house, keeping it together. Everything depended on me.

"When I start the motor," I told Joel, "it sounds just fine. Then I go faster and I'm waiting for that click, you know? That click that tells me the car's shifted gears? But I don't seem to hear it. And it seems to me the motor whines a little, has the wrong sound; I don't know how to explain it."

"Just hope it's not the transmission," Joel said. "That can get expensive."

We were waiting for a stoplight; he was driving. He was going to test the automatic shift for me. It was August and very hot and sunny (Joel's face was glazed with sweat and his yellow hair had a glittery look), but I didn't open my window. I liked the feeling of soaking in heat; I'd felt cold and anxious all morning. I liked the fact that Joel, waiting serenely for the light, whistled "Let It Be" and drummed his fingers on the steering wheel. My car seemed humble and obedient.

"I hope I don't have to buy a new one," I said.

"You won't," he told me.

The light changed. Joel started right off, but we were following some-one—some old lady in a Studebaker who just wouldn't get up any speed. "Shoot," Joel said. He switched lanes. Now we really were trav-elling, and Joel had his head cocked to hear the sound of the motor. "Well?" he said. "Seems to me like she's shifting just about on schedule."

"No, wait a minute, give it a minute ..."

I was listening too, but I couldn't hear what I heard when I was alone.

We turned off onto a smaller road, a residential street with no traf-fic lights. Joel stopped the car, then started again and went up to sixty, all the time keeping his head cocked. He braked and shifted to neutral; his knuckles moved beneath the skin like well-oiled machine parts. "Let's run her through again," he said.

The second run carried us to the end of the road—a surprise, a field full of goldenrod and beer cans. He stopped the car and wiped his upper lip with the back of his hand. "Well," he said, gazing out at the field. Behind his eyes (which were long and blue, as clear as windows) I imagined sheets of information, all the facts he knew being reviewed in an orderly way. "No," he said finally, and shook his head. "She seems O.K. to me."

You'd think I'd be relieved, but I wasn't. If something is wrong, it can be fixed; then you know it won't go wrong again for a while. But if nothing's been pinpointed, if it's just this nebulous feeling of *error* in your mind ... I sighed and gripped my purse. Joel looked over at me. "I must be going crazy," I told him.

"Oh, no ..."

"I seem to be taking this car so seriously. Lately, I've stopped driving on freeways. I don't want to be too far from a service station. I've had to give up the League of Women Voters and my favorite supermarket. Even here in town, I only go by routes that have service stations. Streets with nothing but houses make me anxious."

"Shoot, this car's in *fine* shape," he told me, giving the wheel a pat. "You don't have to feel like that."

"I'm worried pretty soon I'll just have to stay at home all day."

That made him laugh. "So what?" he said. "What's so bad about home?"

"I'd lose my job, for one thing."

"Well, I just wish my wife would have your problem," he said. "That's all she does all day—drive around. Drops me off at the station and then drives here, drives there ... spends all our money, wears out the baby ..."

"But she does have you to call if something goes wrong," I said.

"Where, forty miles out on the Beltway? Out at Korvettes, or K Mart, or Two Guys? And none of what she buys is worth much. All these skimpy sweaters, tacky plastic earrings ... I don't begrudge the money, but she could save it up and buy something *good*, like your tan coat—you know your tan coat?—and be a whole lot better off. I tell her that, but think she'll listen?"

"Maybe she's lonely," I said.

"Maybe so," he said, "but I'd sure like a wife who stayed home some. And she doesn't take care of herself—she's so sloppy. She's let her hair grow long, and every time I come home I think, Well, who's this? I mean it never stops being a surprise, I never get used to it. I think, Is this *it*, is this who I'm with, this lady with the stringy hair? It's like I have amnesia. I just can't figure how it all happened."

"No one told us it would be so permanent," I said.

"Why, no," he said. "Not so as to make us believe it."

He looked over at me. His hands fell off the wheel. Outside I could hear the locusts whirring, pointing up our silence. "Well!" I said, and Joel said, "Well! Victor will be having kittens by now." And he started up the car again, and turned around, and we drove on back to the station.

Last September, I went South to visit my parents for a week. It didn't go well, though. I'd been away too long; something had stiffened between us. I watched my younger sister teasing them at the supper table and I felt more orphaned than ever. My father stayed down in his workshop, taking things apart and putting them back together; my mother and I were so polite it was painful. I was glad when it was time to leave.

Alfred met me at the train station, carrying roses. I was so happy to see him. His crumpled clothes gave me a soothed and trustful feeling; I rested on his smell of old tobacco. "Don't let me leave you again," I told him. He smiled and laid the roses in my arms.

Driving home, he asked about my family: Were they used to the idea of our marriage yet? "Oh, sure," I told him offhandedly. What did my family have to do with us?

He parked in front of our house, with two wheels on the curb. He took my suitcase from the trunk, and we climbed the front steps, holding hands. "You notice I've mowed the grass for you," he said.

I was surprised. I looked around at the lawn—straggly, dotted with the first few leaves of fall. Plainly, something had been chewing at it. I saw the narrow, tufted rows he'd missed. "Why, Alfred!" I said.

He seemed uneasy.

"That's wonderful!" I told him.

"Yes, but—Lucy? I'm not so sure about the lawnmower."

"Lawnmower?"

"I mean, it seems to me that something's wrong with it."

"Oh, well, I'll check it later," I told him.

"It's right over there, if you want to take a look."

In the grass at the side of the house, he meant; he'd left it out. It was an electric mower, and fairly expensive—not a thing you'd leave sitting around. But I didn't tell him so. "What seems to be the trouble?" I asked.

"Well—"

He set my suitcase on the porch and went over to the mower. He turned the mower upside down without unplugging it (I winced but said nothing) and pointed to the blades. "See there?" he said.

Well, they *used* to be blades. Now they were mangled hunks of metal, notched and torn and twisted. I said, "What on earth?" I bent closer. One of the hunks of metal wasn't a blade at all, it turned out, but something flatter and wider. "Why, that's the foot guard," I said. "It's supposed to be attached to the rear of the mower."

"Evidently it came loose," Alfred said.

"Yes, but—what happened, you just went on mowing? You mowed on over your own foot guard and let the blades gnash it up?"

"I didn't realize what was going on," he said.

"But the noise must have been horrendous!"

"Well, I thought it was the ... I don't know. I just thought it was having a little spell of some sort, caught a twig or something."

I pictured it exactly: Alfred doggedly pushing on, with terrible shrieks and clatters coming from the mower. It gave me a feeling of despair. I couldn't seem to rise above this. "Oh, Alfred," I said, "can't you do something right? Will I always have to be the one?"

He straightened up and looked at me. His face had grown white. His eyes (ordinarily a mild gray) had widened and darkened; they seemed to be all iris. "I knew you would say that, Lucy," he said.

"If you knew, then why—"

"Nothing I do will satisfy you. You always want everything perfect and you always do it yourself; or stand over me and nag and belittle, find fault with every move I make. You just have to be in control; it's always you that holds the power."

"Is that how you see it?" I said. "Do you think I choose to be this way? Do you think I *want* the power? Take it! Why won't you take it? Do you think I'd hold it if anybody else would? *Take* it!"

And I shook my hands in his face, offering all that was in them, but he merely looked at me. I let them drop. I watched him turn to right the mower and unplug it and trundle it toward the garage: a large, sad man in a baggy suit, slumping slightly as he walked.

My car's been running well lately, though I haven't given up worrying. In fact, the last time I went to Exxon it was just to fill the gas tank. I went on a foggy October morning, the first really cold day of fall. Joel was the one on duty. He seemed grim, maybe hung over; and I had a headache from sitting up to watch the late show after Alfred had gone to bed. So all I did was nod, and Joel nodded back and went to start the pump. While the tank was filling, he stood waiting with his arms folded. I stared straight ahead, watching my breath steam the windshield. Then I paid him six dollars and twenty-four cents and put my billfold back in my purse and drove away.

NOTES

nebulous   vague; hazy

"Let It Be"   popular Beatles song of hope and acceptance

RESPONDING PERSONALLY

3. Identify some of the several issues raised by the story. Focus on one of them. Respond in writing: share your thoughts and opinions about that issue.

4. Near the very end of the story, the narrator describes first her husband and then herself: "Alfred doggedly pushing on.... It gave me a feeling of despair. I couldn't seem to rise above this." Reflect back to a time or situation when you *knew* that what you were doing was perhaps not right, but you, too, couldn't "rise above" it and instead fell deeper in. Share your reflection in writing.

RESPONDING CRITICALLY/ANALYTICALLY

5. The story is written in the first person (see "point of view" in the Glossary), meaning that all the events the reader encounters have been filtered through the thoughts and opinions of the narrator. Despite this, the picture the narrator paints of herself is not especially flattering. How has the writer achieved this effect? How has she allowed verisimilitude of character to survive a biased narration? Share your thoughts in small-group discussion.

6. The writer draws an ironic parallel between the narrator's near-neurotic exasperation with her husband's apparent helplessness in matters of the home and his resulting dependence on her, and her own need for help with matters automotive and her resulting dependence on her mechanic. With a partner, identify some of the many parallels the writer develops. Share with your classmates.

7. Compose two abbreviated character sketches:
   a) Piece together a character sketch of the narrator using just lines and phrases taken verbatim from the story (e.g., "I didn't like teaching … now I work in a library").
   b) Write the character sketch of Alfred that the narrator might have written, again using just lines from the story. How closely does this match the reality as you would believe it to be?
   c) In what way does Alfred's character sketch pose the question: Why are they married?

8. The three minor characters, Victor, Joel, and Bee, function as foils in the story.
   a) What similarities of personality do these three share?
   b) Whom are they more like—the narrator or Alfred?
   c) Why has the writer introduced the personalities of these characters into the story?

RESPONDING CREATIVELY

9. Suppose that Alfred was not a part of the narrator's life. Write two relatively concise advertisements written by the narrator that might appear in the "Personals" section of the newspaper:
   a) The advertisement for the husband that she *thinks* she wants.
   b) The advertisement for the husband that she in actuality *does* want.

   Share the second of the ads with your classmates. Perhaps create a class collage of the ads.

   ### PEER ASSESSMENT

   Which advertisement better captures the psychological and emotional needs of the narrator? What does that ad do better than the rest?

10. What advice would Bee be likely to offer the narrator about her relationship with Alfred? Present this information in the style of an "Advice" columnist.

PROBLEM SOLVING OR DECISION MAKING

11. The husband and wife are 15 years apart in age, she still relatively young and he approaching middle age. He has lived some 50 percent more life than she. Is discrepancy in age a factor that needs to be considered in marriage? While not necessarily the cause of marital problems, might it nonetheless contribute to the difficulty in overcoming them? Discuss, using examples from your own life experience as support for your views.

Translated from the Vietnamese by
Nguyen Nguyet Cam and Linh Dinh

Duong Thu Huong
Reflections of Spring

PRE-READING

1. Describe a situation that you have experienced where a certain sensory impression—a particular taste or sight, for example—triggered a vivid memory. What was the impression? What was the memory?

2. Have you ever had strong feelings for someone, feelings that you didn't, for whatever reason, express? Or conversely, did you ever express feelings for someone that were not returned? Recall such an experience. Describe your situation at the time, as closely as you remember. How strong is the memory today? Explain.

It's not because of that evening. But since then, thoughts of her hadn't left his mind. They would linger for a while, then rush at him like a gust of wind, throwing his thoughts into chaos and disrupting his equanimity, leaving behind vague and anguished longings. That evening, he was returning to Hanoi from a midland province. An economic planner, he was used to these long, tedious trips. Dozing in his seat on the bus, he was awoke by loud clanking sounds coming from the engine. The driver lifted the hood and moaned:

"Can't make it to Hanoi this evening. The radiator is broken ..."

The passengers got off the bus to walk around and to breathe in the pleasant air of the midland area. Yellow fields ran to the horizon. In the distance, one could see the uneven peaks of dark green hills, like a clique of moss-covered snails resting on a carpet of rice paddies. The yellow of ripe rice was pale in the fading sun, but it flared up in spots, as if still soaked in light. At the edge of the road, the harvested field had a soft pink glow, as gentle as adolescent love. The autumn breeze made him feel light-headed: He was free from projects, reports, criticisms, approvals—all hindrances and distractions. It was an unusual feeling, this clarity. He walked briskly along.

By the side of the road was a row of houses. Their uneven roofs and white walls gave a strong warmth to the landscape. Butted up against each other, the houses were fronted by a mishmash of verandahs in different styles. In the small yards were tree stumps and piles of bricks. Nearby, pigeon coops perched on tree branches. At the base of a mound of shiny yellow straw, smelling of harvest, an old hen led her chicks, cluck-clucking, searching for food. A crude red and green sign announced a bicycle repair shop. In front, a dangling flat wire wobbled with each gust of wind. Bunches of bananas, suspended from hooks, hovered over the heads of diners in the cheap restaurants.

The serenity and melancholic air of the small town enchanted him. He didn't know what he was thinking, but he walked up and down the streets admiring the familiar views, especially the shrubs and poinciana plants behind the houses. The yellow flowers bloomed in the quiet evening.

"Uncle, come in for a drink. We have country rice pies and sticky-rice cakes."

An old woman behind a small glass display case leaned forward to greet her customer. He was a little surprised, it had been a long time since he heard such a natural, friendly greeting from a shopkeeper. He walked in and sat down on a long bench. He didn't know why he had walked in: he wasn't hungry, thirsty or in need of a smoke from the water pipe. But he had a strong intuition he was waiting for something. It was vague yet urgent. His heart beat anxiously. The shop-keeper leisurely poured out a bowl of green tea for her customer. Then she sat back, chewed her betel nut and said nothing. He raised the bowl of tea, took a sip and looked around. A gust of wind whirled some yellow leaves. From a distance, they looked like tiny gold grains that nature had generously scattered.

He had known all of this at one time. They were images from his past, although he wasn't aware of it. He felt increasingly uneasy.

"Grandma, should I make more rice wafers?"

A girl's voice echoed from inside the house. The sound of her voice startled him. He almost got up to rudely peer into the other room. But he restrained himself. The shop owner's granddaughter came out from the back:

"I baked ten more rice wafers, Grandma. There's none left in the basket!"

Seeing him, the girl stepped back cautiously. The old woman opened the bag and took out a bunch of small rice pancakes. "Bake twenty small ones for Grandma. They're easier to sell." The girl answered "yes" in a low voice and leaned over the earthenware basin to blow into the fire. The white ashes flew up, danced in the air and gently landed on her shiny black hair. Her teenage face was smooth and ruddy as a ripe fruit. Her nose was straight and graceful. She had a simple haircut, parted down the middle. He couldn't take his eyes off her; his heart beat excitedly.

"This is it!"

This unspoken sentiment had echoed within him as the girl came out ... Twenty-three years ago, when he was in the tenth grade and a boarder in a small town, there was a similarly pretty and well-behaved girl. The same earthenware basin and red coals throwing off cinders, the same ruddy cheeks and round wrists ... but the girl from his memory had a long hollow trace on her forehead. There were the same poinciana flowers and tiny yellow leaves, scattered by gusts of wind, dotting the ground in autumn, when sounds from the radio mixed with rustling from the unharvested rice paddies and the incessant noises of insects—the lazy, forlorn music of a small town.

It was odd how deeply buried these memories were. He was very poor then. Each month, his mother would send him only three *dong* for pocket money and 10 kilograms of rice. But he studied harder than all the other boys in his class, who called him a bookworm. The pretty girl lived next door to the house where he rented his room. She used to lean her arms against the fence and listen to him memorize poems out loud. Her mother was a food vendor; she would squat in front of the earthenware basin to bake rice wafers for her mother. At night, when he studied, she also lit an oil lamp and sat under the carambola tree to do her homework. At 10 o'clock, as his face was still buried in a book, she would hoist a carrying pole onto her shoulder to go get water for her family. She was a good student and never needed his help. Still, she would look at him admiringly as he diagrammed a geometric problem, or as he closed his eyes and recited, smooth as soup, a long poem. By the time she came back with the water, he would be ready for bed. He was so hungry he had to literally tighten his belt. It was then she would bring him a piping hot rice wafer. The two of them didn't say much. Usually, he just smiled:

"What luck, my stomach was growling."

He never bothered to thank her. But they both felt that they needed to see each other, look at each other's faces and talk about nothing. Neither of them dared to ask too deeply about the other. Truth is, there was nothing more to ask ... Her piping hot wafers; the hollow trace on her forehead; the bright face; the understanding looks when he was homesick, sitting all bunched up during cold, rainy evenings.

He suddenly remembered all these things. All of them. He now understood what he had been waiting for that evening. It had arrived. That beautiful, sweet, distant memory. A memory, buried for more than twenty years, awakened suddenly by a gust of wind.

The young girl, who was fanning the fire, looked up: "Grandma, I've finished ten ... Give me a hand ..."

She gave the stack of yellow cakes to the old woman and glanced curiously at the strange customer. He rotated the tea bowl in his hands while staring at her. She became flustered and clumsily swatted a lump of coal to the ground with her fan. She picked it up immediately, threw it back into the basin, then blew on her two fingers to cool them off, her brows knit in a frown.

"Now she looks like a twelve-year-old. The other girl was older, and more pretty," he thought.

Once, he didn't have enough money to buy textbooks. It wasn't clear how she found out. That night, along with the wafers, she also gave him a small envelope. He opened it: inside was a small stack of bills. The notes were so new you could smell the aroma of paper and ink. It was her New Year's money. He sat motionless. It looked like she had been hoarding it for ten months and hadn't touched it. "But what did I do that day?" After graduating, he was pre-occupied with taking the university admissions exam. After his acceptance, knowing he was going away, he excitedly took care of the paperwork, merrily said goodbye to everyone, then took a train straight for Hanoi.

"Why didn't I say goodbye to the girl? No, I was about to, but it was getting too close to my departure date. I was rushed by my relatives. And intimidated by such an opportunity ..."

And after that? A fresh environment; a strange city; life's frantic rhythm made him dizzy; bright lights; streetcars; the first parties where he felt awkward, provincial, out of place; teahouses; the blackboard in the classroom; new girlfriends ...

"Eat the hot rice wafers, Uncle. It's aromatic in your mouth. In Hanoi, you don't get country treats like this." The old shopkeeper gave him a small rice wafer. Its fluffy surface was speckled with golden sesame seeds—very appetizing. He broke off a small piece and put it in his mouth. It was a taste he had long forgotten about.

"I used to think rice wafers were the most delicious food on earth," he thought. He remembered studying at night, particularly nights when he had to memorize history and biology lessons—two damnable subjects when he was so hungry waiting for her footsteps near the fence that his mouth could taste the deliciously baked rice flour and the fatty sesame seeds ... that taste and smell ... and her wet eyes looking at him, as she rested her arms on the windowsill and smiled:

"I knew you were hungry, Brother. I get pretty hungry at night also. Mother told me to go into town tomorrow to buy cassava so we can have something extra to eat at night." The next day she brought him pieces of boiled cassava. At eighteen, eating them, he also thought her boiled cassava was the most delicious food on earth. Once, she gave him cassava wrapped in banana leaves. It was steaming hot. As he yanked his arms back, she grabbed both his hands and the hot cassava. She let go immediately, her eyes wide in astonishment. As for him, he was as dizzy as he had been that one holiday morning, when he had drunk too much sweet wine ...

"I really did love her back then ... I really did love ..." Then why hadn't he gone back to that town to find her? Finished with his studies, he was assigned a job by the government. Then he had to apply for housing. Then he was involved with a female colleague. Life worries. There was a secret agreement, then the marriage license. That was his wife, unattractive yet dogged in her pursuit of his love, who used every trick imaginable to make him yield to the harsh demands of necessity ... And then what? Children. Problems at work. A promotion. Steps forward and backward. Years spent overseas to get a doctorate degree ... Everything has to be tabulated.

"Is the wafer good, Uncle?" the old woman asked.

"Very good, Grandmother," he answered. Crumbs fell onto his knees and he brushed them off. The old hen came over, cluck clucking for her chicks to come pick the crumbs.

"Why didn't I look for her? Why didn't I ... Well, I had to achieve, at all costs, the planning targets for operative 038 ... And, to raise my kids, I had to teach to supplement my income. My daughters don't resemble me; they are like their mother, ugly, stuck-up ... But do I love my wife? Probably not ... Most likely not. I've never tingled because of that woman like I did years ago waiting for the sounds of the little girl's footsteps. Especially in the afternoon, with everyone gone, when she washed her hair—with her cheeks dripping wet and strands of hair nappy on her temples. As she dried her hair, one hand on the fence, she would smile because she knew I was secretly admiring her ... As for my wife, there's never any suspense; I never look forward to seeing her, nor feel empty when we're apart. Back then, going home to get rice, how I anticipated seeing the little girl again, even after only a day ... My wife needed a husband and she found me. As for me ..."

This thought nearly drove him mad. He stood up abruptly. The girl fanning the fire stared at him, her eyes black as coal, a deep dimple on one cheek.

He paid the old woman and started walking toward the bus. He wanted to return to Hanoi immediately. He wanted to forget these thoughts ...

But the bus wasn't fixed until 2 in the morning. They returned to Hanoi by dawn. He returned to his daily life, to his daily business and worries ... The thoughts of the little girl never left him. They would circle back like the hands on a watch.

"Why didn't I go find her back then? I surely would have had a different wife. And who knows ..." The little girl is thirty-eight now, but to him she's still fifteen. She is his true love, but why do people only find out these things twenty years later? He flicked the cigarette ashes into the fancy pink ashtray and watched the tiny embers slowly die. On the bed, his wife sleepily raised her head:

"Why are you up so late, dear? Are you admiring me?"

"Yes, yes, I'm admiring you," he answered, squashing the cigarette butt in the ashtray. His wife had just bought an embroidered dress from Thailand and had asked what he thought of it three times already.

"Go to bed, dear."

"I still have work to do."

"I wonder where the little girl is living now? What is she doing? Maybe I can take a bus there tomorrow. No, no, that's not possible." He saw clearly that to walk away silently twenty-three years ago was wrong. How could he possibly go back, when he had dismissed love so easily?

He retrieved the cigarette butt and lit it again. The ember returned to his lips.

A garden full of shades. Carambolas on the ground like fallen stars. And the smell of ripe carambolas. And her wet eyes. Her head tilted as she stood near the fence ...

"But I was very shy then. I didn't dare to make any vow ... Stop denying it—it is useless when it comes to love." He knew he had loved her and she had loved him, but he was impatient to get out of there because he was dazzled by his own prospects. During the last hectic days, he did brood over a petty calculation. He did plan to ... but never realized it.

"It wasn't like that, because ..."

"Sure it was."

"It wasn't like that ..."

"Yes, and you can't be forgiven ..."

He threw the cigarette butt into the ashtray and flopped into an armchair. The polyester-covered cushions weren't as comfortable as usual. He stood up again, went to the window and pushed the glass panes open.

"It's cold, honey," his wife shrieked.

He didn't turn around, but answered gruffly:

"Then use the blanket."

Many stars lit up the night sky. He suddenly smelled the scent of fresh straw, of harvest. This familiar smell shrouded the neighborhood, a fragrance to stir one's soul. The poinciana flowers bloomed in the evening ... Everything revived—vague, spurious, yet stark enough to make him bitter. His head was spinning.

He lit a second cigarette and slapped himself on the forehead.

"What is going on?"

There was no answer. Only a rising tremolo of rice stalks and leaves rustling. Again, the swirling sky over the crown of the carambola tree; her smooth, firm arms on the windowsill as she smiled at him. White teeth like two rows of corn. His love had returned, right now, within him. He walked unconsciously to the mirror. His hair had begun to gray. Lines were etched all over his cheeks. Behind the glasses, his eyes had started to become lifeless. He drew deeply on the cigarette then exhaled. The pale blue smoke billowed shapelessly, like the confusions in his life.

His report contained many interesting proposals and was very well received, a complete success. Both his bosses and rivals were equally impressed. He himself didn't know how he had managed to do it. All the endless nights, walking back and forth, watching smoke rise then evaporate, when he had thought of her. She, the object of his true love—a love not shared, not articulated, what does it all add up to? But these soothing, melancholic memories had kept him awake at night, and he had written his report during these late hours, as he tried to recover what had disappeared from his life.

At the conference, people were admiring the exhibits illustrating his proposals. He had succeeded almost completely. Even his enemies were congratulating him. He smiled, shook hands and thanked everybody before slipping out into the hallway. Alone.

His closest colleague ran out to find him. The man looked him in the eye and said:

"The newspaper photographers are waiting for you. What's wrong, Brother? Are you in love?"

"Me, in love?" he chuckled, then snapped, "Me, love?! Are you mad? Me still in love ... a steel-and-cement man, a ... and with my hair turning ..."

He didn't finish his sentence, but rushed out the gate. He walked down a little lane. For some reasons, his eyes were stinging, as if smoke had blown into them. Where's that hamlet, that town? With pigeon coops and piles of straw in the yards. And poinciana flowers blooming in the evening sun. And the windswept rice paddies, with their ripe stalks rustling. And the harvested fields glowing, a soft pink, distant ...

NOTES

carambolas   exotic, star-shaped fruits

cassava   plant used as a staple food in tropics; tapioca is derived from it

RESPONDING PERSONALLY

3. What is your opinion of the narrator: Is he a likable character? Can you empathize with him? Are you pleased for his success in his job? Are you saddened at his sense of loss, of unfulfilled love? Respond freely.

4. In William Shakespeare's *Hamlet*, Queen Gertrude says, "The lady doth protest too much." At the end of the short story, the narrator says, "Me, love?! Are you mad?" Why is he so emphatic? What does this show?

RESPONDING CRITICALLY/ANALYTICALLY

5. Examine the language and imagery of the two opening descriptive paragraphs. Notice the definite contrast in tone. What is the writer's purpose in establishing this contrast? Why might the writer have selected the paragraph sequence he did, rather than the reverse?

6. A back-and-forth, present-to-past movement runs throughout the story. The sections of flashback remain basically similar—a consistent tone, a consistent mood—but sections that narrate the present time do not.
   a) How does the narration change?
   b) Why does it change?
   c) Comment on the change the *narrator* undergoes.

7. At what point in the flashback narrative does negativity begin to creep into the story? How is this brought about? What does the writer appear to be suggesting about the situation, about the character?

8. In a sentence or two, write a thematic statement that you feel effectively identifies the controlling idea (or one of the controlling ideas) of the story. Be prepared to defend your statement in terms of the choices the writer appears to have made.

Responding Creatively

9. If you were to adapt this story for film, how would you manage the constant shifting of present and past? Work in small groups of three.
   a) Would your changes parallel the short story precisely, or would you perhaps *combine* passages of text for your adaptation?
   b) How would your transitions between times appear to the viewer? Describe one of your transitions from before the switch to after. What visual cues would you employ? Explain why.
   c) What would be your aural cues?

   If you have access to the appropriate technology, videotape a dramatic representation of one of the transition passages. Present it to the class.

Group Assessment

Readers' visualizations of the same story can often be quite dissimilar. Did differences appear in your group members' thinking? Were you comfortably able to reach agreement on the most effectively designed transition? Overall, how well did your group function?

10. Write the initial e-mail that the narrator sends when he discovers his lost love's address.

Problem Solving or Decision Making

11. a) The narrator is a married man. Has he acted immorally? Share your thoughts in a group discussion.
    b) In writing, tell what you would have done in his situation/predicament, and explain why.

Sinclair Ross
The Painted Door

PRE-READING

1. Could you live in an isolated setting, away from all contact with society, for a long period of time? Why or why not? If you had to, how long do you think you could stay? Explain.

2. Can you imagine being in a situation where, due to circumstances you cannot control, you are unable to share your true feelings at the conclusion of a relationship—unable to say "Goodbye," or "I'm sorry," or "I love you"? How do you think you would feel? Explain.

Straight across the hills it was five miles from John's farm to his father's. But in winter, with the roads impassable, a team had to make a wide detour and skirt the hills, so that from five the distance was more than trebled to seventeen.

"I think I'll walk," John said at breakfast to his wife. "The drifts in the hills wouldn't hold a horse, but they'll carry me all right. If I leave early I can spend a few hours helping him with his chores, and still be back by suppertime."

Moodily she went to the window, and thawing a clear place in the frost with her breath, stood looking across the snowswept farmyard to the huddle of stables and sheds. "There was a double wheel around the moon last night," she countered presently. "You said yourself we could expect a storm. It isn't right to leave me here alone. Surely I'm as important as your father."

He glanced up uneasily, then drinking off his coffee tried to reassure her. "But there's nothing to be afraid of—even if it does start to storm. You won't need to go near the stable. Everything's fed and watered now to last till night. I'll be back at the latest by seven or eight."

She went on blowing against the frosted pane, carefully elongating the clear place until it was oval-shaped and symmetrical. He watched her a moment or two longer, then more insistently repeated, "I say you won't need to go near the stable. Everything's fed and watered, and I'll see that there's plenty of wood in. That will be all right, won't it?"

"Yes—of course—I heard you—" It was a curiously cold voice now, as if the words were chilled by their contact with the frosted pane. "Plenty to eat—plenty of wood to keep me warm—what more could a woman ask for?"

"But he's an old man—living there all alone. What is it, Ann? You're not like yourself this morning."

She shook her head without turning. "Pay no attention to me. Seven years a farmer's wife—it's time I was used to staying alone."

Slowly the clear place on the glass enlarged: oval, then round, then oval again. The sun was risen above the frost mists now, so keen and hard a glitter on the snow that instead of warmth its rays seemed shedding cold. One of the two-year-old colts that had cantered away when John turned the horses out for water stood covered with rime at the stable door again, head down and body hunched, each breath a little plume of steam against the frosty air. She shivered, but did not turn. In the clear, bitter light the long white miles of prairie landscape seemed a region strangely alien to life. Even the distant farmsteads she could see served only to intensify a sense of isolation. Scattered across the face of so vast and bleak a wilderness it was difficult to conceive them as a testimony of human hardihood and endurance. Rather they seemed futile, lost. Rather they seemed to cower before the implacability of snowswept earth and clear pale sun-chilled sky.

And when at last she turned from the window there was a brooding stillness in her face as if she had recognized this mastery of snow and cold. It troubled John. "If you're really afraid," he yielded, "I won't go today. Lately it's been so cold, that's all. I just wanted to make sure he's all right in case we do have a storm."

"I know—I'm not really afraid." She was putting in a fire now, and he could no longer see her face. "Pay no attention to me. It's ten miles there and back, so you'd better get started."

"You ought to know by now I wouldn't stay away," he tried to brighten her. "No matter how it stormed. Twice a week before we were married I never missed—and there were bad blizzards that winter too."

He was a slow, unambitious man, content with his farm and cattle, naïvely proud of Ann. He had been bewildered by it once, her caring for a dull-witted fellow like him; then assured at last of her affection he had relaxed against it gratefully, unsuspecting it might ever be less constant than his own. Even now, listening to the restless brooding in her voice, he felt only a quick, unformulated kind of pride that after seven years his absence for a day should still concern her. While she, his trust and earnestness controlling her again:

"I know. It's just that sometimes when you're away I get lonely.... There's a long cold tramp in front of you. You'll let me fix a scarf around your face."

He nodded. "And on my way I'll drop in at Steven's place. Maybe he'll come over tonight for a game of cards. You haven't seen anybody but me for the last two weeks."

She glanced up sharply, then busied herself clearing the table. "It will mean another two miles if you do. You're going to be cold and tired enough as it is. When you're gone I think I'll paint the kitchen woodwork. White this time—you remember we got the paint last fall. It's going to make the room a lot lighter. I'll be too busy to find the day long."

"I will though," he insisted, "and if the storm gets up you'll feel safer, knowing that he's coming. That's what you need, Ann—some-one to talk to besides me."

She stood at the stove motionless for a moment, then turned to him uneasily. "Will you shave then, John—now—before you go?"

He glanced at her questioningly, and avoiding his eyes she tried to explain, "I mean—he may be here before you're back—and you won't have a chance then."

"But it's only Steven—he's seen me like this—"

"He'll be shaved, though—that's what I mean—and I'd like you too to spend a little time on yourself."

He stood up, stroking the heavy stubble on his chin. "Maybe I should all right, but it makes the skin too tender. Especially when I've got to face the wind."

She nodded and began to help him dress, bringing heavy socks and a big woollen sweater from the bedroom, wrapping a scarf around his face and forehead. "I'll tell Steven to come early," he said, as he went out. "In time for supper. Likely there'll be chores for me to do, so if I'm not back by six don't wait."

From the bedroom window she watched him nearly a mile along the road. The fire had gone down when at last she turned away, and already through the house there was an encroaching chill. A blaze sprang up again when the drafts were opened, but as she went on clearing the table her movements were furtive and constrained. It was the silence weighing upon her—the frozen silence of the bitter fields and sun-chilled sky—lurking outside as if alive, relentlessly in wait, mile-deep between her now and John. She listened to it, suddenly tense, motionless. The fire crackled and the clock ticked. Always it was there. "I'm a fool," she whispered hoarsely, rattling the dishes in defiance, going back to the stove to put in another fire. "Warm and safe—I'm a fool. It's a good chance when he's away to paint. The day will go quickly. I won't have time to brood."

Since November now the paint had been waiting warmer weather. The frost in the walls on a day like this would crack and peel it as it dried, but she needed something to keep her hands occupied, something to stave off the gathering cold and loneliness. "First of all," she said aloud, opening the paint and mixing it with a little turpentine, "I must get the house warmer. Fill up the stove and open the oven door so that all the heat comes out. Wad something along the window sills to keep out the drafts. Then I'll feel brighter. It's the cold that depresses."

She moved briskly, performing each little task with careful and exaggerated absorption, binding her thoughts to it, making it a screen between herself and the surrounding snow and silence. But when the stove was filled and the windows sealed it was more difficult again. Above the quiet, steady swishing of her brush against the bedroom door the clock began to tick. Suddenly her movements became precise, deliberate, her posture self-conscious, as if someone had entered the room and were watching her. It was the silence again, aggressive, hovering. The fire spit and crackled at it. Still it was there. "I'm a fool," she repeated. "All farmers' wives have to stay alone. I mustn't give in this way. I mustn't brood. A few hours now and they'll be here."

The sound of her voice reassured her. She went on: "I'll get them a good supper—and for coffee tonight after cards bake some of the little cakes with raisins that he likes.... Just three of us, so I'll watch, and let John play. It's better with four, but at least we can talk. That's all I need—someone to talk to. John never talks. He's stronger—he doesn't understand. But he likes Steven—no matter what the neighbours say. Maybe he'll have him come again, and some other young people

too. It's what we need, both of us, to help keep young ourselves....
And then before we know it we'll be into March. It's cold still in March
sometimes, but you never mind the same. At least you're beginning to
think about spring."

She began to think about it now. Thoughts that outstripped her
words, that left her alone again with herself and the ever-lurking silence. Eager and hopeful first; then clenched, rebellious, lonely.
Windows open, sun and thawing earth again, the urge of growing, living things. Then the days that began in the morning at half-past four
and lasted till ten at night; the meals at which John gulped his food
and scarcely spoke a word; the brute-tired stupid eyes he turned on
her if ever she mentioned town or visiting.

For spring was drudgery again. John never hired a man to help
him. He wanted a mortgage-free farm; then a new house and pretty
clothes for her. Sometimes, because with the best of crops it was going
to take so long to pay off anyway, she wondered whether they mightn't
better let the mortgage wait a little. Before they were worn out, before
their best years were gone. It was something of life she wanted, not
just a house and furniture; something of John, not pretty clothes
when she would be too old to wear them. But John of course couldn't
understand. To him it seemed only right that she should have the
clothes—only right that he, fit for nothing else, should slave away fifteen hours a day to give them to her. There was in his devotion a baf-
fling, insurmountable humility that made him feel the need of
sacrifice. And when his muscles ached, when his feet dragged stolid-
ly with weariness, then it seemed that in some measure at least he was
making amends for his big hulking body and simple mind. That by
his sacrifice he succeeded only in the extinction of his personality
never occurred to him. Year after year their lives went on in the same
little groove. He drove his horses in the field; she milked the cow and
hoed potatoes. By dint of his drudgery he saved a few months' wages,
added a few dollars more each fall to his payments on the mortgage;
but the only real difference that it all made was to deprive her of his
companionship, to make him a little duller, older, uglier than he
might otherwise have been. He never saw their lives objectively. To
him it was not what he actually accomplished by means of the sacrifice that mattered, but the sacrifice itself, the gesture—something
done for her sake.

And she, understanding, kept her silence. In such a gesture, how-ever futile, there was a graciousness not to be shattered lightly. "John" she would begin sometimes, "you're doing too much. Get a man to help you—just for a month—" but smiling down at her he would an-swer simply, "I don't mind. Look at the hands on me. They're made for work." While in his voice there would be a stalwart ring to tell her that by her thoughtfulness she had made him only the more resolved to serve her, to prove his devotion and fidelity.

They were useless such thoughts. She knew. It was his very devo-tion that made them useless, that forbade her to rebel. Yet over and over, sometimes hunched still before their bleakness, sometimes her brush making swift sharp strokes to pace the chafe and rancour that they brought, she persisted in them.

This now, the winter, was their slack season. She could sleep some-times till eight, and John till seven. They could linger over their meals a little, read, play cards, go visiting the neighbours. It was the time to relax, to indulge and enjoy themselves; but instead, fretful and impa-tient, they kept on waiting for the spring. They were compelled now, not by labour, but by the spirit of labour. A spirit that pervaded their lives and brought with idleness a sense of guilt. Sometimes they did sleep late, sometimes they did play cards, but always uneasily, always reproached by the thought of more important things that might be done. When John got up at five to attend to the fire he wanted to stay up and go out to the stable. When he sat down to a meal he hurried his food and pushed his chair away again, from habit, from sheer work-instinct, even though it was only to put more wood in the stove, or go down cellar to cut up beets and turnips for the cows.

And anyway, sometimes she asked herself, why sit trying to talk with a man who never talked? Why talk when there was nothing to talk about but crops and cattle, the weather and the neighbours? The neighbours, too—why go visiting them when still it was the same— crops and cattle, the weather and the other neighbours? Why go to the dances in the schoolhouse to sit among the older women, one of them now, married seven years, or to waltz with the work-bent tired old farmers to a squeaky fiddle tune? Once she had danced with Steven six or seven times in the evening, and they had talked about it for as many months. It was easier to stay at home. John never danced or enjoyed himself. He was always uncomfortable in his good suit and shoes. He didn't like shaving in the cold weather oftener than once or twice a week. It was easier to stay at home, to stand at the window staring out across the bitter fields, to count the days and look forward to another spring.

But now, alone with herself in the winter silence, she saw the spring for what it really was. This spring—next spring—all the springs and summers still to come. While they grew old, while their bodies warped, while their minds kept shrivelling dry and empty like their lives. "I mustn't," she said aloud again. "I married him—and he's a good man. I mustn't keep on this way. It will be noon before long, and then time to think about supper.... Maybe he'll come early—and as soon as John is finished at the stable we can all play cards."

It was getting cold again, and she left her painting to put in more wood. But this time the warmth spread slowly. She pushed a mat up to the outside door, and went back to the window to pat down the woollen shirt that was wadded along the sill. Then she paced a few times round the room, then poked the fire and rattled the stove lids, then paced again. The fire crackled, the clock ticked. The silence now seemed more intense than ever, seemed to have reached a pitch where it faintly moaned. She began to pace on tiptoe, listening, her shoulders drawn together, not realizing for a while that it was the wind she heard, thin-strained and whimpering through the eaves.

Then she wheeled to the window, and with quick short breaths thawed the frost to see again. The glitter was gone. Across the drifts sped swift and snakelike little tongues of snow. She could not follow them, where they sprang from, or where they disappeared. It was as if all across the yard the snow were shivering awake—roused by the warnings of the wind to hold itself in readiness for the impending storm. The sky had become a sombre, whitish grey. It, too, as if in readiness, had shifted and lay close to earth. Before her as she watched a mane of powdery snow reared up breast-high against the darker background of the stable, tossed for a moment angrily, and then subsided again as if whipped down to obedience and restraint. But another followed, more reckless and impatient than the first. Another reeled and dashed itself against the window where she watched. Then ominously for a while there were only the angry little snakes of snow. The wind rose, creaking the troughs that were wired beneath the eaves. In the distance, sky and prairie now were merged into one another linelessly. All round her it was gathering; already in its press and whimpering there strummed a boding of eventual fury. Again she saw a mane of snow spring up, so dense and high this time that all the sheds and stables were obscured. Then others followed, whirling fiercely out of hand; and, when at last they cleared, the stables seemed in dimmer outline than before. It was the snow beginning, long lancet shafts of it, straight from the north, borne almost level by the straining wind. "He'll be there soon," she whispered, "and coming home it will be in his back. He'll leave again right away. He saw the double wheel—he knows the kind of storm there'll be."

She went back to her painting. For a while it was easier, all her thoughts half-anxious ones of John in the blizzard, struggling his way across the hills; but petulantly again she soon began, "I knew we were going to have a storm—I told him so—but it doesn't matter what I say. Big stubborn fool—he goes his own way anyway. It doesn't matter what becomes of me. In a storm like this he'll never get home. He won't even try. And while he sits keeping his father company I can look after his stable for him, go ploughing through snowdrifts up to my knees—nearly frozen—"

Not that she meant or believed her words. It was just an effort to convince herself that she did have a grievance, to justify her rebellious thoughts, to prove John responsible for her unhappiness. She was young still, eager for excitement and distractions; and John's stead-fastness rebuked her vanity, made her complaints seem weak and triv-ial. Fretfully she went on, "If he'd listen to me sometimes and not be so stubborn we wouldn't be living still in a house like this. Seven years in two rooms—seven years and never a new stick of furniture.... There—as if another coat of paint could make it different anyway."

She cleaned her brush, filled up the stove again, and went back to the window. There was a void white moment that she thought must be frost formed on the window pane; then, like a fitful shadow through the whirling snow, she recognized the stable roof. It was in-credible. The sudden, maniac raging of the storm struck from her face all its pettishness. Her eyes glazed with fear a little; her lips blanched. "If he starts for home now," she whispered silently— "But he won't— he knows I'm safe—he knows Steven's coming. Across the hills he would never dare."

She turned to the stove, holding out her hands to the warmth. Around her now there seemed a constant sway and tremor, as if the air were vibrating with the violent shudderings of the walls. She stood quite still, listening. Sometimes the wind struck with sharp, savage blows. Sometimes it bore down in a sustained, minute-long blast, silent with effort and intensity, then with a foiled shriek of threat wheeled away to gather and assault again. Always the eavestroughs creaked and sawed. She started towards the window again, then detecting the morbid trend of her thoughts, prepared fresh coffee and forced herself to drink a few mouthfuls. "He would never dare," she whispered again. "He wouldn't leave the old man anyway in such a storm. Safe in here—there's nothing for me to keep worrying about. It's after one already. I'll do my baking now, and then it will be time to get supper ready for Steven."

Soon, however, she began to doubt whether Steven would come. In such a storm even a mile was enough to make a man hesitate. Especially Steven, who, for all his attractive qualities, was hardly the one to face a blizzard for the sake of someone else's chores. He had a stable of his own to look after anyway. It would be only natural for him to think that when the storm rose John had turned again for home. Another man would have—would have put his wife first.

But she felt little dread or uneasiness at the prospect of spending the night alone. It was the first time she had been left like this on her own resources, and her reaction, now that she could face and appraise her situation calmly, was gradually to feel it a kind of adventure and responsibility. It stimulated her. Before nightfall she must go to the stable and feed everything. Wrap up in some of John's clothes—take a ball of string in her hand, one end tied to the door, so that no matter how blinding the storm she could at least find her way back to the house. She had heard of people having to do that. It appealed to her now because suddenly it made life dramatic. She had not felt the storm yet, only watched it for a minute through the window.

It took nearly an hour to find enough string, to choose the right socks and sweaters. Long before it was time to start out she tried on John's clothes, changing and rechanging, striding around the room to make sure there would be play enough for pitching hay and struggling over snowdrifts; then she took them off again, and for a while busied herself baking the little cakes with raisins that he liked.

Night came early. Just for a moment on the doorstep she shrank back, uncertain. The slow dimming of the light clutched her with an illogical sense of abandonment. It was like the covert withdrawal of an ally, leaving the alien miles unleashed and unrestrained. Watching the hurricane of writhing snow rage past the little house she forced herself, "They'll never stand the night unless I get them fed. It's nearly dark already, and I've work to last an hour."

Timidly, unwinding a little of the string, she crept out from the shelter of the doorway. A gust of wind spun her forward a few yards, then plunged her headlong against a drift that in the dense white whirl lay invisible across her path. For nearly a minute she huddled still, breathless and dazed. The snow was in her mouth and nostrils, inside her scarf and up her sleeves. As she tried to straighten a smothering scud flung itself against her face, cutting off her breath a second time. The wind struck from all sides, blustering and furious. It was as if the storm had discovered her, as if all its forces were concentrated upon her extinction. Seized with panic suddenly she thrashed out a moment with her arms, then stumbled back and sprawled her length across the drift.

But this time she regained her feet quickly, roused by the whip and batter of the storm to retaliative anger. For a moment her impulse was to face the wind and strike back blow for blow; then, as suddenly as it had come, her frantic strength gave way to limpness and exhaustion. Suddenly, a comprehension so clear and terrifying that it struck all thought of the stable from her mind, she realized in such a storm her puny insignificance. And the realization gave her new strength, stilled this time to a desperate persistence. Just for a moment the wind held her, numb and swaying in its vise; then slowly, buckled far forward, she groped her way again towards the house.

Inside, leaning against the door, she stood tense and still a while. It was almost dark now. The top of the stove glowed a deep, dull red. Heedless of the storm, self-absorbed and self-satisfied, the clock ticked on like a glib little idiot. "He shouldn't have gone," she whispered silently. "He saw the double wheel—he knew. He shouldn't have left me here alone."

For so fierce now, so insane and dominant did the blizzard seem, that she could not credit the safety of the house. The warmth and lull around her was not real yet, not to be relied upon. She was still at the mercy of the storm. Only her body pressing hard like this against the door was staving it off. She didn't dare move. She didn't dare ease the ache and strain. "He shouldn't have gone," she repeated, thinking of the stable again, reproached by her helplessness. "They'll freeze in their stalls—and I can't reach them. He'll say it's all my fault. He won't believe I tried."

Then Steven came. Quickly, startled to quietness and control, she let him in and lit the lamp. He stared at her a moment, then flinging off his cap crossed to where she stood by the table and seized her arms. "You're so white—what's wrong? Look at me—" It was like him in such little situations to be masterful. "You should have known better than to go out on a day like this. For a while I thought I wasn't going to make it here myself—"

"I was afraid you wouldn't come—John left early, and there was the stable—"

But the storm had unnerved her, and suddenly at the assurance of his touch and voice the fear that had been gripping her gave way to an hysteria of relief. Scarcely aware of herself she seized his arm and sobbed against it. He remained still a moment, unyielding, then slipped his other arm around her shoulder. It was comforting and she relaxed against it, hushed by a sudden sense of lull and safety. Her shoulders trembled with the easing of the strain, then fell limp and still. "You're shivering,"—he drew her gently towards the stove. "There's nothing to be afraid of now, though. I'm going to do the chores for you."

It was a quiet, sympathetic voice, yet with an undertone of insolence, a kind of mockery even, that made her draw away quickly and busy herself putting in a fire. With his lips drawn in a little smile he watched her till she looked at him again. The smile too was insolent, but at the same time companionable; Steven's smile, and therefore difficult to reprove. It lit up his lean, still-boyish face with a peculiar kind of arrogance: features and smile that were different from John's, from other men's—wilful and derisive, yet naïvely so—as if it were less the difference itself he was conscious of, than the long-accustomed privilege that thereby fell his due. He was erect, tall, square-shouldered. His hair was dark and trim, his young lips curved soft and full. While John, she made the comparison swiftly, was thickset, heavy-jowled, and stooped. He always stood before her helpless, a kind of humility and wonderment in his attitude. And Steven now smiled on her appraisingly with the worldly-wise assurance of one for whom a woman holds neither mystery nor illusion.

"It was good of you to come, Steven," she responded, the words running into a sudden, empty laugh. "Such a storm to face—I suppose I should feel flattered."

For his presumption, his misunderstanding of what had been only a momentary weakness, instead of angering quickened her, roused from latency and long disuse all the instincts and resources of her femininity. She felt eager, challenged. Something was at hand that hitherto had always eluded her, even in the early days with John, something vital, beckoning, meaningful. She didn't understand, but she knew. The texture of the moment was satisfyingly dreamlike: an incredibility perceived as such, yet acquiesced in. She was John's wife—she knew—but also she knew that Steven standing here was different from John. There was no thought or motive, no understanding of herself as the knowledge persisted. Wary and poised round a sudden little core of blind excitement she evaded him, "But it's nearly dark—hadn't you better hurry if you're going to do the chores? Don't trouble—I can get them off myself—"

An hour later when he returned from the stable she was in another dress, hair rearranged, a little flush of colour in her face. Pouring warm water for him from the kettle into the basin she said evenly, "By the time you're washed supper will be ready. John said we weren't to wait for him."

He looked at her a moment. "But in a storm like this you're not expecting John?"

"Of course." As she spoke she could feel the colour deepening in her face. "We're going to play cards. He was the one that suggested it."

He went on washing, and then as they took their places at the table, resumed, "So John's coming. When are you expecting him?"

"He said it might be seven o'clock—or a little later." Conversation with Steven at other times had always been brisk and natural, but now suddenly she found it strained. "He may have work to do for his father. That's what he said when he left. Why do you ask, Steven?"

"I was just wondering—it's a rough night."

"He always comes. There couldn't be a storm bad enough. It's easier to do the chores in daylight, and I knew he'd be tired—that's why I started out for the stable."

She glanced up again and he was smiling at her. The same insolence, the same little twist of mockery and appraisal. It made her
flinch suddenly, and ask herself why she was pretending to expect
John—why there should be this instinct of defence to force her. This
time, instead of poise and excitement, it brought a reminder that she
had changed her dress and rearranged her hair. It crushed in sudden silence, through which she heard the whistling wind again, and
the creaking saw of the eaves. Neither spoke now. There was something strange, almost terrifying, about this Steven and his quiet,
unrelenting smile; but strangest of all was the familiarity: the Steven
she had never seen or encountered, and yet had always known,
always expected, always waited for. It was less Steven himself that
she felt than his inevitability. Just as she had felt the snow, the
silence and the storm. She kept her eyes lowered, on the window
past his shoulder, on the stove, but his smile now seemed to exist
apart from him, to merge and hover with the silence. She clinked a
cup—listened to the whistle of the storm—always it was there. He
began to speak, but her mind missed the meaning of his words.
Swiftly she was making comparisons again; his face so different to
John's, so handsome and young and clean-shaven. Swiftly, helplessly,
feeling the imperceptible and relentless ascendancy that thereby he
was gaining over her, sensing sudden menace in this new, more vital
life, even as she felt drawn towards it.

The lamp between them flickered as an onslaught of the storm sent
shudderings through the room. She rose to build up the fire again and
he followed her. For a long time they stood close to the stove, their
arms almost touching. Once as the blizzard creaked the house she
spun around sharply, fancying it was John at the door; but quietly he
intercepted her. "Not tonight—you might as well make up your mind
to it. Across the hills in a storm like this—it would be suicide to try."

Her lips trembled suddenly in an effort to answer, to parry the
certainty in his voice, then set thin and bloodless. She was afraid now.
Afraid of his face so different from John's—of his smile, of her own
helplessness to rebuke it. Afraid of the storm, isolating her here alone
with him in its impenetrable fastness. They tried to play cards, but she
kept starting up at every creak and shiver of the walls. "It's too rough
a night," he repeated. "Even for John. Just relax a few minutes—stop
worrying and pay a little attention to me."

But in his tone there was a contradiction to his words. For it implied that she was not worrying—that her only concern was lest it really might be John at the door.

And the implication persisted. He filled up the stove for her, shuffled the cards—won—shuffled—still it was there. She tried to respond to his conversation, to think of the game, but helplessly into her cards instead she began to ask, Was he right? Was that why he smiled? Why he seemed to wait, expectant and assured?

The clock ticked, the fire crackled. Always it was there. Furtively for a moment she watched him as he deliberated over his hand. John, even in the days before they were married, had never looked like that. Only this morning she had asked him to shave. Because Steven was coming—because she had been afraid to see them side by side—because deep within herself she had known even then. The same knowledge, furtive and forbidden, that was flaunted now in Steven's smile. "You look cold," he said at last, dropping his cards and rising from the table. "We're not playing, anyway. Come over to the stove for a few minutes and get warm."

"But first I think we'll hang blankets over the door. When there's a blizzard like this we always do." It seemed that in sane, commonplace activity there might be release, a moment or two in which to recover herself. "John has nails in to put them on. They keep out a little of the draft."

He stood on a chair for her, and hung the blankets that she carried from the bedroom. Then for a moment they stood silent, watching the blankets sway and tremble before the blade of wind that spurted around the jamb. "I forgot," she said at last, "that I painted the bedroom door. At the top there, see—I've smeared the blankets coming through."

He glanced at her curiously, and went back to the stove. She followed him, trying to imagine the hills in such a storm, wondering whether John would come. "A man couldn't live in it," suddenly he answered her thoughts, lowering the oven door and drawing up their chairs one on each side of it. "He knows you're safe. It isn't likely that he'd leave his father, anyway."

"The wind will be in his back," she persisted. "The winter before we were married—all the blizzards that we had that year—and he never missed—"

"Blizzards like this one? Up in the hills he wouldn't be able to keep his direction for a hundred yards. Listen to it a minute and ask yourself."

His voice seemed softer, kindlier now. She met his smile a moment, its assured little twist of appraisal, then for a long time sat silent, tense, careful again to avoid his eyes.

Everything now seemed to depend on this. It was the same as a few hours ago when she braced the door against the storm. He was watching her, smiling. She dared not move, unclench her hands, or raise her eyes. The flames cracked, the clock ticked. The storm wrenched the walls as if to make them buckle in. So rigid and desperate were all her muscles set, withstanding, that the room around her seemed to swim and reel. So rigid and strained that for relief at last, despite herself, she raised her head and met his eyes again.

Intending that it should be for only an instant, just to breathe again, to ease the tension that had grown unbearable—but in his smile now, instead of the insolent appraisal that she feared, there seemed a kind of warmth and sympathy. An understanding that quickened and encouraged her—that made her wonder why but a moment ago she had been afraid. It was as if the storm had lulled, as if she had suddenly found calm and shelter.

Or perhaps, the thought seized her, perhaps instead of his smile it was she that had changed. She who, in the long, wind-creaked silence, had emerged from the increment of codes and loyalties to her real, unfettered self. She who now felt suddenly an air of appraisal as nothing more than an understanding of the unfulfilled woman that until this moment had lain within her brooding and unadmitted, reproved out of consciousness by the insistence of an outgrown, routine fidelity.

For there had always been Steven. She understood now. Seven years—almost as long as John—ever since the night they first danced together.

The lamp was burning dry, and through the dimming light, isolated in the fastness of silence and storm, they watched each other. Her face was white and struggling still. His was handsome, clean-shaven, young. Her eyes were fanatic, believing desperately, fixed upon him as if to exclude all else, as if to find justification. His were cool, bland, drooped a little with expectancy. The light kept dimming, gathering the shadows round them, hushed, conspiratorial. He was smiling still. Her hands again were clenched up white and hard.

"But he always came," she persisted. "The wildest, coldest nights— even such a night as this. There was never a storm—"

"Never a storm like this one." There was a quietness in his smile now, a kind of simplicity almost, as if to reassure her. "You were out in it yourself for a few minutes. He would have five miles, across the hills.... I'd think twice myself, on such a night, before risking even one."

Long after he was asleep she lay listening to the storm. As a check on the draft up the chimney they had left one of the stovelids partly off, and through the open bedroom door she could see the flickerings of flame and shadow on the kitchen wall. They leaped and sank fantastically. The longer she watched the more alive they seemed to be. There was one great shadow that struggled towards her threateningly, massive, and black and engulfing all the room. Again and again it advanced, about to spring, but each time a little whip of light subdued it to its place among the others on the wall. Yet though it never reached her still she cowered, feeling that gathered there was all the frozen wilderness, its heart of terror and invincibility.

Then she dozed a while, and the shadow was John. Interminably he advanced. The whips of light still flicked and coiled, but now suddenly there were the swift little snakes that this afternoon she had watched twist and shiver across the snow. And they too were advancing. They writhed and vanished and came again. She lay still, paralysed. He was over her now, so close that she could have touched him. Already it seemed that a deadly tightening hand was on her throat. She tried to scream but her lips were locked. Steven beside her slept on heedlessly.

Until suddenly as she lay staring up at him a gleam of light revealed his face. And in it was not a trace of threat or anger—only calm, and stonelike hopelessness.

That was like John. He began to withdraw, and frantically she tried to call him back. "It isn't true—not really true—listen, John—" but the words clung frozen to her lips. Already there was only the shriek of the wind again, the sawing eaves, the leap and twist of shadow on the wall.

She sat up, startled now and awake. And so real had he seemed there, standing close to her, so vivid the sudden age and sorrow in his face, that at first she could not make herself understand she had been only dreaming. Against the conviction of his presence in the room it was necessary to insist over and over that he must still be with his father on the other side of the hills. Watching the shadows she had fallen asleep. It was only her mind, her imagination, distorted to a nightmare by the illogical and unadmitted dread of his return. But he wouldn't come. Steven was right. In such a storm he would never try. They were safe, alone. No one would ever know. It was only fear, morbid and irrational; only the sense of guilt that even her new-found and challenged womanhood could not entirely quell.

She knew now. She had not let herself understand or acknowledge it as guilt before, but gradually through the wind-torn silence of the night his face compelled her. The face that had watched her from the darkness with its stonelike sorrow—the face that was really John—John more than his features of mere flesh and bone could ever be.

She wept silently. The fitful gleam of light began to sink. On the ceiling and wall at last there was only a faint dull flickering glow. The little house shuddered and quailed, and a chill crept in again. Without wakening Steven she slipped out to build up the fire. It was burned to a few spent embers now, and the wood she put on seemed a long time catching light. The wind swirled through the blankets they had hung around the door, and struck her flesh like laps of molten ice. Then hollow and moaning it roared up the chimney again, as if against its will drawn back to serve still longer with the onrush of the storm.

For a long time she crouched over the stove, listening. Earlier in the evening, with the lamp lit and the fire crackling, the house had seemed a stand against the wilderness, against its frozen, blizzard-breathed implacability, a refuge of feeble walls wherein persisted the elements of human meaning and survival. Now, in the cold, creaking darkness, it was strangely extinct, looted by the storm and abandoned again. She lifted the stove lid and fanned the embers till at last a swift little tongue of flame began to lick around the wood. Then she replaced the lid, extended her hands, and as if frozen in that attitude stood waiting.

It was not long now. After a few minutes she closed the drafts, and as the flames whirled back upon each other, beating against the top of the stove and sending out flickers of light again, a warmth surged up to relax her stiffened limbs. But shivering and numb it had been easier. The bodily well-being that the warmth induced gave play again to an ever more insistent mental suffering. She remembered the shadow that was John. She saw him bent towards her, then retreating, his features pale and overcast with unaccusing grief. She re-lived their seven years together and, in retrospect, found them to be years of worth and dignity. Until crushed by it all at last, seized by a sudden need to suffer and atone, she crossed to where the draft was bitter, and for a long time stood unflinching on the icy floor.

The storm was close here. Even through the blankets she could feel a sift of snow against her face. The eaves sawed, the walls creaked. Above it all, like a wolf in howling flight, the wind shrilled lone and desolate.

And yet, suddenly she asked herself, hadn't there been other storms, other blizzards? And through the worst of them hadn't he always reached her?

Clutched by the thought she stood rooted a minute. It was hard now to understand how she could have so deceived herself—how a moment of passion could have quieted within her not only conscience, but reason and discretion too. John always came. There could never be a storm to stop him. He was strong, inured to the cold. He had crossed the hills since his boyhood, knew every creek-bed and gully. It was madness to go on like this—to wait. While there was still time she must waken Steven, and hurry him away.

But in the bedroom again, standing at Steven's side, she hesitated. In his detachment from it all, in his quiet, even breathing, there was such sanity, such realism. For him nothing had happened; nothing would. If she wakened him he would only laugh and tell her to listen to the storm. Already it was long past midnight, either John had lost his way or not set out at all. And she knew that in his devotion there was nothing foolhardy. He would never risk a storm beyond his endurance, never permit himself a sacrifice likely to endanger her lot or future. They were both safe. No one would ever know. She must control herself—be sane like Steven.

For comfort she let her hand rest a while on Steven's shoulder. It would be easier were he awake now, with her, sharing her guilt; but gradually as she watched his handsome face in the glimmering light she came to understand that for him no guilt existed. Just as there had been no passion, no conflict. Nothing but the sane appraisal of their situation, nothing but the expectant little smile, and the arrogance of features that were different from John's. She winced deeply, remembering how she had fixed her eyes on those features, how she had tried to believe that so handsome and young, so different from John's, they must in themselves be her justification.

In the flickering light they were still young, still handsome. No longer her justification—she knew now—John was the man—but wistfully still, wondering sharply at their power and tyranny, she touched them a moment with her fingertips again.

She could not blame him. There had been no passion, no guilt; therefore there could be no responsibility. Suddenly looking down at him as he slept, half-smiling still, his lips relaxed in the conscience-less complacency of his achievement, she understood that thus he was revealed in his entirety—all there ever was or ever could be. John was the man. With him lay all the future. For tonight, slowly and contritely through the days and years to come, she would try to make amends.

Then she stole back to the kitchen, and without thought, impelled by overwhelming need again, returned to the door where the draft was bitter still. Gradually towards morning the storm began to spend itself. Its terror blast became a feeble, wornout moan. The leap of light and shadow sank, and a chill crept in again. Always the eaves creaked, tortured with wordless prophecy. Heedless of it all the clock ticked on in idiot content.

They found him the next day, less than a mile from home. Drifting with the storm he had run against his own pasture fence and overcome had frozen there, erect still, both hands clasping fast the wire.

"He was south of here," they said wonderingly when she told them how he had come across the hills. "Straight south—you'd wonder how he could have missed the buildings. It was the wind last night, coming every way at once. He shouldn't have tried. There was a double wheel around the moon."

She looked past them a moment, then as if to herself said simply, "If you knew him, though—John would try."

It was later, when they had left her a while to be alone with him, that she knelt and touched his hand. Her eyes dimmed, still it was such a strong and patient hand; then, transfixed, they suddenly grew wide and clear. On the palm, white even against its frozen whiteness, was a little smear of paint.

NOTES

contritely	showing deep regret or sorrow
implacability	(in this context) relentlessness
reproached	blamed; criticized
rime	(hoar)frost
steadfastness	state of unchangeability or being fixed firmly

RESPONDING PERSONALLY

3. Throughout the story, right up to the next-to-last paragraph, Ann repeats, "If you knew him, though—John would try." Does she know him? Then if so, was her act with Steven committed on purpose, as a clear statement of defiance after seven years of "ever-lurking silence"? Respond to your instincts: what do they tell you? Share your thoughts in a small group.

4. "John is a victim—not of the snow, but of his wife's betrayal." Support or refute the statement.

RESPONDING CRITICALLY/ANALYTICALLY

5. The story is told from a third-person omniscient point of view. Initially, there is a shared omniscience wherein both John's and Ann's perspectives are given. Once John leaves, Ann continues through the end of the story. Steven is never permitted a "voice." Why does the writer do this? Why does the writer shift from a fully omniscient narration at the beginning to a limited omniscience at the end? How does the writer's choice serve the story best?

6. Using a T-chart to assist you, contrast John's genuineness of character with Steven's superficiality.
   a) In one column, identify John's character traits. If you were to title the column with either the word "Warm" or "Cold," which would it be? Why?
   b) In the second column, identify Steven's traits. Title his column with the second of the two words. Explain why this suits.
   c) What does Ann's fateful decision reveal about her character? Support your conclusion with at least one direct quotation from the story.

7. In small groups, explore the imagery of nature in the story.
   a) The imagery of the winter landscape is vast, harsh, bleak, and lonely. In what way does the natural landscape serve as a metaphor for Ann's emotional "landscape"? Identify some examples of the metaphor—one description that represents both the outer and inner landscapes simultaneously.
   b) In what way is the storm in nature a metaphor of the inner storm that Ann is living? Identify some examples of the metaphor—of both storms striking simultaneously.

   Share the examples in class.

8. Examine the extensive use of foreshadowing in the story. Identify some of the signs of the inevitability of the tragic resolution to the story.

Responding Creatively

9. "She would try to make amends." Had John *not* returned that night as he did, and the story were to continue, *would* Ann have made amends? Or might she have continued to some extent with Steven? Write the paragraph(s) that describe her standing at her kitchen window, one year later, thinking about what is taking place in her life.

10. Create a visual mind-map of the story. Include in your mind-map the story's three characters—judiciously placed on the page—as well as three or four other key images selected from the story. The layout of the images can be sequential, or juxtaposed, or even superimposed. The end product should reveal your understanding of the key idea(s) of the story.

Self-Assessment

Which process do you find more "complete" in terms of gathering and expressing your own understanding of the story—responding verbally or visually? Why does that process seem to serve you better?

Problem Solving or Decision Making

11. Was John's death accidental or intentional? Discuss your thoughts in a small-group setting. Following your discussion, turn your examination to the question of the "right" way for an adult to respond to a partner's infidelity.

Lorraine McMullen
An Analysis of "The Painted Door"

In "The Painted Door" Ann gives vent to her frustration at the loneliness and drabness of her life as a prairie farm wife. Her slow, plodding husband has been made duller and more silent by the exhausting demands of farm labour. Ironically, his devotion to her has pushed him to work even harder to pay off the mortgage, so that he can do even more for her, build her a new house and buy her pretty clothes. The story relates events leading to Ann's seduction by the younger, more handsome neighbor as she waits alone for her husband, John, to return from his father's farm five miles away. When the young neighbor, Steven, arrives to spend the evening Ann sees in him all that John lacks: for Steven is handsome, clean-shaven, erect, assured. No sooner has she capitulated to Steven, persuaded by him that not even John can get home in the blizzard now raging, than she realizes the superficiality of his attractions in contrast with John's substantial qualities. For John may be slow and dull, but he is reliable and devoted. His lack of grace and polish is insignificant in contrast with his enduring loyalty and love. Ann now perceives: "John was the man. With him lay all the future. For tonight, slowly and contritely through the days and years to come, she would try to make amends." But Ann's repentance comes too late and the stunning finale tells the reader as it tells Ann that she must bear for the rest of her life the consequences of her one momentary weakness.

This story exemplifies Ross's use of landscape to mirror inner reality. The coldness, barrenness, and loneliness of the setting are the cause of Ann's situation as well as a reflection of her own inner sense of loneliness and isolation. The storm impending as John leaves her for his father's farm mirrors her own impending emotional storm; and throughout the day, as the storm outside becomes increasingly violent, so too does her own emotional state become increasingly distraught. The words applied to the physical storm outside, "The storm wrenched the walls as if to make them buckle in" (p. 239), apply equally to her own inner state as she struggles against Steven's attractiveness.

Steven, who is cold, insolent, and passionless, is linked with the coldness of the exterior winter climate. In contrast, John's devotion and Ann's attempts to remind herself of his love and withstand her own rebellious feelings are linked with the fire and warmth, and with her endeavors throughout the day to build up the fire. Her attempt to ward off the encroaching cold parallels her attempt to withstand her attraction to Steven. This complex interweaving of inner and outer states is initiated at the beginning of the story with Ann's warning to John of the coming storm and John's words, which in retrospect are proven to be disastrously wrong, "But there's nothing to be afraid of—" (p. 225). Ann's resentment against John for leaving her alone is apparent in the coldness of her voice as well as by the words of her reply, "It was a curiously cold voice now, as if the words were chilled by their contact with the frosted pane. 'Plenty to eat—plenty of wood to keep me warm—what more could a woman ask for?'" (p. 226). The loneliness, bleakness and bitter cold of the landscape are then viewed through Ann's eyes:

> The sun was risen above the frost mists now, so keen and hard a glitter on the snow that instead of warmth its rays seemed shedding cold. One of the two-year-old colts that had cantered away when John turned the horses out for water stood covered with rime at the stable door again, head down and body hunched, each breath a little plume of steam against the frosty air. She shivered, but did not turn. In the clear, bitter light the long white miles of prairie landscape seemed a region strangely alien to life. Even the distant farmsteads she could see served only to intensify a sense of isolation. Scattered across the face of so vast and bleak a wilderness it was difficult to conceive them as a testimony of human hardihood and endurance. Rather they seemed futile, lost. Rather they seemed to cower before the implacability of snow-swept earth and clear pale sun-chilled sky. (p. 226)

Simple, spare diction echoes the bleak, remorseless landscape. Description repetitively insists upon its emptiness and loneliness: "long white miles of prairie landscape seemed a region alien to life"; "so vast and bleak a wilderness"; "distant farmsteads ... intensify a sense of isolation"; "scattered ... they seemed futile, lost."

As soon as John leaves, Ann becomes aware of the silence and chill: "It was the silence weighing upon her—the frozen silence of the bitter fields and sun-chilled sky—lurking outside as if alive, relentlessly in wait, mile-deep between her now and John" (p. 228). Steven, too, like the cold is "relentless in wait," as not only the physical but also the emotional gulf between Ann and John widens. Throughout the day Ann tries to maintain her serenity and her loyalty to John; she busies herself with her painting and builds up the fire against the silence, isolation, and encroaching cold. Ann's discontent, increasingly difficult to stifle as the day passes, continues to be reflected by the description of the cold: "It was getting cold again, and she left her painting to put in more wood. But this time the warmth spread slowly" (p. 231).

When Ann must leave the house to feed the farm animals she is unable to withstand the violence of the blizzard; she struggles back to the house, defeated by the storm and terrified at its intensity: "Only her body pressing hard like this against the door was staving it off. She didn't dare move" (p. 235). Later, when she feels Steven's attraction, Ann herself links him with the storm: "It was less Steven himself that she felt than his inevitability. Just as she had felt the snow, the silence and the storm" (p. 237), and finally, when his attraction overwhelms her as did the storm earlier, she associates her sensations with the feeling she had earlier when attempting to stave off the storm: "It was the same as a few hours ago when she braced the door against the storm. He was watching her, smiling. She dared not move, unclench her hands, or raise her eyes. The flames cracked, the clock ticked. The storm wrenched the walls as if to make them buckle in. So rigid and desperate were all her muscles set, withstanding, that the room around her seemed to swim and reel. So rigid and strained that for relief at last, despite herself, she raised her head and met his eyes again" (p. 239). Again the stark simplicity of diction and phrasing underlines the tension. Except for the one word, "smiling," which describes Steven, there are no modifiers in this passage, no adverbs or adjectives, until the repeated, "So rigid and desperate.... So rigid and strained...," which by the insistent, incantatory rhythm contributes to the depiction of her inevitable surrender. This is the moment of her capitulation and now, no longer struggling against the storm within herself, she feels "as if the storm had lulled, as if she had suddenly found calm and shelter" (p. 239).

The cold and storm outside operate as a synecdoche to represent the harshness of land and climate which after seven years have caused Ann to rebel against the bleakness and loneliness of her life and against her plodding, devoted husband. It is appropriate that John should wander back out into the storm after he has discovered Ann and Steven together, since the storm is a reflection of Ann's internal storm which caused her to betray him. She was defeated by cold and loneliness of which the cold, passionless Steven is both symbol and agent. John, who, because of his dogged loyalty and devotion, has fought his way through the blizzard to her, freezes to death, a victim not of the snow and cold but of his wife's betrayal.

Handling of time contributes to the effectiveness of this story. There are two kinds of time: linear, objective time, the one day in which events occur; and subjective time, the monotonous, repetitive seven years of their marriage and all the dreary years yet to come as Ann imaginatively relives the past and looks into the future: "But now, alone with herself in the winter silence, she saw the spring for what it really was. This spring—next spring—all the springs and summers still to come. While they grew old, while their bodies warped, while their minds kept shrivelling dry and empty like their lives" (p. 231). The texture of Ross's prose approximates the tone and emotional tension of the situation. In this quotation rhythm and repetition echo the endless monotony Ann sees ahead of her. The repetition of the word "spring" and the incantatory rhythm reflect the endless monotonous life Ann sees ahead: "This spring—next spring—all the springs and summers still to come." Short, terse phrases underline the sexual tension; as over and over again the same words "the flames crackled, the clock ticked" intensify the silence and pressure. Subjective time superimposed upon the present makes this day insupportable for Ann and helps the reader to understand the loneliness, despair, and need which result in her surrender to Steven. For Steven, young, well-groomed, smooth talking—all that John is not—becomes a symbol of all that is missing in her life. Although Ann's true sense of values soon reasserts itself and she sees the superficiality of Steven's attractions in contrast to the genuineness of John's qualities, her realization comes too late. The vastness, loneliness, and harshness of the environment which have made John slower and duller, Ann more morose and dissatisfied, finally defeat them.

Reality vs. Illusion

Human kind Cannot bear very much reality. — T.S. Eliot	My illusion is more real to me than reality. — Mary Antin

Reality vs. illusion is one of the most common conflicts in literature and life. There is much about human experience that is mysteriously illusory, despite our best efforts to live rational lives.

From Egypt comes "Half a Day," a fantasy by the celebrated writer Naguib Mahfouz. The story follows a boy's remarkable first day at school, which does not unfold by "clock time," taking both the narrator and the reader by surprise.

The aging process is explored again, this time for its reverse effects, in Nathaniel Hawthorne's famous story "Dr. Heidegger's Experiment." Dr. Heidegger is a mysterious physician who invites four old friends over to drink from the reputed Fountain of Youth. The experiment in this moralistic tale turns out to be a rather interesting one, revealing in both psychology and human nature.

"An Occurrence at Owl Creek Bridge" plays with reality, point of view, and reader expectation. Peyton Farquhar, a Southern planter during the American Civil War, is being hanged for his war crime, but apparently performs a remarkable, miraculous escape from certain death.

Margaret Laurence's "Horses of the Night" rounds out this unit with a story about Chris, a young farm boy who prefers the world of illusion to reality. The narrator, his younger cousin Vanessa, tries her best to understand him, but is doomed to fail because of harsh, unforgiving circumstances created by poverty and the limiting circumstances of the Depression and World War II.

As seen in these four stories, when writers decide to take on the question of reality vs. illusion, they can show us the deeper, elusive, illusory nature of life itself.

Translated by Denys Johnson-Davies

Naguib Mahfouz
Half a Day

PRE-READING

1. What is the meaning of the word "archetype"? Research the term, and prepare a brief introduction and/or explanation of the term for the class.

2. Explore your memory. Remember as much as you can of your own first day of school. What was the classroom like: colours, objects, furniture, windows? What people do you remember? What were your thoughts and feelings? How trying a day was it? Explain.

I proceeded alongside my father, clutching his right hand, running to keep up with the long strides he was taking. All my clothes were new: the black shoes, the green school uniform, and the red tarboosh. My delight in my new clothes, however, was not altogether unmarred, for this was no feast day but the day on which I was to be cast into school for the first time.

My mother stood at the window watching our progress, and I would turn toward her from time to time, as though appealing for help. We walked along a street lined with gardens; on both sides were extensive fields planted with crops, prickly pears, henna trees, and a few date palms.

"Why school?" I challenged my father openly. "I shall never do anything to annoy you."

"I'm not punishing you," he said, laughing. "School's not a punishment. It's the factor that makes useful men out of boys. Don't you want to be like your father and brothers?"

I was not convinced. I did not believe there was really any good to be had in tearing me away from the intimacy of my home and throwing me into this building that stood at the end of the road like some huge, high-walled fortress, exceedingly stern and grim.

When we arrived at the gate we could see the courtyard, vast and crammed full of boys and girls. "Go in by yourself," said my father, "and join them. Put a smile on your face and be a good example to others."

I hesitated and clung to his hand, but he gently pushed me from him. "Be a man," he said. "Today you truly begin life. You will find me waiting for you when it's time to leave."

I took a few steps, then stopped and looked but saw nothing. Then the faces of boys and girls came into view. I did not know a single one of them, and none of them knew me. I felt I was a stranger who had lost his way. But glances of curiosity were directed toward me, and one boy approached and asked, "Who brought you?"

"My father," I whispered.

"My father's dead," he said quite simply.

I did not know what to say. The gate was closed, letting out a pitiable screech. Some of the children burst into tears. The bell rang. A lady came along, followed by a group of men. The men began sorting us into ranks. We were formed into an intricate pattern in the great courtyard surrounded on three sides by high buildings of several floors; from each floor we were overlooked by a long balcony roofed in wood.

"This is your new home," said the woman. "Here too there are mothers and fathers. Here there is everything that is enjoyable and beneficial to knowledge and religion. Dry your tears and face life joyfully."

We submitted to the facts, and this submission brought a sort of contentment. Living beings were drawn to other living beings, and from the first moments my heart made friends with such boys as were to be my friends and fell in love with such girls as I was to be in love with, so that it seemed my misgivings had had no basis. I had never imagined school would have this rich variety. We played all sorts of different games: swings, the vaulting horse, ball games. In the music room we chanted our first songs. We also had our first introduction to language. We saw a globe of the Earth, which revolved and showed the various continents and countries. We started learning the numbers. The story of the Creator of the universe was read to us, we were told of His present world and of His Hereafter, and we heard examples of what He said. We ate delicious food, took a little nap, and woke up to go on with friendship and love, play and learning.

As our path revealed itself to us, however, we did not find it as totally sweet and unclouded as we had presumed. Dust-laden winds and unexpected accidents came about suddenly, so we had to be watchful, at the ready, and very patient. It was not all a matter of playing and fooling around. Rivalries could bring about pain and hatred or give rise to fighting. And while the lady would sometimes smile, she would often scowl and scold. Even more frequently she would resort to physical punishment.

In addition, the time for changing one's mind was over and gone and there was no question of ever returning to the paradise of home. Nothing lay ahead of us but exertion, struggle, and perseverance. Those who were able took advantage of the opportunities for success and happiness that presented themselves amid worries.

The bell rang announcing the passing of the day and the end of work. The throngs of children rushed toward the gate, which was opened again. I bade farewell to friends and sweethearts and passed through the gate. I peered around but found no trace of my father, who had promised to be there. I stepped aside to wait. When I had waited for a long time without avail, I decided to return home on my own. After I had taken a few steps, a middle-aged man passed by, and I realized at once that I knew him. He came toward me, smiling, and shook me by the hand, saying, "It's a long time since we last met— how are you?"

With a nod of my head, I agreed with him and in turn asked, "And you, how are you?"

"As you can see, not all that good, the Almighty be praised!"

Again he shook me by the hand and went off. I proceeded a few steps, then came to a startled halt. Good Lord! Where was the street lined with gardens? Where had it disappeared to? When did all these vehicles invade it? And when did all these hordes of humanity come to rest upon its surface? How did these hills of refuse come to cover its sides? And where were the fields that bordered it? High buildings had taken over, the street surged with children, and disturbing noises shook the air. At various points stood conjurers showing off their tricks and making snakes appear from baskets. Then there was a band announcing the opening of a circus, with clowns and weight lifters walking in front. A line of trucks carrying central security troops crawled majestically by. The siren of a fire engine shrieked, and it was not clear how the vehicle would cleave its way to reach the blazing fire. A battle raged between a taxi driver and his passenger, while the passenger's wife called out for help and no one answered. Good God! I was in a daze. My head spun. I almost went crazy. How could all this have happened in half a day, between early morning and sunset? I would find the answer at home with my father. But where was my home? I could see only tall buildings and hordes of people. I hastened on to the crossroads between the gardens and Abu Khoda. I had to cross Abu Khoda to reach my house, but the stream of cars would not let up. The fire engine's siren was shrieking at full pitch as it moved at a snail's pace, and I said to myself, "Let the fire take its pleasure in what it consumes." Extremely irritated, I wondered when I would be able to cross. I stood there a long time, until the young lad employed at the ironing shop on the corner came up to me. He stretched out his arm and said gallantly, "Grandpa, let me take you across."

NOTE

tarboosh   close-fitting brimless cap worn by some Muslim men on its own or as a base for a turban

RESPONDING PERSONALLY

3. Describe to a partner your reaction to the end of the story. How is it like or unlike what you expected?

4. Describe a time when you were expecting assistance of some sort— whether you were meeting someone, or getting direction, or being helped to complete a task—but were left instead to fend for yourself. What emotions did you experience, both initially and as time went by? Did you "grow" in any way because of the experience? Explain.

RESPONDING CRITICALLY/ANALYTICALLY

5. The writer ends with a sentence that, while a surprise of sorts, is not unexpected. How has the writer prepared the reader to be accepting of the story's outcome?

6. The story employs an unconventional narrative sequence that alters time and makes possible the transformations that occur.
   a) At which point do you first suspect that the events of the story stretch beyond just the one half-day of school? What in the narration suggests this to you? At which point in the story are you first certain?

    b) Examine the writer's use of antithesis near the end of the story: "The fire engine's siren was shrieking at full pitch as it moved at a snail's pace." In what way does that sentence suit the blending of the two narrative time sequences?

    c) With a partner, find some descriptive passages that unify the narration by referring to *both* of the story's timelines simultaneously.

7. In small groups, examine the "quest" motif that guides the story.

    a) In what way is the naiveté of the early protagonist made visible? Why is it important that this be firmly established?

    b) Describe the "known world" that the protagonist is compelled to leave in order to begin his "journey." What are his thoughts and emotions as he steps across the threshold to leave his known world?

    c) In what way is the protagonist's journey one of necessity rather than choice?

    d) Who is the archetypal wise guide, the sage, who mentors the protagonist through his journey? Explain.

    e) What is the climactic test, the great ordeal, that the protagonist must endure and overcome in order to complete his journey?

    f) When the protagonist is finally able "to reach my house," will he be back where he began, or will he be elsewhere? Support your answer with one or more passages from the story.

How well has the metaphor of the first half-day of school served as an appropriate vehicle for the protagonist's "journey"?

Self-Assessment

How clear is your own understanding of the journey archetype? Has responding to the questions either supported or expanded your understanding? Or are you still unclear as to the details of this motif? If so, what kind of research might help you to complete your understanding?

Responding Creatively

8. In a small group of three or four, design a children's book that tells the protagonist's story.

    a) Create a web—verbal/visual/a blend of both—that reveals the various stages of the archetypal journey upon which the young boy has embarked. Share your web, and your understanding of the boy's growth, with your classmates.

    b) Plan and design your book in such a way that you tell *both* stories—the day of school and the lifetime journey. Decide on a page layout that permits you to do both. For example, you might choose to place comparable stages of the two stories on facing pages, with a common narrative accompanied by two sets of visuals.

PROBLEM SOLVING OR DECISION MAKING

9. Sometimes, an ordeal is simply a difficult and unfulfilling experience. Other times, it is an opportunity for growth. How is the difference between the two determined? Does the difference lie in the experience itself, or in the one who lives the experience? In writing, reflect on the question.

Nathaniel Hawthorne
Dr. Heidegger's Experiment

PRE-READING

1. What truth is there to the thought that "youth is wasted on the young"? Base your response on your own life as well as on the lived experience of those around you.

2. Do people ever really change? Or do our values that are largely formed in our youth remain with us through life? Share your thoughts. Base your response on the lives of people you know.

That very singular man, old Dr. Heidegger, once invited four venerable friends to meet him in his study. There were three white-bearded gentlemen, Mr. Medbourne, Colonel Killigrew, and Mr. Gascoigne, and a withered gentlewoman, whose name was the Widow Wycherly. They were all melancholy old creatures, who had been unfortunate in life, and whose greatest misfortune it was that they were not long ago in their graves. Mr. Medbourne, in the vigor of his age, had been a prosperous merchant, but had lost his all by a frantic speculation, and was now little better than a mendicant. Colonel Killigrew had wasted his best years, and his health and substance, in the pursuit of sinful pleasures which had given birth to a brood of pains, such as the gout, and diverse other torments of soul and body. Mr. Gascoigne was a ruined politician, a man of evil fame, or at least had been so, till time had buried him from the knowledge of the present generation, and made him obscure instead of infamous. As for the Widow Wycherly, tradition tells us that she was a great beauty in her day; but, for a long while past, she had lived in deep seclusion, on account of certain scandalous stories which had prejudiced the gentry of the town against her. It is a circumstance worth mentioning, that each of these three old gentlemen, Mr. Medbourne, Colonel Killigrew, and Mr. Gascoigne, were early lovers of the Widow Wycherly, and had once been on the point of cutting each other's throats for her sake. And before proceeding farther, I will merely hint that Dr. Heidegger and all his four guests were sometimes thought to be a little beside themselves; as is not unfrequently the case with old people, when worried either by present troubles or woeful recollections.

"My dear old friends," said Dr. Heidegger, motioning them to be seated, "I am desirous of your assistance in one of those little experiments with which I amuse myself here in my study."

If all stories were true, Dr. Heidegger's study must have been a very curious place. It was a dim, old-fashioned chamber, festooned with cobwebs, and besprinkled with antique dust. Around the walls stood several oaken bookcases, the lower shelves of which were filled with rows of gigantic folios and black-letter quartos, and the upper with little parchment-covered duodecimos. Over the central bookcase was a bronze bust of Hippocrates, with which, according to some authorities, Dr. Heidegger was accustomed to hold consultations in all difficult cases of his practice. In the obscurest corner of the room stood a tall and narrow oaken closet, with its door ajar, within which doubtfully appeared a skeleton. Between two of the bookcases hung a looking glass, presenting its high and dusty plate within a tarnished gilt frame. Among many wonderful stories related of this mirror, it was fabled that the spirits of all the doctor's deceased patients dwelt within its verge, and would stare him in the face whenever he looked thitherward. The opposite side of the chamber was ornamented with the full-length portrait of a young lady, arrayed in the faded magnificence of silk, satin, and brocade, and with a visage as faded as her dress. Above half a century ago, Dr. Heidegger had been on the point of marriage with this young lady; but, being affected with some slight disorder, she had swallowed one of her lover's prescriptions, and died on the bridal evening. The greatest curiosity of the study remains to be mentioned; it was a ponderous folio volume, bound in black leather, with massive silver clasps. There were no letters on the back, and nobody could tell the title of the book. But it was well-known to be a book of magic; and once, when the chambermaid had lifted it, merely to brush away the dust, the skeleton had rattled in its closet, the picture of the young lady had stepped one foot upon the floor, and several ghastly faces had peeped forth from the mirror; while the brazen head of Hippocrates frowned, and said—"Forbear!"

Such was Dr. Heidegger's study. On the summer afternoon of our tale, a small round table, as black as ebony, stood in the center of the room, sustaining a cut-glass vase of beautiful form and elaborate workmanship. The sunshine came through the window, between the heavy festoons of two faded damask curtains, and fell directly across this vase; so that a mild splendor was reflected from it on the ashen visages of the five old people who sat around. Four champagne glasses were also on the table.

"My dear old friends," repeated Dr. Heidegger, "may I reckon on your aid in performing an exceedingly curious experiment?"

Now Dr. Heidegger was a very strange old gentleman, whose eccentricity had become the nucleus for a thousand fantastic stories. Some of these fables, to my shame be it spoken, might possibly be traced back to mine own veracious self; and if any passages of the present tale should startle the reader's faith, I must be content to bear the stigma of a fiction-monger.

When the doctor's four guests heard him talk of his proposed experiment, they anticipated nothing more wonderful than the murder of a mouse in an air pump, or the examination of a cobweb by the microscope, or some similar nonsense, with which he was constantly in the habit of pestering his intimates. But without waiting for a reply, Dr. Heidegger hobbled across the chamber, and returned with the same ponderous folio, bound in black leather, which common report affirmed to be a book of magic. Undoing the silver clasps, he opened the volume, and took from among its black-letter pages a rose, or what was once a rose, though now the green leaves and crimson petals had assumed one brownish hue, and the ancient flower seemed ready to crumble to dust in the doctor's hands.

"This rose," said Dr. Heidegger, with a sigh, "this same withered and crumbling flower, blossomed five and fifty years ago. It was given me by Sylvia Ward, whose portrait hangs yonder; and I meant to wear it in my bosom at our wedding. Five and fifty years it has been treasured between the leaves of this old volume. Now, would you deem it possible that this rose of half a century could ever bloom again?"

"Nonsense!" said the Widow Wycherly, with a peevish toss of her head. "You might as well ask whether an old woman's wrinkled face could ever bloom again."

"See!" answered Dr. Heidegger.

He uncovered the vase, and threw the faded rose into the water which it contained. At first it lay lightly on the surface of the fluid, appearing to imbibe none of its moisture. Soon, however, a singular change began to be visible. The crushed and dried petals stirred, and assumed a deepening tinge of crimson, as if the flower were reviving from a deathlike slumber; the slender stalk and twigs of foliage became green; and there was the rose of half a century, looking as fresh as when Sylvia Ward had first given it to her lover. It was scarcely full-blown; for some of its delicate red leaves curled modestly around its moist bosom, within which two or three dewdrops were sparkling.

"That is certainly a very pretty deception," said the doctor's friends; carelessly, however, for they had witnessed greater miracles at a conjurer's show; "pray how was it effected?"

"Did you never hear of the 'Fountain of Youth,'" asked Dr. Heidegger, "which Ponce de Leon, the Spanish adventurer, went in search of, two or three centuries ago?"

"But did Ponce de Leon ever find it?" said the Widow Wycherly.

"No," answered Dr. Heidegger, "for he never sought it in the right place. The famous Fountain of Youth, if I am rightly informed, is situated in the southern part of the Floridian peninsula, not far from Lake Macaco. Its source is overshadowed by several gigantic magnolias, which, though numberless centuries old, have been kept as fresh as violets by the virtues of this wonderful water. An acquaintance of mine, knowing my curiosity in such matters, has sent me what you see in the vase."

"Ahem!" said Colonel Killigrew, who believed not a word of the doctor's story; "and what may be the effect of this fluid on the human frame?"

"You shall judge for yourself, my dear colonel," replied Dr. Heidegger; "and all of you, my respected friends, are welcome to so much of this admirable fluid as may restore to you the bloom of youth. For my own part, having had much trouble in growing old, I am in no hurry to grow young again. With your permission, therefore, I will merely watch the progress of the experiment."

While he spoke, Dr. Heidegger had been filling the four champagne glasses with the water of the Fountain of Youth. It was apparently impregnated with an effervescent gas, for little bubbles were continually ascending from the depths of the glasses, and bursting in silvery spray at the surface. As the liquor diffused a pleasant perfume, the old people doubted not that it possessed cordial and comfortable properties; and, though utter skeptics as to its rejuvenescent power, they were inclined to swallow it at once. But Dr. Heidegger besought them to stay a moment.

"Before you drink, my respectable old friends," said he, "it would be well that, with the experience of a lifetime to direct you, you should draw up a few general rules for your guidance, in passing a second time through the perils of youth. Think what a sin and a shame it would be, if with your peculiar advantages, you should not become patterns of virtue and wisdom to all the young people of the age!"

The doctor's four venerable friends made him no answer, except by a feeble and tremulous laugh; so very ridiculous was the idea, that, knowing how closely repentance treads behind the steps of error, they should ever go astray again.

"Drink, then," said the doctor, bowing; "I rejoice that I have so well-selected the subjects of my experiment."

With palsied hands they raised the glasses to their lips. The liquor, if it really possessed such virtues as Dr. Heidegger imputed to it, could not have been bestowed on four human beings who needed it more woefully. They looked as if they had never known what youth or pleasure was, but had been the offspring of Nature's dotage, and always the gray, decrepit, sapless, miserable creatures, who now sat stooping round the doctor's table, without life enough in their souls or bodies to be animated even by the prospect of growing young again. They drank off the water, and replaced their glasses on the table.

Assuredly, there was an almost immediate improvement in the aspect of the party, not unlike what might have been produced by a glass of generous wine, together with a sudden glow of cheerful sunshine, brightening over all their visages at once. There was a healthful suffusion on their cheeks, instead of the ashen hue that had made them look so corpselike. They gazed at one another, and fancied that some magic power had really begun to smooth away the deep and sad inscription which Father Time had been so long engraving on their brows. The Widow Wycherly adjusted her cap, for she felt almost like a woman again.

"Give us more of this wondrous water!" cried they eagerly. "We are younger—but we are still too old! Quick—give us more!"

"Patience, patience!" quoth Dr. Heidegger, who sat watching the experiment with philosophic coolness. "You have been a long time growing old. Surely you might be content to grow young in half an hour! But the water is at your service."

Again he filled their glasses with the liquor of youth, enough of which still remained in the vase to turn half the old people in the city to the age of their own grandchildren. While the bubbles were yet sparkling on the brim, the doctor's four guests snatched their glasses from the table, and swallowed the contents at a single gulp. Was it delusion? Even while the draught was passing down their throats, it seemed to have wrought a change on their whole systems. Their eyes grew clear and bright; a dark shade deepened among their silvery locks; they sat around the table, three gentlemen of middle age, and a woman hardly beyond her buxom prime.

"My dear widow, you are charming!" cried Colonel Killigrew, whose eyes had been fixed upon her face, while the shadows of age were flitting from it like darkness from the crimson daybreak.

The fair widow knew, of old, that Colonel Killigrew's compliments were not always measured by sober truth; so she started up and ran to the mirror, still dreading that the ugly visage of an old woman would meet her gaze. Meanwhile, the three gentlemen behaved in such a manner as proved that the water of the Fountain of Youth possessed some intoxicating qualities; unless, indeed, their exhilaration of spirits were merely a lightsome dizziness, caused by the sudden removal of the weight of years. Mr. Gascoigne's mind seemed to run on political topics, but whether relating to the past, present, or future, could not easily be determined, since the same ideas and phrases have been in vogue these fifty years. Now he rattled forth full-throated sentences about patriotism, national glory, and the people's rights; now he muttered some perilous stuff or other, in a sly and doubtful whisper, so cautiously that even his own conscience could scarcely catch the secret; and now again he spoke in measured accents, and a deeply deferential tone, as if a royal ear were listening to his well-turned periods. Colonel Killigrew all this time had been trolling forth a jolly bottle song, and ringing his glass in symphony with the chorus, while his eyes wandered towards the buxom figure of the Widow Wycherly. On the other side of the table, Mr. Medbourne was involved in a calculation of dollars and cents, with which was strangely intermingled a project for supplying the East Indies with ice, by harnessing a team of whales to the polar icebergs.

As for the Widow Wycherly, she stood before the mirror curtsying and simpering to her own image, and greeting it as the friend whom she loved better than all the world beside. She thrust her face close to the glass, to see whether some long-remembered wrinkle or crow's-foot had indeed vanished. She examined whether the snow had so entirely melted from her hair, that the venerable cap could be safely thrown aside. At last, turning briskly away, she came with a sort of dancing step to the table.

"My dear old doctor," cried she, "pray favor me with another glass!"

"Certainly, my dear madam, certainly!" replied the complaisant doctor; "See! I have already filled the glasses."

There, in fact, stood the four glasses, brimful of this wonderful water, the delicate spray of which, as it effervesced from the surface, resembled the tremulous glitter of diamonds. It was now so nearly sunset that the chamber had grown duskier than ever; but a mild and moonlike splendor gleamed from within the vase, and rested alike on the four guests, and on the doctor's venerable figure. He sat in a high-backed, elaborately carved, oaken armchair, with a gray dignity of aspect that might have well befitted that very Father Time whose power had never been disputed save by this fortunate company. Even while quaffing the third draught of the Fountain of Youth, they were almost awed by the expression of his mysterious visage.

But, the next moment, the exhilarating gush of young life shot through their veins. They were now in the happy prime of youth. Age, with its miserable train of cares, and sorrows, and diseases, was remembered only as the trouble of a dream from which they had joyously awoke. The fresh gloss of the soul, so early lost, and without which the world's successive scenes had been but a gallery of faded pictures, again threw its enchantment over all their prospects. They felt like new-created beings, in a new-created universe.

"We are young! We are young!" they cried, exultingly.

Youth, like the extremity of age, had effaced the strongly marked characteristics of middle life, and mutually assimilated them all. They were a group of merry youngsters, almost maddened with the exuberant frolicsomeness of their years. The most singular effect of their gaiety was an impulse to mock the infirmity and decrepitude of which they had so lately been the victims. They laughed loudly at their old-fashioned attire, the wide-skirted coats and flapped waistcoats of the young men, and the ancient cap and gown of the blooming girl. One limped across the floor, like a gouty grandfather; one set a pair of spectacles astride his nose, and pretended to pore over the black-letter pages of the book of magic; a third seated himself in an armchair, and strove to imitate the venerable dignity of Dr. Heidegger. Then all shouted mirthfully, and leaped about the room. The Widow Wycherly—if so fresh a damsel could be called a widow—tripped up to the doctor's chair, with a mischievous merriment in her rosy face.

"Doctor, you dear old soul," cried she, "get up and dance with me!" And then the four young people laughed louder than ever, to think what a queer figure the poor old doctor would cut.

"Pray excuse me," answered the doctor quietly. "I am old and rheumatic, and my dancing days were over long ago. But either of these young gentlemen will be glad of so pretty a partner."

"Dance with me, Clara!" cried Colonel Killigrew.

"No, no, I will be her partner!" shouted Mr. Gascoigne.

"She promised me her hand, fifty years ago!" exclaimed Mr. Medbourne.

They all gathered round her. One caught both her hands in his passionate grasp—another threw his arm about her waist—the third buried his hand among the glossy curls that clustered beneath the widow's cap. Blushing, panting, struggling, chiding, laughing, her warm breath fanning each of their faces by turns, she strove to disengage herself, yet still remained in their triple embrace. Never was there a livelier picture of youthful rivalship, with bewitching beauty for the prize. Yet, by a strange deception, owing to the duskiness of the chamber, and the antique dresses which they still wore, the tall mirror is said to have reflected the figures of the three old, gray, withered grandsires, ridiculously contending for the skinny ugliness of a shrivelled grandam.

But they were young: their burning passions proved them so. Inflamed to madness by the coquetry of the girl-widow, who neither granted nor quite withheld her favors, the three rivals began to interchange threatening glances. Still keeping hold of the fair prize, they grappled fiercely at one another's throats. As they struggled to and fro, the table was overturned, and the vase dashed into a thousand fragments. The precious Water of Youth flowed in a bright stream across the floor, moistening the wings of a butterfly, which, grown old in the decline of summer, had alighted there to die. The insect fluttered lightly through the chamber, and settled on the snowy head of Dr. Heidegger.

"Come, come, gentlemen!—come, Madam Wycherly," exclaimed the doctor, "I really must protest against this riot."

They stood still, and shivered; for it seemed as if gray Time were calling them back from their sunny youth, far down into the chill and darksome vale of years. They looked at old Dr. Heidegger, who sat in his carved armchair, holding the rose of half a century, which he had rescued from among the fragments of the shattered vase. At the motion of his hand, the four rioters resumed their seats; the more readily, because their violent exertions had wearied them, youthful though they were.

"My poor Sylvia's rose!" cried Dr. Heidegger, holding it in the light of the sunset clouds; "it appears to be fading again."

And so it was. Even while the party were looking at it, the flower continued to shrivel up, till it became as dry and fragile as when the doctor had first thrown it into the vase. He shook off the few drops of moisture which clung to its petals.

"I love it as well thus as in its dewy freshness," observed he, pressing the withered rose to his withered lips. While he spoke, the butterfly fluttered down from the doctor's snowy head, and fell upon the floor.

His guests shivered again. A strange chillness, whether of the body or spirit they could not tell, was creeping gradually over them all. They gazed at one another, and fancied that each fleeting moment snatched away a charm, and left a deepening furrow where none had been before. Was it an illusion? Had the changes of a lifetime been crowded into so brief a space, and were they now four aged people, sitting with their old friend, Dr. Heidegger?

"Are we grown old again, so soon?" cried they dolefully.

In truth, they had. The Water of Youth possessed merely a virtue more transient than that of wine. The delirium which it created had effervesced away. Yes! They were old again. With a shuddering impulse that showed her a woman still, the widow clasped her skinny hands before her face, and wished that the coffin lid were over it, since it could be no longer beautiful.

"Yes, friends, ye are old again," said Dr. Heidegger; "and lo! the Water of Youth is all lavished on the ground. Well—I bemoan it not; for if the fountain gushed at my very doorstep, I would not stoop to bathe my lips in it—no, though its delirium were for years instead of moments. Such is the lesson ye have taught me!"

But the doctor's four friends had taught no such lesson to themselves. They resolved forthwith to make a pilgrimage to Florida, and quaff at morning, noon, and night, from the Fountain of Youth.

Notes

dolefully	sadly; mournfully
festooned	hung in curves
Hippocrates	famous ancient Greek physician, considered "The Father of Medicine"
mendicant	beggar
Ponce de Leon	Spanish explorer (1460–1521) who sought the legendary Fountain of Youth
quaff	drink deeply
singular	extraordinary; strange; unique; remarkable
suffusion	a spreading-over as of liquid or light
venerable	respectable
veracious	true
visage	face; appearance

Responding Personally

3. If you, in your later years, were to be offered the same opportunity the four "friends" were given—knowing only as much as they knew—do you think you would accept? Why or why not?

4. We all have made decisions that we would like to be able to undo. Describe one such decision that you have made. What about that event would you have liked to be able to change? In your honest opinion, if you were given the opportunity to relive that one particular experience, would you act differently? Explain why or why not.

RESPONDING CRITICALLY/ANALYTICALLY

5. Examine the narrator's "involvement" in the story.
   a) What is the narrative point of view from which the story is told? In what way does this narrative perspective suit the story?
   b) In several instances, the narrator makes reference to an external presence:
      - "Dr. Heidegger and all his four guests were sometimes *thought to be....*"
      - "But it was *well-known to be* a book of magic."
      - "The tall mirror *is said to* have reflected...."

      To whom are these references being made? Who is *thinking, knowing, saying*? What purpose do such references serve?

6. With a partner, develop a chart that compares or contrasts the traits of the five characters. Areas of comparison might include their physical appearance, their history, their past and present behaviours, their motivations or aspirations, their flaws. What are some key observations that emerge?

7. With a partner, examine the symbolism of the story. Comment on the significance of each of the following:
   a) the "bookends" effect of the "summer afternoon" opening and the "sunset clouds" closing
   b) the "black as ebony" table supporting the vase
   c) the water of the Fountain of Youth
   d) the rose itself, as well as the changes it undergoes
   e) the unchanging mirror
   f) the shattering of the vase "into a thousand fragments"

   Identify at least one other element in the story—an object, action, name, or description—that you would call a symbol. Explain its symbolic significance and justify your naming it a symbol. Share the symbol and your explanation of it with your classmates.

SELF-ASSESSMENT

How well do you function when working on this kind of assignment with a partner? Do you work together, sharing your knowledge? Or do you work "separately together," each completing some of the sections and then pooling your answers? Which process do you think is the more educationally sound?

8. Was this a true "experiment"? If so, what was being tested?
   a) Why did he select four people of such similar personality? Would it not have been a more productive and interesting experiment had differing personalities been included?
   b) What did Dr. Heidegger expect to see? What might have been his initial hypothesis? Support your thinking with reference to the story.

c) What, if anything, did he expect his "subjects" to learn from the experiment? What might have been his purpose?

RESPONDING CREATIVELY

9. Had Dr. Heidegger withheld the water from his friends until after they had seen the totality of its effect on the rose, would they still have drunk it? Assume the role of one of the four characters, and, writing in the first person, tell what you would have done, and why. Remain true to character.

10. In a group of five, assume the roles of the characters of the story. Improvise a moderated talk-show discussion over the "few general rules" that Dr. Heidegger wants the group to draw up. Let the Dr. Heidegger in your group be a little more adamant about the necessity for rules than the one in the story.

PROBLEM SOLVING OR DECISION MAKING

11. Dr. Heidegger offers a brief explanation for why he chooses not to drink. Support or refute his point of view. In a small group, offer a series of "proofs" for why one either should or should not be in a "hurry to grow young again."

Ambrose Bierce
An Occurrence at Owl Creek Bridge

PRE-READING

1. When you prepare to read a story or watch a movie, what are some of the most basic expectations you have of the writer and of the story? Have you ever encountered a story that did not meet one or more of your basic expectations? Recall your reaction at the time: did it influence your appreciation of the writer or director? Explain.

2. Most people have at some time awakened from a very deep sleep not knowing whether they are dreaming or awake. Have you ever had such an experience? Describe as many of your thoughts, feelings, or sensations as you are able to remember. Share your memories in class.

I

A man stood upon a railroad bridge in Northern Alabama, looking down into the swift waters twenty feet below. The man's hands were behind his back, the wrists bound with a cord. A rope loosely encircled his neck. It was attached to a stout cross-timber above his head, and the slack fell to the level of his knees. Some loose boards laid upon the sleepers supporting the metals of the railway supplied a footing for him and his executioners—two private soldiers of the Federal army, directed by a sergeant, who in civil life may have been a deputy sheriff. At a short remove upon the same temporary platform was an officer in the uniform of his rank, armed. He was a captain. A sentinel at each end of the bridge stood with his rifle in the position known as "Support," that is to say, vertical in front of the left shoulder, the hammer resting on the forearm thrown straight across the chest—a formal and unnatural position, enforcing an erect carriage of the body. It did not appear to be the duty of these two men to know what was occurring at the centre of the bridge; they merely blockaded the two ends of the foot plank which traversed it.

Beyond one of the sentinels nobody was in sight; the railroad ran straight away into a forest for a hundred yards, then, curving, was lost to view. Doubtless there was an outpost further along. The other bank of the stream was open ground—a gentle acclivity crowned with a stockade of vertical tree trunks, loop-holed for rifles, with a single embrasure through which protruded the muzzle of a brass cannon commanding the bridge. Midway of the slope between bridge and fort were the spectators—a single company of infantry in line, at "parade rest," the butts of the rifles on the ground, the barrels inclining slightly backward against the right shoulder, the hands crossed upon the stock. A lieutenant stood at the right of the line, the point of his sword upon the ground, his left hand resting upon his right. Excepting the group of four at the centre of the bridge not a man moved. The company faced the bridge, staring stonily, motionless. The sentinels, facing the banks of the stream, might have been statues to adorn the bridge. The captain stood with folded arms, silent, observing the work of his subordinates but making no sign. Death is a dignitary who, when he comes announced, is to be received with formal manifestations of respect, even by those most familiar with him. In the code of military etiquette silence and fixity are forms of deference.

The man who was engaged in being hanged was apparently about thirty-five years of age. He was a civilian, if one might judge from his dress, which was that of a planter. His features were good—a straight nose, firm mouth, broad forehead, from which his long, dark hair was combed straight back, falling behind his ears to the collar of his well-fitting frock coat. He wore a moustache and pointed beard, but no whiskers; his eyes were large and dark grey and had a kindly expression which one would hardly have expected in one whose neck was in the hemp. Evidently this was no vulgar assassin. The liberal military code makes provision for hanging many kinds of people, and gentlemen are not excluded.

The preparations being complete, the two private soldiers stepped aside and each drew away the plank upon which he had been standing. The sergeant turned to the captain, saluted and placed himself immediately behind that officer, who in turn moved apart one pace. These movements left the condemned man and the sergeant standing on the two ends of the same plank, which spanned three of the crossties of the bridge. The end upon which the civilian stood almost, but not quite, reached a fourth. This plank had been held in place by the weight of the captain; it was now held by that of the sergeant. At a signal from the former, the latter would step aside, the plank would tilt and the condemned man go down between two ties. The arrangement commended itself to his judgment as simple and effective. His face had not been covered nor his eyes bandaged. He looked a moment at his "unsteadfast footing," then let his gaze wander to the swirling water of the stream racing madly beneath his feet. A piece of dancing driftwood caught his attention and his eyes followed it down the current. How slowly it appeared to move! What a sluggish stream!

He closed his eyes in order to fix his last thoughts upon his wife and children. The water, touched to gold by the early sun, the brooding mists under the banks at some distance down the stream, the fort, the soldiers, the piece of drift—all had distracted him. And now he became conscious of a new disturbance. Striking through the thought of his dear ones was a sound which he could neither ignore nor understand, a sharp, distinct, metallic percussion like the stroke of a blacksmith's hammer upon the anvil; it had the same ringing quality. He wondered what it was, and whether immeasurably distant or near by—it seemed both. Its recurrence was regular, but as slow as the tolling of a death knell. He awaited each stroke with impatience and—he knew not why—apprehension. The intervals of silence grew progressively longer; the delays became maddening. With their greater infrequency the sounds increased in strength and sharpness. They hurt his ear like the thrust of a knife; he feared he would shriek. What he heard was the ticking of his watch.

He unclosed his eyes and saw again the water below him. "If I could free my hands," he thought, "I might throw off the noose and spring into the stream. By diving I could evade the bullets, and, swimming vigorously, reach the bank, take to the woods, and get away home. My home, thank God, is as yet outside their lines; my wife and little ones are still beyond the invader's farthest advance."

As these thoughts, which have here to be set down in words, were flashed into the doomed man's brain rather than evolved from it, the captain nodded to the sergeant. The sergeant stepped aside.

II

Peyton Farquhar was a well-to-do planter, of an old and highly respected Alabama family. Being a slave owner, and, like other slave owners, a politician, he was naturally an original secessionist and ardently devoted to the Southern cause. Circumstances of an imperious nature which it is unnecessary to relate here, had prevented him from taking service with the gallant army which had fought the disastrous campaigns ending with the fall of Corinth, and he chafed under the inglorious restraint, longing for the release of his energies, the larger life of the soldier, the opportunity for distinction. That opportunity, he felt, would come, as it comes to all in war time. Meanwhile he did what he could. No service was too humble for him to perform in aid of the South, no adventure too perilous for him to undertake if consistent with the character of a civilian who was at heart a soldier, and who in good faith and without too much qualification assented to at least a part of the frankly villainous dictum that all is fair in love and war.

One evening while Farquhar and his wife were sitting on a rustic bench near the entrance to his grounds, a grey-clad soldier rode up to the gate and asked for a drink of water. Mrs. Farquhar was only too happy to serve him with her own white hands. While she was gone to fetch the water, her husband approached the dusty horseman and inquired eagerly for news from the front.

"The Yanks are repairing the railroads," said the man, "and are getting ready for another advance. They have reached the Owl Creek bridge, put it in order, and built a stockade on the other bank. The commandant has issued an order, which is posted everywhere, declaring that any civilian caught interfering with the railroad, its bridges, tunnels, or trains, will be summarily hanged. I saw the order."

"How far is it to the Owl Creek bridge?" Farquhar asked.

"About thirty miles."

"Is there no force on this side the creek?"

"Only a picket post half a mile out, on the railroad, and a single sentinel at this end of the bridge."

"Suppose a man—a civilian and student of hanging—should elude the picket post and perhaps get the better of the sentinel," said Farquhar, smiling, "what could he accomplish?"

The soldier reflected. "I was there a month ago," he replied. "I observed that the flood of last winter had lodged a great quantity of driftwood against the wooden pier at this end of the bridge. It is now dry and would burn like tow."

The lady had now brought the water, which the soldier drank. He thanked her ceremoniously, bowed to her husband, and rode away. An hour later, after nightfall, he repassed the plantation, going northward in the direction from which he had come. He was a Federal scout.

III

As Peyton Farquhar fell straight downward through the bridge, he lost consciousness and was as one already dead. From this state he was awakened—ages later, it seemed to him—by the pain of a sharp pressure upon his throat, followed by a sense of suffocation. Keen, poignant agonies seemed to shoot from his neck downward through every fibre of his body and limbs. These pains appeared to flash along well-defined lines of ramification, and to beat with an inconceivably rapid periodicity. They seemed like streams of pulsating fire heating him to an intolerable temperature. As to his head, he was conscious of nothing but a feeling of fullness—of congestion. These sensations were unaccompanied by thought. The intellectual part of his nature was already effaced; he had power only to feel, and feeling was torment. He was conscious of motion. Encompassed in a luminous cloud, of which he was now merely the fiery heart, without material substance, he swung through unthinkable arcs of oscillation, like a vast pendulum. Then all at once, with terrible suddenness, the light about him shot upward with the noise of a loud plash; a frightful roaring was in his ears, and all was cold and dark. The power of thought was restored; he knew that the rope had broken and he had fallen into the stream. There was no additional strangulation; the noose about his neck was already suffocating him, and kept the water from his lungs. To die of hanging at the bottom of a river!—the idea seemed to him ludicrous. He opened his eyes in the blackness and saw above him a gleam of light, but how distant, how inaccessible! He was still sinking, for the light became fainter and fainter until it was a mere glimmer. Then it began to grow and brighten, and he knew that he was rising toward the surface—knew it with reluctance, for he was now very comfortable. "To be hanged and drowned," he thought, "that is not so bad; but I do not wish to be shot. No; I will not be shot; that is not fair."

He was not conscious of an effort, but a sharp pain in his wrists apprised him that he was trying to free his hands. He gave the struggle his attention, as an idler might observe the feat of a juggler, without interest in the outcome. What a splendid effort!—what magnificent, what superhuman strength! Ah, that was a fine endeavour! Bravo! The cord fell away; his arms parted and floated upward, the hands dimly seen on each side in the growing light. He watched them with a new interest as first one and then the other pounced upon the noose at his neck. They tore it away and thrust it fiercely aside, its undulations resembling those of a water-snake. "Put it back, put it back!" He thought he shouted these words to his hands, for the undoing of the noose had been succeeded by the direst pang which he had yet experienced. His neck ached horribly; his brain was on fire; his heart, which had been fluttering faintly, gave a great leap, trying to force itself out at his mouth. His whole body was racked and wrenched with an insupportable anguish! But his disobedient hands gave no heed to the command. They beat the water vigorously with quick, downward strokes, forcing him to the surface. He felt his head emerge; his eyes were blinded by the sunlight; his chest expanded convulsively, and with a supreme and crowning agony his lungs engulfed a great draught of air, which instantly he expelled in a shriek!

He was now in full possession of his physical senses. They were, indeed, preternaturally keen and alert. Something in the awful disturbance of his organic system had so exalted and refined them that they made record of things never before perceived. He felt the ripples upon his face and heard their separate sounds as they struck. He looked at the forest on the bank of the stream, saw the individual trees, the leaves and the veining of each leaf—saw the very insects upon them, the locusts, the brilliant-bodied flies, the grey spiders stretching their webs from twig to twig. He noted the prismatic colours in all the dewdrops upon a million blades of grass. The humming of the gnats that danced above the eddies of the stream, the beating of the dragonflies' wings, the strokes of the water spiders' legs, like oars which had lifted their boat—all these made audible music. A fish slid along beneath his eyes and he heard the rush of its body parting the water.

He had come to the surface facing down the stream; in a moment the visible world seemed to wheel slowly round, himself the pivotal point, and he saw the bridge, the fort, the soldiers upon the bridge, the captain, the sergeant, the two privates, his executioners. They were in silhouette against the blue sky. They shouted and gesticulated, pointing at him; the captain had drawn his pistol, but did not fire; the others were unarmed. Their movements were grotesque and horrible, their forms gigantic.

Suddenly he heard a sharp report and something struck the water smartly within a few inches of his head, spattering his face with spray. He heard a second report, and saw one of the sentinels with his rifle at his shoulder, a light cloud of blue smoke rising from the muzzle. The man in the water saw the eye of the man on the bridge gazing into his own through the sights of the rifle. He observed that it was a grey eye, and remembered having read that grey eyes were keenest and that all famous marksmen had them. Nevertheless, this one had missed.

A counter swirl had caught Farquhar and turned him half round; he was again looking into the forest on the bank opposite the fort. The sound of a clear, high voice in a monotonous singsong now rang out behind him and came across the water with a distinctness that pierced and subdued all other sounds, even the beating of the ripples in his ears. Although no soldier, he had frequented camps enough to know the dread significance of that deliberate, drawling, aspirated chant; the lieutenant on shore was taking a part in the morning's work. How coldly and pitilessly—with what an even, calm intonation, presaging and enforcing tranquility in the men—with what accurately-measured intervals fell those cruel words:

"Attention, company.——Shoulder arms.——Ready.——Aim.——Fire."

Farquhar dived—dived as deeply as he could. The water roared in his ears like the voice of Niagara, yet he heard the dulled thunder of the volley, and rising again toward the surface, met shining bits of metal, singularly flattened, oscillating slowly downward. Some of them touched him on the face and hands, then fell away, continuing their descent. One lodged between his collar and neck; it was uncomfortably warm, and he snatched it out.

As he rose to the surface, gasping for breath, he saw that he had been a long time under water; he was perceptibly farther down stream—nearer to safety. The soldiers had almost finished reloading; the metal ramrods flashed all at once in the sunshine as they were drawn from the barrels, turned in the air, and thrust into their sockets. The two sentinels fired again, independently and ineffectually.

The hunted man saw all this over his shoulder; he was now swimming vigorously with the current. His brain was as energetic as his arms and legs; he thought with the rapidity of lightning.

"The officer," he reasoned, "will not make that martinet's error a second time. It is as easy to dodge a volley as a single shot. He has probably already given the command to fire at will. God help me, I cannot dodge them all!"

An appalling plash within two yards of him, followed by a loud rushing sound, *diminuendo*, which seemed to travel back through the air to the fort and died in an explosion which stirred the very river to its deeps! A rising sheet of water, which curved over him, fell down upon him, blinded him, strangled him! The cannon had taken a hand in the game. As he shook his head free from the commotion of the smitten water, he heard the deflected shot humming through the air ahead, and in an instant it was cracking and smashing the branches in the forest beyond.

"They will not do that again," he thought; "the next time they will use a charge of grape. I must keep my eye upon the gun; the smoke will apprise me—the report arrives too late; it lags behind the missile. It is a good gun."

Suddenly he felt himself whirled round and round—spinning like a top. The water, the banks, the forest, the now distant bridge, fort and men—all were commingled and blurred. Objects were represented by their colours only; circular horizontal streaks of colour—that was all he saw. He had been caught in a vortex and was being whirled on with a velocity of advance and gyration which made him giddy and sick. In a few moments he was flung upon the gravel at the foot of the left bank of the stream—the southern bank—and behind a projecting point which concealed him from his enemies. The sudden arrest of his motion, the abrasion of one of his hands on the gravel, restored him and he wept with delight. He dug his fingers into the sand, threw it over himself in handfuls and audibly blessed it. It looked like gold, like diamonds, rubies, emeralds; he could think of nothing beautiful which it did not resemble. The trees upon the bank were giant garden plants; he noted a definite order in their arrangement, inhaled the fragrance of their blooms. A strange, roseate light shone through the spaces among their trunks, and the wind made in their branches the music of aeolian harps. He had no wish to perfect his escape, was content to remain in that enchanting spot until retaken.

A whizz and rattle of grapeshot among the branches high above his head roused him from his dream. The baffled cannoneer had fired him a random farewell. He sprang to his feet, rushed up the sloping bank, and plunged into the forest.

All that day he travelled, laying his course by the rounding sun. The forest seemed interminable; nowhere did he discover a break in it, not even a woodsman's road. He had not known that he lived in so wild a region. There was something uncanny in the revelation.

By nightfall he was fatigued, footsore, famishing. The thought of his wife and children urged him on. At last he found a road which led him in what he knew to be the right direction. It was as wide and straight as a city street, yet it seemed untravelled. No fields bordered it, no dwelling anywhere. Not so much as the barking of a dog suggested human habitation. The black bodies of the great trees formed a straight wall on both sides, terminating on the horizon in a point, like a diagram in a lesson in perspective. Overhead, as he looked up through this rift in the wood, shone great golden stars looking unfamiliar and grouped in strange constellations. He was sure they were arranged in some order which had a secret and malign significance. The wood on either side was full of singular noises, among which— once, twice, and again—he distinctly heard whispers in an unknown tongue.

His neck was in pain, and, lifting his hand to it, he found it horribly swollen. He knew that it had a circle of black where the rope had bruised it. His eyes felt congested; he could no longer close them. His tongue was swollen with thirst; he relieved its fever by thrusting it forward from between his teeth into the cool air. How softly the turf had carpeted the untravelled avenue! He could no longer feel the roadway beneath his feet!

Doubtless, despite his suffering, he fell asleep while walking, for now he sees another scene—perhaps he has merely recovered from a delirium. He stands at the gate of his own home. All is as he left it, and all bright and beautiful in the morning sunshine. He must have travelled the entire night. As he pushes open the gate and passes up the wide white walk, he sees a flutter of female garments; his wife, looking fresh and cool and sweet, steps down from the verandah to meet him. At the bottom of the steps she stands waiting, with a smile of ineffable joy, an attitude of matchless grace and dignity. Ah, how beautiful she is! He springs forward with extended arms. As he is about to clasp her, he feels a stunning blow upon the back of the neck; a blinding white light blazes all about him, with a sound like the shock of a cannon— then all is darkness and silence!

Peyton Farquhar was dead; his body, with a broken neck, swung gently from side to side beneath the timbers of the Owl Creek bridge.

NOTES

aeolian harps	stringed instruments that make music when the wind blows through them
diminuendo	with a gradual decrease In volume
Federal army	or the Union, a reference to the northern United States, the winning side in the American Civil War (1861–1865)
secessionist	person in favour of withdrawing from a political union
Southern cause	reference to the southern United States, the losing side in the American Civil War
Yanks	or Yankees, derogatory term for soldiers in the army of the northern United States

RESPONDING PERSONALLY

3. Were you surprised by the ending of the story? Or did the ending unfold logically and meet with your expectations? Describe freely your thoughts as you were reading and making meaning of the sequence of events. Was there anything you may have glossed over or missed on your first reading that may have resulted in your being tricked by the narrative sequence?

4. Peyton Farquhar *wants* to believe the dusty "grey-clad soldier" in part because he himself longs for "the opportunity for distinction" that military life might offer him. Consequently, he is easily deceived. Have you ever been too easily deceived about something, perhaps more so because you wanted to believe despite what your own senses and better judgement suggested? Share the experience in writing.

RESPONDING CRITICALLY/ANALYTICALLY

5. The opening paragraph of section II provides a brief characterization of Peyton Farquhar's romanticized sense of military service. At the same time, however, the narrator omits mentioning those circumstances that "had prevented him from taking service with that gallant army," saying they are "unnecessary to relate here." In light of the rest of section II, and of the outcome of the story as a whole, what were those "circumstances of an imperious nature" that barred Peyton Farquhar from the gallant life of the soldier? Was there a particular character flaw? Discuss in a small group, and then share your thoughts with your classmates.

6. Working in small discussion groups, construct a chart that will assist you in analyzing the structure of the story, and subsequently in reaching a more thorough understanding of the way in which the writer has prepared you to expect a particular outcome.
   a) Set up three columns, one for each section of the story. Identify the following for each story section:
      - a brief, one-sentence summary of each section's story content
      - the time setting in which the events occur (e.g., present/past)
      - the speed with which time moves
      - the objectivity or subjectivity of the omniscient narrative point of view
      - the degree of preciseness of the descriptive detail
      - the reliability of narrative information as it is shared with the reader
   b) Describe the narrative *pattern* that the writer has created, or that he appears to be following.
   c) In what way is the reader conditioned by the apparent structure of the story to expect the action in section III to be a structural and logical continuation of the action of section I?

SELF-ASSESSMENT

In a discussion such as this, do you find a large group setting preferable to a small group, or the reverse? Which setting do you find the most productive for yourself? Why?

7. With a partner, explore the symbolic representation of the "untravelled" land four paragraphs from the end of the story.
   a) Where has he arrived?
   b) Explain why you feel that this section of the story succeeds.

RESPONDING CREATIVELY

8. Write the letter that rejects Peyton Farquhar's application for military service. Base your letter on your understanding of the story events.

9. If you were to direct the film adaptation of this story, what are some of the choices you would make? Describe your film.

- Where would you deviate from the story's original sequence? Why? If you did deviate, what changes would you make?
- Would you create additional dialogue? If so, what?
- At what point in the film would the sergeant step off the plank? Explain.
- Would the viewer be shown the protagonist's face, or would the film be shot through his eyes? Why?
- Would your film remain "short story" length, or would you expand it to feature film length? What running time would you envision the film to be? Explain.

PROBLEM SOLVING OR DECISION MAKING

10. Literature seems to imply an unwritten "contract" between writer and reader. What obligation, if any, does the writer have to the reader insofar as clarity of information is concerned? Share your thoughts in a whole-class discussion.

Margaret Laurence
Horses of the Night

PRE-READING

1. Daydreaming is a natural act, an opportunity for the imagination to run free. Everyone daydreams to some degree. When, though, does simple daydreaming become something more, something unhealthy? Can you identify the line that delineates what is normal imaginative activity from what is not? Explain.

2. Reflect on a relative or friend you've known well who has changed significantly over a period of years. In writing, chronicle the change, along with your thoughts as to the reason(s) for the change.

I never knew I had distant cousins who lived up north, until Chris came down to Manawaka to go to high school. My mother said he belonged to a large family, relatives of ours, who lived at Shallow Creek, up north. I was six, and Shallow Creek seemed immeasurably far, part of a legendary winter country where no leaves grew and where the breath of seals and polar bears snuffled out steamily and turned to ice.

"Could plain people live there?" I asked my mother, meaning people who were not Eskimos. "Could there be a farm?"

"How do you mean?" she said, puzzled. "I told you. That's where they live. On the farm. Uncle Wilf—that was Chris's father, who died a few years back—he got the place as a homestead, donkey's years ago."

"But how could they grow anything? I thought you said it was up north."

"Mercy," my mother said, laughing, "it's not *that* far north, Vanessa. It's about a hundred miles beyond Galloping Mountain. You be nice to Chris, now, won't you? And don't go asking him a whole lot of questions the minute he steps inside the door."

How little my mother knew of me, I thought. Chris had been fifteen. He could be expected to feel only scorn towards me. I detested the fact that I was so young. I did not think I would be able to say anything at all to him.

"What if I don't like him?"

"What if you don't?" my mother responded sharply. "You're to watch your manners, and no acting up, understand? It's going to be quite difficult enough without that."

"Why does he have to come here, anyway?" I demanded crossly. "Why can't he go to school where he lives?"

"Because there isn't any high school up there," my mother said. "I hope he gets on well here, and isn't too homesick. Three years is a long time. It's very good of your grandfather to let him stay at the Brick House."

She said this last accusingly, as though she suspected I might be thinking differently. But I had not thought of it one way or another. We were all having dinner at the Brick House because of Chris's arrival. It was the end of August, and sweltering. My grandfather's house looked huge and cool from the outside, the high low-sweeping spruce trees shutting out the sun with their dusky out-fanned branches. But inside it wasn't cool at all. The woodstove in the kitchen was going full blast, and the whole place smelled of roasting meat.

Grandmother Connor was wearing a large mauve apron. I thought it was a nicer colour than the dark bottle-green of her dress, but she believed in wearing sombre shades lest the spirit give way to vanity, which in her case was certainly not much of a risk. The apron came up over her shapeless bosom and obscured part of her cameo brooch, the only jewellery she ever wore, with its portrait of a fiercely bearded man whom I imagined to be either Moses or God.

"Isn't it nearly time for them to be getting here, Beth?" Grandmother Connor asked.

"Train's not due until six," my mother said. "It's barely five-thirty, now. Has Father gone to the station already?"

"He went an hour ago," my grandmother said.

"He would," my mother commented.

"Now, now, Beth," my grandmother cautioned and soothed.

At last the front screen door was hurled open and Grandfather Connor strode into the house, followed by a tall lanky boy. Chris was wearing a white shirt, a tie, grey trousers. I thought, unwillingly, that he looked handsome. His face was angular, the bones showing through the brown skin. His grey eyes were slightly slanted, and his hair was the colour of couchgrass at the end of summer when it has been bleached to a light yellow by the sun. I had not planned to like him, not even a little, but somehow I wanted to defend him when I heard what my mother whispered to my grandmother before they went into the front hall.

"Heavens, look at the shirt and trousers—must've been his father's, the poor kid."

I shot out into the hall ahead of my mother, and then stopped and stood there.

"Hi, Vanessa," Chris said.

"How come you knew who I was?" I asked.

"Well. I knew your mother and dad only had one of a family, so I figured you must be her," he replied grinning.

The way he spoke did not make me feel I had blundered. My mother greeted him warmly but shyly. Not knowing if she were expected to kiss him or to shake hands, she finally did neither. Grandmother Connor, however, had no doubts. She kissed him on both cheeks and then held him at arm's length to have a proper look at him.

"Bless the child," she said.

Coming from anyone else, this remark would have sounded ridiculous, especially as Chris was at least a head taller. My grandmother was the only person I have ever known who could say such things without appearing false.

"I'll show you your room, Chris," my mother offered.

Grandfather Connor, who had been standing in the living room doorway in absolute silence, looking as granite as a statue in the cemetery, now followed Grandmother out to the kitchen.

"Train was forty minutes late," he said weightily.

"What a shame," my grandmother said. "But I thought it wasn't due until six, Timothy."

"Six!" my grandfather cried. "That's the mainline train. The local's due at five-twenty."

This was not correct, as both my grandmother and I knew. But neither of us contradicted him.

"What on earth are you cooking a roast for, on a night like this?" my grandfather went on. "A person could fry an egg on the sidewalk, it's that hot. Potato salad would've gone down well."

Privately I agreed with this opinion, but I could never permit myself to acknowledge agreement with him on anything. I automatically and emotionally sided with Grandmother in all issues, not because she was inevitably right but because I loved her.

"It's not a roast," my grandmother said mildly. "It's mock-duck. The stove's only been going for an hour. I thought the boy would be hungry after the trip."

My mother and Chris had come downstairs and were now in the living room. I could hear them there, talking awkwardly, with pauses.

"Potato salad," my grandfather declaimed, "would've been plenty good enough. He'd have been lucky to get it, if you ask me anything. Wilf's family hasn't got two cents to rub together. It's me that's paying for the boy's keep."

The thought of Chris in the living room, and my mother unable to explain, was too much for me. I sidled over to the kitchen door, intending to close it. But my grandmother stopped me.

"No," she said, with unexpected firmness. "Leave it open, Vanessa."

I could hardly believe it. Surely she couldn't want Chris to hear? She herself was always able to move with equanimity through a hurricane because she believed that a mighty fortress was her God. But the rest of us were not like that, and usually she did her best to protect us. At the time I felt only bewilderment. I think now that she must have realised Chris would have to learn the Brick House sooner or later, and he might as well start right away.

I had to go into the living room. I had to know how Chris would take my grandfather. Would he, as I hoped, be angry and perhaps even speak out? Or would he, meekly, only be embarrassed?

"Wilf wasn't much good, even as a young man," Grandfather Connor was trumpeting. "Nobody but a simpleton would've taken up a homestead in a place like that. Anybody could've told him that land's no use for a thing except hay."

Was he going to remind us again how well he had done in the hardware business? Nobody had ever given him a hand, he used to tell me. I am sure he believed that this was true. Perhaps even was true.

"If the boy takes after his father, it's a poor lookout for him," my grandfather continued.

I felt the old rage of helplessness. But as for Chris—he gave no sign of feeling anything. He was sitting on the big wing-backed sofa that

curled into the bay window like a black and giant seashell. He began
to talk to me, quite easily, just as though he had not heard a word my
grandfather was saying.

This method proved to be the one Chris always used in any dealings with my grandfather. When the bludgeoning words came, which
was often, Chris never seemed, like myself, to be holding back with a
terrible strained force for fear of letting go and speaking out and having the known world unimaginably fall to pieces. He would not argue
or defend himself, but he did not apologise, either. He simply appeared to be absent, elsewhere. Fortunately there was very little need
for response, for when Grandfather Connor pointed out your short-
comings, you were not expected to reply.

But this aspect of Chris was one which I noticed only vaguely at the
time. What won me was that he would talk to me and wisecrack as
though I were his same age. He was—although I didn't know the
phrase then—a respecter of persons.

On the rare evenings when my parents went out, Chris would
come over to mind me. These were the best times, for often when he
was supposed to be doing his homework, he would make fantastic
objects for my amusement, or his own—pipecleaners twisted into the
shape of wildly prancing midget men, or an old set of Christmas-tree
lights fixed onto a puppet theatre with a red velvet curtain that really
pulled. He had skill in making miniature things of all kinds. Once for
my birthday he gave me a leather saddle no bigger than a matchbox,
which he had sewn himself, complete in every detail, stirrups and
horn, with the criss-cross lines that were the brand name of his ranch,
he said, explaining it was a reference to his own name.

"Can I go to Shallow Creek sometime?" I asked one evening.

"Sure. Some summer holidays, maybe. I've got a sister about your
age. The others are all grownup."

I did not want to hear. His sisters—for Chris was the only boy—
did not exist for me, not even as photographs, because I did not want
them to exist. I wanted him to belong only here. Shallow Creek existed, though, no longer filled with ice mountains in my mind but as
some beckoning country beyond all ordinary considerations.

"Tell me what it's like there, Chris."

"My gosh, Vanessa, I've told you before, about a thousand times."

"You never told me what your house is like."

"Didn't I? Oh well—it's made out of trees grown right there beside the lake."

"Made out of trees? Gee. Really?"

I could see it. The trees were still growing, and the leaves were firmly and greenly on them. The branches had been coaxed into formations of towers and high-up nests where you could look out and see for a hundred miles or more.

"That lake, you know," Chris said. "It's more like an inland sea. It goes on for ever and ever amen, before there were any human beings at all, that lake was full of water monsters. All different kinds of dinosaurs. Then they all died off. Nobody knows for sure why. Imagine them—all those huge creatures, with necks like snakes and some of them had hackles on their heads, like a rooster's comb only very tough, like hard leather. Some guys from Winnipeg came up a few years back, there, and dug up dinosaur bones, and they found footprints in the rocks."

"Footprints in the *rocks*?"

"The rocks were mud, see, when the dinosaurs went trampling through, but after trillions of years the mud turned into stone and there were these mighty footprints with the claws still showing. Amazing, eh?"

I could only nod, fascinated and horrified. Imagine going swimming in those waters. What if one of the creatures had lived on?

"Tell me about the horses," I said.

"Oh, them. Well, we've got these two riding horses. Duchess and Firefly. I raised them, and you should see them. Really sleek, know what I mean? I bet I could make racers out of them."

He missed the horses, I thought with selfish satisfaction, more than he missed his family. I could visualise the pair, one sorrel and one black, swifting through all the meadows of summer.

"When can I go, Chris?"

"Well, we'll have to see. After I get through high school, I won't be at Shallow Creek much."

"Why not?"

"Because," Chris said, "what I am going to be is an engineer, civil engineer. You ever seen a really big bridge, Vanessa? Well, I haven't either, but I've seen pictures. You take the Golden Gate Bridge in San Francisco, now. Terrifically high—all those thin ribs of steel, joined together to go across this very wide stretch of water. It doesn't seem possible, but it's there. That's what engineers do. Imagine doing something like that, eh?"

I could not imagine it. It was beyond me.

"Where will you go?" I asked. I did not want to think of his going anywhere.

"Winnipeg, to college," he said with assurance.

The Depression did not get better, as everyone had been saying it would. It got worse, and so did the drought. That part of the prairies where we lived was never dustbowl country. The farms around Manawaka never had a total crop failure, and afterwards, when the drought was over, people used to remark on the fact proudly, as though it had been due to some virtue or special status, like the Children of Israel being afflicted by Jehovah but never in real danger of annihilation. But although Manawaka never knew the worst, what it knew was bad enough. Or so I learned later. At the time I saw none of it. For me, the Depression and drought were external and abstract, malevolent gods whose names I secretly learned although they were concealed from me, and whose evil I sensed only superstitiously, knowing they threatened us but not how or why. What I really saw was only what went on in our family.

"He's done quite well all through, despite everything," my mother said. She sighed, and I knew she was talking about Chris.

"I know," my father said. "We've been over all this before, Beth. But quite good just isn't good enough. Even supposing he managed to get a scholarship, which isn't likely, it's only tuition and books. What about room and board? Who's going to pay for that? Your father?"

"I see I shouldn't have brought up the subject at all," my mother said in an aloof voice.

"I'm sorry," my father said impatiently. "But you know, yourself, he's the only one who might possibly—"

"I can't bring myself to ask Father about it, Ewen. I simply cannot do it."

"There wouldn't be much point in asking," my father said, "when the answer is a foregone conclusion. He feels he's done his share, and actually, you know, Beth, he has, too. Three years, after all. He may not have done it gracefully, but he's done it."

We were sitting in the living room, and it was evening. My father was slouched in the grey armchair that was always his. My mother was slenderly straight-backed in the blue chair in which nobody else ever sat. I was sitting on the footstool, beige needlepoint with mathematical roses, to which I had staked my own claim. This seating arrangement was obscurely satisfactory to me, perhaps because predictable, like the three bears. I was pretending to be colouring into a scribbler on my knee, and from time to time my lethargic purple crayon added a feather to an outlandish swan. To speak would be to invite dismissal. But their words forced questions in my head.

"Chris isn't going away, is he?"

My mother swooped, shocked at her own neglect.

"My heavens—are you still up, Vanessa? What am I thinking of?"

"Where is Chris going?"

"We're not sure yet," my mother evaded, chivvying me up the stairs. "We'll see."

He would not go, I thought. Something would happen, miraculously, to prevent him. He would remain, with his long loping walk and half-slanted grey eyes and his talk that never excluded me. He would stay right here. And soon, because I desperately wanted to, and because every day mercifully made me older, quite soon I would be able to reply with such a lightning burst of knowingness that it would astound him, when he spoke of the space or was it some black sky that never ended anywhere beyond this earth. Then I would not be innerly belittled for being unable to figure out what he would best like to hear. At that good and imagined time, I would not any longer be limited. I would not any longer be young.

I was nine when Chris left Manawaka. The day before he was due to go, I knocked on the door of his room in the Brick House.

"Come in," Chris said. "I'm packing. Do you know how to fold socks, Vanessa?"

"Sure. Of course."

"Well, get folding on that bunch there, then."

I had come to say goodbye, but I did not want to say it yet. I got to work on the socks. I did not intend to speak about the matter of college, but the knowledge that I must not speak about it made me uneasy. I was afraid I would blurt out a reference to it in my anxiety not to. My mother had said, "He's taken it amazingly well—he doesn't even mention it, so we mustn't either."

"Tomorrow night you'll be in Shallow Creek," I ventured.

"Yeh." He did not look up. He went on stuffing clothes and books into his suitcase.

"I bet you'll be glad to see the horses, eh?" I wanted him to say he didn't care about the horses any more and that he would rather stay here.

"It'll be good to see them again," Chris said. "Mind handing over those socks now, Vanessa? I think I can just squash them in at the side here. Thanks. Hey, look at that, will you? Everything's in. Am I an expert packer or am I an expert packer?"

I sat on his suitcase for him so it would close, and then he tied a piece of rope around it because the lock wouldn't lock.

"Ever thought what it would be like to be a traveller, Vanessa?" he asked.

I thought of Richard Halliburton, taking an elephant over the Alps and swimming illicitly in the Taj Mahal lily pool by moonlight.

"It would be keen," I said, because this was the word Chris used to describe the best possible. "That's what I'm going to do someday."

He did not say, as for a moment I feared he might, that girls could not be travellers.

"Why not?" he said. "Sure you will, if you really want to. I got this theory, see, that anybody can do anything at all, anything, if they really set their minds to it. But you have to have this total concentration. You have to focus on it with your whole mental powers, and not let it slip away by forgetting to hold it in your mind. If you hold it in your mind, like, then it's real, see? You take most people, now. They can't concentrate worth a darn."

"Do you think I can?" I enquired eagerly, believing that this was what he was talking about.

"What?" he said. "Oh—sure. Sure I think you can. Naturally."

Chris did not write after he left Manawaka. About a month later we had a letter from his mother. He was not at Shallow Creek. He had not gone back. He had got off the northbound train at the first stop after Manawaka, cashed in his ticket, and thumbed a lift with a truck to Winnipeg. He had written to his mother from there, but had given no address. She had not heard from him since. My mother read Aunt

Tess's letter aloud to my father. She was too upset to care whether I was listening or not.

"I can't think what possessed him, Ewen. He never seemed irresponsible. What if something should happen to him? What if he's broke? What do you think we should do?"

"What can we do? He's nearly eighteen. What he does is his business. Simmer down, Beth, and let's decide what we're going to tell your father."

"Oh, Lord," my mother said. "There's that to consider, of course."

I went out without either of them noticing. I walked to the hill at the edge of the town, and down into the valley where the scrub oak and poplar grew almost to the banks of the Wachakwa River. I found the oak where we had gone last autumn, in a gang, to smoke cigarettes made of dried leaves and pieces of newspaper. I climbed to the lowest branch and stayed there for a while.

I was not consciously thinking about Chris. I was not thinking of anything. But when at last I cried, I felt relieved afterwards and could go home again.

Chris departed from my mind, after that, with quickness that was due to the other things that happened. My Aunt Edna, who was a secretary in Winnipeg, returned to Manawaka to live because the insurance company cut down on staff and she could not find another job. I was intensely excited and jubilant about her return, and could not see why my mother seemed the opposite, even though she was as fond of Aunt Edna as I was. Then my brother Roderick was born, and that same year Grandmother Connor died. The strangeness, the unbelievability, of both these events took up all of me.

When I was eleven, almost two years after Chris had left, he came back without warning. I came home from school and found him sitting in our living room. I could not accept that I had nearly forgotten him until this instant. Now that he was present, and real again, I felt I had betrayed him by not thinking of him more.

He was wearing a navy-blue serge suit. I was old enough now to notice that it was a cheap one and had been worn a considerable time. Otherwise, he looked the same, the same smile, the same knife-boned face with no flesh to speak of, the same unresting eyes.

"How come you're here?" I cried. "Where have you been, Chris?"

"I'm a traveller," he said. "Remember?"

He was a traveller all right. One meaning of the word *traveller* in our part of the world, was a travelling salesman. Chris was selling vacuum cleaners. That evening he brought out his line and showed us. He went through his spiel for our benefit, so we could hear how it sounded.

"Now look, Beth," he said, turning the appliance on and speaking loudly above its moaning roar, "see how it brightens up this old rug of yours? Keen, eh?"

"Wonderful," my mother laughed. "Only we can't afford one."

"Oh well—" Chris said quickly, "I'm not trying to sell one to you. I'm only showing you. Listen, I've only been in this job a month, but I figure this is really a going thing. I mean, it's obvious, isn't it? You take all those old wire carpet-beaters of yours, Beth. You could kill yourself over them and your carpet isn't going to look one-tenth as good as it does with this."

"Look, I don't want to seem—" my father put in, "but, hell, they're not exactly a new invention, and we're not the only ones who can't afford—"

"This is a pretty big outfit, you know?" Chris insisted. "Listen, I don't plan to stay, Ewen. But a guy could work at it for a year or so, and save—right? Lots of guys work their way through university like that."

I needed to say something really penetrating, something that would show him I knew the passionate truth of his conviction.

"I bet—" I said, "I bet you'll sell a thousand, Chris."

Two years ago, this statement would have seemed self-evident, unquestionable. Yet now, when I had spoken, I knew that I did not believe it.

The next time Chris visited Manawaka, he was selling magazines. He had the statistics worked out. If every sixth person in town would get a subscription to *Country Guide*, he could make a hundred dollars in a month. We didn't learn how he got on. He didn't stay in Manawaka a full month. When he turned up again, it was winter. Aunt Edna phoned.

"Nessa? Listen, kiddo, tell your mother she's to come down if it's humanly possible. Chris is here, and Father's having fits."

So in five minutes we were scurrying through the snow, my mother and I, with our overshoes not even properly done up and our feet getting wet. We need not have worried. By the time we reached the Brick House, Grandfather Connor had retired to the basement, where he sat in the rocking chair beside the furnace, making occasional black pronouncements like a subterranean oracle. These loud utterances made my mother and aunt wince, but Chris didn't seem to notice any more than he ever had. He was engrossed in telling us about the mechanism he was holding. It had a cranker handle like an old-fashioned sewing machine.

"You attach the ball of wool here, see? Then you set this little switch here, and adjust this lever, and you're away to the races. Neat, eh?"

It was a knitting machine. Chris showed us the finished products. The men's socks he had made were coarse wool, one pair in grey heather and another in maroon. I was impressed.

"Gee—can I do it, Chris?"

"Sure. Look, you just grab hold of the handle right here."

"Where did you get it?" my mother asked.

"I've rented it. The way I figure it, Beth, I can sell these things at about half the price you'd pay in a store, and they're better quality."

"Who are you going to sell them to?" Aunt Edna enquired.

"You take all these guys who do outside work—they need heavy socks all year round, not just in winter. I think this thing could be quite a gold mine."

"Before I forget," my mother said, "how's your mother and the family keeping?"

"They're okay," Chris said in a restrained voice. "They're not short of hands, if that's what you mean, Beth. My sisters have their husbands there."

Then he grinned, casting away the previous moment, and dug into his suitcase.

"Hey, I haven't shown you—these are for you, Vanessa, and this pair is for Roddie."

My socks were cherry-coloured. The very small ones for my brother were turquoise.

Chris only stayed until after dinner, and then he went away again.

After my father died, the whole order of life was torn. Nothing was known or predictable any longer. For months I lived almost entirely within myself, so when my mother told me one day that Chris couldn't find any work at all because there were no jobs and so he had gone back to Shallow Creek to stay, it made scarcely any impression on me. But that summer, my mother decided I ought to go away for a holiday. She hoped it might take my mind off my father's death. What, if anything, was going to take her mind off his death, she did not say.

"Would you like to go to Shallow Creek for a week or so?" she asked me. "I could write to Chris's mother."

Then I remembered, all in a torrent, the way I had imagined it once, when he used to tell me about it—the house fashioned of living trees, the lake like a sea where monsters had dwelt, the grass that shone like green wavering light while the horses flew in the splendour of their pride.

"Yes," I said. "Write to her."

The railway did not go through Shallow Creek, but Chris met me at Challoner's Crossing. He looked different, not only thinner, but— what was it? Then I saw that it was the fact that his face and neck were tanned red-brown, and he was wearing denims, farm pants, and a blue plaid shirt open at the neck. I liked him like this. Perhaps the change was not so much in him as in myself, now that I was thirteen. He looked masculine in a way I had not been aware of, before.

"C'mon kid," he said. "The limousine's over here."

It was a wagon and two horses, which was what I had expected, but the nature of each was not what I had expected. The wagon was a long and clumsy one, made of heavy planking, and the horses were both plough horses, thick in the legs, and badly matched as a team. The mare was short and stout, matronly. The gelding was very tall and gaunt, and he limped.

"Allow me to introduce you," Chris said. "Floss—Trooper—this is Vanessa."

He did not mention the other horses, Duchess and Firefly, and neither did I, not all the fortnight I was there. I guess I had known for some years now, without realising it, that the pair had only ever existed in some other dimension.

Shallow Creek wasn't a town. It was merely a name on a map. There was a grade school a few miles away, but that was all. They had to go to Challoner's Crossing for their groceries. We reached the farm, and Chris steered me through the crowd of aimless cows and wolfish dogs in the yard, while I flinched with panic.

It was perfectly true that the house was made out of trees. It was a fair-sized but elderly shack, made out of poplar poles and chinked with mud. There was an upstairs, which was not so usual around here, with three bedrooms, one of which I was to share with Chris's sister, Jeannie, who was slightly younger than I, a pallid-eyed girl who was either too shy to talk or who had nothing to say. I never discovered which, because I was so reticent with her myself, wanting to push her away, not to recognise her, and at the same time experiencing a shocked remorse at my own unacceptable feelings.

Aunt Tess, Chris's mother, was severe in manner and yet wanting to be kind, worrying over it, making tentative overtures which were either ignored or repelled by her older daughters and their monosyllabic husbands. Youngsters swam in and out of the house like shoals of nameless fishes. I could not see how so many people could live here, under one roof, but then I learned they didn't. The married daughters had their own dwelling places, nearby, but some kind of communal life was maintained. They wrangled endlessly but they never left one another alone, not even for a day.

Chris took no part at all, none. When he spoke, it was usually to the children, and they would often follow him around the yard or to the barn, not pestering but just trailing along in clusters of three or four. He never told them to go away. I liked him for this, but it bothered me, too. I wished he would return his sisters' bickering for once, or tell them to clear out, or even yell at one of the kids. But he never did. He closed himself off from squabbling voices just as he used to do with Grandfather Connor's spearing words.

The house had no screens on the doors or windows, and at meal times the flies were so numerous you could hardly see the food for the iridescent-winged blue-black bodies squirming all over it. Nobody noticed my squeamishness except Chris, and he was the only one from whom I really wanted to conceal it.

"Fan with your hand," he murmured.

"It's okay," I said quickly.

For the first time in all the years we had known each other, we could not look the other in the eye. Around the table, the children stabbed and snivelled, until Chris's oldest sister, driven frantic, shrieked, *Shut up shut up shut up*. Chris began asking me about Manawaka then, as though nothing were going on around him.

They were due to begin haying, and Chris announced that he was going to camp out in the bluff near the hayfields. To save himself the long drive in the wagon each morning, he explained, but I felt this wasn't the real reason.

"Can I go, too?" I begged. I could not bear the thought of living in the house with all the others who were not known to me, and Chris not here.

"Well, I don't know—"

"Please. Please, Chris. I won't be any trouble, I promise."

Finally he agreed. We drove out in the big hayrack, its slatted sides rattling, its old wheels jolting metallically. The road was narrow and dirt, and around it the low bushes grew, wild rose and blueberry and wolf willow with silver leaves. Sometimes we would come to a bluff of pale-leaved poplar trees, and once a red-winged blackbird flew up out of the branches and into the hot dusty blue of the sky.

Then we were there. The hayfields lay beside the lake. It was my first view of the water which had spawned saurian giants so long ago. Chris drove the hayrack through the fields of high coarse grass and on down almost to the lake's edge, where there was no shore but only the green rushes like floating meadows in which the water birds nested. Beyond the undulating reeds the open lake stretched, deep, green-grey, out and out, beyond sight.

No human word could be applied. The lake was not lonely or un-tamed. These words relate to people, and there was nothing of people here. There was no feeling about the place. It existed in some world in which man was not yet born. I looked at the grey reaches of it and felt threatened. It was like the view of God which I had held since my father's death. Distant, indestructible, totally indifferent.

Chris had jumped down off the hayrack.

"We're not going to camp *here*, are we?" I asked and pleaded.

"No. I just want to let the horses drink. We'll camp up there in the bluff."

I looked. "It's still pretty close to the lake, isn't it?"

"Don't worry," Chris said, laughing. "You won't get your feet wet."

"I didn't mean that."

Chris looked at me.

"I know you didn't," he said. "But let's learn to be a little tougher, and not let on, eh? It's necessary."

Chris worked through the hours of sun, while I lay on the half-formed stack of hay and looked up at the sky. The blue air trembled and spun with the heat haze, and the hay on which I was lying held the scents of grass and dust and wild mint.

In the evening, Chris took the horses to the lake again, and then he drove the hayrack to the edge of the bluff and we spread out our blankets underneath it. He made a fire and we had coffee and a tin of stew, and then we went to bed. We did not wash, and we slept in our clothes. It was only when I was curled up uncomfortably with the itching blanket around me that I felt a sense of unfamiliarity at being here, with Chris only three feet away, a self-consciousness I would not have felt even the year before. I do not think he felt this sexual strangeness. If he wanted me not to be a child—and he did—it was not with the wish that I would be a woman. It was something else.

"Are you asleep, Vanessa?" he asked.

"No. I think I'm lying on a tree root."

"Well, shift yourself, then," he said. "Listen, kid, I never said anything before, because I didn't really know what to say, but—you know how I felt about your dad dying, and that, don't you?"

"Yes," I said chokingly. "It's okay. I know."

"I used to talk with Ewen sometimes. He didn't see what I was driving at, mostly, but he'd always listen, you know? You don't find many guys like that."

We were both silent for a while.

"Look," Chris said finally. "Ever noticed how much brighter the stars are when you're completely away from any houses? Even the lamps up at the farm, there, make enough of a glow to keep you from seeing properly like you can out here. What do they make you think about, Vanessa?"

"Well—"

"I guess most people don't give them much thought at all, except maybe to say—*very pretty*—or like that. But the point is, they aren't like that. The stars and planets, in themselves, are just not like that, not *pretty*, for heaven's sake. They're gigantic—some of them burning—imagine those worlds tearing through space and made of pure fire. Or the ones that are absolutely dead—just rock or ice and no warmth in them. There must be some, though, that have living creatures. You wonder what *they* could look like, and what they feel. We won't ever get to know. But somebody will know, someday. I really believe that. Do you ever think about this kind of thing at all?"

He was twenty-one. The distance between us was still too great. For years I had wanted to be older so I might talk with him, but now I felt unready.

"Sometimes," I said, hesitantly, making it sound like *Never*.

"People usually say there must be a God," Chris went on, "because otherwise how did the universe get here? But that's ridiculous. If the stars and planets go on to infinity, they could have existed forever, for no reason at all. Maybe they weren't ever created. Look—what's the alternative? To believe in a God who is brutal. What else could He be? You've only got to look anywhere around you. It would be an insult to Him to believe in a God like that. Most people don't like talking about this kind of thing—it embarrasses them, you know? Or else they're not interested. I don't mind. I can always think about things myself. You don't actually need anyone to talk to. But about God, though—if there's a war, like it looks there will be, would people claim that was planned? What kind of a God would pull a trick like that? And yet, you know, plenty of guys would think it was a godsend, and who's to say they're wrong? It would be a job, and you'd get around and see places."

He paused, as though waiting for me to say something. When I did not, he resumed.

"Ewen told me about the last war, once. He hardly ever talked about it, but this once he told me about seeing the horses in the mud, actually going under, you know? And the way their eyes looked when they realised they weren't going to get out. Ever seen horses' eyes when they're afraid, I mean really berserk with fear, like in a bushfire? Ewen said a guy tended to concentrate on the horses because he didn't dare think what was happening to the men. Including himself. Do you ever listen to the news at all, Vanessa?"

"I—"

I could only feel how foolish I must sound, still unable to reply as I would have wanted, comprehendingly. I felt I had failed myself utterly. I could not speak even the things I knew. As for the other things, the things I did not know, I resented Chris's facing me with them. I took refuge in pretending to be asleep, and after a while Chris stopped talking.

Chris left Shallow Creek some months after the war began, and joined the Army. After his basic training he was sent to England. We did not hear from him until about a year later, when a letter arrived for me.

"Vanessa—what's wrong?" my mother asked.

"Nothing."

"Don't fib," she said firmly. "What did Chris say in his letter, honey?"

"Oh—not much."

She gave me a curious look and then she went away. She would never have demanded to see the letter. I did not show it to her and she did not ask about it again.

Six months later my mother heard from Aunt Tess. Chris had been sent home from England and discharged from the Army because of a mental breakdown. He was now in the provincial mental hospital and they did not know how long he would have to remain there. He had been violent, before, but now he was not violent. He was, the doctors had told his mother, passive.

Violent. I could not associate the word with Chris, who had been so much the reverse. I could not bear to consider what anguish must have catapulted him into that even greater anguish. But the way he was now seemed almost worse. How might he be? Sitting quite still, wearing the hospital's grey dressing-gown, the animation gone from his face?

My mother cared about him a great deal, but her immediate thought was not for him.

"When I think of you, going up to Shallow Creek that time," she said, "and going out camping with him, and what might have happened—"

I, also, was thinking of what might have happened. But we were not thinking of the same thing. For the first time I recognised, at least a little, the dimensions of his need to talk that night. He must have understood perfectly well how impossible it would be, with a thirteen-year-old. But there was no one else. All his life's choices had grown narrower and narrower. He had been forced to return to the alien lake of home, and when finally he saw a means of getting away, it could only be into a turmoil which appalled him and which he dreaded even more than he knew. I had listened to his words, but I had not really heard them, not until now. It would not have made much difference to what happened, but I wished it were not too late to let him know.

Once when I was on holiday from college, my mother got me to help her clean out the attic. We sifted through boxes full of junk, old clothes, schoolbooks, bric-a-brac that once had been treasures. In one of the boxes I found the miniature saddle that Chris had made for me a long time ago.

"Have you heard anything recently?" I asked, ashamed that I had not asked sooner.

She glanced up at me. "Just the same. It's always the same. They don't think there will be much improvement."

Then she turned away.

"He always used to seem so—hopeful. Even when there was really nothing to be hopeful about. That's what I find so strange. He *seemed* hopeful, didn't you think?"

"Maybe it wasn't hope," I said.

"How do you mean?"

I wasn't certain myself. I was thinking of all the schemes he'd had, the ones that couldn't possibly have worked, the unreal solutions to which he'd clung because there were no others, the brave and useless strokes of fantasy against a depression that was both the world's and his own.

"I don't know," I said. "I just think things were always more difficult for him than he let on, that's all. Remember that letter?"

"Yes."

"Well—what it said was that they could force his body to march and even to kill, but what they didn't know was that he'd fooled them. He didn't live inside it any more."

"Oh Vanessa—" my mother said. "You must have suspected right then."

"Yes, but—"

I could not go on, could not say that the letter seemed only the final heartbreaking extension of that way he'd always had of distancing himself from the absolute unbearability of battle.

I picked up the tiny saddle and turned it over in my hand.

"Look. His brand, the name of his ranch. The Criss-Cross."

"What ranch?" my mother said, bewildered.

"The one where he kept his racing horses. Duchess and Firefly."

Some words came into my head, a single line from a poem I had once heard. I knew it referred to a lover who did not want the morning to come, but to me it had another meaning, a different relevance.

Slowly, slowly, horses of the night—

The night must move like this for him, slowly, all through the days and nights. I could not know whether the land he journeyed through was inhabited by terrors, the old monster-kings of the lake, or whether he had discovered at last a way for himself to make the necessary dream perpetual.

I put the saddle away once more, gently and ruthlessly, back into the cardboard box.

NOTES

bluff	copse; clump of trees standing on the prairie
Jehovah	name for God in the Old Testament; alteration of the Hebrew name *Yaweh*
Manawaka	Margaret Laurence's name for the fictional town in most of her writing, based on Neepawa, Laurence's small hometown northwest of Winnipeg
Richard Halliburton	(1900–1939) American adventurer and writer of romantic travel books and articles; he disappeared at sea
Slowly, slowly, horses of the night—	an allusion to elegy XIII of *The Art of Love* by the Roman classical author Ovid; the speaker in the original quotation states that night is beautiful and should linger

RESPONDING PERSONALLY

3. What is your final impression of Chris? Jot down some of the emotions you feel at the conclusion of your reading. What in particular about Chris has caused you to feel those emotions?

4. Have you ever known a person—perhaps even yourself—who occasionally seems to slip away into another "space," into a world of her or his own? Describe this person and suggest, if you are able, a reason why she or he would behave this way.

RESPONDING CRITICALLY/ANALYTICALLY

5. With a partner, identify and explore the several conflicts that Chris experiences during the course of the story. Comment on the effect that each has on Chris's increasing inability to deal with the ongoing realities of his life:
   a) Chris's conflicts with his immediate physical and societal environment, including his poverty and consequent lack of opportunity, as well as the Depression and his failure to recognize its impact on his potential for livelihood
   b) Chris's manner of dealing with his personal conflicts, most noticeably with Grandfather Connor but also with the other adults of both the Brick House as well as the Shallow Creek communities
   c) Chris's internal conflicts as he finds himself increasingly unable to cope with the harsh realities of the world

   What do Chris's struggles suggest not only about him but also about human nature in general? Find one passage that you feel most completely articulates Chris's final understanding of the impending destruction of his soul. Share your passage with the class.

6. In a small group, explore the allusions the writer enlists in her telling of the story:
   - "the Children of Israel being afflicted by Jehovah"
   - "Richard Halliburton, taking an elephant over the Alps"
   - "Grandfather Connor ... making occasional black pronouncements like a subterranean oracle."
   a) Share your understanding of the origin of each allusion.
   b) In what way does each allusion contribute to the developing sense of Chris as the outsider, the exile?
   c) What purpose is served in using allusions that relate to the distant past?

   Share your observations in whole-class discussion.

7. Vanessa plays several roles in the story, as the narrative "eyes" through which Chris is observed, as his confidante, and as his foil. With a partner, explore each role.
   a) What is the writer's advantage of selecting a naïve six-year-old to be the narrator? What is she able to offer that an adult narrator could not?
      - What is the added advantage of making the narrator grow older over time? What does this do to her narrator's perspective?
      - At which point(s) in the story is there a difference between what the narrator relates and what the reader perceives?

b) Why has Chris, a relatively mature 15-year-old when he first arrives, turned to a child of 6 for companionship? What purpose does she serve in his life that an adult does not? Ultimately, is she able to adequately fulfill the role that he seems so urgently to need? Explain.

c) Using a T-chart, contrast the emotional development of Vanessa and of Chris. For each "stage" of the story—when Vanessa is 6, then 9, 11, 13, and finally in college—identify a passage from the story that captures Vanessa's ability to understand with the vision of her age the complexity of Chris's struggles. In the column opposite, identify a passage that relates Chris's method of coping with his struggles. What generalization can be drawn regarding the *pattern* of behaviours that appears?

SELF-ASSESSMENT

Do you find the process of T-charting helpful in identifying contrasts? Is there another organizational process, perhaps a different kind of graphic organizer, that you might find more useful in fulfilling a task like the one you just did? If so, share that process with your classmates.

RESPONDING CREATIVELY

8. Design a visual representation, perhaps a collage, that depicts the two "faces" of Chris: one, the outer face that he displays in public; and the second, the more private, inward-looking face with which he must confront his "horses of the night." Determine beforehand whether the structure of your representation will be bipolar or progressive.

PROBLEM SOLVING OR DECISION MAKING

9. Is it our responsibility to help others? To what degree? Due in large part to the immaturity of her years, Vanessa is unable to help Chris overcome the turbulence that is his life. Yet she understands intuitively that he needs "something" to ease his growing despair. What obligation does she have to her friendship with Chris? Are you satisfied with her treatment of Chris? Could she have helped him more? Should she have? How?

Ideals, Dreams, and Obsessions

Ideals, like mountains, are best at a distance.
— *Ellen Glasgow*

Dreams are true while they last, and do we not live in dreams?
— *Alfred, Lord Tennyson*

Though this be madness, yet there be method in't.
— *William Shakespeare*

The four selections in this unit focus on the motivations, aspirations, or irrational drives of their protagonists. Each main character has an ideal, a dream, or an obsession that creates conflict for that person and others.

Caribbean writer John Wickham's "The Light on the Sea" is about a man who visits his elderly former teacher, whose ideal of painting has fallen by the wayside over time. There is a sense of pathos in this story; just as the teacher has lost his ideals and his art, the narrator has lost (in a way) a person who was a significant adult influence in his early life.

"Janus" is a strange but modern piece by American Ann Beattie about a real estate agent and her dreamy attitudes toward a mysterious bowl she uses as a prop to sell houses. The central image of the bowl symbolizes the unrealized world that epitomizes the woman's inner life and her decision about a past relationship.

Obsession is clearly the subject of the last two stories. In "Metonymy, or The Husband's Revenge," a jealous, insecure husband is driven to a desperate act in order to end an extra-marital affair. This story by Brazilian author Rachel de Queiróz cleverly employs the literary device of metonymy to create suspense and to help the reader understand finally why the distraught husband commits his crime.

Obsessions may not only destroy others but can destroy the obsessed person as well. The latter is made clear in Charlotte Perkins

Gilman's "The Yellow Wallpaper," an early feminist tale about a re-pressed woman who cannot stop seeing things in the wallpaper of her bedroom.

This unit reveals the psychology and inner lives of four focal char-acters. As readers, we are drawn into their private worlds to learn about the nature of—and the fine lines among—ideals, dreams, and obsessions.

John Wickham
The Light on the Sea

PRE-READING

1. Identify a "teacher"—either at school or from life in general—who has had a significant impact on your life. Why does this individual stand out? Have you recently spoken to this person? Have you ever thanked this person? What might you say to her or him now?

2. Contrast between "light" and "dark" serves as a theme throughout much of literature. Why is that? What is it about these two conditions that writers seem to find so useful?

Two elderly women were sitting in the room with their backs to the sea when I stepped through the front door. They were sitting at opposite ends of the room, which was large enough, but looked even larger because it was so sparsely furnished: three or four chairs in dully grey upholstery and a table or two, but no flowers on them and no pictures on the walls. I said, "Good Morning," and they looked in my direction, blinking but not speaking. I guessed that they could not make me out with my figure silhouetted against the bright light of the doorway and they must have been a trifle alarmed at my sudden appearance. I stepped further into the room and then they spoke, both of them together and both of them pleasantly, as if they were glad to see me, although they had never seen me before.

I asked whether there was a Mr. Farley in the house and they both shook their heads and looked as if they were sorry for my sake that there was no Mr. Farley to offer me. Then one of them said that, perhaps if I went downstairs, someone might be able to tell me, because the truth was that they didn't really know the names of all the guests. Both of them brightened up at this and one of them got out of her chair to show me where the staircase was. I told her that she needn't have bothered, but she came with me all the same, anxious to help.

At the bottom of the stairs, an old man, gaunt, bony-faced, with thin white hair, was sitting at a small table which was covered with a check tablecloth frayed at the edges. A small yellow plastic bowl was before him and he was staring at its contents with an expression of disgust amounting to revulsion. With a silver teaspoon, he began to stir an egg yolk which had separated from its accompanying white, and he let the yellow viscous liquid drip off the spoon back into the bowl and emitted a series of heavy, forlorn sighs. He was quite unaware of my presence and paid not the slightest attention to me. Opposite the table, a door opened on a kitchen, and as I pushed my head inside the room, a woman in a blue apron looked up from what she was doing and I asked her whether she had a Mr. Farley living there. She wiped her hands in her apron and told me that she would go to let him know that he had a visitor.

The white-haired old man at the table was still sighing and stirring the yellow mess in his bowl while I waited. Another woman, whom I had not seen before, came out of the kitchen and stopped by the old man's table and asked him, solicitously, I thought, whether there was something wrong with his egg. The question irritated him and it was clear that his irritation puzzled the woman. There was nothing wrong with the egg, so far as she could see. And, indeed, from where I stood, the egg, as an egg, seemed perfectly good. But what the woman could not understand was that the old man's disgust had nothing to do with the egg, as an egg.

"Oh, my God," he half-muttered, half-whispered. "Look at this." He rapped the plastic bowl with his spoon and then tilted it as if he would empty it of its yellow contents. "But look at this, couldn't you ...?" But words failed him, and with something like a mixture of resolve and resignation, he plunged the spoon into the bowl and raised it to his mouth. But his hand was trembling and the spoon, when it reached his mouth, was empty. And still the woman was watching him, concerned and, it seemed to me, anxious to help, could not understand what was wrong.

Mr. Farley came forward to see me. He was wearing a scarlet dressing gown and deep red carpet slippers, and he smiled broadly when I moved out of the light of the doorway and he was able to see me. I had taken some fruit for him, a hand of bananas, a pawpaw and a shaddock, and when he took the bag from me, he smiled even more.

He sat in a chair beside the bed and motioned me to make myself comfortable on the bed.

"I am so glad to see you," he said.

I told him that I had been wondering how he was getting on. I had heard only a few days before that he had gone into the home.

"I am as well as an old man can be," he said, and grinned broadly.

I had known Mr. Farley ever since I was a child; he had taught me in my first class at the elementary school and I was fond of him in a pitying sort of way. He was not a good teacher of small boys: he could not keep them in order and did not really try to, and I used to feel sorry for him when the boys teased him by asking silly questions which he took seriously and to which he always tried to give considered replies. I never understood how he could not see through the questions. He never lost his temper and I used often to be angry with him, because he didn't seem to see how ineffectual he was.

It did not surprise me that Mr. Farley never succeeded in his career, never became talked about but always remained a kind of butt, outside the swim of things, a harmless figure of fun. Until one evening, at his invitation, some of us who had already graduated from his class, went to his house to look at his pictures.

He lived near our school in an old house set back from the main road to town and behind what seemed to us a thick forest of trees—breadfruit, sugar apple, hog plum, soursop. The possibilities of such a house and such a forest were enormous to us, and Mr. Farley immediately went up in our estimation.

That afternoon we sat around a room full of dark mahogany furniture—what-not, an old sideboard with a lion's head carved on its back panel and an assortment of rocking chairs. An old oil lamp stood on the sideboard. The room smelt of dust and mildew, but it was cosy. Mr. Farley gave us lemonade and sweet biscuits, and when we had finished eating, he brought some of his pictures for us to look at: water colours and a few oils and some sketches in ink.

I did not like the sketches and remember thinking that they were childish; the outlines were weak. But the water colours were like Mr. Farley himself, muted and shy. Some of them were of the sea, which he made look like an inland lake of quiet dappled water. He took us into a dark cellar under the house where hundreds of canvases were stacked carelessly on the floor around the walls. It was too dark to see them very clearly, but many of them looked as if they consisted only of shapes randomly arranged. In a way, they were frightening, like creatures bred of the dark shadows of the cellar and never seeing the light. I was glad to escape back up the stairs and into the relative brightness of the parlour.

Now, as I sat on his bed, I thought: how like a child he is! He was babbling with excitement at being visited, like a child given a present. I asked him if he remembered the afternoon when a group of us visited him and he showed us his pictures, but he had forgotten. It was too long ago, I suppose. And I asked him if he still painted and what had become of the pictures. Had he sold them?

"Oh," he said, "I left them behind at the house when I came here." He dismissed them as if they were part of something he had discarded and would prefer to forget; there had been so many pictures in the cellar, hundreds of them, and I was tempted to ask him to let me go and look at them. Who could tell? There might be a masterpiece lurking in that gloom, waiting to be discovered. I could not believe that he had left them behind, just like that. I asked him what he planned to do with them.

"Nothing," he said. "They weren't any good." He did not sound regretful but, rather, relieved, as if he had rid himself of a great, unbearable burden at last.

I asked him, "Did you think when you were young, that you would ever come to a life without painting—a canvas and brushes and paints?"

He answered simply. "It was always only a hope, never a conviction. But hope sustained until ..." His voice trailed away as if he no longer remembered the sequence of events.

The bare, poorly-furnished room was without books or pictures, uncurtained, with only a single window through which the morning sunlight poured bright and undiluted, a spare bed across the width of the room in a far corner, no flowers and the ceiling stained brown with water from the floor above. Yet, while I was saddened by the bare and loveless look of the room and the lonely figures of the other members of the household, the two old women in the living room and the gaunt man in the kitchen sighing over his egg as he recalled better days, as I thought about the terrible loneliness to which old age had sentenced them, I had to accept that Mr. Farley was cheerful. Perhaps it was because he had never had a family; he had always been lonely and this state was not new to him. He was smiling when he began to speak.

"All those pictures," he said, "and, believe me, I never felt as if I had ever finished a single one of them. There was always something to be done to complete every one. So I never had any satisfaction. I would put it aside, meaning to go back and finish it, but I was never able to. Another picture would come to mind and crowd the last effort and failure out, and I never looked at that last one again; I was never able to remember what I wanted to paint."

"It must have been like a nightmare," I said, "or a series of nightmares, never being able to recall the vision that started the picture."

"Frustration it was, and confusion. That's what it was. I am glad for this peace now." And he looked around the room, the bare and cheerless room, like a child welcoming an open space where he could run and romp.

"How do you spend your time now?" It was, all of a sudden, important for me to know.

"I look at the sea," he said, so solemnly that I thought he was making fun of the question. But he wasn't.

"You know," he said, "I never knew what light was. All those years behind those trees in that dark house. The light used to trickle through the leaves, only trickle, never flow. Mark you, I used to like it, I didn't complain. I thought the gloom was pleasant. But I never knew what light was."

"And how did you come to find out, to see the light?" I asked.

"I was lucky. When my sister died, there was no one to look after things; I had never learned to cook. My friend told me about this place. The moment I saw it, with the light on the sea, I knew that I was not going back to that dark house."

"So you just upped and left your pictures and the furniture and everything?"

"It was easy and, besides, what was there to wait for? They look after me very well here, the girls are kind and they leave me alone, which is a kindness. Do you understand how being left alone can be a real kindness? And, now, look, you have come to see me. You never came to the old house."

"Don't you feel lonely here?"

"No, not lonelier than I have always felt. I have never been what you could call gregarious. And I never get tired of looking at the sea."

He laughed, and I said goodbye and told him that I would come soon to see him again.

"When you came," he said, "I was going to have a shower." He clutched his dressing gown with a dramatic gesture, like Gielgud clutching his toga in Julius Caesar. I never thought that he had such panache in his make-up. As he spoke, he was making his way to the bathroom, and by the time I reached the door and looked back to see what he was doing, he had already put me out of his mind.

When I stepped outside the front door, I found one of the old ladies pulling dry yellow leaves off a hibiscus bush in the untidy garden. She was so intent on what she was doing that she did not even reply when I said goodbye.

The bright Sunday morning glistened and the sea sparkled vast and wide and flat to the horizon.

NOTES

Gielgud	John Gielgud (1904–2000), famous English stage and movie actor, known best for his Shakespeare work
gregarious	very sociable
Julius Caesar	name of the proud protagonist of Shakespeare's play
shaddock	tart-tasting, pear-shaped fruit

RESPONDING PERSONALLY

3. There is a sense of melancholy in the picture the writer has painted of Mr. Farley. Yet there is a sense of contentment as well. Respond to your own emotions and to what you are made to feel by the writer's "picture."

4. Recall and write about a personal experience when you learned of a new "way" of life and chose not to go back to an old. Have you ever regretted your decision?

RESPONDING CRITICALLY/ANALYTICALLY

5. The concluding sentence of the narrator's initial statement describing his perception of Mr. Farley as a teacher is that "he didn't seem to see how ineffectual he was."

a) What is the irony of that statement?
b) What is significant about the fact that some "who had already graduated" were among the group who went to view the teacher's pictures?
c) What is significant about the fact that the narrator remembers the visit while Mr. Farley himself "had forgotten" about it?

What is the reality of Mr. Farley's effectiveness as a teacher?

6. With a partner, discuss Mr. Farley's purpose in inviting "the group" to look at his pictures.
   a) In what way were the "sketches" the narrator did not like actually representative of Mr. Farley's manner?
   b) What was his purpose in leaving his "hundreds" of pictures behind?
   c) What is the likelihood of there having been "a masterpiece lurking in that gloom, waiting to be discovered"? Share your thoughts in whole-class discussion.

7. Examine the contrast between the "dark" of Mr. Farley's house, and in particular his cellar, with the "light" that now pervades his life.
   a) In what way(s) has the light of his present life overcome the dark of his past?
   b) In reference to his paintings, Mr. Farley answers, "I left them behind." What else has he left behind?
   c) Why has the writer chosen to end the story with the particular sentence that he does?

8. The residents of the home appear to be preoccupied with elements of their immediate present surroundings and situations. In what way does Mr. Farley's sharing of his story shed new light on the way that these people might be understood?

9. An atmosphere of "sparseness" runs through the entire story.
   a) What things has the writer done to create this atmosphere?
   b) In what way does the resulting mood serve the theme of the story?

RESPONDING CREATIVELY

10. Acting as the set designer for either the stage or film adaptation of this story, design the set for either the parlour in Mr. Farley's house or the room in which he now lives. The design can be completed in either two- or three-dimensional representation.

PEER ASSESSMENT

Upon completion, select two representations—one of each scene—that when juxtaposed depict most clearly the contrasting metaphors of light and dark. What is it about these two representations that serves the contrast so well?

PROBLEM SOLVING OR DECISION MAKING

11. "But what the woman could not understand was that the old man's disgust had nothing to do with the egg, as an egg." Is there a generalization that can be drawn about how people might go about trying to better understand one another, to break through formed assumptions that may or may not be accurate? Discuss this question with others in a group. Share your group's findings with the rest of the class.

Ann Beattie
Janus

PRE-READING

1. Research the background of the Roman god Janus. Speculate on some of the possible subjects that a story with this title might include. Share your thoughts with a partner.

2. In writing, relate the "story" behind an object of significance in your life.
   - how long you have had it
   - how you came by it
   - what gives it the meaning it holds for you
   - how you look after it

   Can you ever see, in time, this object assuming an even greater significance in what it represents to you? Speculate about how that may be.

The bowl was perfect. Perhaps it was not what you'd select if you faced a shelf of bowls, and not the sort of thing that would inevitably attract a lot of attention at a crafts fair, yet it had real presence. It was as predictably admired as a mutt who has no reason to suspect he might be funny. Just such a dog, in fact, was often brought out (and in) along with the bowl.

Andrea was a real-estate agent, and when she thought that some prospective buyers might be dog lovers, she would drop off her dog at the same time she placed the bowl in the house that was up for sale.

She would put a dish of water in the kitchen for Mondo, take his squeaking plastic frog out of her purse and drop it on the floor. He would pounce delightedly, just as he did every day at home, batting around his favorite toy. The bowl usually sat on a coffee table, though recently she had displayed it on top of a pine blanket chest and on a lacquered table. It was once placed on a cherry table beneath a Bonnard still life, where it held its own.

Everyone who has purchased a house or who has wanted to see a house must be familiar with some of the tricks used to convince a buyer that the house is quite special: a fire in the fireplace in early evening; jonquils in a pitcher on the kitchen counter, where no one ordinarily has space to put flowers; perhaps the slight aroma of spring, made by a single drop of scent vaporizing from a lamp bulb.

The wonderful thing about the bowl, Andrea thought, was that it was both subtle and noticeable—a paradox of a bowl. Its glaze was the color of cream and seemed to glow no matter what light it was placed in. There were a few bits of color in it—tiny geometric flashes—and some of these were tinged with flecks of silver. They were as mysterious as cells seen under a microscope; it was difficult not to study them, because they shimmered, flashing for a split second, and then resumed their shape. Something about the colors and their random placement suggested motion. People who liked country furniture always commented on the bowl, but then it turned out that people who felt comfortable with Biedermeier loved it just as much. But the bowl was not at all ostentatious, or even so noticeable that anyone would suspect that it had been put in place deliberately. They might notice the height of the ceiling on first entering a room, and only when their eye moved down from that, or away from the refraction of sunlight on a pale wall, would they see the bowl. Then they would go immediately to it and comment. Yet they always faltered when they tried to say something. Perhaps it was because they were in the house for a serious reason, not to notice some object.

Once Andrea got a call from a woman who had not put in an offer on a house she had shown her. That bowl, she said—would it be possible to find out where the owners had bought that beautiful bowl? Andrea pretended that she did not know what the woman was referring to. A bowl, somewhere in the house? Oh, on a table under the window. Yes, she would ask, of course. She let a couple of days pass, then called back to say that the bowl had been a present and the people did not know where it had been purchased.

When the bowl was not being taken from house to house, it sat on Andrea's coffee table at home. She didn't keep it carefully wrapped (although she transported it that way, in a box); she kept it on the table, because she liked to see it. It was large enough so that it didn't seem fragile or particularly vulnerable if anyone sideswiped the table or Mondo blundered into it at play. She had asked her husband to please not drop his house key in it. It was meant to be empty.

When her husband first noticed the bowl, he had peered into it and smiled briefly. He always urged her to buy things she liked. In recent years, both of them had acquired many things to make up for all the lean years when they were graduate students, but now that they had been comfortable for quite a while, the pleasure of new possessions dwindled. Her husband had pronounced the bowl "pretty," and he had turned away without picking it up to examine it. He had no more interest in the bowl than she had in his new Leica.

She was sure that the bowl brought her luck. Bids were often put in on houses where she had displayed the bowl. Sometimes the owners, who were always asked to be away or to step outside when the house was being shown, didn't even know that the bowl had been in their house. Once—she could not imagine how—she left it behind, and then she was so afraid that something might have happened to it that she rushed back to the house and sighed with relief when the woman owner opened the door. The bowl, Andrea explained—she had purchased a bowl and set it on the chest for safekeeping while she toured the house with the prospective buyers, and she ... She felt like rushing past the frowning woman and seizing her bowl. The owner stepped aside, and it was only when Andrea ran to the chest that the lady glanced at her a little strangely. In the few seconds before Andrea picked up the bowl, she realized that the owner must have just seen that it had been perfectly placed, that the sunlight struck the bluer part of it. Her pitcher had been moved to the far side of the chest, and the bowl predominated. All the way home, Andrea wondered how she could have left the bowl behind. It was like leaving a friend at an outing—just walking off. Sometimes there were stories in the paper about families forgetting a child somewhere and driving to the next city. Andrea had only gone a mile down the road before she remembered.

In time, she dreamed of the bowl. Twice, in a waking dream—early in the morning, between sleep and a last nap before rising—she had a clear vision of it. It came into sharp focus and startled her for a moment—the same bowl she looked at every day.

She had a very profitable year selling real estate. Word spread, and she had more clients than she felt comfortable with. She had the foolish thought that if only the bowl were an animate object she could thank it. There were times when she wanted to talk to her husband about the bowl. He was a stockbroker, and sometimes told people that he was fortunate to be married to a woman who had such a fine aesthetic sense and yet could also function in the real world. They were a lot alike, really—they had agreed on that. They were both quiet people—reflective, slow to make value judgments, but almost intractable once they had come to a conclusion. They both liked details, but while ironies attracted her, he was more impatient and dismissive when matters became many-sided or unclear. They both knew this, and it was the kind of thing they could talk about when they were alone in the car together, coming home from a party or after a weekend with friends. But she never talked to him about the bowl. When they were at dinner, exchanging their news of the day, or while they lay in bed at night listening to the stereo and murmuring sleepy disconnections, she was often tempted to come right out and say that she thought that the bowl in the living room, the cream-colored bowl, was responsible for her success. But she didn't say it. She couldn't begin to explain it. Sometimes in the morning, she would look at him and feel guilty that she had such a constant secret.

Could it be that she had some deeper connection with the bowl—a relationship of some kind? She corrected her thinking: how could she imagine such a thing, when she was a human being and it was a bowl? It was ridiculous. Just think of how people lived together and loved each other ... But was that always so clear, always a relationship? She was confused by these thoughts, but they remained in her mind. There was something within her now, something real, that she never talked about.

The bowl was a mystery, even to her. It was frustrating, because her involvement with the bowl contained a steady sense of unrequited good fortune; it would have been easier to respond if some sort of demand were made in return. But that only happened in fairy tales. The bowl was just a bowl. She did not believe that for one second. What she believed was that it was something she loved.

In the past, she had sometimes talked to her husband about a new property she was about to buy or sell—confiding some clever strategy she had devised to persuade owners who seemed ready to sell. Now she stopped doing that, for all her strategies involved the bowl. She became more deliberate with the bowl, and more possessive. She put it in houses only when no one was there, and removed it when she left the home. Instead of just moving a pitcher or a dish, she would remove all the other objects from a table. She had to force herself to handle them carefully, because she didn't really care about them. She just wanted them out of sight.

She wondered how the situation would end. As with a lover, there was no exact scenario of how matters would come to a close. Anxiety became the operative force. It would be irrelevant if the lover rushed into someone else's arms, or wrote her a note and departed to another city. The horror was the possibility of the disappearance. That was what mattered.

She would get up at night and look at the bowl. It never occurred to her that she might break it. She washed and dried it without anxiety, and she moved it often, from coffee table to mahogany corner table or wherever, without fearing an accident. It was clear that she would not be the one who would do anything to the bowl. The bowl was only handled by her, set safely on one surface or another; it was not very likely that anyone would break it. A bowl was a poor conductor of electricity: it would not be hit by lightning. Yet the idea of damage persisted. She did not think beyond that—to what her life would be without the bowl. She only continued to fear that some accident would happen. Why not, in a world where people set plants where they did not belong, so that visitors touring a house would be fooled into thinking that dark corners got sunlight—a world full of tricks?

She had first seen the bowl several years earlier, at a crafts fair she had visited half in secret, with her lover. He had urged her to buy the bowl. She didn't *need* any more things, she told him. But she had been drawn to the bowl, and they had lingered near it. Then she went on to the next booth, and he came up behind her, tapping the rim against her shoulder as she ran her fingers over a wood carving. "You're still insisting that I buy that?" she said. "No," he said. "I bought it for you." He had bought her other things before this—things she liked more, at first—the child's ebony-and-turquoise ring that fitted her little finger; the wooden box, long and thin, beautifully dovetailed, that she used to hold paper clips; the soft gray sweater with a pouch pocket. It was his idea that when he could not be there to hold her hand she could hold her own—clasp her hands inside the lone pocket that stretched across the front. But in time she became more attached to the bowl than to any of his other presents. She tried to talk herself out of it. She owned other things that were more striking or valuable. It wasn't an object whose beauty jumped out at you; a lot of people must have passed it by before the two of them saw it that day.

Her lover had said that she was always too slow to know what she really loved. Why continue with her life the way it was? Why be two-faced, he asked her. He had made the first move toward her. When she would not decide in his favor, would not change her life and come to him, he asked her what made her think she could have it both ways. And then he made the last move and left. It was a decision meant to break her will, to shatter her intransigent ideas about honoring previous commitments.

Time passed. Alone in the living room at night, she often looked at the bowl sitting on the table, still and safe, unilluminated. In its way, it was perfect: the world cut in half, deep and smoothly empty. Near the rim, even in dim light, the eye moved toward one small flash of blue, a vanishing point on the horizon.

Notes

Biedermeier	reference to Viennese period furniture
Bonnard still life	picture by French painter who painted domestic scenes
dovetail	a way to join wood planks by interlocking finger-like projections
intractable	stubborn
Janus	ancient Roman god with two faces who looked into both the past and the future
jonquils	small, fragrant yellow flowers
ostentatious	showy

RESPONDING PERSONALLY

3. What questions are you left with as you finish reading the story? Share your questions with a partner. Explore possible answers.

4. At the conclusion of the story, do you feel the same sense of incompletion, the lack of resolution with the story, that Andrea seems to be left with in her life? Share your thoughts first in writing, then with a partner.

RESPONDING CRITICALLY/ANALYTICALLY

5. At what point in the story do you first sense that the bowl signifies a loss of some sort in Andrea's life? What has the writer done to create that impression? What is the loss?

6. There is an impression that arises at several points in the story that the bowl also represents for Andrea a vague sense of control over situations that are in reality out of her direct control. Locate an example of this in the story and share it with your classmates. In light of the end of the story, why is this sense of control important to Andrea?

7. The initial reference to Andrea's infidelity is made almost in passing, as though the extramarital relationship is nothing out of the ordinary. How has the writer prepared the reader to be accepting of the fact of Andrea's marital dishonesty? Identify at least two specific passages in the story that help to do this.

8. The story begins with the statement "The bowl was perfect." The statement changes in the closing paragraph to "In its way, it was perfect." Trace the progression of plot events that have modified an *absolute* statement into one that is less so.
   a) How are the two statements as the story's "bookend" statements aptly suited to the metaphor of the title?
   b) How is the story's final paragraph an apt metaphor for this chapter in Andrea's life?
   c) How is the bowl representative of the Janus allusion? What understanding does the allusion provide to the "paradox" of Andrea's life?

RESPONDING CREATIVELY

9. Virtually *no* physical description of any character is provided during the telling of the story. Let your imagination work. How do you picture Andrea?
   - Age? Body type? Hair/eyes/skin colour and tone?
   - Her hands? Her nails? Her style of hair?
   - How does she dress—for work? at home?
   - How does she carry herself—move? sit? stand?

Support your description of her with inferences and elements of the story, as much as you are able.

Peer Assessment

It is very likely that most descriptions of Andrea will be quite similar. Is there one description, however, that is dissimilar from most of the others, yet fitting with the character as she has been presented? What has this description been able to capture that most others in the class did not?

10. Compose the personal journal entry that Andrea writes following her lover's departure. Indicate by the content of the entry whether her "will" has indeed been broken, whether her "intransigent ideas about honoring previous commitments" have been shattered.

Problem Solving or Decision Making

11. The story deals with marital infidelity in a very matter-of-fact way. While such may be a fact of life, is it right that the subject be presented nonjudgementally in a school text, even a grade 12 text? Should a story like this be dropped from study? Present your argument in a small group.

Translated by William L. Grossman

Rachel de Queiróz
Metonymy, or The Husband's Revenge

PRE-READING

1. What is metonymy? Share your understanding of the term with the class.
2. Recall a time when you were so upset or frustrated with a situation in your life that you reacted in a way well beyond the bounds of reason. Did your actions solve the original problem? Did you feel any better after reacting? Why or why not?

Metonymy. I learned the word in 1930 and shall never forget it. I had just published my first novel. A literary critic had scolded me because my hero went out into the night "chest unbuttoned."

"What deplorable nonsense!" wrote this eminently sensible gentleman. "Why does she not say what she means? Obviously, it was his shirt that was unbuttoned, not his chest."

I accepted his rebuke with humility, indeed with shame. But my illustrious Latin professor, Dr. Matos Peixoto, came to my rescue. He said that what I had written was perfectly correct; that I had used a respectable figure of speech known as metonymy; and that this figure consisted in the use of one word for another word associated with it—for example, a word representing a cause instead of the effect, or representing the container when the content is intended. The classic instance, he told me, is "the sparkling cup"; in reality, not the cup but the wine in it is sparkling.

The professor and I wrote a letter, which was published in the newspaper where the review had appeared. It put my unjust critic in his place. I hope he learned a lesson. I know I did. Ever since, I have been using metonymy—my only bond with classical rhetoric.

Moreover, I have devoted some thought to it, and I have concluded that metonymy may be more than a figure of speech. There is, I believe, such a thing as practical or applied metonymy. Let me give a crude example, drawn from my own experience. A certain lady of my acquaintance suddenly moved out of the boardinghouse where she had been living for years and became a mortal enemy of the woman who owned it. I asked her why. We both knew that the woman was a kindly soul; she had given my friend injections when she needed them, had often loaned her a hot water bottle, and had always waited on her when she had her little heart attacks. My friend replied:

"It's the telephone in the hall. I hate her for it. Half the time when I answered it, the call was a hoax or joke of some sort."

"But the owner of the boardinghouse didn't perpetrate these hoaxes. She wasn't responsible for them."

"No. But whose telephone was it?"

I know another case of applied metonymy, a more disastrous one for it involved a crime. It happened in a city of the interior, which I shall not name for fear that someone may recognize the parties and revive the scandal. I shall narrate the crime but conceal the criminal.

Well, in this city of the interior there lived a man. He was not old but he was spent, which is worse than being old. In his youth he had suffered from beriberi. His legs were weak, his chest was tired and asthmatic, his skin was yellowish, and his eyes were rheumy. He was, however, a man of property; he owned the house in which he lived and the one next to it, in which he had set up a grocery store. Therefore, although so unattractive personally, he was able to find himself a wife. In all justice to him, he did not tempt fate by marrying a beauty. Instead, he married a poor, emaciated girl who worked in a men's clothing factory. By her face one would have thought that she had consumption. So our friend felt safe. He did not foresee the effects of good nutrition and a healthful life on a woman's appearance. The girl no longer spent eight hours a day at a sewing table. She was the mistress of her house. She ate well: fresh meat, cucumber salad, pork fat with beans and manioc mush, all kinds of sweets, and oranges, which her husband bought by the gross for his customers. The effects were like magic. Her body filled out, especially in the best places. She even seemed to grow taller. And her face—what a change! I may have forgotten to mention that her features, in themselves, were good to begin with. Moreover, money enabled her to embellish her natural advantages with art; she began to wear make-up, to wave her hair, and to dress well.

Lovely, attractive, she now found her sickly, prematurely old husband a burden and a bore. Each evening, as soon as the store was closed, he dined, mostly on milk (he could not stomach meat), took his newspaper, and rested on his chaise longue until time to go to bed. He did not care for movies or for soccer or for radio. He did not even show much interest in love. Just a sort of tepid, tasteless cohabitation.

And then Fate intervened: it produced a sergeant.

Granted, it was unjust for a young wife, after being reconditioned at her husband's expense, to employ her charms against the aforesaid husband. Unjust; but, then, this world thrives on injustice, doesn't it? The sergeant—I shall not say whether he was in the Army, the Air Force, the Marines, or the Fusiliers, for I still mean to conceal the identities of the parties—the sergeant was muscular, young, ingratiating, with a manly, commanding voice and a healthy spring in his walk. He looked gloriously martial in his high-buttoned uniform.

One day, when the lady was in charge of the counter (while her husband lunched), the sergeant came in. Exactly what happened and what did not happen, is hard to say. It seems that the sergeant asked for a pack of cigarettes. Then he wanted a little vermouth. Finally he asked permission to listen to the sports broadcast on the radio next to the counter. Maybe it was just an excuse to remain there awhile. In any case, the girl said it would be all right. It is hard to refuse a favour to a sergeant, especially a sergeant like this one. It appears that the sergeant asked nothing more that day. At most, he and the girl exchanged expressive glances and a few agreeable words, murmured so softly that the customers, always alert for something to gossip about, could not hear them.

Three times more the husband lunched while his wife chatted with the sergeant in the store. The flirtation progressed. Then the husband fell ill with a grippe, and the two others went far beyond flirtation. How and where they met, no one was able to discover. The important thing is that they were lovers and that they loved with a forbidden love, like Tristan and Isolde or Paolo and Francesca.

Then Fate, which does not like illicit love and generally punishes those who engage in it, transferred the sergeant to another part of the country.

It is said that only those who love can really know the pain of separation. The girl cried so much that her eyes grew red and swollen. She lost her appetite. Beneath her rouge could be seen the consumptive complexion of earlier times. And these symptoms aroused her husband's suspicion, although, curiously, he had never suspected anything when the love affair was flourishing and everything was wine and roses.

He began to observe her carefully. He scrutinized her in her periods of silence. He listened to her sighs and to the things she murmured in her sleep. He snooped around and found a postcard and a book, both with a man's name in the same handwriting. He found the insignia of the sergeant's regiment and concluded that the object of his wife's murmurs, sighs, and silences was not only a man but a soldier. Finally he made the supreme discovery: that they had indeed betrayed him. For he discovered the love letters, bearing airmail stamps, a distant postmark, and the sergeant's name. They left no reasonable doubt.

For five months the poor fellow twisted the poisoned dagger of jealousy inside his own thin, sickly chest. Like a boy who discovers a bird's nest and, hiding nearby, watches the eggs increasing in number every day, so the husband, using a duplicate key to the wood chest where his wife put her valuables, watched the increase in the number of letters concealed there. He had given her the chest during their honeymoon, saying, "Keep your secrets here." And the ungrateful girl had obeyed him.

Every day at the fateful hour of lunch, she replaced her husband at the counter. But he was not interested in eating. He ran to her room, pulled out a drawer in her bureau, removed the chest from under a lot of panties, slips, and such, took the little key out of his pocket, opened the chest, and anxiously read the new letter. If there was no new letter, he reread the one dated August 21st; it was so full of realism that it sounded like dialogue from a French movie. Then he put everything away and hurried to the kitchen, where he swallowed a few spoonfuls of broth and gnawed at a piece of bread. It was almost impossible to swallow with the passion of those two thieves sticking in his throat.

When the poor man's heart had become utterly saturated with jealousy and hatred, he took a revolver and a box of bullets from the counter drawer; they had been left, years before, by a customer as security for a debt which had never been paid. He loaded the revolver.

One bright morning at exactly ten o'clock, when the store was full of customers, he excused himself and went through the doorway that connected the store with his home. In a few seconds the customers heard the noise of a row, a woman's scream, and three shots. On the sidewalk in front of the shopkeeper's house they saw his wife on her knees, still screaming, and him, with the revolver in his trembling hand, trying to raise her. The front door of the house was open. Through it, they saw a man's legs, wearing khaki trousers and boots. He was lying face down, with his head and torso in the parlor not visible from the street.

The husband was the first to speak. Raising his eyes from his wife, he looked at the terror-stricken people and spotted among them his favourite customer. He took a few steps, stood in the doorway, and said:

"You may call the police."

At the police station he explained that he was a deceived husband. The police chief remarked:

"Isn't this a little unusual? Ordinarily you kill your wives. They're weaker than their lovers."

The man was deeply offended.

"No," he protested. "I would be utterly incapable of killing my wife. She is all that I have in the world. She is refined, pretty, and hardworking. She helps me in the store, she understands bookkeeping, she writes the letters to the wholesalers. She is the only person who knows how to prepare my food. Why should I want to kill my wife?"

"I see," said the chief of police. "So you killed her lover."

The man shook his head.

"Wrong again. The sergeant—her lover—was transferred to a place far from here. I discovered the affair only after he had gone. By reading his letters. They tell the whole story. I know one of them by heart, the worst of them...."

The police chief did not understand. He said nothing and waited for the husband to continue, which he presently did:

"Those letters! If they were alive, I would kill them, one by one. They were shameful to read—almost like a book. I thought of taking an airplane trip. I thought of killing some other sergeant here, so that they would all learn a lesson not to fool around with another man's wife. But I was afraid of the rest of the regiment; you know how these military men stick together. Still, I had to do something. Otherwise I would have gone crazy. I couldn't get those letters out of my head. Even on days when none arrived I felt terrible, worse than my wife. I had to put an end to it, didn't I? So today, at last, I did it. I waited till the regular time and, when I saw the wretch appear on the other side of the street, I went into the house, hid behind a door, and lay there waiting for him."

"The lover?" asked the police chief stupidly.

"No, of course not. I told you I didn't kill her lover. It was those letters. The sergeant sent them—but *he* delivered them. Almost every day, there he was at the door, smiling, with the vile envelope in his hand. I pointed the revolver and fired three times. He didn't say a word; he just fell. No, chief it wasn't her lover. It was the mailman."

NOTES

beriberi	serious disease that can lead to heart failure or paralysis
consumption	tuberculosis
grippe	influenza; severe cold with fever
Paolo and Francesca	legendary tragic Italian lovers
Tristan and Isolde	hero and heroine of one of the English world's greatest love stories

RESPONDING PERSONALLY

3. With which character of the story do you most closely identify: the husband, the wife, the sergeant, or the narrator? Why is that? Has the writer manipulated the situation purposely, or is there something in your own lived experience that establishes an empathic understanding between you and that character? Explain.

4. Three times the narrator mentions that "Fate" may or may not be taking an active role in the events as they come to pass. Share your thoughts, in relation to the events of the story or otherwise, on the subject of fate. Do you believe that there are times in your life when fate—or irony or whatever else you may call it—intervenes to take the control of your actions out of your hands? Explain.

RESPONDING CRITICALLY/ANALYTICALLY

5. What purpose is served by the opening dissertation on metonymy and "applied metonymy"? Is it necessary? Could the story have survived without it? Does it add to or detract from the story?

6. With a partner, explore the humour in the story.
   a) Find examples of the use of humour in the opening descriptions of the man and of his wife.
   b) Find examples from the section that speaks of the man's growing jealousy.
   c) Find examples from the final section of the story, at the police station.
   d) The writer uses a variety of strategies in the creation of her humour. Identify as many of her different strategies as you are able. Share these with your classmates.

7. In a small group, examine the role and purpose of the narrator in the story.
   a) Why is the "framing" story told from a first-person perspective? What can she say or do that a third-person narration cannot?
   b) Describe the narrator's "voice." What attribute embedded in the narrator's voice adds to the story's humour? Explain.
   c) Identify several passages selected from different points in the story in which the obvious "I" of the first person is *not* used, yet the narrator's voice emerges. Is there a unity of voice throughout? Explain.
   d) Describe the narrative tone. What is the difference between tone and voice?

8. At which point in the story do you first suspect that some form of "applied metonymy" will be the husband's goal, rather than the more obvious choice of his wife or her lover? What has foreshadowed to you that suspicion? Were you able to correctly anticipate who might be killed instead? Explain why or why not.

RESPONDING CREATIVELY

9. In keeping with the tone of the story and with the voice of the narrator, complete the story in one of two ways:
   a) Bring about some form of resolution between the principal characters that remains in keeping with their motivations as depicted during the story.
   b) Create a closing "bookend" to the opening dissertation of the story. Return to the perspective of the narrator. Bring closure to her explanation of "applied metonymy."

10. With a partner, create a phrase collage using short passages taken from the story. Identify a particular theme of the story—perhaps the narrator's use of non sequitur. Find as many examples of theme-related phrases as you are able, and arrange them onto a single page in collage form.

PROBLEM SOLVING OR DECISION MAKING

11. Certainly, murder cannot be committed to serve justice. But in this instance, has it rightly served some form of poetic justice? Put forward an argument that supports the husband's action in the service of poetic justice. Your argument may be presented tongue-in-cheek. Convince the class with your presentation.

PEER ASSESSMENT

Whose argument best captures the tone of the original story and at the same time most convincingly rationalizes the actions of the husband? What does this presentation do that others do not?

Charlotte Perkins Gilman
The Yellow Wallpaper

PRE-READING

1. In a small group, brainstorm/research the characteristics that make up the genre of literature known as "gothic." Share your group's information with the rest of the class.

2. Tell about a time you strongly believed something but were unable to convince anyone else about. How did you feel? Did you at any point doubt yourself? What happened in the end?

It is very seldom that mere ordinary people like John and myself secure ancestral halls for the summer.

A colonial mansion, a hereditary estate, I would say a haunted house, and reach the height of romantic felicity—but that would be asking too much of fate!

Still I will proudly declare that there is something queer about it.

Else, why should it be let so cheaply? And why have stood so long untenanted?

John laughs at me, of course, but one expects that in marriage.

John is practical in the extreme. He has no patience with faith, an intense horror of superstition, and he scoffs openly at any talk of things not to be felt and seen and put down in figures.

John is a physician, and *perhaps*—(I would not say it to a living soul, of course, but this is dead paper and a great relief to my mind)—*perhaps* that is one reason I do not get well faster.

You see he does not believe I am sick!

And what can one do?

If a physician of high standing, and one's own husband, assures friends and relatives that there is really nothing the matter with one but temporary nervous depression—a slight hysterical tendency— what is one to do?

My brother is also a physician, and also of high standing, and he says the same thing.

So I take phosphates or phosphites—whichever it is, and tonics, and journeys, and air, and exercise, and am absolutely forbidden to "work" until I am well again.

Personally, I disagree with their ideas.

Personally, I believe that congenial work, with excitement and change, would do me good.

But what is one to do?

I did write for a while in spite of them; but it *does* exhaust me a good deal—having to be so sly about it, or else meet with heavy opposition.

I sometimes fancy that in my condition if I had less opposition and more society and stimulus—but John says the very worst thing I can do is to think about my condition, and I confess it always makes me feel bad.

So I will let it alone and talk about the house.

The most beautiful place! It is quite alone, standing well back from the road, quite three miles from the village. It makes me think of English places that you read about, for there are hedges and walls and gates that lock, and lots of separate little houses for the gardeners and people.

There is a *delicious* garden! I never saw such a garden—large and shady, full of box-bordered paths, and lined with long grape-covered arbors with seats under them.

There were greenhouses, too, but they are all broken now.

There was some legal trouble, I believe, something about the heirs and coheirs; anyhow, the place has been empty for years.

That spoils my ghostliness, I am afraid, but I don't care—there is something strange about the house—I can feel it.

I even said so to John one moonlight evening, but he said what I felt was a *draught*, and shut the window.

I get unreasonably angry with John sometimes. I'm sure I never used to be so sensitive. I think it is due to this nervous condition.

But John says if I feel so, I shall neglect proper self-control; so I take pains to control myself—before him, at least, and that makes me very tired.

I don't like our room a bit. I wanted one downstairs that opened on the piazza and had roses all over the window, and such pretty old-fashioned chintz hangings! But John would not hear of it.

He said there was only one window and not room for two beds, and no near room for him if he took another.

He is very careful and loving, and hardly lets me stir without special direction.

I have a schedule prescription for each hour in the day; he takes all care from me, and so I feel basely ungrateful not to value it more.

He said we came here solely on my account, that I was to have perfect rest and all the air I could get. "Your exercise depends on your strength, my dear," said he, "and your food somewhat on your appetite; but air you can absorb all the time." So we took the nursery at the top of the house.

It is a big, airy room, the whole floor nearly, with windows that look all ways, and air and sunshine galore. It was nursery first and then playroom and gymnasium, I should judge; for the windows are barred for little children, and there are rings and things in the walls.

The paint and paper look as if a boys' school had used it. It is stripped off—the paper—in great patches all around the head of my bed, about as far as I can reach, and in a great place on the other side of the room low down. I never saw a worse paper in my life.

One of those sprawling flamboyant patterns committing every artistic sin.

It is dull enough to confuse the eye in following, pronounced enough to constantly irritate and provoke study, and when you follow the lame uncertain curves for a little distance they suddenly commit suicide—plunge off at outrageous angles, destroy themselves in unheard of contradictions.

The color is repellent, almost revolting; a smouldering unclean yellow, strangely faded by the slow-turning sunlight.

It is a dull yet lurid orange in some places, a sickly sulphur tint in others.

No wonder the children hated it! I should hate it myself if I had to live in this room long.

There comes John, and I must put this away,—he hates to have me write a word.

We have been here two weeks, and I haven't felt like writing before, since that first day.

I am sitting by the window now, up in this atrocious nursery, and there is nothing to hinder my writing as much as I please, save lack of strength.

John is away all day, and even some nights when his cases are serious.

I am glad my case is not serious!

But these nervous troubles are dreadfully depressing.

John does not know how much I really suffer. He knows there is *reason* to suffer, and that satisfies him.

Of course it is only nervousness. It does weigh on me so not to do my duty in any way!

I meant to be such a help to John, such a real rest and comfort, and here I am a comparative burden already!

Nobody would believe what an effort it is to do what little I am able—to dress and entertain, and order things.

It is fortunate Mary is so good with the baby. Such a dear baby!

And yet I *cannot* be with him, it makes me so nervous.

I suppose John never was nervous in his life. He laughs at me so about this wallpaper!

At first he meant to repaper the room, but afterwards he said that I was letting it get the better of me, and that nothing was worse for a nervous patient than to give way to such fancies.

He said that after the wallpaper was changed it would be the heavy bedstead, and then the barred windows, and then that gate at the head of the stairs, and so on.

"You know the place is doing you good," he said, "and really, dear, I don't care to renovate the house just for a three months' rental."

"Then do let us go downstairs," I said, "there are such pretty rooms there."

Then he took me in his arms and called me a blessed little goose, and said he would go down to the cellar, if I wished, and have it whitewashed into the bargain.

But he is right enough about the beds and windows and things.

It is an airy and comfortable room as any one need wish, and, of course, I would not be so silly as to make him uncomfortable just for a whim.

I'm really getting quite fond of the big room, all but that horrid paper.

Out of one window I can see the garden, those mysterious deep-shaded arbors, the riotous old-fashioned flowers, and bushes and gnarly trees.

Out of another I get a lovely view of the bay and a little private wharf belonging to the estate. There is a beautiful shaded lane that runs down there from the house. I always fancy I see people walking in these numerous paths and arbors, but John has cautioned me not to give way to fancy in the least. He says that with my imaginative power and habit of story-making, a nervous weakness like mine is sure to lead to all manner of excited fancies, and that I ought to use my will and good sense to check the tendency. So I try.

I think sometimes that if I were only well enough to write a little it would relieve the press of ideas and rest me.

But I find I get pretty tired when I try.

It is so discouraging not to have any advice and companionship about my work. When I get really well, John says we will ask Cousin Henry and Julia down for a long visit; but he says he would as soon put fireworks in my pillowcase as to let me have those stimulating people about now.

I wish I could get well faster.

But I must not think about that. This paper looks to me as if it *knew* what a vicious influence it had!

There is a recurrent spot where the pattern lolls like a broken neck and two bulbous eyes stare at you upside down.

I get positively angry with the impertinence of it and the everlastingness. Up and down and sideways they crawl, and those absurd, unblinking eyes are everywhere. There is one place where two breadths didn't match, and the eyes go all up and down the line, one a little higher than the other.

I never saw so much expression in an inanimate thing before, and we all know how much expression they have! I used to lie awake as a child and get more entertainment and terror out of blank walls and plain furniture than most children could find in a toy-store.

I remember what a kindly wink the knobs of our big, old bureau used to have, and there was one chair that always seemed like a strong friend.

I used to feel that if any of the other things looked too fierce I could always hop into that chair and be safe.

The furniture in this room is no worse than inharmonious, however, for we had to bring it all from downstairs. I suppose when this was used as a playroom they had to take the nursery things out, and no wonder! I never saw such ravages as the children have made here.

The wallpaper, as I said before, is torn off in spots, and it sticketh closer than a brother—they must have had perseverance as well as hatred.

Then the floor is scratched and gouged and splintered, the plaster itself is dug out here and there, and this great heavy bed which is all we found in the room, looks as if it had been through the wars.

But I don't mind it a bit—only the paper.

There comes John's sister. Such a dear girl as she is, and so careful of me! I must not let her find me writing.

She is a perfect and enthusiastic housekeeper, and hopes for no better profession. I verily believe she thinks it is the writing which made me sick!

But I can write when she is out, and see her a long way off from these windows.

There is one that commands the road, a lovely shaded winding road, and one that just looks off over the country. A lovely country, too, full of great elms and velvet meadows.

This wallpaper has a kind of sub-pattern in a different shade, a particularly irritating one, for you can only see it in certain lights, and not clearly then.

But in the places where it isn't faded and where the sun is just so—I can see a strange, provoking, formless sort of figure, that seems to skulk about behind that silly and conspicuous front design.

There's sister on the stairs!

Well, the Fourth of July is over! The people are all gone and I am tired out. John thought it might do me good to see a little company, so we just had mother and Nellie and the children down for a week.

Of course I didn't do a thing. Jennie sees to everything now.

But it tired me all the same.

John says if I don't pick up faster he shall send me to Weir Mitchell in the fall.

But I don't want to go there at all. I had a friend who was in his hands once, and she says he is just like John and my brother, only more so!

Besides, it is such an undertaking to go so far.

I don't feel as if it was worth while to turn my hand over for anything, and I'm getting dreadfully fretful and querulous.

I cry at nothing, and cry most of the time.

Of course I don't when John is here, or anybody else, but when I am alone.

And I am alone a good deal just now. John is kept in town very often by serious cases, and Jennie is good and lets me alone when I want her to.

So I walk a little in the garden or down that lovely lane, sit on the porch under the roses, and lie down up here a good deal.

I'm getting really fond of the room in spite of the wallpaper. Perhaps *because* of the wallpaper.

It dwells in my mind so!

I lie here on this great immovable bed—it is nailed down, I believe—and follow that pattern about by the hour. It is as good as gymnastics, I assure you. I start, we'll say, at the bottom, down in the corner over there where it has not been touched, and I determine for the thousandth time that I *will* follow that pointless pattern to some sort of a conclusion.

I know a little of the principle of design, and I know this thing was not arranged on any laws of radiation, or alternation, or repetition, or symmetry, or anything else that I ever heard of.

It is repeated, of course, by the breadths, but not otherwise.

Looked at in one way each breadth stands alone, the bloated curves and flourishes—a kind of "debased Romanesque" with *delirium tremens*—go waddling up and down in isolated columns of fatuity.

But, on the other hand, they connect diagonally, and the sprawling outlines run off in great slanting waves of optic horror, like a lot of wallowing seaweeds in full chase.

The whole thing goes horizontally, too, at least it seems so, and I exhaust myself in trying to distinguish the order of its going in that direction.

They have used a horizontal breadth for a frieze, and that adds wonderfully to the confusion.

There is one end of the room where it is almost intact, and there, when the crosslights fade and the low sun shines directly upon it, I can almost fancy radiation after all—the interminable grotesques seem to form around a common centre and rush off in headlong plunges of equal distraction.

It makes me tired to follow it. I will take a nap I guess.

I don't know why I should write this.

I don't want to.

I don't feel able.

And I know John would think it absurd. But I *must* say what I feel and think in some way—it is such a relief!

But the effort is getting to be greater than the relief.

Half the time now I am awfully lazy, and lie down ever so much.

John says I mustn't lose my strength, and has me take cod liver oil and lots of tonics and things, to say nothing of ale and wine and rare meat.

Dear John! He loves me very dearly, and hates to have me sick. I tried to have a real earnest reasonable talk with him the other day, and tell him how I wish he would let me go and make a visit to Cousin Henry and Julia.

But he said I wasn't able to go, nor able to stand it after I got there; and I did not make out a very good case for myself, for I was crying before I had finished.

It is getting to be a great effort for me to think straight. Just this nervous weakness I suppose.

And dear John gathered me up in his arms, and just carried me upstairs and laid me on the bed, and sat by me and read to me till it tired my head.

He said I was his darling and his comfort and all he had, and that I must take care of myself for his sake, and keep well.

He says no one but myself can help me out of it, that I must use my will and self-control and not let any silly fancies run away with me.

There's one comfort, the baby is well and happy, and does not have to occupy this nursery with the horrid wallpaper.

If we had not used it, that blessed child would have! What a fortunate escape! Why, I wouldn't have a child of mine, an impressionable little thing, live in such a room for worlds.

I never thought of it before, but it is lucky that John kept me here after all, I can stand it so much easier than a baby, you see.

Of course I never mention it to them any more—I am too wise—but I keep watch of it all the same.

There are things in that paper that nobody knows but me, or ever will.

Behind that outside pattern the dim shapes get clearer every day.

It is always the same shape, only very numerous.

And it is like a woman stooping down and creeping about behind that pattern. I don't like it a bit. I wonder—I begin to think—I wish John would take me away from here!

It is so hard to talk with John about my case, because he is so wise, and because he loves me so.

But I tried it last night.

It was moonlight. The moon shines in all around just as the sun does.

I hate to see it sometimes, it creeps so slowly, and always comes in by one window or another.

John was asleep and I hated to waken him, so I kept still and watched the moonlight on that undulating wallpaper till I felt creepy.

The faint figure behind seemed to shake the pattern, just as if she wanted to get out.

I got up softly and went to feel and see if the paper *did* move, and when I came back John was awake.

"What is it, little girl?" he said. "Don't go walking about like that—you'll get cold."

I thought it was a good time to talk, so I told him that I really was not gaining here, and that I wished he would take me away.

"Why darling!" said he, "our lease will be up in three weeks, and I can't see how to leave before.

"The repairs are not done at home, and I cannot possibly leave town just now. Of course if you were in any danger, I could and would, but you really are better, dear, whether you can see it or not. I am a doctor, dear, and I know. You are gaining flesh and color, your appetite is better, I feel really much easier about you."

"I don't weigh a bit more," said I, "nor as much; and my appetite may be better in the evening when you are here, but it is worse in the morning when you are away!"

"Bless her little heart!" said he with a big hug, "she shall be as sick as she pleases! But now let's improve the shining hours by going to sleep, and talk about it in the morning!"

"And you won't go away?" I asked gloomily.

"Why, how can I, dear? It is only three weeks more and then we will take a nice little trip of a few days while Jennie is getting the house ready. Really, dear, you are better!"

"Better in body perhaps—" I began, and stopped short, for he sat up straight and looked at me with such a stern, reproachful look that I could not say another word.

"My darling," said he, "I beg of you, for my sake and for our child's sake, as well as for your own, that you will never for one instant let that idea enter your mind! There is nothing so dangerous, so fascinating, to a temperament like yours. It is a false and foolish fancy. Can you not trust me as a physician when I tell you so?"

So of course I said no more on that score, and we went to sleep before long. He thought I was asleep first, but I wasn't, and lay there for hours trying to decide whether that front pattern and the back pattern really did move together or separately.

On a pattern like this, by daylight, there is a lack of sequence, a defiance of law, that is a constant irritant to a normal mind.

The color is hideous enough, and unreliable enough, and infuriating enough, but the pattern is torturing.

You think you have mastered it, but just as you get well underway in following, it turns a back-somersault and there you are. It slaps you in the face, knocks you down, and tramples upon you. It is like a bad dream.

The outside pattern is a florid arabesque, reminding one of a fungus. If you can imagine a toadstool in joints, an interminable string to toadstools, budding and sprouting in endless convolutions—why, that is something like it.

That is, sometimes!

There is one marked peculiarity about this paper, a thing nobody seems to notice but myself, and that is that it changes as the light changes.

When the sun shoots in through the east window—I always watch for that first long, straight ray—it changes so quickly that I never can quite believe it.

That is why I watch it always.

By moonlight—the moon shines in all night when there is a moon—I wouldn't know it was the same paper.

At night in any kind of light, in twilight, candle light, lamplight, and worst of all by moonlight, it becomes bars! The outside pattern I mean, and the woman behind it is as plain as can be.

I didn't realize for a long time what the thing was that showed behind, that dim sub-pattern, but now I am quite sure it is a woman.

By daylight she is subdued, quiet. I fancy it is the pattern that keeps her so still. It is so puzzling. It keeps me quiet by the hour.

I lie down ever so much now. John says it is good for me, and to sleep all I can.

Indeed he started the habit by making me lie down for an hour after each meal.

It is a very bad habit I am convinced, for you see I don't sleep.

And that cultivates deceit, for I don't tell them I'm awake—O no!

The fact is I am getting a little afraid of John.

He seems very queer sometimes, and even Jennie has an inexplicable look.

It strikes me occasionally, just as a scientific hypothesis,—that perhaps it is the paper!

I have watched John when he did not know I was looking, and come into the room suddenly on the most innocent excuses, and I've caught him several times *looking at the paper!* And Jennie too. I caught Jennie with her hand on it once.

She didn't know I was in the room, and when I asked her in a quiet, a very quiet voice, with the most restrained manner possible, what she was doing with the paper—she turned around as if she had been caught stealing, and looked quite angry—asked me why I should frighten her so!

Then she said that the paper stained everything it touched, and that she had found yellow smooches on all my clothes and John's, and she wished we would be more careful!

Did not that sound innocent? But I know she was studying that pattern, and I am determined that nobody shall find it out but myself!

Life is very much more exciting now than it used to be. You see I have something more to expect, to look forward to, to watch. I really do eat better, and am more quiet than I was.

John is so pleased to see me improve! He laughed a little the other day, and said I seemed to be flourishing in spite of my wallpaper.

I turned it off with a laugh. I had no intention of telling him it was *because* of the wallpaper—he would make fun of me. He might even want to take me away.

I don't want to leave now until I have found it out. There is a week more, and I think that will be enough.

I'm feeling ever so much better! I don't sleep much at night, for it is so interesting to watch developments; but I sleep a good deal in the daytime.

In the daytime it is tiresome and perplexing.

There are always new shoots on the fungus, and new shades of yellow all over it. I cannot keep count of them, though I have tried conscientiously.

It is the strangest yellow, that wallpaper! It makes me think of all the yellow things I ever saw—not beautiful ones like buttercups, but old foul, bad yellow things.

But there is something else about that paper—the smell! I noticed it the moment we came into the room, but with so much air and sun it was not bad. Now we have had a week of fog and rain, and whether the windows are open or not, the smell is here.

It creeps all over the house.

I find it hovering in the dining-room, skulking in the parlor, hiding in the hall, lying in wait for me on the stairs.

It gets into my hair.

Even when I go to ride, if I turn my head suddenly and surprise it—there is that smell!

Such a peculiar odor, too! I have spent hours in trying to analyze it, to find what it smelled like.

It is not bad—at first, and very gentle, but quite the subtlest, most enduring odor I ever met.

In this damp weather it is awful, I wake up in the night and find it hanging over me.

It used to disturb me at first. I thought seriously of burning the house—to reach the smell.

But now I am used to it. The only thing I can think of that it is like is the *color* of the paper! A yellow smell.

There is a very funny mark on this wall, low down, near the mopboard. A streak that runs round the room. It goes behind every piece of furniture, except the bed, a long, straight, even *smooch*, as if it had been rubbed over and over.

I wonder how it was done and who did it, and what they did it for. Round and round and round—round and round and round—it makes me dizzy!

I really have discovered something at last.

Through watching so much at night, when it changes so, I have finally found out.

The front pattern *does* move—and no wonder! The woman behind shakes it!

Sometimes I think there are a great many women behind, and sometimes only one, and she crawls around fast, and her crawling shakes it all over.

Then in the very bright spots she keeps still, and in the very shady spots she just takes hold of the bars and shakes them hard.

And she is all the time trying to climb through. But nobody could climb through that pattern—it strangles so: I think that is why it has so many heads.

They get through, and then the pattern strangles them off and turns them upside down, and makes their eyes white!

If those heads were covered or taken off it would not be half so bad.

I think that woman gets out in the daytime!

And I'll tell you why—privately—I've seen her!

I can see her out of every one of my windows!

It is the same woman, I know, for she is always creeping, and most women do not creep by daylight.

I see her on that long road under the tree, creeping along, and when a carriage comes she hides under the blackberry vines.

I don't blame her a bit. It must be very humiliating to be caught creeping by daylight.

I always lock the door when I creep by daylight. I can't do it at night, for I know John would suspect something at once.

And John is so queer now, that I don't want to irritate him. I wish he would take another room! Besides, I don't want anybody to get that woman out at night but myself.

I often wonder if I could see her out of all the windows at once.

But, turn as fast as I can, I can only see out of one at one time.

And though I always see her, she *may* be able to creep faster than I can turn!

I have watched her sometimes away off in the open country, creeping as fast as a cloud shadow in a high wind.

If only that top pattern could be gotten off from the under one! I mean to try it, little by little.

I have found out another funny thing, but I shan't tell it this time! It does not do to trust people too much.

There are only two more days to get this paper off, and I believe John is beginning to notice. I don't like the look in his eyes.

And I heard him ask Jennie a lot of professional questions about me. She had a very good report to give.

She said I slept a good deal in the daytime.

John knows I don't sleep very well at night, for all I'm so quiet!

He asked me all sorts of questions, too, and pretended to be very loving and kind.

As if I couldn't see through him!

Still, I don't wonder he acts so, sleeping under this paper for three months.

It only interests me, but I feel sure John and Jennie are secretly affected by it.

Hurrah! This is the last day, but it is enough. John to stay in town over night, and won't be out until this evening.

Jennie wanted to sleep with me—the sly thing! But I told her I should undoubtedly rest better for a night all alone.

That was clever, for really I wasn't alone a bit! As soon as it was moonlight and that poor thing began to crawl and shake the pattern, I got up and ran to help her.

I pulled and she shook, I shook and she pulled, and before morning we had peeled off yards of that paper.

A strip about as high as my head and half around the room.

And then when the sun came and that awful pattern began to laugh at me, I declared I would finish it to-day!

We go away to-morrow, and they are moving all my furniture down again to leave things as they were before.

Jennie looked at the wall in amazement, but I told her merrily that I did it out of pure spite at the vicious thing.

She laughed and said she wouldn't mind doing it herself, but I must not get tired.

How she betrayed herself that time!

But I am here, and no person touches this paper but me—not *alive!*

She tried to get me out of the room—it was too patent! But I said it was so quiet and empty and clean now that I believed I would lie down again and sleep all I could; and not to wake me even for dinner—I would call when I woke.

So now she is gone, and the servants are gone, and the things are gone, and there is nothing left but that great bedstead nailed down, with the canvas mattress we found on it.

We shall sleep downstairs to-night, and take the boat home to-morrow.

I quite enjoy the room, now it is bare again.

How those children did tear about here!

This bedstead is fairly gnawed!

But I must get to work.

I have locked the door and thrown the key down into the front path.

I don't want to go out, and I don't want to have anybody come in, till John comes.

I want to astonish him.

I've got a rope up here that even Jennie did not find. If that woman does get out, and tries to get away, I can tie her.

But I forgot I could not reach far without anything to stand on! This bed will *not* move!

I tried to lift and push it until I was lame, and then I got so angry I bit off a little piece at one corner—but it hurt my teeth.

Then I peeled off all the paper I could reach standing on the floor. It sticks horribly and the pattern just enjoys it! All those strangled heads and bulbous eyes and waddling fungus growths just shriek with derision!

I am getting angry enough to do something desperate. To jump out of the window would be admirable exercise, but the bars are too strong even to try.

Besides I wouldn't do it. Of course not. I know well enough that a step like that is improper and might be misconstrued.

I don't like to *look* out of the windows even—there are so many of those creeping women, and they creep so fast.

I wonder if they all come out of that wallpaper as I did?

But I am securely fastened now by my well-hidden rope—you don't get *me* out in the road there!

I suppose I shall have to get back behind the pattern when it comes night, and that is hard!

It is so pleasant to be out in this great room and creep around as I please!

I don't want to go outside. I won't, even if Jennie asks me to.

For outside you have to creep on the ground, and everything is green instead of yellow.

But here I can creep smoothly on the floor, and my shoulder just fits in that long smooch around the wall, so I cannot lose my way.

Why there's John at the door!

It is no use, young man, you can't open it!

How he does call and pound!

Now he's crying for an axe.

It would be a shame to break down that beautiful door!

"John dear!" said I in the gentlest voice, "the key is down by the front steps, under a plantain leaf!"

That silenced him for a few moments.

Then he said—very quietly indeed, "Open the door, my darling!"

"I can't," said I. "The key is down by the front door under a plantain leaf!"

And then I said it again, several times, very gently and slowly, and said it so often that he had to go and see, and he got it of course, and came in. He stopped short by the door.

"What is the matter?" he cried. "For God's sake, what are you doing?"

I kept on creeping just the same, but I looked at him over my shoulder.

"I've got out at last," said I, "in spite of you and Jennie. And I've pulled off most of the paper, so you can't put me back!"

Now why should that man have fainted? But he did, and right across my path by the wall, so that I had to creep over him every time!

NOTES

arabesque	elaborate and fanciful design of flowers
derision	ridicule
phosphates or phosphites	drinks made of carbonated water flavoured with fruit syrup and phosphoric acid, used in early medicinal treatments
Romanesque	architectural style characterized by thick walls and round arches
tonics	drinks restoring health and vigour

RESPONDING PERSONALLY

3. As readers, we all consciously or subconsciously ask ourselves questions about the text. As you were reading, what was the first question you asked? At what point in the story?

4. Most often with stories narrated in the first person, the reader forms an empathic relationship with the narrator. Such is initially the case in this story. But that changes. At which point in the story did you first begin to feel uncomfortable about the narrator? At which point did you break your emotional association with her, and begin to view her from a "distanced" perspective? What were your thoughts about her by that point in the story?

RESPONDING CRITICALLY/ANALYTICALLY

5. Consider the writer's decision regarding narrative point of view. Why do you think she chose this point of view over other possibilities? Comment on the problem her choice creates for the realism of the story's end.

6. Examine the portrayal of the narrator's husband.
   a) Write a very brief, one-paragraph, encapsulating personality description.
   b) In what way and to what degree is such a characterization necessary in order for this story to arrive at the outcome it does? Could the story achieve its same effect without the presence of such a character? Explain.
   c) Could the same story be written today, in the twenty-first century? Would the characters be as plausible? Comment.

7. There is clear evidence of the narrator's growing paranoia as the story proceeds. Document the development of her paranoid behaviours through the successive journal entries. In each entry, identify
   - who and what she is increasingly mistrustful of, and
   - the degree of abnormal suspicion she feels (use a scale of 1 to 4—let 1 represent what is usual; let 4 stand for a completely delusional state of mind).

   Refer to specific passages from the story for support.

8. Over the course of the story, the narrator and the woman behind the wallpaper move closer and closer together.
   a) At which point in the story did you first begin to consider that the two may be one and the same?
   b) At which point were you first certain? Explain what it was that convinced you.
   c) Did the writer move too slowly from point a) to point b) or was the progression of events reasonably paced and developed? Comment on the writer's technique.

RESPONDING CREATIVELY

9. With a partner, improvise the conversation John and Jennie have just before the final journal entry. In preparation for this task, decide together your responses to the following:
   - What concerns does each have about the narrator's deteriorating condition?
   - What action are they planning to take, both in the short term and the long?
   - What is their greatest fear at the moment?

   Share your improvisation with the class.

PEER ASSESSMENT

How did other group presentations compare with yours?

- Were the personalities of their characters in keeping with the characters in the story?
- Did they recognize the dramatic changes that had taken place in the narrator?
- Was your peers' thinking of a story resolution similar to your own?
- Did anyone perform an improvisation that you felt was more true to the story than was yours? If so, explain.

PROBLEM SOLVING OR DECISION MAKING

10. Why do thoughtful, intelligent readers willingly suspend their rational faculties to engage with irrational story characters involved in irrational actions and situations? What draws us, fascinates us? What, if anything, can we learn from such reading? Respond to these questions with reference to a particular story—print, visual, or oral—that you know.

Charlotte Perkins Gilman
Why I Wrote "The Yellow Wallpaper"

Many and many a reader has asked that. When the story first came out, in the *New England Magazine* about 1891, a Boston physician made protest in *The Transcript*. Such a story ought not to be written, he said; it was enough to drive anyone mad to read it.

Another physician, in Kansas I think, wrote to say that it was the best description of incipient insanity he had ever seen, and—begging my pardon—had I been there?

Now the story of the story is this:

For many years I suffered from a severe and continuous nervous breakdown tending to melancholia—and beyond. During about the third year of this trouble I went, in devout faith and some faint stir of hope, to a noted specialist in nervous diseases, the best known in the country. This wise man put me to bed and applied the rest cure, to which a still-good physique responded so promptly that he concluded there was nothing much the matter with me, and sent me home with solemn advice to "live as domestic a life as far as possible," to "have but two hours' intellectual life a day," and "never to touch pen, brush, or pencil again" as long as I lived. This was in 1887.

I went home and obeyed those directions for some three months, and came so near the borderline of utter mental ruin that I could see over.

Then, using the remnants of intelligence that remained, and helped by a wise friend, I cast the noted specialist's advice to the winds and went to work again—work, the normal life of every human being; work, in which is joy and growth and service, without which one is a pauper and a parasite—ultimately recovering some measure of power.

Being naturally moved to rejoicing by this narrow escape, I wrote "The Yellow Wallpaper," with its embellishments and additions, to carry out the ideal (I never had hallucinations or objections to my mural decorations) and sent a copy to the physician who so nearly drove me mad. He never acknowledged it.

The little book is valued by alienists and as a good specimen of one kind of literature. It has, to my knowledge, saved one woman from a similar fate—so terrifying her family that they let her out into normal activity and she recovered.

But the best result is this. Many years later I was told that the great specialist had admitted to friends of his that he had altered his treatment of neurasthenia since reading "The Yellow Wallpaper."

It was not intended to drive people crazy, but to save people from being driven crazy, and it worked.

NOTES

alienists	psychiatrists who testify in court
neurasthenia	nervous breakdown

Goals, Journeys, and Quests

The heart has its reasons which reason does not know.
— *Blaise Pascal*

The journey is my home.
— *Muriel Rukeyser*

What we seek we do not find—that would be too trim and tidy for so reckless and opulent a thing as life.
— *Susan Glaspell*

Most people have something they wish to find, accomplish, or explore in life. In the following unit's stories, all of the protagonists undertake a journey or quest that is best understood by them alone and shared with the reader.

"Tuesday Siesta," by the Colombian short story master Gabriel García Márquez, is about a journey to another, unknown town in order to complete what psychologists would call "unfinished business." What begins as a secretive private journey, however, becomes very awkwardly public by the story's odd conclusion.

Graham Greene's "The Destructors" is an extended psychology piece fraught with conflicts on many levels. A teenage gang decides to play an elaborate practical joke on Mr. Thomas, a grumpy, elderly neighbour, a joke which requires organization and careful planning.

D.H. Lawrence's "The Rocking-Horse Winner" is a symbolic fantasy about Paul, a young, tormented boy who rides his rocking horse in order to learn the names of race-winning horses to bet on. His manic quest is rooted in a twisted Freudian drive to make his mother happy and to win her withheld love.

"'If I Forget Thee, Oh Earth...'" by Sir Arthur C. Clarke is a science fiction story set in the future about a boy's journey with his father to look at the stars. It is not until the story's ending, though, that we come to understand the goal and quest that are the boy's deeper longings.

The four stories of this unit reveal how focused and purposeful human beings can be. The goals, journeys, and quests that we ultimately seek to fulfill give our lives meaning, hope, and satisfaction.

Translated by J.S. Bernstein

Gabriel García Márquez
Tuesday Siesta

PRE-READING

1. The concept of "siesta" is a phenomenon not common to most of North America. What do you know of siesta: Where is it practised? What actually happens? Why does it take place? Is it really necessary, or is it simply a custom that, in the modern world, has outlived its purpose? What mood does the word immediately lend to the story?

2. If you were to find yourself in a situation where you knew something of importance was terribly wrong but no one would listen to you or believe you, what, if anything, would you do? Explain why.

The train emerged from the quivering tunnel of sandy rocks, began to cross the symmetrical, interminable banana plantations, and the air became humid and they couldn't feel the sea breeze anymore. A stifling blast of smoke came in the car window. On the narrow road parallel to the railway there were oxcarts loaded with green bunches of bananas. Beyond the road, in uncultivated spaces set at odd intervals there were offices with electric fans, red-brick buildings, and residences with chairs and little white tables on the terraces among dusty palm trees and rosebushes. It was eleven in the morning, and the heat had not yet begun.

"You'd better close the window," the woman said. "Your hair will get full of soot."

The girl tried to, but the shade wouldn't move because of the rust.

They were the only passengers in the lone third-class car. Since the smoke of the locomotive kept coming through the window, the girl left her seat and put down the only things they had with them: a plastic sack with some things to eat and a bouquet of flowers wrapped in newspaper. She sat on the opposite seat, away from the window, facing her mother. They were both in severe and poor mourning clothes.

The girl was twelve years old, and it was the first time she'd ever been on a train. The woman seemed too old to be her mother, because of the blue veins on her eyelids and her small, soft, and shapeless body, in a dress cut like a cassock. She was riding with her spinal column braced firmly against the back of the seat, and held a peeling patent-leather handbag in her lap with both hands. She bore the conscientious serenity of someone accustomed to poverty.

By twelve the heat had begun. The train stopped for ten minutes to take on water at a station where there was no town. Outside, in the mysterious silence of the plantations, the shadows seemed clean. But the still air inside the car smelled like untanned leather. The train did not pick up speed. It stopped at two identical towns with wooden houses painted bright colors. The woman's head nodded and she sank into sleep. The girl took off her shoes. Then she went to the washroom to put the bouquet of flowers in some water.

When she came back to her seat, her mother was waiting to eat. She gave her a piece of cheese, half a cornmeal pancake, and a cookie, and took an equal portion out of the plastic sack for herself. While they ate, the train crossed an iron bridge very slowly and passed a town just like the ones before, except that in this one there was a crowd in the plaza. A band was playing a lively tune under the oppressive sun. At the other side of town the plantations ended in a plain which was cracked from the drought.

The woman stopped eating.

"Put on your shoes," she said.

The girl looked outside. She saw nothing but the deserted plain, where the train began to pick up speed again, but she put the last piece of cookie into the sack and quickly put on her shoes. The woman gave her a comb.

"Comb your hair," she said.

The train whistle began to blow while the girl was combing her hair. The woman dried the sweat from her neck and wiped the oil from her face with her fingers. When the girl stopped combing, the train was passing the outlying houses of a town larger but sadder than the earlier ones.

"If you feel like doing anything, do it now," said the woman. "Later, don't take a drink anywhere even if you're dying of thirst. Above all, no crying."

The girl nodded her head. A dry, burning wind came in the window, together with the locomotive's whistle and the clatter of the old cars. The woman folded the plastic bag with the rest of the food and put it in the handbag. For a moment a complete picture of the town, on that bright August Tuesday, shone in the window. The girl wrapped the flowers in the soaking-wet newspapers, moved a little farther away from the window, and stared at her mother. She received a pleasant expression in return. The train began to whistle and slowed down. A moment later it stopped.

There was no one at the station. On the other side of the street, on the sidewalk shaded by the almond trees, only the pool hall was open. The town was floating in the heat. The woman and the girl got off the train and crossed the abandoned station—the tiles split apart by the grass growing up between—and over to the shady side of the street.

It was almost two. At that hour, weighted down by drowsiness, the town was taking a siesta. The stores, the town offices, the public school were closed at eleven, and didn't reopen until a little before four, when the train went back. Only the hotel across from the station, with its bar and pool hall, and the telegraph office at one side of the plaza stayed open. The houses, most of them built on the banana company's model, had their doors locked from inside and their blinds drawn. In some of them it was so hot that the residents ate lunch in the patio. Others leaned a chair against the wall, in the shade of the almond trees, and took their siesta right out in the street.

Keeping to the protective shade of the almond trees, the woman and the girl entered the town without disturbing the siesta. They went directly to the parish house. The woman scratched the metal grating on the door with her fingernail, waited a moment, and scratched again. An electric fan was humming inside. They did not hear the steps. They hardly heard the slight creaking of a door, and immediately a cautious voice, right next to the metal grating: "Who is it?" The woman tried to see through the grating.

"I need the priest," she said.

"He's sleeping now."

"It's an emergency," the woman insisted.

Her voice showed a calm determination.

The door was opened a little way, noiselessly, and a plump, older woman appeared, with very pale skin and hair the color of iron. Her eyes seemed too small behind her thick eyeglasses.

"Come in," she said, and opened the door all the way.

They entered a room permeated with an old smell of flowers. The woman of the house led them to a wooden bench and signaled them to sit down. The girl did so, but her mother remained standing, absent-mindedly, with both hands clutching the handbag. No noise could be heard above the electric fan.

The woman of the house reappeared at the door at the far end of the room. "He says you should come back after three," she said in a very low voice. "He just lay down five minutes ago."

"The train leaves at three-thirty," said the woman.

It was a brief and self-assured reply, but her voice remained pleasant, full of undertones. The woman of the house smiled for the first time.

"All right," she said.

When the far door closed again, the woman sat down next to her daughter. The narrow waiting room was poor, neat, and clean. On the other side of the wooden railing which divided the room, there was a worktable, a plain one with an oilcloth cover, and on top of the table a primitive typewriter next to a vase of flowers. The parish records were beyond. You could see that it was an office kept in order by a spinster.

The far door opened and this time the priest appeared, cleaning his glasses with a handkerchief. Only when he put them on was it evident that he was the brother of the woman who had opened the door.

"How can I help you?" he asked.

"The keys to the cemetery," said the woman.

The girl was seated with the flowers in her lap and her feet crossed under the bench. The priest looked at her, then looked at the woman, and then through the wire mesh of the window at the bright, cloudless sky.

"In this heat," he said. "You could have waited until the sun went down."

The woman moved her head silently. The priest crossed to the other side of the railing, took out of the cabinet a notebook covered in oilcloth, a wooden penholder, and an inkwell, and sat down at the table. There was more than enough hair on his hands to account for what was missing on his head.

"Which grave are you going to visit?" he asked.

"Carlos Centeno's," said the woman.

"Who?"

"Carlos Centeno," the woman repeated.

The priest still did not understand.

"He's the thief who was killed here last week," said the woman in the same tone of voice. "I am his mother."

The priest scrutinized her. She stared at him with quiet self-control, and the Father blushed. He lowered his head and began to write. As he filled the page, he asked the woman to identify herself, and she replied unhesitatingly, with precise details, as if she were reading them. The Father began to sweat. The girl unhooked the buckle of her left shoe, slipped her heel out of it, and rested it on the bench rail. She did the same with the right one.

It had all started the Monday of the previous week, at three in the morning, a few blocks from there. Rebecca, a lonely widow who lived in a house full of odds and ends, heard above the sound of the drizzling rain someone trying to force the front door from the outside. She got up, rummaged around in her closet for an ancient revolver that no one had fired since the days of Colonel Aureliano Buendía, and went into the living room without turning on the lights. Orienting herself not so much by the noise at the lock as by a terror developed in her by twenty-eight years of loneliness, she fixed in her imagination not only the spot where the door was but also the exact height of the lock. She clutched the weapon with both hands, closed her eyes, and squeezed the trigger. It was the first time in her life that she had fired a gun. Immediately after the explosion, she could hear nothing except the murmur of the drizzle on the galvanized roof. Then she heard a little metallic bump on the cement porch, and a very low voice, pleasant but terribly exhausted: "Ah, Mother." The man they found dead in front of the house in the morning, his nose blown to bits, wore a flannel shirt with colored stripes, everyday pants with a rope for a belt, and was barefoot. No one in town knew him.

"So his name was Carlos Centeno," murmured the Father when he finished writing.

"Centeno Ayala," said the woman. "He was my only boy."

The priest went back to the cabinet. Two big rusty keys hung on the inside of the door; the girl imagined, as her mother had when she was a girl and as the priest himself must have imagined at some time, that they were Saint Peter's keys. He took them down, put them on the open notebook on the railing, and pointed with his forefinger to a place on the page he had just written, looking at the woman.

"Sign here."

The woman scribbled her name, holding the handbag under her arm. The girl picked up the flowers, came to the railing shuffling her feet, and watched her mother attentively.

The priest sighed.

"Didn't you ever try to get him on the right track?"

The woman answered when she finished signing.

"He was a very good man."

The priest looked first at the woman and then at the girl, and realized with a kind of pious amazement that they were not about to cry. The woman continued in the same tone:

"I told him never to steal anything that anyone needed to eat, and he minded me. On the other hand, before, when he used to box, he used to spend three days in bed, exhausted from being punched."

"All his teeth had to be pulled out," interrupted the girl.

"That's right," the woman agreed. "Every mouthful I ate those days tasted of the beatings my son got on Saturday nights."

"God's will is inscrutable," said the Father.

But he said it without much conviction, partly because experience had made him a little skeptical and partly because of the heat. He suggested that they cover their heads to guard against sunstroke. Yawning, and now almost completely asleep, he gave them instructions about how to find Carlos Centeno's grave. When they came back, they didn't have to knock. They should put the key under the door; and in the same place, if they could, they should put an offering for the Church. The woman listened to his directions with great attention, but thanked him without smiling.

The Father had noticed that there was someone looking inside, his nose pressed against the metal grating, even before he opened the door to the street. Outside was a group of children. When the door was opened wide, the children scattered. Ordinarily, at that hour there was no one in the street. Now there were not only children. There were groups of people under the almond trees. The Father scanned the street swimming in the heat and then he understood. Softly, he closed the door again.

"Wait a moment," he said without looking at the woman.

His sister appeared at the far door with a black jacket over her nightshirt and her hair down over her shoulders. She looked silently at the Father.

"What was it?" he asked.

"The people have noticed," murmured his sister.

"You'd better go out by the door to the patio," said the Father.

"It's the same there," said his sister. "Everybody is at the windows."

The woman seemed not to have understood until then. She tried to look into the street through the metal grating. Then she took the bouquet of flowers from the girl and began to move toward the door. The girl followed her.

"Wait until the sun goes down," said the Father.

"You'll melt," said his sister, motionless at the back of the room. "Wait and I'll lend you a parasol."

"Thank you," replied the woman. "We're all right this way."

She took the girl by the hand and went into the street.

NOTES

interminable   endless

scrutinized   examined carefully and closely

RESPONDING PERSONALLY

3. Do you admire the woman? Is she doing something extraordinary, or is she acting as all mothers would? Share your thoughts in writing.

4. Do you feel the woman has or has not been treated with respect by the priest and his sister? What is it about her that has resulted in the treatment she has received? From your experience, what kind of personal "manner" do you think is worthy of respect from others?

RESPONDING CRITICALLY/ANALYTICALLY

5. The writer has selected an uncommon narrative point of view that is highly objective: He provides no knowledge of any of the characters' thoughts but simply observes what they say and do. Since the story is about the woman, why might the writer have purposely chosen not to let the reader into the thoughts and feelings that form her motivation?

6. With a partner, reconstruct the factual details of the incident that "all started the Monday of the previous week," as well as the information the mother shares in defence of her son, the boxer.

a) Was the son's purpose to steal? Consider the following:
- What days did he box?
- What day was he shot?
- What sounds did the widow hear?
- What were the son's dying words?
- What was the mother's earlier admonition of her son?
- What was the mother's answer to the priest's question?

Support your response to the question with specific story detail.

b) The mother seems to know what had occurred. Why does she not say, "He wasn't a thief"? Why does she not bother to try to persuade the priest?

c) Why has the mother brought her daughter with her, into what she knows will be an unsympathetic and unwelcoming situation?

d) Why does she choose to exit via the front door?

PEER ASSESSMENT

Do you find general agreement among the students of the class, or do opinions, and therefore readings of the story, vary quite considerably from student to student? If there are variances, what might be the cause? Is it difference in interpretations of facts, or is it the personal experiences students appear to have brought to the reading?

7. The woman's character is portrayed through minute and occasional expressions of her words and her actions. Explore the writer's portrayal.
   a) Identify references to her extreme poverty that go beyond just direct narrative statements of the fact.
   b) Identify references to her personality: statements of values and of motivations.
   c) Identify references to her physical appearance, mannerisms, and bearing that support her characterization.
   d) How is her action at the very end of the story true to character? Why would you not expect her to act otherwise?
   e) If the train were not to leave at 3:30, but later, would the woman have waited until dark, as the priest requested? Explain.
   f) Does the writer appear to be purposely relating the woman's station in life and her dignity of being? Support your thoughts with references to the story.

RESPONDING CREATIVELY

8. How do you think the woman learned that the dead man was her son? What reasonable set of circumstances might have led to her finding out? Write the missing paragraph(s).

9. Prepare the second part of the story, the conversation between woman and priest, for a readers' theatre presentation. Maintain the dialogue,

though you may wish to judiciously trim some of the lengthier pieces of narration, such as the one long piece of antecedent information regarding the circumstances of the son's death. Present your dramatic reading to the class. Allow your physical bearing as well as your manner of speech, not just your words, to indicate your character.

PROBLEM SOLVING OR DECISION MAKING

10. Does poverty excuse theft? Following the *intent* of the woman's statement, is it permissible to steal in such circumstances as long as you do not take "anything that anyone needed to eat"? Support your thoughts with reference to the story, your life experience, or both.

Graham Greene
The Destructors

PRE-READING

1. Why do people belong to gangs? Do certain kinds of people seem particularly suited to gang membership? What benefit might membership in a gang offer an individual that is not available elsewhere?

2. Vandalism seems to have become an unfortunate element of contemporary everyday life. Why is that so? What causes people to commit seemingly purposeless acts of vandalism? Share your thoughts in small-group discussion.

1

It was on the eve of August Bank Holiday that the latest recruit became the leader of the Wormsley Common Gang. No one was surprised except Mike, but Mike at the age of nine was surprised by everything. "If you don't shut your mouth," somebody once said to him, "you'll get a frog down it." After that Mike had kept his teeth tightly clamped except when the surprise was too great.

The new recruit had been with the gang since the beginning of the summer holidays, and there were possibilities about his brooding silence that all recognised. He never wasted a word even to tell his name until that was required of him by the rules. When he said "Trevor" it was a statement of fact, not as it would have been with the others a statement of shame or defiance. Nor did anyone laugh except Mike, who finding himself without support and meeting the dark gaze of the newcomer opened his mouth and was quiet again. There was every reason why T., as he was afterwards referred to, should have been an object of mockery—there was his name (and they substituted the initial because otherwise they had no excuse not to laugh at it), the fact that his father, a former architect and present clerk, had "come down in the world" and that his mother considered herself better than

the neighbours. What but an odd quality of danger, of the unpredictable, established him in the gang without any ignoble ceremony
of initiation?

The gang met every morning in an impromptu car-park, the site of
the last bomb of the first blitz. The leader, who was known as Blackie,
claimed to have heard it fall, and no one was precise enough in his
dates to point out that he would have been one year old and fast
asleep on the down platform of Wormsley Common Underground
Station. On one side of the car-park leant the first occupied house,
No. 3, of the shattered Northwood Terrace—literally leant, for it had
suffered from the blast of the bomb and the side walls were supported
on wooden struts. A smaller bomb and some incendiaries had fallen
beyond, so that the house stuck up like a jagged tooth and carried
on the further wall relics of its neighbour, a dado, the remains of a
fireplace. T., whose words were almost confined to voting "Yes" or
"No" to the plan of operations proposed each day by Blackie, once
startled the whole gang by saying broodingly, "Wren built that house,
father says."

"Who's Wren?"

"The man who built St. Paul's."

"Who cares?" Blackie said. "It's only Old Misery's."

Old Misery—whose real name was Thomas—had once been a
builder and decorator. He lived alone in the crippled house, doing for
himself: once a week you could see him coming back across the common with bread and vegetables, and once as the boys played in the
car-park he put his head over the smashed wall of his garden and
looked at them.

"Been to the loo," one of the boys said, for it was common knowledge that since the bombs fell something had gone wrong with the
pipes of the house and Old Misery was too mean to spend money on
the property. He could do the redecorating himself at cost price, but
he had never learnt plumbing. The loo was a wooden shed at the bottom of the narrow garden with a star-shaped hole in the door: it had
escaped the blast which had smashed the house next door and sucked
out the window-frames of No. 3.

The next time the gang became aware of Mr. Thomas was more
surprising. Blackie, Mike and a thin yellow boy, who for some reason
was called by his surname Summers, met him on the common coming

back from the market. Mr. Thomas stopped them. He said glumly, "You belong to the lot that play in the car-park?"

Mike was about to answer when Blackie stopped him. As the leader he had responsibilities. "Suppose we are?" he said ambiguously.

"I got some chocolates," Mr. Thomas said. "Don't like 'em myself. Here you are. Not enough to go round, I don't suppose. There never is," he added with sombre conviction. He handed over three packets of Smarties.

The gang were puzzled and perturbed by this action and tried to explain it away. "Bet someone dropped them and he picked 'em up," somebody suggested.

"Pinched 'em and then got in a bleeding funk," another thought aloud.

"It's a bribe," Summers said. "He wants us to stop bouncing balls on his wall."

"We'll show him we don't take bribes," Blackie said, and they sacrificed the whole morning to the game of bouncing that only Mike was young enough to enjoy. There was no sign from Mr. Thomas.

Next day T. astonished them all. He was late at the rendezvous, and the voting for that day's exploit took place without him. At Blackie's suggestion the gang was to disperse in pairs, take buses at random and see how many free rides could be snatched from unwary conductors (the operation was to be carried out in pairs to avoid cheating). They were drawing lots for their companions when T. arrived.

"Where you been, T.?" Blackie asked. "You can't vote now. You know the rules."

"I've been *there*," T. said. He looked at the ground, as though he had thoughts to hide.

"Where?"

"At Old Misery's." Mike's mouth opened and then hurriedly closed again with a click. He had remembered the frog.

"At Old Misery's?" Blackie said. There was nothing in the rules against it, but he had a sensation that T. was treading on dangerous ground. He asked hopefully, "Did you break in?"

"No. I rang the bell."

"And what did you say?"

"I said I wanted to see his house."

"What did he do?"

"He showed it me."

"Pinch anything?"

"No."

"What did you do it for then?"

The gang had gathered round: it was as though an impromptu court were about to form and to try some case of deviation. T. said, "It's a beautiful house," and still watching the ground, meeting no one's eyes, he licked his lips first one way, then the other.

"What do you mean, a beautiful house?" Blackie asked with scorn.

"It's got a staircase two hundred years old like a corkscrew. Nothing holds it up."

"What do you mean, nothing holds it up. Does it float?"

"It's to do with opposite forces, Old Misery said."

"What else?"

"There's panelling."

"Like in the Blue Boar?"

"Two hundred years old."

"Is Old Misery two hundred years old?"

Mike laughed suddenly and then was quiet again. The meeting was in a serious mood. For the first time since T. had strolled into the car-park on the first day of the holidays his position was in danger. It only needed a single use of his real name and the gang would be at his heels.

"What did you do it for?" Blackie asked. He was just, he had no jealousy, he was anxious to retain T. in the gang if he could. It was the word "beautiful" that worried him—that belonged to a class world that you could still see parodied at the Wormsley Common Empire by a man wearing a top hat and a monocle, with a haw-haw accent. He was tempted to say, "My dear Trevor, old chap," and unleash his hell hounds. "If you'd broken in," he said sadly—that indeed would have been an exploit worthy of the gang.

"This was better," T. said. "I found out things." He continued to stare at his feet, not meeting anybody's eye, as though he were absorbed in some dream he was unwilling—or ashamed—to share.

"What things?"

"Old Misery's going to be away all tomorrow and Bank Holiday."

Blackie said with relief, "You mean we could break in?"

"And pinch things?" somebody asked.

Blackie said, "Nobody's going to pinch things. Breaking in—that's good enough, isn't it? We don't want any court stuff."

"I don't want to pinch anything," T. said. "I've got a better idea."

"What is it?"

T. raised eyes, as grey and disturbed as the drab August day. "We'll pull it down," he said. "We'll destroy it."

Blackie gave a single hoot of laughter and then, like Mike, fell quiet, daunted by the serious implacable gaze. "What'd the police be doing at the time?" he said.

"They'd never know. We'd do it from inside. I've found a way in." He said with a sort of intensity, "We'd be like worms, don't you see, in an apple. When we came out again there'd be nothing there, no staircase, no panels, nothing but just walls, and then we'd make the walls fall down—somehow."

"We'd go to jug," Blackie said.

"Who's to prove? and anyway we wouldn't have pinched anything." He added without the smallest flicker of glee, "There wouldn't be anything to pinch after we'd finished."

"I've never heard of going to prison for breaking things," Summers said.

"There wouldn't be time," Blackie said, "I've seen housebreakers at work."

"There are twelve of us," T. said. "We'd organise."

"None of us know how ..."

"I know," T. said. He looked across at Blackie, "Have you got a better plan?"

"Today," Mike said tactlessly, "we're pinching free rides...."

"Free rides," T. said. "You can stand down, Blackie, if you'd rather...."

"The gang's got to vote."

"Put it up then."

Blackie said uneasily, "It's proposed that tomorrow and Monday we destroy Old Misery's house."

"Here, here," said a fat boy called Joe.

"Who's in favour?"

T. said, "It's carried."

"How do we start?" Summers asked.

"He'll tell you," Blackie said. It was the end of his leadership. He went away to the back of the car-park and began to kick a stone, dribbling it this way and that. There was only one old Morris in the park, for few cars were left there except lorries: without an attendant there was no safety. He took a flying kick at the car and scraped a little paint off the rear mudguard. Beyond, paying no more attention to him than to a stranger, the gang had gathered round T.; Blackie was dimly aware of the fickleness of favour. He thought of going home, of never returning, of letting them all discover the hollowness of T.'s leadership, but suppose after all what T. proposed was possible—nothing like it had ever been done before. The fame of the Wormsley Common car-park gang would surely reach around London. There would be headlines in the papers. Even the grown-up gangs who ran the betting at the all-in wrestling and the barrow-boys would hear with respect of how Old Misery's house had been destroyed. Driven by the pure, simple and altruistic ambition of fame for the gang, Blackie came back to where T. stood in the shadow of Misery's wall.

T. was giving orders with decision: it was as though this plan had been with him all his life, pondered through the seasons, now in his fifteenth year crystallised with the pain of puberty. "You," he said to Mike, "bring some big nails, the biggest you can find, and a hammer. Anyone else who can better bring a hammer and a screwdriver. We'll need plenty of them. Chisels too. We can't have too many chisels. Can anybody bring a saw?"

"I can," Mike said.

"Not a child's saw," T. said. "A real saw."

Blackie realised he had raised his hand like any ordinary member of the gang.

"Right, you bring one, Blackie. But now there's a difficulty. We want a hacksaw."

"What's a hacksaw?" someone asked.

"You can get 'em at Woolworth's," Summers said.

The fat boy called Joe said gloomily, "I knew it would end in a collection."

"I'll get one myself," T. said. "I don't want your money. But I can't buy a sledge-hammer."

Blackie said, "They are working on No. 15. I know where they'll leave their stuff for Bank Holiday."

"Then that's all," T. said. "We meet here at nine sharp."

"I've got to go to church," Mike said.

"Come over the wall and whistle. We'll let you in."

2

On Sunday morning all were punctual except Blackie, even Mike. Mike had had a stroke of luck. His mother felt ill, his father was tired after Saturday night, and he was told to go to church alone with many warnings of what would happen if he strayed. Blackie had had difficulty in smuggling out the saw, and then in finding the sledge-hammer at the back of No. 15. He approached the house from a lane at the rear of the garden, for fear of the policeman's beat along the main road. The tired evergreens kept off a stormy sun: another wet Bank Holiday was being prepared over the Atlantic, beginning in swirls of dust under the trees. Blackie climbed the wall into Misery's garden.

There was no sign of anybody anywhere. The loo stood like a tomb in a neglected graveyard. The curtains were drawn. The house slept. Blackie lumbered nearer with the saw and the sledge-hammer. Perhaps after all nobody had turned up: the plan had been a wild invention: they had woken wiser. But when he came close to the back door he could hear a confusion of sound, hardly louder than a hive in swarm: a clickety-clack, a bang bang bang, a scraping, a creaking, a sudden painful crack. He thought: it's true, and whistled.

They opened the door to him and he came in. He had at once the impression of organisation, very different from the old happy-go-lucky ways under his leadership. For a while he wandered up and down stairs looking for T. Nobody addressed him: he had a sense of great urgency, and already he could begin to see the plan. The interior of the house was being carefully demolished without touching the outer walls. Summers with hammer and chisel was ripping out the skirting-boards in the ground floor dining-room: he had already smashed the panels of the door. In the same room Joe was heaving up the parquet blocks, exposing the soft wood floor-boards over the cellar. Coils of wire came out of the damaged skirting and Mike sat happily on the floor, clipping the wires.

On the curved stairs two of the gang were working hard with an inadequate child's saw on the banisters—when they saw Blackie's big saw they signalled for it wordlessly. When he next saw them a quarter of the banisters had been dropped into the hall. He found T. at last in the bathroom—he sat moodily in the least cared-for room in the house, listening to the sounds coming up from below.

"You've really done it," Blackie said with awe. "What's going to happen?"

"We've only just begun," T. said. He looked at the sledge-hammer and gave his instructions. "You stay here and break the bath and the wash-basin. Don't bother about the pipes. They come later."

Mike appeared at the door. "I've finished the wire, T.," he said.

"Good. You've just got to go wandering round now. The kitchen's in the basement. Smash all the china and glass and bottles you can lay hold of. Don't turn on the taps—we don't want a flood—yet. Then go into all the rooms and turn out drawers. If they are locked get one of the others to break them open. Tear up any papers you find and smash all the ornaments. Better take a carving-knife with you from the kitchen. The bedroom's opposite here. Open the pillows and tear up the sheets. That's enough for the moment. And you, Blackie, when you've finished in here crack the plaster in the passage up with your sledge-hammer."

"What are you going to do?" Blackie asked.

"I'm looking for something special," T. said.

It was nearly lunch-time before Blackie had finished and went in search of T. Chaos had advanced. The kitchen was a shambles of broken glass and china. The dining-room was stripped of parquet, the skirting was up, the door had been taken off its hinges, and the destroyers had moved up a floor. Streaks of light came in through the closed shutters where they worked with the seriousness of creators—and destruction after all is a form of creation. A kind of imagination had seen this house as it had now become.

Mike said, "I've got to go home for dinner."

"Who else?" T. asked, but all the others on one excuse or another had brought provisions with them.

They squatted in the ruins of the room and swapped unwanted sandwiches. Half an hour for lunch and they were at work again. By the time Mike returned, they were on the top floor, and by six the superficial damage was completed. The doors were all off, all the skirtings raised, the furniture pillaged and ripped and smashed—no one could have slept in the house except on a bed of broken plaster. T. gave his orders—eight o'clock next morning, and to escape notice they climbed singly over the garden wall, into the car-park. Only Blackie and T. were left: the light had nearly gone, and when they touched a switch, nothing worked—Mike had done his job thoroughly.

"Did you find anything special?" Blackie asked.

T. nodded. "Come over here," he said, "and look." Out of both pockets he drew bundles of pound notes. "Old Misery's savings," he said. "Mike ripped out the mattress, but he missed them."

"What are you going to do? Share them?"

"We aren't thieves," T. said. "Nobody's going to steal anything from this house. I kept these for you and me—a celebration." He knelt down on the floor and counted them out—there were seventy in all. "We'll burn them," he said, "one by one," and taking it in turns they held a note upwards and lit the top corner, so that the flame burnt slowly towards their fingers. The grey ash floated above them and fell on their heads like age. "I'd like to see Old Misery's face when we are through," T. said.

"You hate him a lot?" Blackie asked.

"Of course I don't hate him," T. said. "There'd be no fun if I hated him." The last burning note illuminated his brooding face. "All this hate and love," he said, "it's soft, it's hooey. There's only things, Blackie," and he looked round the room crowded with the unfamiliar shadows of half things, broken things, former things. "I'll race you home, Blackie," he said.

3

Next morning the serious destruction started. Two were missing—Mike and another boy whose parents were off to Southend and Brighton in spite of the slow warm drops that had begun to fall and the rumble of thunder in the estuary like the first guns of the old blitz. "We've got to hurry," T. said.

Summers was restive. "Haven't we done enough?" he said. "I've been given a bob for slot machines. This is like work."

"We've hardly started," T. said. "Why, there's all the floors left, and the stairs. We haven't taken out a single window. You voted like the others. We are going to *destroy* this house. There won't be anything left when we've finished."

They began again on the first floor picking up the top floorboards next the outer wall, leaving the joists exposed. Then they sawed through the joists and retreated into the hall, as what was left of the floor heeled and sank. They had learnt with practise, and the second floor collapsed more easily. By the evening an odd exhilaration seized them as they looked down the great hollow of the house. They ran risks and made mistakes: when they thought of the windows it was too late to reach them. "Cor," Joe said, and dropped a penny down into the dry rubble-filled well. It cracked and span among the broken glass.

"Why did we start this?" Summers asked with astonishment; T. was already on the ground, digging at the rubble, clearing a space along the outer wall. "Turn on the taps," he said. "It's too dark for anyone to see now, and in the morning it won't matter." The water overtook them on the stairs and fell through the floorless rooms.

It was then they heard Mike's whistle at the back. "Something's wrong," Blackie said. They could hear his urgent breathing as they unlocked the door.

"The bogies?" Summers asked.

"Old Misery," Mike said, "He's on his way." He put his head between his knees and retched. "Ran all the way," he said with pride.

"But why?" T. said. "He told me ..." He protested with the fury of the child he had never been, "It isn't fair."

"He was down at Southend," Mike said, "and he was on the train coming back. Said it was too cold and wet." He paused and gazed at the water. "My, you've had a storm here. Is the roof leaking?"

"How long will he be?"

"Five minutes. I gave Ma the slip and ran."

"We better clear," Summers said. "We've done enough, anyway."

"Oh no, we haven't. Anybody could do this—" "this" was the shattered hollowed house with nothing left but the walls. Yet walls could be preserved. Façades were valuable. They could build inside again more beautifully than before. This could again be a home. He said angrily, "We've got to finish. Don't move. Let me think."

"There's no time," a boy said.

"There's got to be a way," T. said. "We couldn't have got this far ..."

"We've done a lot," Blackie said.

"No. No, we haven't. Somebody watch the front."

"We can't do any more."

"He may come in at the back."

"Watch the back too." T. began to plead. "Just give me a minute and I'll fix it. I swear I'll fix it." But his authority had gone with his ambiguity. He was only one of the gang. "Please," he said.

"Please," Summers mimicked him, and then suddenly struck home with the fatal name. "Run along home, Trevor."

T. stood with his back to the rubble like a boxer knocked groggy against the ropes. He had no words as his dreams shook and slid. Then Blackie acted before the gang had time to laugh, pushing Summers backward. "I'll watch the front, T." he said, and cautiously he opened the shutters of the hall. The grey wet common stretched ahead, and the lamps gleamed in the puddles. "Someone's coming, T. No, it's not him. What's your plan, T.?"

"Tell Mike to go out to the loo and hide close beside it. When he hears me whistle he's got to count ten and start to shout."

"Shout what?"

"Oh, 'Help', anything."

"You hear, Mike," Blackie said. He was the leader again. He took a quick look between the shutters. "He's coming, T."

"Quick, Mike. The loo. Stay here, Blackie, all of you till I yell."

"Where are you going, T.?"

"Don't worry. I'll see to this. I said I would, didn't I?"

Old Misery came limping off the common. He had mud on his shoes and he stopped to scrape them on the pavement's edge. He didn't want to soil his house, which stood jagged and dark between the bomb-sites, saved so narrowly, as he believed, from destruction. Even the fanlight had been left unbroken by the bomb's blast. Somewhere somebody whistled. Old Misery looked sharply round. He didn't trust whistles. A child was shouting: it seemed to come from his own garden. Then a boy ran into the road from the car-park. "Mr. Thomas," he called, "Mr. Thomas."

"What is it?"

"I'm terribly sorry, Mr. Thomas. One of us got taken short, and we thought you wouldn't mind, and now he can't get out."

"What do you mean, boy?"

"He's got stuck in your loo."

"He'd no business ... Haven't I seen you before?"

"You showed me your house."

"So I did. So I did. That doesn't give you the right to ..."

"Do hurry, Mr. Thomas. He'll suffocate."

"Nonsense. He can't suffocate. Wait till I put my bag in."

"I'll carry your bag."

"Oh no, you don't. I carry my own."

"This way, Mr. Thomas."

"I can't get in the garden that way. I've got to go through the house."

"But you *can* get in the garden this way, Mr. Thomas. We often do."

"You often do?" He followed the boy with a scandalised fascination. "When? What right? ..."

"Do you see ...? the wall's low."

"I'm not going to climb walls into my own garden. It's absurd."

"This is how we do it. One foot here, one foot there, and over." The boy's face peered down, an arm shot out, and Mr. Thomas found his bag taken and deposited on the other side of the wall.

"Give me back my bag," Mr. Thomas said. From the loo a boy yelled and yelled. "I'll call the police."

"Your bag's all right, Mr. Thomas. Look. One foot there. On your right. Now just above. To your left." Mr. Thomas climbed over his own garden wall. "Here's your bag, Mr. Thomas."

"I'll have the wall built up," Mr. Thomas said. "I'll not have you boys coming over here, using my loo." He stumbled on the path, but the boy caught his elbow and supported him. "Thank you, thank you, my boy," he murmured automatically. Somebody shouted again through the dark. "I'm coming, I'm coming," Mr. Thomas called. He said to the boy beside him, "I'm not unreasonable. Been a boy myself. As long as things are done regular. I don't mind you playing round the place Saturday mornings. Sometimes I like company. Only it's got to be regular. One of you asks leave and I say Yes. Sometimes I'll say No. Won't feel like it. And you come in at the front door and out at the back. No garden walls."

"Do get him out, Mr. Thomas."

"He won't come to any harm in my loo," Mr. Thomas said, stumbling slowly down the garden. "Oh, my rheumatics," he said. "Always get 'em on Bank Holiday. I've got to go careful. There's loose stones here. Give me your hand. Do you know what my horoscope said yesterday? 'Abstain from any dealings in first half of week. Danger of serious crash.' That might be on this path," Mr. Thomas said. "They speak in parables and double meanings." He paused at the door of the loo. "What's the matter in there?" he called. There was no reply.

"Perhaps he's fainted," the boy said.

"Not in my loo. Here, you, come out," Mr. Thomas said, and giving a great jerk at the door he nearly fell on his back when it swung easily open. A hand first supported him and then pushed him hard. His head hit the opposite wall and he sat heavily down. His bag hit his feet. A hand whipped the key out of the lock and the door slammed. "Let me out," he called, and heard the key turn in the lock. "A serious crash," he thought, and felt dithery and confused and old.

A voice spoke to him softly through the star-shaped hole in the door. "Don't worry, Mr. Thomas," it said, "we won't hurt you, not if you stay quiet."

Mr. Thomas put his head between his hands and pondered. He had noticed that there was only one lorry in the car-park, and he felt certain that the driver would not come for it before the morning. Nobody could hear him from the road in front, and the lane at the back was seldom used. Anyone who passed there would be hurrying home and would not pause for what they would certainly take to be drunken cries. And if he did call "Help," who, on a lonely Bank Holiday evening, would have the courage to investigate? Mr. Thomas sat on the loo and pondered with the wisdom of age.

After a while it seemed to him that there were sounds in the silence—they were faint and came from the direction of his house. He stood up and peered through the ventilation-hole—between the cracks in one of the shutters he saw a light, not the light of a lamp, but the wavering light that a candle might give. Then he thought he heard the sound of hammering and scraping and chipping. He thought of burglars—perhaps they had employed the boy as a scout, but why should burglars engage in what sounded more and more like a stealthy form of carpentry? Mr. Thomas let out an experimental yell, but nobody answered. The noise could not even have reached his enemies.

4

Mike had gone home to bed, but the rest stayed. The question of leadership no longer concerned the gang. With nails, chisels, screwdrivers, anything that was sharp and penetrating they moved around the inner walls worrying at the mortar between the bricks. They started too high, and it was Blackie who hit on the damp course and realised the work could be halved if they weakened the joints immediately above. It was a long, tiring, unamusing job, but at last it was finished. The gutted house stood there balanced on a few inches of mortar between the damp course and the bricks.

There remained the most dangerous task of all, out in the open at the edge of the bomb-site. Summers was sent to watch the road for passers-by, and Mr. Thomas, sitting on the loo, heard clearly now the sound of sawing. It no longer came from his house, and that a little reassured him. He felt less concerned. Perhaps the other noises too had no significance.

A voice spoke to him through the hole. "Mr. Thomas."

"Let me out," Mr. Thomas said sternly.

"Here's a blanket," the voice said, and a long grey sausage was worked through the hole and fell in swathes over Mr. Thomas's head.

"There's nothing personal," the voice said. "We want you to be comfortable to-night."

"To-night," Mr. Thomas repeated incredulously.

"Catch," the voice said. "Penny buns—we've buttered them, and sausage-rolls. We don't want you to starve, Mr. Thomas."

Mr. Thomas pleaded desperately. "A joke's a joke, boy. Let me out and I won't say a thing. I've got rheumatics. I got to sleep comfortable."

"You wouldn't be comfortable, not in your house, you wouldn't. Not now."

"What do you mean, boy?" but the footsteps receded. There was only the silence of night: no sound of sawing. Mr. Thomas tried one more yell, but he was daunted and rebuked by the silence—a long way off an owl hooted and made away again on its muffled flight through the soundless world.

At seven next morning the driver came to fetch his lorry. He climbed into the seat and tried to start the engine. He was vaguely aware of a voice shouting, but it didn't concern him. At last the engine responded and he backed the lorry until it touched the great wooden shore that supported Mr. Thomas's house. That way he could drive right out and down the street without reversing. The lorry moved forward, was momentarily checked as though something were pulling it from behind, and then went on to the sound of a long rumbling crash. The driver was astonished to see bricks bouncing ahead of him, while stones hit the roof of his cab. He put on his brakes. When he climbed out the whole landscape had suddenly altered. There was no house beside the car-park, only a hill of rubble. He went round and examined the back of his car for damage, and found a rope tied there that was still twisted at the other end round part of a wooden strut.

The driver again became aware of somebody shouting. It came from the wooden erection which was the nearest thing to a house in that desolation of broken brick. The driver climbed the smashed wall and unlocked the door. Mr. Thomas came out of the loo.

He was wearing a grey blanket to which flakes of pastry adhered. He gave a sobbing cry. "My house," he said. "Where's my house?"

"Search me," the driver said. His eye lit on the remains of a bath and what had once been a dresser and he began to laugh. There wasn't anything left anywhere.

"How dare you laugh," Mr. Thomas said. "It was my house. My house."

"I'm sorry," the driver said, making heroic efforts, but when he remembered the sudden check to his lorry, the crash of bricks falling, he became convulsed again. One moment the house had stood there with such dignity between the bomb-sites like a man in a top hat, and then, bang, crash, there wasn't anything left—not anything. He said, "I'm sorry. I can't help it, Mr. Thomas. There's nothing personal, but you got to admit it's funny."

NOTES

altruistic	done for unselfish reasons
Bank Holiday	any day on which banks were once legally closed
bleeding funk	slang for great exaggerated fear or depression
blitz	reference to airplane attacks on England in World War II
bob	shilling (British coinage)
bogies	slang for policemen
Common	open public land (the boys live around or near a common)
haw-haw accent	exaggerated accent used by the comic stereotypical Englishman
incendiaries	bombs to cause fires

joists	series of parallel supporting floorboards
loo	toilet
lorries	trucks
pillaged	plundered; ransacked
pinched	slang for stolen
Wren	Sir Christopher Wren (1632–1723), famous architect who built the domed landmark St. Paul's Cathedral in London; despite the blitz bombing, it survived and became a symbol of the survival of Britain.

RESPONDING PERSONALLY

3. At the conclusion of your reading, what were your immediate thoughts regarding, first, the joke itself, and second, the ultimate effect of the joke on Mr. Thomas? Were you laughing? At the same time, did you empathize at all with him? Share your thoughts in writing.

4. Have older members of your family—such as grandparents or perhaps older friends or acquaintances whom you know—ever been harassed by a group of adolescents? Tell what happened. With whom did your sympathies lie? Could you ever see yourself being at least somewhat sympathetic to *both* sides involved? Explain why or why not.

RESPONDING CRITICALLY/ANALYTICALLY

5. Trevor is the character most central to the action of the story. It is his vision that the group actualizes. Yet, for all the importance of his imagination, the reader never gains access to his thoughts in the same way the reader is shown the thinking of Blackie, Mr. Thomas, the gang, and even the lorry driver. Why is this so? What is the writer's purpose in excluding only Trevor's limited omniscient point of view?

6. Explain the irony in each of the following passages:
   a) When the gang members disperse to steal free bus rides, "The operation was to be carried out in pairs to avoid cheating."
   b) As the boys finalize their plan of vandalism, Mike reminds them, "I've got to go to church."
   c) Trevor finds Mr. Thomas's savings and is asked, "What are you going to do?" He replies, "We aren't thieves."
   d) When Mr. Thomas returns early, Trevor protests in fury, "But why? He told me.... It isn't fair."
   e) When Mr. Thomas is locked in the loo, the boys give him a blanket and food for the night. "Penny buns—we've buttered them, and sausage-rolls. We don't want you to starve, Mr. Thomas."

   What is the writer's purpose in such repeated and consistent characterization of the boys? What truth is the writer trying to establish? Why do you think he has selected irony as his vehicle of choice?

7. Why is the post–World War II setting of London so important to the story?
   - the evidence of destruction throughout the city
   - the reference to Trevor's parents
   - the "timelessness" of the architect's constructions
   - the double reference, at critical points in the story, to a man in "a top hat"?

   How does the story reach beyond just the actions of the boys?

8. As the boys' work continues, the writer describes the continuing efforts of those he calls "the destroyers." He states, "They worked with the seriousness of creators—and destruction after all is a form of creation."
   a) In a small group, discuss the truth of this statement.
   b) Why is the title of the story "The Destructors" rather than "The Destroyers"?

Responding Creatively

9. Retell the story in cinematic form using either video or electronic media. Employ a "talking heads" format: Let the story be told by various characters presented sequentially who simply sit in one place and speak directly to the camera. Each character adds his perspective to the developing story until it has been completely told. Characters may complement or contradict one another's information, but they should not simply repeat.

Self-Assessment

How effective a storytelling format is the method of presentation used in this retelling? What unanticipated difficulties did you encounter in using this format? What were some of the necessary requirements? What kind of story does this format suit best?

Problem Solving or Decision Making

10. The growing prevalence of gangs in contemporary society is a cause of increasing concern to many. With this in mind, should a story such as this, a story that celebrates the creative behaviours of the gang and its members, be read and studied? Is there not a danger of life imitating art? Discuss this question in a small group. Share your conclusions with the rest of the class.

Richard Davies
Personal Response to "The Destructors"

When I first started teaching in a small northern Alberta town, I remember reading this story for the first time and being struck by how far away the setting of World War II London was from Canada of 1972. What possible relevance could a story like this have to students who came from a very different time and background?

The students, however, seemed to enjoy the story, especially the premise of an elaborate practical joke played on an old man against the background of the Blitz—that period when German bombers dropped their payloads on London. I showed them a photo of St. Paul's Cathedral—everyone seems to recognize it when they see its famous dome—an inspirational architectural landmark that had miraculously survived the bombing.

But I don't think the relevance of the story really hit home until the following fall when I was teaching a poetry module to a small class of eight grade 12 students. In those more carefree days, one thought nothing of piling into a couple of cars and heading out for the lake on a creative writing field trip.

I wanted them to be inspired by the leaves changing colour on a late September morning and maybe create some of their own poems. We separated when we arrived at the lake. Some time later, I became aware of some distant banging or racket coming from the depth of the woods back of the beach, not thinking anything of it until one student came to tell me that a few boys had found a derelict hut that they were well into tearing apart.

I went to find them and, sure enough, there they were, systematically destroying the roof of someone's long-deserted summer digs! The boys were *totally* engrossed in what they were doing and oblivious of me and why we were there. Annoyed and not interested in seeing anyone get injured, I told them to head back to the cars. One by one, they walked by me, their hot faces flushed with their efforts. One boy laughed, "We decided to do somebody a favour and take that place down." And then it hit me: "The Destructors" had come to life in my own students' acts of wanton vandalism!

Years later, I often reflect on how my students continue to teach me. And I will never forget what I learned from those three totally engrossed teens that beautiful fall day early in my career: (1) *sometimes people would rather destroy than create*, and, perhaps more importantly, (2) *people can be very creative in their methods of destruction.*

Although specific circumstantial details of this incident were different from those in "The Destructors," I doubt that the above realizations would have even occurred to me if I hadn't already read Graham Greene's story beforehand. As has been remarked before, life has an uncanny way of imitating the truths of art, and vice versa.

D.H. Lawrence
The Rocking-Horse Winner

PRE-READING

1. What is a fairy tale?
   a) With a partner, identify as many typical characteristics of the fairy tale genre as you can. Share these characteristics with your classmates.
   b) Why do fairy tales continue to remain popular with young children? What fascination do they hold? Might fairy tales also "speak" to adults? Explain.

2. What makes an ideal mother?
   a) In a single paragraph, describe what you believe are the most desirable characteristics of motherhood. Explain briefly why those characteristics are so important.
   b) Again in a single paragraph, identify and describe one stereotypically idealized mother as she is portrayed on television today.
   c) Is there a similarity between the two? If not, which is the more realistic—your idealization, or television's? Explain which and why.

There was a woman who was beautiful, who started with all the advantages, yet she had no luck. She married for love, and the love turned to dust. She had bonny children, yet she felt they had been thrust upon her, and she could not yet love them. They looked at her coldly, as if they were finding fault with her. And hurriedly she felt she must cover up some fault in herself. Yet what it was that she must cover up she never knew. Nevertheless, when her children were present, she always felt the centre of her heart go hard. This troubled her, and in her manner she was all the more gentle and anxious for her children as if she loved them very much. Only she herself knew that at the centre of her heart was a hard little place that could not feel love, no, not for anybody. Everybody else said of her: "She is such a good mother. She adores her children." Only she herself, and her children themselves, knew it was not so. They read it in each other's eyes.

There were a boy and two little girls. They lived in a pleasant house, with a garden, and they had discreet servants, and felt themselves superior to anyone in the neighbourhood.

Although they lived in style, they felt always an anxiety in the house. There was never enough money. The mother had a small income, and the father had a small income, but not nearly enough for the social position which they had to keep up. The father went into town to some office. But though he had good prospects, these prospects never materialized. There was always the grinding sense of the shortage of money, though the style was always kept up.

At last the mother said: "I will see if I can't make something." But she did not know where to begin. She racked her brains, and tried this thing and the other, but could not find anything successful. The failure made deep lines come into her face. Her children were growing up, they would have to go to school. There must be more money, there must be more money. The father, who was always very handsome and expensive in his tastes, seemed as if he never would be able to do anything worth doing. And the mother, who had a great belief in herself, did not succeed any better, and her tastes were just as expensive.

And so the house came to be haunted by the unspoken phrase: There must be more money! There must be more money! The children could hear it all the time, though nobody said it aloud. They heard it at Christmas, when the expensive and splendid toys filled the nursery. Behind the shining modern rocking horse, behind the smart doll's-house, a voice would start whispering: "There must be more money! There must be more money!" And the children would stop playing, to listen for a moment. They would look into each other's eyes, to see if they had all heard. And each one saw in the eyes of the other two that they too had heard. "There must be more money! There must be more money!"

It came whispering from the springs of the still-swaying rocking horse, and even the horse, bending his wooden, champing head, heard it. The big doll, sitting so pink and smirking in her new pram, could hear it quite plainly, and seemed to be smirking all the more self-consciously because of it. The foolish puppy, too, that took the place of the Teddy bear, he was looking so extraordinarily foolish for no other reason but that he heard the secret whisper all over the house: "There must be more money!"

Yet nobody ever said it aloud. The whisper was everywhere, and therefore no one spoke it. Just as no one ever says: "We are breathing!" in spite of the fact that breath is coming and going all the time.

"Mother," said the boy Paul one day, "why don't we keep a car of our own? Why do we always use uncle's, or else a taxi?"

"Because we're the poor members of the family," said the mother.

"But why are we, mother?"

"Well—I suppose," she said slowly and bitterly, "it's because your father has no luck."

The boy was silent for some time.

"Is luck money, mother?" he asked, rather timidly.

"No, Paul. Not quite. It's what causes you to have money."

"Oh!" said Paul vaguely. "I thought when Uncle Oscar said filthy lucker, it meant money."

"Filthy lucre does mean money," said the mother. "But it's lucre, not luck."

"Oh!" said the boy. "Then what is luck, mother?"

"It's what causes you to have money. If you're lucky you have money. That's why it's better to be born lucky than rich. If you're rich, you may lose your money. But if you're lucky, you will always get more money."

"Oh! Will you? And is father not lucky?"

"Very unlucky, I should say," she said bitterly.

The boy watched her with unsure eyes.

"Why?" he asked.

"I don't know. Nobody ever knows why one person is lucky and another unlucky."

"Don't they? Nobody at all? Does nobody know?"

"Perhaps God. But He never tells."

"He ought to, then. And aren't you lucky either, mother?"

"I can't be, if I married an unlucky husband."

"But by yourself, aren't you?"

"I used to think I was, before I married. Now I think I am very unlucky indeed."

"Why?"

"Well—never mind! Perhaps I'm not really," she said.

The child looked at her, to see if she meant it. But he saw, by the lines of her mouth, that she was only trying to hide something from him.

"Well, anyhow," he said stoutly. "I'm a lucky person."

"Why?" said his mother, with a sudden laugh.

He stared at her. He didn't even know why he had said it.

"God told me," he asserted, brazening it out.

"I hope He did, dear!" she said, again with a laugh, but rather bitter.

"He did, mother!"

"Excellent!" said the mother, using one of her husband's exclamations.

The boy saw she did not believe him; or, rather, that she paid no attention to his assertion. This angered him somewhat, and made him want to compel her attention.

He went off by himself, vaguely, in a childish way, seeking for the clue to "luck." Absorbed, taking no heed of other people, he went about with a sort of stealth, seeking inwardly for luck. He wanted luck, he wanted it, he wanted it. When the two girls were playing dolls in the nursery, he would sit on his big rocking horse, charging madly into space, with a frenzy that made the little girls peer at him uneasily. Wildly the horse careered, the waving dark hair of the boy tossed, his eyes had a strange glare in them. The little girls dared not speak to him.

When he had ridden to the end of his mad little journey, he climbed down and stood in front of his rocking horse, staring fixedly into its lowered face. Its red mouth was slightly open, its big eye was wide and glassy-bright.

"Now!" he would silently command the snorting steed. "Now, take me to where there is luck! Now take me!"

And he would slash the horse on the neck with the little whip he had asked Uncle Oscar for. He knew the horse could take him to where there was luck, if only he forced it. So he would mount again and start on his furious ride, hoping at last to get there. He knew he could get there.

"You'll break your horse, Paul!" said the nurse.

"He's always riding like that! I wish he'd leave off!" said his elder sister Joan.

But he only glared down on them in silence. Nurse gave him up. She could make nothing of him. Anyhow, he was growing beyond her.

One day his mother and his Uncle Oscar came in when he was on one of his furious rides. He did not speak to them.

"Hallo, you young jockey! Riding a winner?" said his uncle.

"Aren't you growing too big for a rocking horse? You're not a very little boy any longer, you know," said his mother.

But Paul only gave a blue glare from his big, rather close-set eyes.

He would speak to nobody when he was in full tilt. His mother watched him with an anxious expression on her face.

At last he suddenly stopped forcing his horse into the mechanical gallop, and slid down.

"Well, I got there!" he announced fiercely, his blue eyes still flaring, and his sturdy long legs straddling apart.

"Where did you get to?" asked his mother.

"Where I wanted to go," he flared back at her.

"That's right, son!" said Uncle Oscar. "Don't you stop till you get there. What's the horse's name?"

"He doesn't have a name," said the boy.

"Gets on without all right?" asked the uncle.

"Well, he has different names. He was called Sansovino last week."

"Sansovino, eh? Won the Ascot. How did you know his name?"

"He always talks about horse races with Bassett," said Joan.

The uncle was delighted to find that his small nephew was posted with all the racing news. Bassett, the young gardener, who had been wounded in the left foot in the war and had got his present job through Oscar Cresswell, whose batman he had been, was a perfect blade of the "turf." He lived in the racing events, and the small boy lived with him.

Oscar Cresswell got it all from Bassett.

"Master Paul comes and asks me, so I can't do more than tell him, sir," said Bassett, his face terribly serious, as if he were speaking of religious matters.

"And does he ever put anything on a horse he fancies?"

"Well—I don't want to give him away—he's a young sport, a fine sport, sir. Would you mind asking him yourself? He sort of takes a pleasure in it, and perhaps he'd feel I was giving him away, sir, if you don't mind."

Bassett was serious as a church.

The uncle went back to his nephew, and took him off for a ride in the car.

"Say, Paul, old man, do you ever put anything on a horse?" the uncle asked.

"Why, do you think I oughtn't to?" he parried.

"Not a bit of it! I thought perhaps you might give me a tip for the Lincoln."

The car sped on into the country, going down to Uncle Oscar's place in Hampshire.

"Honour bright?" said the nephew.

"Honour bright, son!" said the uncle.

"Well, then, Daffodil."

"Daffodil! I doubt it, sonny. What about Mirza?"

"I only know the winner," said the boy. "That's Daffodil."

"Daffodil, eh?"

There was a pause. Daffodil was an obscure horse comparatively.

"Uncle!"

"Yes, son?"

"You won't let it go any further, will you? I promised Bassett."

"Bassett be damned, old man! What's he got to do with it?"

"We're partners. We've been partners from the first. Uncle, he lent me my first five shillings, which I lost. I promised him, honour bright, it was only between me and him; only you gave me that ten-shilling note I started winning with, so I thought you were lucky. You won't let it go any further, will you?"

The boy gazed at his uncle from those big, hot, blue eyes, set rather close together. The uncle stirred and laughed uneasily.

"Right you are, son! I'll keep your tip private. Daffodil, eh? How much are you putting on him?"

"All except twenty pounds," said the boy. "I keep that in reserve."

The uncle thought it a good joke.

"You keep twenty pounds in reserve, do you, you young romancer? What are you betting, then?"

"I'm betting three hundred," said the boy gravely. "But it's between you and me, Uncle Oscar! Honour bright?"

The uncle burst into a roar of laughter.

"It's between you and me all right, you young Nat Gould," he said, laughing. "But where's your three hundred?"

"Bassett keeps it for me. We're partners."

"You are, are you! And what is Bassett putting on Daffodil?"

"He won't go quite as high as I do, I expect. Perhaps he'll go a hundred and fifty."

"What, pennies?" laughed the uncle.

"Pounds," said the child, with a surprised look at his uncle. "Bassett keeps a bigger reserve than I do."

Between wonder and amusement Uncle Oscar was silent. He pursued the matter no further, but he determined to take his nephew with him to the Lincoln races.

"Now, son," he said, "I'm putting twenty on Mirza, and I'll put five for you on any horse you fancy. What's your pick?"

"Daffodil, uncle."

"No, not the fiver on Daffodil!"

"I should if it was my own fiver," said the child.

"Good! Good! Right you are! A fiver for me and a fiver for you on Daffodil."

The child had never been to a race meeting before, and his eyes were blue fire. He pursed his mouth tight, and watched. A Frenchman just in front had put his money on Lancelot. Wild with excitement, he flayed his arms up and down, yelling "Lancelot! Lancelot!" in his French accent.

Daffodil came in first, Lancelot second, Mirza third. The child, flushed and with eyes blazing, was curiously serene. His uncle brought him four five-pound notes, four to one.

"What am I to do with these?" he cried, waving them before the boy's eyes.

"I suppose we'll talk to Bassett," said the boy. "I expect I have fifteen hundred now; and twenty in reserve; and this twenty."

"Look here, son!" he said. "You're not serious about Bassett and that fifteen hundred, are you?"

"Yes, I am. But it's between you and me, uncle. Honour bright!"

"Honour bright all right, son! But I must talk to Bassett."

"If you'd like to be a partner, uncle, with Bassett and me, we could all be partners. Only, you'd have to promise, honour bright, uncle, not to let it go beyond us three. Bassett and I are lucky, and you must be lucky, because it was your ten shillings I started winning with...."

Uncle Oscar took both Bassett and Paul into Richmond Park for an afternoon, and there they talked.

"It's like this, you see, sir," Bassett said. "Master Paul would get me talking about racing events, spinning yarns, you know, sir. And he was always keen on knowing if I'd made or if I'd lost. It's about a year since, now, that I put five shillings on Blush of Dawn for him—and we lost. Then the luck turned, with that ten shillings he had from you, that we put on Singhalese. And since that time, it's been pretty steady, all things considering. What do you say, Master Paul?"

"We're all right when we're sure," said Paul. "It's when we're not quite sure that we go down."

"Oh, but we're careful then," said Bassett.

"But when are you sure?" smiled Oscar.

"It's Master Paul, sir," said Bassett, in a secret, religious voice. "It's as if he had it from heaven. Like Daffodil, now, for the Lincoln. That was as sure as eggs."

"Did you put anything on Daffodil?" asked Oscar Cresswell.

"Yes, sir, I made my bit."

"And my nephew?"

Bassett was obstinately silent, looking at Paul.

"I made twelve hundred, didn't I, Bassett? I told uncle I was putting three hundred on Daffodil."

"That's right," said Bassett, nodding.

"But where's the money?" asked the uncle.

"I keep it safe locked up, sir. Master Paul he can have it any minute he likes to ask for it."

"What, fifteen hundred pounds?"

"And twenty! And forty, that is, with the twenty he made on the course."

"It's amazing!" said the uncle.

"If Master Paul offers you to be partners, sir, I would, if I were you; if you'll excuse me," said Bassett.

Oscar Cresswell thought about it.

"I'll see the money," he said.

They drove home again, and sure enough, Bassett came round to the garden-house with fifteen hundred pounds in notes. The twenty pounds reserve was left with Joe Glee, in the Turf Commission deposit.

"You see, it's all right, uncle, when I'm sure! Then we go strong, for all we're worth. Don't we, Bassett?"

"We do that, Master Paul."

"And when are you sure?" said the uncle, laughing.

"Oh, well, sometimes I'm absolutely sure, like about Daffodil," said the boy; "and sometimes I have an idea; and sometimes I haven't even an idea, have I, Bassett? Then we're careful, because we mostly go down."

"You do, do you! And when you're sure, like about Daffodil, what makes you sure, sonny?"

"Oh, well, I don't know," said the boy uneasily. "I'm sure, you know, uncle; that's all."

"It's as if he had it from heaven, sir," Bassett reiterated.

"I should say so!" said the uncle.

But he became a partner. And when the Leger was coming on, Paul was "sure" about Lively Spark, which was a quite inconsiderable horse. The boy insisted on putting a thousand on the horse, Bassett went for five hundred, and Oscar Cresswell two hundred. Lively Spark came in first, and the betting had been ten to one against him. Paul had made ten thousand.

"You see," he said, "I was absolutely sure of him."

Even Oscar Cresswell had cleared two thousand.

"Look here, son," he said, "this sort of thing makes me nervous."

"It needn't, uncle! Perhaps I shan't be sure again for a long time."

"But what are you going to do with your money?" asked the uncle.

"Of course," said the boy, "I started it for mother. She said she had no luck, because father is unlucky, so I thought if I was lucky, it might stop whispering."

"What might stop whispering?"

"Our house. I hate our house for whispering."

"What does it whisper?"

"Why—why"—the boy fidgeted—"why, I don't know. But it's always short of money, you know, uncle."

"I know it, son, I know it."

"You know people send mother writs, don't you, uncle?"

"I'm afraid I do," said the uncle.

"And then the house whispers, like people laughing at you behind your back. It's awful, that is! I thought if I was lucky ..."

"You might stop it," added the uncle.

The boy watched him with big blue eyes that had an uncanny cold fire in them, and he said never a word.

"Well, then!" said the uncle. "What are we doing?"

"I shouldn't like mother to know I was lucky," said the boy.

"Why not, son?"

"She'd stop me."

"I don't think she would."

"Oh!"—and the boy writhed in an odd way—"I don't want her to know, uncle."

"All right, son! We'll manage it without her knowing."

They managed it very easily. Paul, at the other's suggestion, handed over five thousand pounds to his uncle, who deposited it with the family lawyer, who was then to inform Paul's mother that a relative had put five thousand pounds into his hands, which sum was to be paid out a thousand pounds at a time, on the mother's birthday, for the next five years.

"So she'll have a birthday present of a thousand pounds for five successive years," said Uncle Oscar. "I hope it won't make it all the harder for her later."

Paul's mother had her birthday in November. The house had been "whispering" worse than ever lately, and, even in spite of his luck, Paul could not bear up against it. He was very anxious to see the effect of the birthday letter, telling his mother about the thousand pounds.

When there were no visitors, Paul now took his meals with his parents, as he was beyond the nursery control. His mother went into town nearly every day. She had discovered that she had an odd knack of sketching furs and dress materials, so she worked secretly in the studio of a friend who was the chief "artist" for the leading drapers. She drew the figures of ladies in furs and ladies in silk and sequins for the newspaper advertisements. This young woman artist earned several thousand pounds a year, but Paul's mother only made several hundreds, and she was again dissatisfied. She so wanted to be first in something, and she did not succeed, even in making sketches for drapery advertisements.

She was down to breakfast on the morning of her birthday. Paul watched her face as she read her letters. He knew the lawyer's letter. As his mother read it, her face hardened and became more expressionless. Then a cold, determined look came on her mouth. She hid the letter under the pile of others, and said not a word about it.

"Didn't you have anything nice in the post for your birthday, mother?" said Paul.

"Quite moderately nice," she said, her voice cold and absent.

She went away to town without saying more.

But in the afternoon Uncle Oscar appeared. He said Paul's mother had had a long interview with the lawyer, asking if the whole five thousand could be advanced at once, as she was in debt.

"What do you think, uncle!" said the boy.

"I leave it to you, son."

"Oh, let her have it, then! We can get some more with the other," said the boy.

"A bird in the hand is worth two in the bush, laddie!" said Uncle Oscar.

"But I'm sure to know for the Grand National or the Lincolnshire; or else the Derby. I'm sure to know for one of them," said Paul.

So Uncle Oscar signed the agreement, and Paul's mother touched the whole five thousand. Then something very curious happened. The voices in the house suddenly went mad, like a chorus of frogs on a spring evening. There were certain new furnishings, and Paul had a tutor. He was really going to Eton, his father's school, in the following autumn. There were flowers in the winter, and a blossoming of the luxury Paul's mother had been used to. And yet the voices in the house, behind the sprays of mimosa and almond blossom, and from under the piles of iridescent cushions, simply trilled and screamed in a sort of ecstasy: "There must be more money! Oh-h-h, there must be more money. Oh, now, now-w! Now-w-w—there must be more money!—more than ever! More than ever!"

It frightened Paul terribly. He studied away at his Latin and Greek with his tutors. But his intense hours were spent with Bassett. The Grand National had gone by: he had not "known," and had lost a hundred pounds. Summer was at hand. He was in agony for the Lincoln. But even for the Lincoln he didn't "know" and he lost fifty pounds. He became wild-eyed and strange, as if something were going to explode in him.

"Let it alone, son! Don't you bother about it!" urged Uncle Oscar. But it was as if the boy couldn't really hear what his uncle was saying.

"I've got to know for the Derby! I've got to know for the Derby!" the child reiterated, his big blue eyes blazing with a sort of madness.

His mother noticed how overwrought he was.

"You'd better go to the seaside. Wouldn't you like to go now to the seaside, instead of waiting? I think you'd better," she said, looking down at him anxiously, her heart curiously heavy because of him.

But the child lifted his uncanny blue eyes.

"I couldn't possibly go before the Derby, mother!" he said. "I couldn't possibly!"

"Why not?" she said, her voice becoming heavy when she was opposed. "Why not? You can still go from the seaside to see the Derby with your Uncle Oscar, if that's what you wish. No need for you to wait here. Besides, I think you care too much about these races. It's a bad sign. My family has been a gambling family, and you won't know till you grow up how much damage it has done. But it has done damage. I shall have to send Bassett away, and ask Uncle Oscar not to talk racing to you, unless you promise to be reasonable about it; go away to the seaside and forget it. You're all nerves!"

"I'll do what you like, mother, so long as you don't send me away till after the Derby," the boy said.

"Send you away from where? Just from this house?"

"Yes," he said, gazing at her.

"Why, you curious child, what makes you care about this house so much, suddenly? I never knew you loved it."

He gazed at her without speaking. He had a secret within a secret, something he had not divulged, even to Bassett or to Uncle Oscar.

But his mother, after standing undecided and a little bit sullen for some moments, said:

"Very well, then! Don't go to the seaside till after the Derby, if you don't wish it. But promise me you won't let your nerves go to pieces. Promise you won't think so much about horse racing and events, as you call them!"

"Oh, no," said the boy casually. "I won't think much about them, mother. You needn't worry. I wouldn't worry, mother, if I were you."

"If you were me and I were you," said his mother, "I wonder what we should do!"

"But you know you needn't worry, mother, don't you?" the boy repeated.

"I should be awfully glad to know it," she said wearily.

"Oh, well, you can, you know. I mean, you ought to know you needn't worry," he insisted.

"Ought I? Then I'll see about it," she said.

Paul's secret of secrets was his wooden horse, that which had no name. Since he was emancipated from a nurse and a nursery governess, he had had his rocking horse removed to his own bedroom at the top of the house.

"Surely, you're too big for a rocking horse!" his mother had remonstrated.

"Well, you see, mother, till I can have a real horse, I like to have some sort of animal about," had been his quaint answer.

"Do you feel he keeps you company?" she laughed.

"Oh, yes! He's very good, he always keeps me company, when I'm there," said Paul.

So the horse, rather shabby, stood in an arrested prance in the boy's bedroom.

The Derby was drawing near, and the boy grew more and more tense. He hardly heard what was spoken to him, he was very frail, and his eyes were really uncanny. His mother had sudden seizures of uneasiness about him. Sometimes, for half-an-hour, she would feel a sudden anxiety about him that was almost anguish. She wanted to rush to him at once, and know he was safe.

Two nights before the Derby, she was at a big party in town, when one of her rushes of anxiety about her boy, her first-born, gripped her heart till she could hardly speak. She fought with the feeling, might and main, for she believed in common sense. But it was too strong. She had to leave the dance and go downstairs to telephone to the country. The children's nursery governess was terribly surprised and startled at being rung up in the night.

"Are the children all right, Miss Wilmot?"

"Oh, yes, they are quite all right."

"Master Paul? Is he all right?"

"He went to bed as right as a trivet. Shall I run up and look at him?"

"No," said Paul's mother reluctantly. "No! Don't trouble. It's all right. Don't sit up. We shall be home fairly soon." She did not want her son's privacy intruded upon.

"Very good," said the governess.

It was about one o'clock when Paul's mother and father drove up to their house. All was still. Paul's mother went to her room and slipped off her white fur coat. She had told her maid not to wait up for her. She heard her husband downstairs, mixing a whiskey-and-soda.

And then, because of the strange anxiety at her heart, she stole upstairs to her son's room. Noiselessly she went along the upper corridor. Was there a faint noise? What was it?

She stood, with arrested muscles, outside his door, listening. There was a strange, heavy, and yet not loud noise. Her heart stood still. It was a soundless noise, yet rushing and powerful. Something huge, in violent, hushed motion. What was it? What in God's name was it? She ought to know. She felt that she knew the noise. She knew what it was.

Yet she could not place it. She couldn't say what it was. And on and on it went, like a madness.

Softly, frozen with anxiety and fear, she turned the door handle.

The room was dark. Yet in the space near the window, she heard and saw something plunging to and fro. She gazed in fear and amazement.

Then suddenly she switched on the light, and saw her son, in his green pyjamas, madly surging on the rocking horse. The blaze of light suddenly lit him up, as he urged the wooden horse, and lit her up, as she stood, blonde, in her dress of pale green and crystal, in the doorway.

"Paul!" she cried. "Whatever are you doing?"

"It's Malabar!" he screamed, in a powerful, strange voice. "It's Malabar."

His eyes blazed at her for one strange and senseless second, as he ceased urging his wooden horse. Then he fell with a crash to the ground, and she, all her tormented motherhood flooding upon her, rushed to gather him up.

But he was unconscious, and unconscious he remained, with some brain-fever. He talked and tossed, and his mother sat stonily by his side.

"Malabar! It's Malabar! Bassett, Bassett, I know! It's Malabar!"

So the child cried, trying to get up and urge the rocking horse that gave him his inspiration.

"What does he mean by Malabar?" asked the heart-frozen mother.

"I don't know," said the father stonily.

"What does he mean by Malabar?" she asked her brother Oscar.

"It's one of the horses running for the Derby," was the answer.

And, in spite of himself, Oscar Cresswell spoke to Bassett, and himself put a thousand on Malabar: at fourteen to one.

The third day of the illness was critical: they were waiting for a change. The boy, with his rather long, curly hair, was tossing ceaselessly on the pillow. He neither slept nor regained consciousness, and his eyes were like blue stones. His mother sat, feeling her heart had gone, turned actually into a stone.

In the evening, Oscar Cresswell did not come, but Bassett sent a message, saying could he come up for one moment, just one moment? Paul's mother was very angry at the intrusion, but on second thought she agreed. The boy was the same. Perhaps Bassett might bring him to consciousness.

The gardener, a shortish fellow with a little brown moustache, and sharp little brown eyes, tiptoed into the room, touched his imaginary cap to Paul's mother, and stole to the bedside, staring with glittering, smallish eyes, at the tossing, dying child.

"Master Paul!" he whispered. "Master Paul! Malabar come in first all right, a clean win. I did as you told me. You've made over seventy thousand pounds, you have; you've got over eighty thousand. Malabar came in all right, Master Paul."

"Malabar! Malabar! Did I say Malabar, mother? Did I say Malabar! Do you think I'm lucky, mother? I knew Malabar, didn't I? Over eighty thousand pounds! I knew, didn't I know I knew? Malabar came in all right. If I ride my horse till I'm sure, then I tell you, Bassett, you can go as high as you like. Did you go for all you were worth, Bassett?"

"I went a thousand on it, Master Paul."

"I never told you, mother, that if I can ride my horse, and get there, then I'm absolutely sure—oh, absolutely! Mother, did I ever tell you? I am lucky."

"No, you never did," said the mother.

But the boy died in the night.

And even as he lay dead, his mother heard her brother's voice saying to her: "My God, Hester, you're eighty-odd thousand to the good and a poor devil of a son to the bad. But, poor devil, poor devil, he's best gone out of a life where he rides his rocking horse to find a winner."

NOTE

lucre   derogatory slang for money, financial profit, and gain

RESPONDING PERSONALLY

3. Were you left with unanswered questions at the conclusion of your reading? List them, and share your list with the class. Respond, as you can, to the questions of your classmates.

4. At which point during your reading of the story were you *most* dissatisfied with the mother's actions? When did she act most irresponsibly? What was the resulting consequence of her actions?

RESPONDING CRITICALLY/ANALYTICALLY

5. The "Once upon a time" opening of the story is immediately reminiscent of fairy tales. Working in a small group, use a T-chart to compare and contrast the characteristic similarities and differences between this story and a typical fairy tale. Based on your lists, explore the following:
   a) What purpose is served by the fairy tale pattern of this story, especially the beginning and ending?
   b) What highly implausible elements does this story introduce?
   c) Since the story's fairy tale qualities *are* so strong, why does the wrIter then choose to break the pattern of the genre? What purpose does his decision serve?

6. The writer's use of poetic language and imagery can be heard immediately upon beginning the story. Examine, for example, the opening three sentences of the story. Which other words in those sentences share the assonant vowel of the story's key word, *luck*?
   a) What is the thematic relationship among these words?
   b) What is the relation between these words and the "unspoken phrase" the house whispers? What of the boy's mispronunciation of "filthy lucre"?

7. Explore the character of the mother:
   a) Why is she, along with the father, left unnamed, at least right up until the very end of the story?
   b) What is missing from the mother's life, and the life of her entire family, that she mistakes for *luck*? Explain.
   c) Apparently, the children and the toys hear the repeated whisperings of the house, but the mother does not. Why is that? What purpose of the writer's is served by this fact?
   d) In what way does the mother's "touch[ing] the whole five thousand" pounds reinforce the story's sense of impending tragedy? Why do the voices *need* to begin screaming more frantically than ever before?
   e) At the climactic point in the story, the mother "rush[es] to gather ... up" her fallen son. In what way does this single action break with the

behaviours she exhibits through the rest of the story? Why does the writer allow this to happen?

    f) Is the mother most responsible for the boy's death? Or can that responsibility be shifted to at least one other character? Explain your thinking, and support it with detail from the story.

8. Numerous ironies are to be found throughout the story. With a partner, identify one compelling example of irony that you feel supports clearly the theme that the writer explores. Explain the irony and its relationship to the story's theme. Share your explanations with your classmates.

RESPONDING CREATIVELY

9. In a small group, assist a moderator of a family talk show to prepare an interview with the principal characters of the story—Paul, his mother, his father, Uncle Oscar, and Bassett. The interview, conducted in Q & A format, will deal with the question of the need for love and affection in human relationships.

    a) Write a series of two or more questions that will be asked of each of the story's characters. The questions should be such that they can be answered from the context and details of the story.

    b) Arrange the questions into a sequence that moves from simpler to more complex, from more obvious to less so.

    c) If possible, present your interview. You may wish to prepare the answers in scripted form or to improvise the responses.

SELF-ASSESSMENT

Which three of the questions will be the most difficult to answer? Why? Does the difficulty lie in the story's details, or in your interpretation and visualization of those details?

10. Several times in the story, the author makes reference to the boy's eyes. In a small group, create a collage of visual images that match the many and varied descriptions the writer has provided. Include as elements of your collage some of the actual words of the story.

PROBLEM SOLVING OR DECISION MAKING

11. Frequently, interpretations of this story support the theme that money and the pursuit of material wealth—at the expense of love and humanity—do not lead to happiness. Do you agree or disagree with this idea? Does the desire for wealth *inevitably* lead to tragedy or unhappiness? Discuss in small groups. Present your group's ideas, conclusions, and/or examples to the class in the form of a panel discussion.

Arthur C. Clarke
"If I Forget Thee, Oh Earth ..."

PRE-READING

1. How do you learn best? If someone needed to "teach" you something considered extremely important, what could they do to make certain that you really learned the lesson? Describe the ideal learning situation.

2. How do people endure living a lifetime of despair, knowing they will never have what they want or need? What kind of person is best suited to survive such a life? Explain.

When Marvin was ten years old, his father took him through the long, echoing corridors that led up through Administration and Power, until at last they came to the uppermost levels of all and were among the swiftly growing vegetation of the Farmlands. Marvin liked it here: it was fun watching the great, slender plants creeping with almost visible eagerness towards the sunlight as it filtered down through the plastic domes to meet them. The smell of life was everywhere, awakening inexpressible longings in his heart: no longer was he breathing the dry, cool air of the residential levels, purged of all smells but the faint tang of ozone. He wished he could stay here for a little while, but Father would not let him. They went onwards until they had reached the entrance to the Observatory, which he had never visited: but they did not stop, and Marvin knew with a sense of rising excitement that there could be only one goal left. For the first time in his life, he was going Outside.

There were a dozen of the surface vehicles, with their wide balloon tyres and pressurised cabins, in the great servicing chamber. His father must have been expected, for they were led at once to the little scout car waiting by the huge circular door of the airlock. Tense with expectancy, Marvin settled himself down in the cramped cabin while his father started the motor and checked the controls. The inner door of the lock slid open and then closed behind them: he heard the roar of the great air-pumps fade slowly away as the pressure dropped to zero. Then the "Vacuum" sign flashed on, the outer door parted, and before Marvin lay the land which he had never yet entered.

He had seen it in photographs, of course: he had watched it imaged on television screens a hundred times. But now it was lying all around him, burning beneath the fierce sun that crawled so slowly across the jet-black sky. He stared into the west, away from the blinding splendour of the sun—and there were the stars, as he had been told but had never quite believed. He gazed at them for a long time, marvelling that anything could be so bright and yet so tiny. They were intense unscintillating points, and suddenly he remembered a rhyme he had once read in one of his father's books:

Twinkle, twinkle, little star,
How I wonder what you are.

Well, he knew what the stars were. Whoever asked that question must have been very stupid. And what did they mean by "twinkle"? You could see at a glance that all the stars shone with the same steady, unwavering light. He abandoned the puzzle and turned his attention to the landscape around him.

They were racing across a level plain at almost a hundred miles an hour, the great balloon tyres sending up little spurts of dust behind them. There was no sign of the Colony: in the few minutes while he had been gazing at the stars, its domes and radio towers had fallen below the horizon. Yet there were other indications of man's presence, for about a mile ahead Marvin could see the curiously shaped structures clustering round the head of a mine. Now and then a puff of vapour would emerge from a squat smoke-stack and would instantly disperse.

They were past the mine in a moment. Father was driving with a reckless and exhilarating skill as if—it was a strange thought to come into a child's mind—he was trying to escape from something. In a few minutes they had reached the edge of the plateau on which the Colony had been built. The ground fell sharply away beneath them in a dizzying slope whose lower stretches were lost in the shadow. Ahead, as far as the eye could reach, was a jumbled wasteland of craters, mountain ranges, and ravines. The crests of the mountains, catching the low sun, burned like islands of fire in a sea of darkness: and above them the stars still shone as steadfastly as ever.

There could be no way forward—yet there was. Marvin clenched his fists as the car edged over the slope and started the long descent. Then he saw the barely visible track leading down the mountainside, and relaxed a little. Other men, it seemed, had gone this way before.

Night fell with a shocking abruptness as they crossed the shadow line and the sun dropped below the crest of the plateau. The twin searchlights sprang into life, casting blue-white bands on the rocks ahead, so that there was scarcely need to check their speed. For hours they drove through valleys and past the feet of mountains whose peaks seemed to comb the stars, and sometimes they emerged for a moment into the sunlight as they climbed over higher ground.

And now on the right was a wrinkled, dusty plain, and on the left, its ramparts and terraces rising mile after mile into the sky, was a wall of mountains that marched into the distance until its peaks sank from sight below the rim of the world. There was no sign that men had ever explored this land, but once they passed the skeleton of a crashed rocket, and beside it a stone cairn surmounted by a metal cross.

It seemed to Marvin that the mountains stretched on forever: but at last, many hours later, the range ended in a towering, precipitous headland that rose steeply from a cluster of little hills. They drove down into a shallow valley that curved in a great arc towards the far side of the mountains: and as they did so, Marvin slowly realised that something very strange was happening in the land ahead.

The sun was now low behind the hills on the right: the valley before them should be in total darkness. Yet it was awash with a cold white radiance that came spilling over the crags beneath which they were driving. Then, suddenly, they were out in the open plain, and the source of the light lay before them in all its glory.

It was very quiet in the little cabin now that the motors had stopped. The only sound was the faint whisper of the oxygen feed and an occasional metallic crepitation as the outer walls of the vehicle radiated away their heat. For no warmth at all came from the great silver crescent that floated low above the far horizon and flooded all this land with pearly light. It was so brilliant that minutes passed before Marvin could accept its challenge and look steadfastly into its glare, but at last he could discern the outlines of continents, the hazy border of the atmosphere, and the white islands of cloud. And even at this distance, he could see the glitter of sunlight on the polar ice.

It was beautiful, and it called to his heart across the abyss of space. There in that shining crescent were all the wonders that he had never known—the hues of sunset skies, the moaning of the sea on pebbled shores, the patter of falling rain, the unhurried benison of snow. These and a thousand others should have been his rightful heritage, but he knew them only from the books and ancient records, and the thought filled him with the anguish of exile.

Why could they not return? It seemed so peaceful beneath those lines of marching cloud. Then Marvin, his eyes no longer blinded by the glare, saw that the portion of the disc that should have been in darkness was gleaming faintly with an evil phosphorescence: and he remembered. He was looking upon the funeral pyre of a world—upon the radioactive aftermath of Armageddon. Across a quarter of a million miles of space, the glow of dying atoms was still visible, a perennial reminder of the ruined past. It would be centuries yet before that deadly glow died from the rocks and life could return again to fill that silent, empty world.

And now Father began to speak, telling Marvin the story which until this moment had meant no more to him than the fairy-tales he had heard in childhood. There were many things he could not understand: it was impossible for him to picture the glowing, multi-coloured pattern of life on the planet he had never seen. Nor could he comprehend the forces that had destroyed it in the end, leaving the Colony, preserved by its isolation, as the sole survivor. Yet he could share the agony of those final days, when the Colony had learned at last that never again would the supply ships come flaming down through the stars with gifts from home. One by one the radio stations had ceased to call: on the shadowed globe the lights of the cities had dimmed and died, and they were alone at last, as no men had ever been alone before, carrying in their hands the future of the race.

Then had followed the years of despair, and the long-drawn battle for survival in their fierce and hostile world. That battle had been won, though barely: this little oasis of life was safe against the worst that Nature could do. But unless there was a goal, a future towards which it could work, the colony would lose the will to live and neither machines nor skill nor science could save it then.

So, at last, Marvin understood the purpose of this pilgrimage. He would never walk beside the rivers of that lost and legendary world, or listen to the thunder raging above its softly rounded hills. Yet one day—how far ahead?—his children's children would return to claim their heritage. The winds and the rains would scour the poisons from the burning lands and carry them to the sea, and in the depths of the sea they would waste their venom until they could harm no living things. Then the great ships that were still waiting here on the silent, dusty plains could lift once more into space, along the road that led to home.

That was the dream: and one day, Marvin knew with a sudden flash of insight, he would pass it on to his own son, here at this same spot with the mountains behind him and the silver light from the sky streaming into his face.

He did not look back as they began the homeward journey. He could not bear to see the cold glory of the crescent Earth fade from the rocks around him, as he went to rejoin his people in their long exile.

RESPONDING PERSONALLY

3. Is the ending pessimistic or hopeful? What thoughts are you left with as Marvin does "not look back" because he cannot "bear to see the cold glory of the crescent Earth fade"?

4. Do you know of any person—either from personal experience or otherwise—who willingly made sacrifices and worked hard so that "things would be better" for her or his children and grandchildren? In writing, share what you know of this person. What quality of character helped this person through a life that must have seemed, at least at times, very bleak?

RESPONDING CRITICALLY/ANALYTICALLY

5. Explore the conflict that the father has been forced to face.
   a) What is his goal in terms of the conflict of this story? Does he successfully attain it?
   b) What has been his motivation in reaching for that goal?
   c) In what way is the story's goal related to the father's own life's goal?
   d) Is it inevitable that the father's conflict will become the son's? Or has the writer allowed the glimmer of a possibility that Marvin's life will

be less despairing than his father's has been? Share your thoughts in class discussion.

6. In several instances in the story, the writer uses the imagery of fire in his descriptions of what the boy sees. Identify at least one such example. What might be his purpose in using this imagery?

7. At one point in the story, the scout car in which the two are travelling passes a mine. Explore the connotations that *your* experience or imagination evokes of mine-related work.
   a) Describe briefly the typical physical environment of the mine setting: is it picturesque or drab? Is it visually appealing? Does it engage any other senses? In what way?
   b) Describe briefly the nature of the labour: is it engaging? creative? uplifting? Does it vary from day to day, providing stimulation to the mind and heart and soul? Explain.
   c) Describe the likely long-term physical and emotional effects on those who toil there.

Why has the writer chosen to make this one brief mention of the mine? What is the symbolic overtone?

Self-Assessment

When is a symbol a symbol, and when is it not? How do you determine when it is that a character in a story, an object, a name, an incident, or a location has become a symbol? Together with a partner, brainstorm your criteria for calling something a symbol. Share your thoughts in a class discussion.

8. The story has been written from the limited omniscient point of view of the boy.
   a) How would the content of the story be altered if it were told from a first-person perspective? Could the same story still be told? Explain why or why not.
   b) How would it be altered if the narration were fully omniscient—that is, if the father's voice were also heard? Again, could the same story still be told? Explain.

Responding Creatively

9. Compose the poem that an optimistic, future-oriented, altruistic Marvin might write to his children's children's children.

10. Write the journal entry that the Marvin who cannot "bear to see the cold glory" and instead turns to face his own "long exile" writes, ultimately to his descendants.

PROBLEM SOLVING OR DECISION MAKING

11. How difficult is it for the father in the story to make a choice between two alternatives: destroy his son's hope in a possible personal future, or destroy humanity's hope in a real one? Would you want your child to ever have knowledge of a very desirable object or situation in life that you know your child could *never* own or experience? Would you be doing the better thing by *not* letting your child know? Discuss your thoughts in writing.

Stories for Further Reading

The selections of this section are offered for reader enjoyment and as a source for extended studies in the short story. They deal with some of the themes of the previous eight units, but introduce more themes and different approaches that have been taken by other authors in crafting stories.

Four of the selections originate from Canada. "The Lost Salt Gift of Blood," about a homecoming, is by Nova Scotia's award-winning Alistair MacLeod. "A Bolt of White Cloth" by Leon Rooke is a hilarious takeoff with biblical overtones on the tall tale. Keath Fraser of British Columbia weighs in with "Roget's Thesaurus," a highly imaginative short short story excursion through the popular reference book of the title. From Quebec comes the wise, atmospheric story about the passage of time by Yvette Naubert entitled "The Pigeons of St. Louis Square."

"Frustration" by Isaac Asimov is a short science fiction story written mostly as philosophical dialogue about the differences between humans and computers. "Spring Storm" by Mori Yoko originates from Japan and is about a celebration that turns into the end of a relationship.

"A Woman without Prejudice" by Russia's Anton Chekhov is a light comical piece about love and the pursuit of happiness.

As you read these additional stories, think about their characters, conflicts, themes, and symbols. Examine what it is that makes them unique—their humour and cleverness; the story's setting and atmosphere; the author's style and approach to point of view and characterization.

Alistair MacLeod
The Lost Salt Gift of Blood

Now in the early evening the sun is flashing everything in gold. It bathes the blunt grey rocks that loom yearningly out toward Europe and it touches upon the stunted spruce and the low-lying lichens and the delicate hardy ferns and the ganglia-rooted moss and the tiny tough rock cranberries. The grey and slanting rain squalls have swept in from the sea and then departed with all the suddenness of surprise marauders. Everything before them and beneath them has been rapidly, briefly, and thoroughly drenched and now the clear droplets catch and hold the sun's infusion in a myriad of rainbow colours. Far beyond the harbour's mouth more tiny squalls seem to be forming, moving rapidly across the surface of the sea out there beyond land's end where the blue ocean turns to grey in rain and distance and the strain of eyes. Even farther out, somewhere beyond Cape Spear lies Dublin and the Irish coast; far away but still the nearest land and closer now than is Toronto or Detroit to say nothing of North America's more western cities; seeming almost hazily visible now in imagination's mist.

Overhead the ivory white gulls wheel and cry, flashing also in the purity of the sun and the clean, freshly washed air. Sometimes they glide to the blue-green surface of the harbour, squawking and garbling; at times almost standing on their pink webbed feet as if they would walk on water, flapping their wings pompously against their breasts like over-conditioned he-men who have successfully passed their body-building courses. At other times they gather in lazy groups on the rocks above the harbour's entrance murmuring softly to themselves or looking also quietly out toward what must be Ireland and the vastness of the sea.

The harbour itself is very small and softly curving, seeming like a tiny, peaceful womb nurturing the life that now lies within it which originated from without; came from without and through the narrow, rock-tight channel that admits the entering and withdrawing sea. That sea is entering again now, forcing itself gently but inevitably through the tightness of the opening and laving the rocky walls and rising and rolling into the harbour's inner cover. The dories rise at their moorings and the tide laps higher on the piles and advances upward toward the high-water marks upon the land; the running moon-drawn tides of spring.

Around the edges of the harbour brightly coloured houses dot the wet and glistening rocks. In some ways they seem almost like defiantly optimistic horseshoe nails: yellow and scarlet and green and pink; buoyantly yet firmly permanent in the grey unsundered rock.

At the harbour's entrance the small boys are jigging for the beautifully speckled salmon-pink sea trout. Barefootedly they stand on the tide-wet rocks flicking their wrists and sending their glistening lines in shimmering golden arcs out into the rising tide. Their voices mount excitedly as they shout to one another encouragement, advice, consolation. The trout fleck dazzlingly on their sides as they are drawn toward the rocks, turning to seeming silver as they flash within the sea.

It is all of this that I see now, standing at the final road's end of my twenty-five-hundred-mile journey. The road ends here — quite literally ends at the door of a now abandoned fishing shanty some six brief yards in front of where I stand. The shanty is grey and weatherbeaten with two boarded-up windows, vanishing wind-whipped shingles and a heavy rusted padlock chained fast to a twisted door. Piled before the twisted door and its equally twisted frame are some marker buoys, a small pile of rotted rope, a broken oar and an old and rust-flaked anchor.

The option of driving my small rented Volkswagen the remaining six yards and then negotiating a right many-twists-of-the-steering-wheel turn still exists. I would be then facing toward the west and could simply retrace the manner of my coming. I could easily drive away before anything might begin.

Instead I walk beyond the road's end and the fishing shanty and begin to descend the rocky path that winds tortuously and narrowly along and down the cliff's edge to the sea. The small stones roll and turn and scrape beside and beneath my shoes and after only a few steps the leather is nicked and scratched. My toes press hard against its straining surface.

As I approach the actual water's edge four small boys are jumping excitedly upon the glistening rocks. One of them has made a strike and is attempting to reel in his silver-turning prize. The other three have laid down their rods in their enthusiasm and are shouting encouragement and giving almost physical moral support: "Don't let him get away, John," they say. "Keep the line steady." "Hold the end of the rod up." "Reel in the slack." "Good." "What a dandy!"

Across the harbour's clear water another six or seven shout the same delirious messages. The silver-turning fish is drawn toward the rock. In the shallows he flips and arcs, his flashing body breaking the water's surface as he walks upon his tail. The small fisherman has now his rod almost completely vertical. Its tip sings and vibrates high above his head while at his feet the trout spins and curves. Both of his hands are clenched around the rod and his knuckles strain white through the water-roughened redness of small-boy hands. He does not know whether he should relinquish the rod and grasp at the lurching trout or merely heave the rod backward and flip the fish behind him. Suddenly he decides upon the latter but even as he heaves his bare feet slide out from beneath him on the smooth wetness of the rock and he slips down into the water. With a pirouetting leap the trout turns glisteningly and tears itself free. In a darting flash of darkened greenness it rights itself with the regained water and is gone. "Oh damn!" says the small fisherman, struggling upright onto his rock. He bites his lower lip to hold back the tears welling within his eyes. There is a small trickle of blood coursing down from a tiny scratch on the inside of his wrist and he is wet up to his knees. I reach down to retrieve the rod and return it to him.

Suddenly a shout rises from the opposite shore. Another line zings tautly through the water throwing off fine showers of iridescent droplets. The shouts and contagious excitement spread anew. "Don't let him get away!" "Good for you." "Hang on!" "Hang on!"

I am caught up in it myself and wish also to shout some enthusiastic advice but I do not know what to say. The trout curves up from the water in a wriggling arch and lands behind the boys in the moss and lichen that grow down to the sea-washed rocks. They race to free it from the line and proclaim about its size.

On our side of the harbour the boys begin to talk. "Where do you live?" they ask me and is it far away and is it bigger than St. John's?

Awkwardly I try to tell them the nature of the North American Midwest. In turn I ask them if they go to school. "Yes," they say. Some of them go to St. Bonaventure's which is the Catholic school and others go to Twilling Memorial. They are all in either grade four or grade five. All of them say that they like school and that they like their teachers.

The fishing is good they say and they come here almost every evening. "Yesterday I caught me a nine-pounder," says John. Eagerly they show me all of their simple equipment. The rods are of all varieties as are the lines. At the lines' ends the leaders are thin transparencies terminating in grotesque three-clustered hooks. A foot or so from each hook there is a silver spike knotted into the leader. Some of the boys say the trout are attracted by the flashing of the spike; others say that it acts only as a weight or sinker. No line is without one.

"Here, sir," says John, "have a go. Don't get your shoes wet." Standing on the slippery rocks in my smooth-soled shoes I twice attempt awkward casts. Both times the line loops up too high and the spike splashes down far short of the running, rising life of the channel.

"Just a flick of the wrist, sir," he says, "just a flick of the wrist. You'll soon get the hang of it." His hair is red and curly and his face is splashed with freckles and his eyes are clear and blue. I attempt three or four more casts and then pass the rod back to the hands where it belongs.

And now it is time for supper. The calls float down from the women standing in the doorways of the multi-coloured houses and obediently the small fishermen gather up their equipment and their catches and prepare to ascend the narrow upward-winding paths. The sun has descended deeper into the sea and the evening has become quite cool. I recognize this with surprise and a slight shiver. In spite of the advice given to me and my own precautions my feet are wet and chilled within my shoes. No place to be unless barefooted or in rubber boots. Perhaps for me no place at all.

As we lean into the steepness of the path my young companions continue to talk, their accents broad and Irish. One of them used to have a tame sea gull at his house, had it for seven years. His older brother found it on the rocks and brought it home. His grandfather called it Joey. "Because it talked so much," explains John. It died last week and they held a funeral about a mile away from the shore where there was enough soil to dig a grave. Along the shore itself it is almost solid rock and there is no ground for a grave. It's the same with people they say. All week they have been hopefully looking along the base of the cliffs for another sea gull but have not found one. You cannot kill a sea gull they say, the government protects them because they are scavengers and keep the harbours clean.

The path is narrow and we walk in single file. By the time we reach the shanty and my rented car I am wheezing and badly out of breath. So badly out of shape for a man of thirty-three; sauna baths do nothing for your wind. The boys walk easily, laughing and talking beside me. With polite enthusiasm they comment upon my car. Again there exists the possibility of restarting the car's engine and driving back the road that I have come. After all, I have not seen a single adult except for the women calling down the news of supper. I stand and fiddle with my keys.

The appearance of the man and the dog is sudden and unexpected. We have been so casual and unaware in front of the small automobile that we have neither seen nor heard their approach along the rock-worn road. The dog is short, stocky and black and white. White hair floats and feathers freely from his sturdy legs and paws as he trots along the rock looking expectantly out into the harbour. He takes no notice of me. The man is short and stocky as well and he also appears as black and white. His rubber boots are black and his dark heavy worsted trousers are supported by a broadly scarred and blackened belt. The buckle is shaped like a dory with a fisherman standing in the bow. Above the belt there is a dark navy woollen jersey and upon his head a toque of the same material. His hair beneath the toque is white as is the three-or-four-day stubble on his face. His eyes are blue and his hands heavy, gnarled, and misshapen. It is hard to tell from looking at him whether he is in his sixties, seventies, or eighties.

"Well, it is a nice evening tonight," he says, looking first at John and then to me. "The barometer has not dropped so perhaps fair weather will continue for a day or two. It will be good for the fishing."

He picks a piece of gnarled grey driftwood from the roadside and swings it slowly back and forth in his right hand. With desperate anticipation the dog dances back and forth before him, his intense eyes glittering at the stick. When it is thrown into the harbour he barks

joyously and disappears, hurling himself down the bank in a scrambling avalanche of small stones. In seconds he reappears with only his
head visible, cutting a silent but rapidly advancing V through the
quiet serenity of the harbour. The boys run to the bank's edge and
shout encouragement to him — much as they had been doing earlier
for one another. "It's farther out," they cry, "to the right, to the right."
Almost totally submerged, he cannot see the stick he swims to find.
The boys toss stones in its general direction and he raises himself out
of the water to see their landing splashdowns and to change his wide-
waked course.

"How have you been?" asks the old man, reaching for a pipe and a
pouch of tobacco and then without waiting for an answer, "perhaps
you'll stay for supper. There are just the three of us now."

We begin to walk along the road in the direction that he has come.
Before long the boys rejoin us accompanied by the dripping dog with
the recovered stick. He waits for the old man to take it from him and
then showers us all with a spray of water from his shaggy coat. The
man pats and scratches the damp head and the dripping ears. He
keeps the returned stick and thwacks it against his rubber boots as we
continue to walk along the rocky road I have so recently travelled in
my Volkswagen.

Within a few yards the houses begin to appear upon our left. Frame
and flat-roofed, they cling to the rocks looking down into the harbour.
In storms their windows are splashed by the sea but now their bright
colours are buoyantly brave in the shadows of the descending dusk.
At the third gate, John, the man, and the dog turn in. I follow them.
The remaining boys continue on; they wave and say, "So long."

The path that leads through the narrow whitewashed gate has had
its stone worn smooth by the passing of countless feet. On either side
there is a row of small, smooth stones, also neatly whitewashed, and
seeming like a procession of large white eggs or tiny unbaked loaves
of bread. Beyond these stones and also on either side, there are some
cast-off tires also white-washed and serving as flower beds. Within
each whitened circumference the colourful low-lying flowers nod;
some hardy strain of pansies or perhaps marigolds. The path leads on
to the square green house, with its white borders and shutters. On one
side of the wooden doorstep a skate blade has been nailed, for the
wiping off of feet, and beyond the swinging screen door there is a

porch which smells saltily of the sea. A variety of sou'westers and rubber boots and mitts and caps hang from the driven nails or lie at the base of the wooden walls.

Beyond the porch there is the kitchen where the woman is at work. All of us enter. The dog walks across the linoleum-covered floor, his nails clacking, and flings himself with a contented sigh beneath the wooden table. Almost instantly he is asleep, his coat still wet from his swim within the sea.

The kitchen is small. It has an iron cookstove, a table against one wall and three or four handmade chairs of wood. There is also a wooden rocking-chair covered by a cushion. The rockers are so thin from years of use that it is hard to believe they still function. Close by the table there is a wash-stand with two pails of water upon it. A wash-basin hangs from a driven nail in its side and above it is an old-fashioned mirrored medicine cabinet. There is also a large cupboard, a low-lying couch, and a window facing upon the sea. On the walls a barometer hangs as well as two pictures, one of a rather jaunty young couple taken many years ago. It is yellowed and rather indistinct; the woman in a long dress with her hair done up in ringlets, the man in a serge suit that is slightly too large for him and with a tweed cap pulled rakishly over his right eye. He has an accordion strapped over his shoulders and his hands are fanned out on the buttons and keys. The other picture is of the Christ-child. Beneath it is written, "Sweet Heart of Jesus Pray for Us."

The woman at the stove is tall and fine featured. Her grey hair is combed briskly back from her forehead and neatly coiled with a large pin at the base of her neck. Her eyes are as grey as the storm scud of the sea. Her age, like her husband's, is difficult to guess. She wears a blue print dress, a plain blue apron and low-heeled brown shoes. She is turning fish within a frying pan when we enter.

Her eyes contain only mild surprise as she first regards me. Then with recognition they glow in open hostility which in turn subsides and yields to self-control. She continues at the stove while the rest of us sit upon the chairs.

During the meal that follows we are reserved and shy in our lonely adult ways; groping for and protecting what perhaps may be the only awful dignity we possess. John, unheedingly, talks on and on. He is in the fifth grade and is doing well. They are learning percentages and the mysteries of decimals; to change a percent to a decimal fraction you move the decimal point two places to the left and drop the percent sign. You always, always do so. They are learning the different breeds of domestic animals: the four main breeds of dairy cattle are Holstein, Ayrshire, Guernsey, and Jersey. He can play the mouth organ and will demonstrate after supper. He has twelve lobster traps of his own. They were originally broken ones thrown up on the rocky shore by storms. Ira, he says nodding toward the old man, helped him fix them, nailing on new lathes and knitting new headings. Now they are set along the rocks near the harbour's entrance. He is averaging a pound a trap and the "big" fishermen say that that is better than some of them are doing. He is saving his money in a little imitation keg that was also washed upon the shore. He would like to buy an outboard motor for the small reconditioned skiff he now uses to visit his traps. At present he has only oars.

"John here has the makings of a good fisherman," says the old man. "He's up at five most every morning when I am putting on the fire. He and the dog are already out along the shore and back before I've made tea."

"When I was in Toronto," says John, "no one was ever up before seven. I would make my own tea and wait. It was wonderful sad. There were gulls there though, flying over Toronto harbour. We went to see them on two Sundays."

After supper we move the chairs back from the table. The woman clears away the dishes and the old man turns on the radio. First he listens to the weather forecast and then turns to short wave where he picks up the conversations from the offshore fishing boats. They are conversations of catches and winds and tides and of the women left behind on the rocky shores. John appears with his mouth organ, standing at a respectful distance. The old man notices him, nods, and shuts off the radio. Rising, he goes upstairs, the sound of his feet echoing down to us. Returning he carries an old and battered accordion. "My fingers have so much rheumatism," he says, "that I find it hard to play anymore."

Seated, he slips his arms through the straps and begins the squeezing accordion motions. His wife takes off her apron and stands behind him with one hand upon his shoulder. For a moment they take on the essence of the once young people in the photograph. They began to sing:

Come all ye fair and tender ladies
Take warning how you court your men
They're like the stars on a summer's morning
First they'll appear and then they're gone.

I wish I were a tiny sparrow
And I had wings and I could fly
I'd fly away to my own true lover
And all he'd ask I would deny.

Alas I'm not a tiny sparrow
I have not wings nor can I fly
And on this earth in grief and sorrow
I am bound until I die.

John sits on one of the home-made chairs playing his mouth organ. He seems as all mouth-organ players the world over: his right foot tapping out the measures and his small shoulders now round and hunched above the cupped hand instrument.

"Come now and sing with us, John," says the old man.

Obediently he takes the mouth organ from his mouth and shakes the moisture drops upon his sleeve. All three of them begin to sing, spanning easily the half century of time that touches their extremes. The old and the young singing now their songs of loss in different comprehensions. Stranded here, alien of my middle generation, I tap my leather foot self-consciously upon the linoleum. The words sweep up and swirl about my head. Fog does not touch like snow yet it is more heavy and more dense. Oh moisture comes in many forms!

All alone as I strayed by the banks of the river
Watching the moonbeams at evening of day
All alone as I wandered I spied a young stranger
Weeping and wailing with many a sigh.

Weeping for one who is now lying lonely
Weeping for one who no mortal can save
As the foaming dark waters flow silently past him
Onward they flow over young Jenny's grave.

Oh Jenny my darling come tarry here with me
Don't leave me alone, love, distracted in pain
For as death is the dagger that plied us asunder
Wide is the gulf, love, between you and I.

After the singing stops we all sit rather uncomfortably for a moment. The mood seeming to hang heavily upon our shoulders. Then with my single exception all come suddenly to action. John gets up and takes his battered school books to the kitchen table. The dog jumps up on a chair beside him and watches solemnly in a supervisory manner. The woman takes some navy yarn the colour of her husband's jersey and begins to knit. She is making another jersey and is working on the sleeve. The old man rises and beckons me to follow him into the tiny parlour. The stuffed furniture is old and worn. There is a tiny wood-burning heater in the centre of the room. It stands on a square of galvanized metal which protects the floor from falling, burning coals. The stovepipe rises and vanishes into the wall on its way to the upstairs. There is an old-fashioned mantelpiece on the wall behind the stove. It is covered with odd shapes of driftwood from the shore and a variety of exotically shaped bottles, blue and green and red, which are from the shore as well. There are pictures here too: of the couple in the other picture; and one of them with their five daughters; and one of the five daughters by themselves. In that far-off picture time all of the daughters seem roughly between the ages of ten and eighteen. The youngest has the reddest hair of all. So red that it seems to triumph over the non-photographic colours of lonely black and white. The pictures are in standard wooden frames.

From behind the ancient chesterfield the old man pulls a collapsible card table and pulls down its warped and shaky legs. Also from behind the chesterfield he takes a faded checkerboard and a large old-fashioned matchbox of rattling wooden checkers. The spine of the board is almost cracked through and is strengthened by layers of adhesive tape. The checkers are circumferences of wood sawed from a length of broom handle. They are about three quarters of an inch thick. Half of them are painted a bright blue and the other half an equally eyecatching red. "John made these," said the old man, "all of them are not really the same thickness but they are good enough. He gave it a good try."

We begin to play checkers. He takes the blue and I the red. The house is silent with only the click-clack of the knitting needles sounding through the quiet rooms. From time to time the old man lights his pipe, digging out the old ashes with a flattened nail and tamping in the fresh tobacco with the same nail's head. The blue smoke winds lazily and haphazardly toward the low-beamed ceiling. The game is solemn as is the next and then the next. Neither of us loses all of the time.

"It is time for some of us to be in bed," says the old woman after a while. She gathers up her knitting and rises from her chair. In the kitchen John neatly stacks his school books on one corner of the table in anticipation of the morning. He goes outside for a moment and then returns. Saying good-night very formally he goes up the stairs to bed. In a short while the old woman follows, her footsteps travelling the same route.

We continue to play checkers, wreathed in smoke and only partially aware of the muffled footfalls sounding softly above our heads. When the old man gets up to go outside I am not really surprised, any more than I am when he returns with the brown, ostensible vinegar jug. Poking at the declining kitchen fire, he moves the kettle about seeking the warmest spot on the cooling stove. He takes two glasses from the cupboard, a sugar bowl and two spoons. The kettle begins to boil.

Even before tasting it, I know the rum to be strong and overproof. It comes at night and in fog from the French islands of St. Pierre and Miquelon. Coming over in the low-throttled fishing boats, riding in imitation gas cans. He mixes the rum and the sugar first, watching them marry and dissolve. Then to prevent the breakage of the glasses he places a teaspoon in each and adds the boiling water. The odour rises richly, its sweetness hung in steam. He brings the glasses to the table, holding them by their tops so that his fingers will not burn.

We do not say anything for some time, sitting upon the chairs, while the sweetened, heated richness moves warmly through and from our stomachs and spreads upward to our brains. Outside the wind begins to blow, moaning and faintly rattling the window's whitened shutters. He rises and brings refills. We are warm within the dark and still within the wind. A clock strikes regularly the strokes of ten.

It is difficult to talk at times with or without liquor; difficult to achieve the actual act of saying. Sitting still we listen further to the rattle of the wind; not knowing where nor how we should begin. Again the glasses are refilled.

"When she married in Toronto," he says at last, "we figured that maybe John should be with her and with her husband. That maybe he would be having more of a chance there in the city. But we would be putting it off and it weren't until nigh on two years that he went. Went with a woman from down the cove going to visit her daughter. Well, what was wrong was that we missed him wonderful awful. More fearful than we ever thought. Even the dog. Just pacing the floor and looking out the window and walking along the rocks of the shore. Like us had no moorings, lost in the fog or on the ice-floes in a snow squall. Nigh sick unto our hearts we was. Even the grandmother who before that was maybe thinking small to herself that he was trouble in her old age. Ourselves having never had no sons only daughters."

He pauses, then rising goes upstairs and returns with an envelope. From it he takes a picture which shows two young people standing self-consciously before a half-ton pickup with a wooden extension ladder fastened to its side. They appear to be in their middle twenties. The door of the truck has the information: "Jim Farrell, Toronto: House painting, Eavestroughing, Aluminum Siding, Phone 535-3484," lettered on its surface.

"This was in the last letter," he says. "That Farrell I guess was a nice enough fellow, from Heartsick Bay he was."

"Anyway they could have no more peace with John than we could without him. Like I says he was here too long before his going and it took ahold of us the way it will. They send word that he was coming on the plane to St. John's with a woman they'd met through a Newfoundland club. I was to go to St. John's to meet him. Well, it was all wrong the night before the going. The signs all bad; the grandmother knocked off the lampshade and it broke in a hunnerd pieces — the sign of death; and the window blind fell and clattered there on the floor and then lied still. And the dog runned around like he was crazy, moanen and cryen worse than the swiles does out on the ice, and throwen hisself against the walls and jumpen on the table and at the window where the blind fell until we would have to be letten him out. But it be no better for he runned and throwed hisself in the sea and then come back and howled outside the same window and jumped against the wall, splashen the water from his coat all over it. Then he be runnen back to the sea again. All the neighbours heard him and said I should bide at home and not go to St. John's at all. We be all wonderful scared and not know what to do and the next mornen, first thing I drops me knife."

"But still I feels I has to go. It be foggy all the day and everyone be thinken the plane won't come or be able to land. And I says, small to myself, now here in the fog be the bad luck and the death but then there the plane be, almost like a ghost ship comen out the fog with all its lights shinen. I think maybe he won't be on it but soon he comen through the fog, first with the woman and then see'n me and starten to run, closer and closer till I can feel him in me arms and the tears on both our cheeks. Powerful strange how things will take one. That night they be killed."

From the envelope that contained the picture he draws forth a tattered clipping:

Jennifer Farrell of Roncesvalles Avenue was instantly killed early this morning and her husband James died later in emergency at St. Joseph's Hospital. The accident occurred about 2 A.M. when the pickup truck in which they were travelling went out of control on Queen St. W. and struck a utility pole. It is thought that bad visibility caused by a heavy fog may have contributed to the accident. The Farrells were originally from Newfoundland.

Again he moves to refill the glasses. "We be all alone," he says. "All our other daughters married and far away in Montreal, Toronto, or the States. Hard for them to come back here, even to visit; they comes only every three years or so for perhaps a week. So we be hav'n only him."

And now my head begins to reel even as I move to the filling of my own glass. Not waiting this time for the courtesy of his offer. Making myself perhaps too much at home with this man's glass and this man's rum and this man's house and all the feelings of his love. Even as I did before. Still locked again for words.

Outside we stand and urinate, turning our backs to the seeming gale so as not to splash our wind-snapped trousers. We are almost driven forward to rock upon our toes and settle on our heels, so blow the gusts. Yet in spite of all, the stars shine clearly down. It will indeed be a good day for the fishing and this wind eventually will calm. The salt hangs heavy in the air and the water booms against the rugged rocks. I take a stone and throw it against the wind into the sea.

Going up the stairs we clutch the wooden banister unsteadily and say good night.

The room has changed very little. The window rattles in the wind and the unfinished beams sway and creak. The room is full of sound. Like a foolish Lockwood I approach the window although I hear no voice. There is no Catherine who cries to be let in. Standing unsteadily on one foot when required I manage to undress, draping my trousers across the wooden chair. The bed is clean. It makes no sound. It is plain and wooden, its mattress stuffed with hay or kelp. I feel it with my hand and pull back the heavy patchwork quilts. Still I do not go into it. Instead I go back to the door which has no knob but only an ingenious latch formed from a twisted nail. Turning it, I go out into the hallway. All is dark and the house seems even more inclined to creak where there is no window. Feeling along the wall with my outstretched hand I find the door quite easily. It is closed with the same kind of latch and not difficult to open. But no one waits on the other side. I stand and bend my ear to hear the even sound of my one son's sleeping. He does not beckon any more than the nonexistent voice in the outside wind. I hesitate to touch the latch for fear that I may waken him and disturb his dreams. And if I did what would I say? Yet I would like to see him in his sleep this once and see the room with the quiet bed once more and the wooden chair beside it from off an old wrecked trawler. There is no boiled egg or shaker of salt or glass of water waiting on the chair within this closed room's darkness.

Once though there was a belief held in the outports, that if a girl would see her own true lover she should boil an egg and scoop out half the shell and fill it with salt. Then she should take it to bed with her and eat it, leaving a glass of water by her bedside. In the night her future husband or a vision of him would appear and offer her the glass. But she must only do it once.

It is the type of belief that bright young graduate students were collecting eleven years ago for the theses and archives of North America and also, they hoped, for their own fame. Even as they sought the near-Elizabethan songs and ballads that had sailed from County Kerry and from Devon and Cornwall. All about the wild, wide sea and the flashing silver dagger and the lost and faithless lover. Echoes to and from the lovely, lonely hills and glens of West Virginia and the standing stones of Tennessee.

Across the hall the old people are asleep. The old man's snoring rattles as do the windows; except that now and then there are catching gasps within his breath. In three or four short hours he will be awake and will go down to light his fire. I turn and walk back softly to my room.

Within the bed the warm sweetness of the rum is heavy and intense. The darkness presses down upon me but still it brings no sleep. There are no voices and no shadows that are real. There are only walls of memory touched restlessly by flickers of imagination.

Oh I would like to see my way more clearly. I, who have never understood the mystery of fog. I would perhaps like to capture it in a jar like the beautiful childhood butterflies that always die in spite of the airholes punched with nails in the covers of their captivity—leaving behind the vapours of their lives and deaths; or perhaps as the unknowing child who collects the grey moist condoms from the lovers' lanes only to have them taken from him and to be told to wash his hands. Oh I have collected many things I did not understand.

And perhaps now I should go and say, oh son of my *summa cum laude* loins, come away from the lonely gulls and the silver trout and I will take you to the land of the Tastee Freeze where you may sleep till ten of nine. And I will show you the elevator to the apartment on the sixteenth floor and introduce you to the buzzer system and the yards of the wrought-iron fences where the Doberman pinscher runs silently at night. Or may I offer you the money that is the fruit of my collecting and my most successful life? Or shall I wait to meet you in some known or unknown bitterness like Yeats' Cuchulain by the wind-whipped sea or as Sohrab and Rustum by the future flowing river?

Again I collect dreams. For I do not know enough of the fog on Toronto's Queen St. West and the grinding crash of the pickup and of lost and misplaced love.

I am up early in the morning as the man kindles the fire from the driftwood splinters. The outside light is breaking and the wind is calm. John tumbles down the stairs. Scarcely stopping to splash his face and pull on his jacket, he is gone, accompanied by the dog. The old man smokes his pipe and waits for the water to boil. When it does he pours some into the teapot then passes the kettle to me. I take it to the washstand and fill the small tin basin in readiness for my shaving. My face looks back from the mirrored cabinet. The woman softly descends the stairs.

"I think I will go back today," I say while looking into the mirror at my face and at those in the room behind me. I try to emphasize the "I." "I just thought I would like to make this trip—again. I think I can leave the car in St. John's and fly back directly." The woman begins to move about the table, setting out the round white plates. The man quietly tamps his pipe.

The door opens and John and the dog return. They have been down along the shore to see what has happened throughout the night. "Well, John," says the old man, "what did you find?"

He opens his hand to reveal a smooth round stone. It is of the deepest green inlaid with veins of darkest ebony. It has been worn and polished by the unrelenting restlessness of the sea and buffed and burnished by the gravelled sand. All of its inadequacies have been removed and it glows with the lustre of near perfection.

"It is very beautiful," I say.

"Yes," he says, "I like to collect them." Suddenly he looks up to my eyes and thrusts the stone toward me. "Here," he says, "would you like to have it?"

Even as I reach out my hand I turn my head to the others in the room. They are both looking out through the window to the sea.

"Why, thank you," I say. "Thank you very much. Yes, I would. Thank you. Thanks." I take it from his outstretched hand and place it in my pocket.

We eat our breakfast in near silence. After it is finished the boy and dog go out once more. I prepare to leave.

"Well, I must go," I say, hesitating at the door. "It will take me a while to get to St. John's." I offer my hand to the man. He takes it in his strong fingers and shakes it firmly.

"Thank you," says the woman. "I don't know if you know what I mean but thank you."

"I think I do," I say. I stand and fiddle with the keys. "I would somehow like to help or keep in touch but ..."

"But there is no phone," he says, "and both of us can hardly write. Perhaps that's why we never told you. John is getting to be a pretty good hand at it though."

"Good-bye," we say again, "good-bye, good-bye."

The sun is shining clearly now and the small boats are putt-putting about the harbour. I enter my unlocked car and start its engine. The gravel turns beneath the wheels. I pass the house and wave to the man and woman standing in the yard.

On a distant cliff the children are shouting. Their voices carol down through the sun-washed air and the dogs are curving and dancing about them in excited circles. They are carrying something that looks like a crippled gull. Perhaps they will make it well. I toot the horn. "Good-bye," they shout and wave, "good-bye, good-bye."

The airport terminal is strangely familiar. A symbol of impermanence, it is itself glisteningly permanent. Its formica surfaces have been designed to stay. At the counter a middle-aged man in mock exasperation is explaining to the girl that it is Newark he wishes to go to, *not* New York.

There are not many of us and soon we are ticketed and lifting through and above the sun-shot fog. The meals are served in tinfoil and in plastic. We eat above the clouds looking at the tips of wings.

The man beside me is a heavy-equipment salesman who has been trying to make a sale to the developers of Labrador's resources. He has been away a week and is returning to his wife and children.

Later in the day we land in the middle of the continent. Because of the changing time zones the distance we have come seems eerily unreal. The heat shimmers in little waves upon the runway. This is the equipment salesman's final destination while for me it is but the place where I must change flights to continue even farther into the heartland. Still we go down the wheeled-up stairs together, donning our sunglasses, and stepping across the heated concrete and through the terminal's electronic doors. The salesman's wife stands waiting along with two small children who are the first to see him. They race toward him with their arms outstretched. "Daddy, Daddy," they cry, "what did you bring me? What did you bring me?"

Notes

Cuchulain	Celtic legendary hero popularized by Irish poet W.B. Yeats (1865–1939)
dories	rowboats used by fishermen
moorings	place where boats are fastened when not at sea
myriad	countless
"Sohrab and Rustum"	legendary narrative poem by Matthew Arnold (1822–1888) about a father who slays his son in ignorance
squalls	sudden downpours of rain
summa cum laude	Latin for "with the highest honour"

Isaac Asimov
Frustration

Herman Gelb turned his head to watch the departing figure. Then he said, "Wasn't that the Secretary?"

"Yes, that was the Secretary of Foreign Affairs. Old man Hargrove. Are you ready for lunch?"

"Of course. What was he doing here?"

Peter Jonsbeck didn't answer immediately. He merely stood up, and beckoned Gelb to follow. They walked down the corridor and into a room that had the steamy smell of spicy food.

"Here you are," said Jonsbeck. "The whole meal has been prepared by computer. Completely automated. Untouched by human hands. And my own programming. I promised you a treat, and here you are."

It *was* good. Gelb could not deny it and didn't want to. Over dessert, he said, "But what was Hargrove doing here?"

Jonsbeck smiled. "Consulting me on programming. What else am I good for?"

"But why? Or is it something you can't talk about?"

"It's something I suppose I *shouldn't* talk about, but it's a fairly open secret. There isn't a computer man in the capital who doesn't know what the poor frustrated simp is up to."

"What is he up to then?"

"He's fighting wars."

Gelb's eyes opened wide. "With whom?"

"With nobody, really. He fights them by computer analysis. He's been doing it for I don't know how long."

"But why?"

"He wants the world to be the way we are—noble, honest, decent, full of respect for human rights and so on."

"So do I. So do we all. We have to keep up the pressure on the bad guys, that's all."

"And they're keeping the pressure on us, too. They don't think we're perfect."

"I suppose we're not, but we're better than they are. You know that."

Jonsbeck shrugged. "A difference in point of view. It doesn't matter. We've got a world to run, space to develop, computerization to extend. Cooperation puts a premium on continued cooperation and there is slow improvement. We'll get along. It's just that Hargrove doesn't want to wait. He hankers for quick improvement—by force. You know, *make* the bums shape up. We're strong enough to do it."

"By force? By war, you mean. We don't fight wars any more."

"That's because it's gotten too complicated. Too much danger. We're all too powerful. You know what I mean? Except that Hargrove thinks he can find a way. You punch certain starting conditions in to the computer and let it fight the war mathematically and yield the results."

"How do you make equations for war?"

"Well, you try, old man. Men. Weapons. Surprise. Counterattack. Ships. Space stations. Computers. We mustn't forget computers. There are a hundred factors and thousands of intensities and millions of combinations. Hargrove thinks it is possible to find *some* combination of starting conditions and courses of development that will result in clear victory for us and not too much damage to the world, and he labors under constant frustration."

"But what if he gets what he wants?"

"Well, if he can find the combination—if the computer says, 'This is it,' then I suppose he thinks he can argue our government into fighting exactly the war the computer has worked out so that, barring random events that upset the indicated course, we'd have what we want."

"There'd be casualties."

"Yes, of course. But the computer will presumably compare the casualties and other damage—to the economy and ecology, for instance—to the benefits that would derive from our control of the world, and if it decides the benefits will outweigh the casualties, then it will give the go-ahead for a 'just war.' After all, it may be that even the losing nations would benefit from being directed by us, with our stronger economy and stronger moral sense."

Gelb stared his disbelief and said, "I never knew we were sitting at the lip of a volcanic crater like that. What about the 'random events' you mentioned?"

"The computer program tries to allow for the unexpected, but you never can, of course. So I don't think the go-ahead will come. It hasn't so far, and unless old man Hargrove can present the government with a computer simulation of a war that is totally satisfactory, I don't think there's much chance he can force one."

"And he comes to you, then, for what reason?"

"To improve the program, of course."

"And you help him?"

"Yes, certainly. There are big fees involved, Herman."

Gelb shook his head. "Peter! Are you going to try to arrange a war, just for money?"

"There won't be a war. There's no realistic combination of events that would make the computer decide on war. Computers place a greater value on human lives than human beings do themselves, and what will seem bearable to Secretary Hargrove, or even to you and me, will never be passed by a computer."

"How can you be sure of that?"

"Because I'm a programmer and I don't know of any way of programming a computer to give it what is most needed to start any war, any persecution, any devilry, while ignoring any harm that may be done in the process. And because it lacks what is most needed, the computers will always give Hargrove, and all others who hanker for war, nothing but frustration."

"What is it that a computer doesn't have, then?"

"Why, Gelb. It totally lacks a sense of self-righteousness."

Translated by Peter Sekirin

Anton Chekhov
A Woman without Prejudice

Maxim Koozmich Saliutov is a tall man with broad shoulders and a straight back. He looks like an athlete. He is tremendously strong: he can bend coins, uproot young trees from the soil, pick up barbells with his teeth, and he swears that there is not a single man who could beat him at wrestling. He is very brave and full of *chutzpah*. No one has ever known him to be afraid of anything. On the contrary: when he is in a bad mood, others fear *him*. Men and women alike exclaim and turn red when he shakes their hands — so painful is his grip! His voice is so loud that it hurts to listen to him speak at close range. Such a powerful man! I have never met a stronger one.

And yet this terrible, inhuman, animal force utterly vanished one day, leaving Maxim Koozmich with all the strength of a dead rat, when he told Elena Gavrilovna that he was in love with her. Maxim Koozmich blushed, grew pale, trembled, and could scarcely have lifted a chair as he tried to squeeze out those three words, "I love you," from his enormous mouth. His terrible power was humbled and rendered useless, his huge body diminished, a gigantic but empty vessel.

He told her that he loved her at the skating rink. She was skating, as light as a feather, and he was trying to keep up to her, trembling, befuddled, whispering to himself. His face was a picture of suffering. His smart, athletic legs bent at the knees and knocked together each time he tried to execute a sharp turn on the ice. Do you think that he was afraid of rejection? Not at all. Elena Gavrilovna loved him, too, and she longed for a wedding, for his hand and his heart. The tiny, pretty brunette was burning with eagerness. She knew that he was thirty, humbly employed, and poorly paid. But he was nice-looking, witty, and graceful. He was a wonderful dancer, an excellent shot, and a peerless horseman. Once, as they were walking through the park, he had leaped across a ravine at which even the finest English stallion would have balked.

No one could resist falling in love with such a man.

He knew that she loved him, but the thought made him suffer, suffocate: it blocked his ability to think, drink, eat, or sleep. It made his life miserable. Because even as he told her that he loved her, a terrible secret burned in his brain and pounded at his temples.

"Be my wife," he said to Elena Gavrilovna. "I love you terribly, I love you madly!"

But even as he said this, he was thinking, "Do I have the right to be her husband? No, I don't! If she only knew about my background, my former life, she would slap me in the face! Oh, my awful past! She is a wealthy, educated, noble lady, and she would simply spit at me if she only knew what kind of a man I really am."

So when Elena Gavrilovna rushed to him, threw her arms around his neck, and told him that she loved him, it did not make him happy. His secret sullied everything.

When he came back home from the skating rink, he bit his lip and thought, "I am a terrible man! If I were a decent man, I would have told her everything by now. I should have revealed my secret before I revealed my love. But I did not, and that makes me a scoundrel!"

Elena Gavrilovna's parents gave their consent to her marriage to Maxim Koozmich. They liked this athlete: he was respectful, and as a civil servant, he had a promising future. Elena Gavrilovna was in seventh heaven. She was euphoric. But the poor athlete was wretched. Even before the wedding, he was tortured by the knowledge that had bothered him at the skating rink.

Then a friend who knew of his past started blackmailing and tormenting him. The athlete had to hand over all his earnings to keep him quiet.

"Treat me to dinner at the Hermitage restaurant!" his friend would demand. "Otherwise, I will tell her everything. And lend me some money: say, twenty-five rubles."

Poor Maxim Koozmich became thin, and his face became gaunt. His cheeks grew hollow, and his hands were skin and bone. He had morbid thoughts. If it hadn't been for the beautiful woman he loved, he would have shot himself.

"I am a terrible, bad man. I should tell her everything before the wedding. Even if she does spit on me and abandon me, I have to do it!"

But he did not tell her anything before the wedding — he was too apprehensive. The thought of parting with the woman he loved was too terrifying.

The wedding day came. The two young people were married, they received congratulations, and everyone was delighted to see their happy faces. Maxim Koozmich drank, danced, and accepted the congratulations, but he felt terribly unhappy.

"I am a lout, but I will force myself to explain everything to her. We're married, but it's still not too late to tell her everything. The wedding can be annulled."

AND THEN, HE TOLD HER HIS STORY ...

When the long-awaited hour came and they were pushed into the bedroom, honesty and conscience took the upper hand. Breathless, his whole body trembling, Maxim Koozmich came to her, heedless of the outcome, and took her hand. "Before we can belong to each other," he said, "there's something I must tell you."

"Whatever's come over you, Max? You've been pale and silent for days. Are you sick?"

"I want to tell you everything, dear Elena. Let's sit down for a while—right here. I am about to shame you and poison your happiness, but what can I do? My duty is the most important thing. I will tell you the whole story about my past."

Elena's eyes widened and she smiled. "Well, tell me whatever you want to, but get it over with. And stop trembling."

"I was born in the provincial town of Tam ... Tam ... Tambov. My parents were not noble at all; in fact, they were very poor. When I tell you what kind of man I am, you will be disgusted. Listen, when I was a kid, I sold apples and pears in the streets."

"You did?"

"You're disgusted, I can tell. But that's not the worst of it. My dear, that's not the most terrible thing about me. You're going to curse me for this!"

"What do you mean?"

"When I was twenty I was ... I was ... Please forgive me! Don't throw me out.... I was a clown in the circus!"

"You? A clown?"

Maxim Koozmich was waiting for a slap in the face, and he even lifted his hands to protect himself. He was ready to faint.

"You? A clown?"

Elena tumbled off the sofa, them jumped to her feet and started pacing the room. What had happened to her? She was laughing so hard that she was holding her belly. The bedroom was filled with her nearly hysterical laughter.

"You were a circus clown? You? Dear Max, can you imagine? Darling, please show me something! Just prove to me that you were a clown — ha-ha-ha. Sweetheart, please do a trick for me, show me a stunt."

She flew into Maxim Koozmich's arms and embraced him, saying, "Show me something, please, my dear, my darling."

"Are you making fun of me? You hate me, don't you?"

"Can you do something for me? Can you walk a tightrope? Please, do this for me?"

She covered her husband's face with tiny kisses, pressed her body against his, and asked him again. She did not appear to be angry. He was delighted. Finally, he agreed to his wife's request — he could see no harm in this.

Approaching their bed, he counted to three, and then, pressing his forehead to the edge, did a headstand.

"Bravo, Max! Ha-ha, my love! Please, show me some more." Holding his position, Max dropped to the floor and started walking on his hands.

The next morning, Elena's parents were alarmed.

"Who is making all that terrible noise upstairs?" they asked each other. "The newlyweds should be sleeping. It sounds like the noises the servants make. What a racket! You can hear it all over the house!"

Her father went up to the second floor to have a look, but there were no servants there. To his surprise, the noise was coming from the newlyweds' room. He stood outside the door for a while and then, shrugging his shoulders, opened it a crack.

When he looked inside, he nearly died of shock. There was Maxim Koozmich, performing astonishing leaps and twists in the air. Elena was standing in front of him and applauding. Their faces were shining with happiness.

Leon Rooke
A Bolt of White Cloth

A man came by our road carrying an enormous bolt of white cloth on his back. Said he was from the East. Said whoever partook of this cloth would come to know true happiness. Innocence without heartbreak, he said, if that person proved worthy. My wife fingered his cloth, having in mind something for new curtains. It was good quality, she said. Beautifully woven, of a fine, light texture, and you certainly couldn't argue with the color.

"How much it is?" she asked.

"Before I tell you that," the man said, "you must tell me truthfully if you've ever suffered."

"Oh, I've suffered," she said. "I've known suffering of some description every day of my natural life."

I was standing over by the tool shed, with a big smile. My wife is a real joker, who likes nothing better than pulling a person's leg. She's known hardships, this and that upheaval, but nothing I would call down-and-out suffering. Mind you, I don't speak for her. I wouldn't pretend to speak for another person.

This man with the bolt of cloth, however, he clearly had no sense of my wife's brand of humor. She didn't get an itch of a smile out of him. He kept the cloth neatly balanced on his shoulder, wincing a little from the weight and from however far he'd had to carry it, staring hard and straight at my wife the whole time she fooled with him, as if he hoped to peer clear through to her soul. His eyes were dark and brooding and hollowed out some. He was like no person either my wife or me had ever seen before.

"Yes," he said, "but suffering of what kind?"

"Worse than I hope forever to carry, I'll tell you that," my wife said. "But why are you asking me these questions? I like your cloth and if the price is right I mean to buy it."

"You can only buy my cloth with love," he said.

We began right then to understand that he was some kind of oddity. He was not like anybody we'd ever seen and he didn't come from around here. He'd come from a place we'd never heard of, and if that was the East, or wherever, then he was welcome to it.

"Love?" she said. "Love? There's love and there's *love*, mister. What kind are you talking about?" She hitched a head my way, rolling her eyes, as if to indicate that if it was *passionate* love he was talking about then he'd first have to do something with me. He'd have to get me off my simmer and onto full boil. That's what she was telling him, with this mischief in her eyes.

I put down my pitchfork about here, and strolled nearer. I liked seeing my wife dealing with difficult situations. I didn't want to miss anything. My life with that woman had been packed with the unusual. Unusual circumstances, she calls them. Any time she's ever gone out anywhere without me, whether for a day or an hour or for five minutes, she's come back with whopping good stories about what she's seen and heard and what's happened to her. She's come back with reports on these unusual circumstances, these little adventures in which so many people have done so many extraordinary things or behaved in such fabulous or foolish ways. So what was rare this time, I thought, was that it had come visiting. She hadn't had to go out and find it.

"Hold these," my wife told me. And she put this washtub of clothes in my hands, and went back to hanging wet pieces on the line, which is what she'd been doing when this man with the bolt of cloth ventured up into our yard.

"Love," she told him. "You tell me what kind I need, if I'm to buy that cloth. I got good ears and I'm listening."

The man watched her stick clothespins in her mouth, slap out a good wide sheet, and string it up. He watched her hang two of these, plus a mess of towels, and get her mouth full again before he spoke. He looked about the unhappiest I've ever seen any man look. He didn't have any joy in him. I wondered why he didn't put down that heavy bolt of cloth, and why he didn't step around into a spot of shade. The sun was lick-killing bright in that yard. I was worried he'd faint.

"The ordinary kind," he said. "Your ordinary kind of love will buy this cloth."

My wife flapped her wash and laughed. He was really tickling her. She was having herself a wonderful time.

"What's ordinary?" she said. "I've never known no *ordinary* love."

He jumped right in. He got excited just for a second.

"The kind such as might exist between the closest friends," he said. "The kind such as might exist between a man and his wife or between parents and children or for that matter the love a boy might have for his dog. That kind of love."

"I've got that," she said. "I've had all three. Last year this time I had me a fourth, but it got run over. Up on the road there, by the tall trees, by a man in a car who didn't even stop."

"That would have been your cat," he said. "I don't know much about cats."

I put down the washtub. My wife let her arms drop. We looked at him, wondering how he knew about the cat. Then I laughed, for I figured someone down the road must have told him of my wife's mourning over the cat. She'd dug it a grave under the grapevine and said sweet words over it. She sorely missed that cat.

"What's wrong with loving cats?" she asked him. "Or beasts of the fields? I'm surprised at you."

The man shifted his burden and worked one shoe into the ground. He stared off at the horizon. He looked like he knew he'd said something he shouldn't.

She pushed me out of the way. She wanted to get nearer to him. She had something more to say.

"Now listen to me," she said. "I've loved lots of things in my life. Lots and lots. *Him!*" she said (pointing at me), "*it*" (pointing to our house), "*them!*" (pointing to the flower beds), "*that*" (pointing to the sky), "*those*" (pointing to the woods), "*this*" (pointing to the ground)—"practically *everything!* There isn't any of it I've hated, and not much I've been in-different to. Including cars. So put that in your pipe and smoke it."

Then swooping up her arms and laughing hard, making it plain she bore no grudge but wasn't just fooling.

Funny thing was, hearing her say it, I felt the same way. *It, them, that, those*—they were all beautiful. I couldn't deny it was love I was feeling.

The man with the cloth had turned each way she'd pointed. He'd staggered a time or two but he'd kept up. In fact, it struck me that he'd got a little ahead of her. That he knew where her arm was next going. Some trickle of pleasure was showing in his face. And something else was happening, something I'd never seen. He had his face lifted up to this burning sun. It was big and orange, that sun, and scorching-hot, but he was staring smack into it. He wasn't blinking or squinting. His eyes were wide open.

Madness or miracle, I couldn't tell which.

He strode over to a parcel of good grass.

"I believe you mean it," he said. "How much could you use?"

He placed the bolt of white cloth down on the grass and pulled out shiny scissors from his back pocket.

"I bet he's blind," I whispered to my wife. "I bet he's got false eyes."

My wife shushed me. She wasn't listening. She had her excitement hat on; her *unusual circumstances* look. He was offering free cloth for love, ordinary love, and she figured she'd go along with the gag.

How much?

"Oh," she said, "maybe eight yards. Maybe ten. It depends on how many windows I end up doing, plus what hang I want, plus the pleating I'm after."

"You mean to make these curtains yourself?" he asked. He was already down on his knees, smoothing the bolt. Getting set to roll it out.

"Why, sure," she said. "I don't know who else would do it for me. I don't know who else I would ask."

He nodded soberly, not thinking about it. "That's so," he said casually. "Mend your own fences first." He was perspiring in the sun, and dishevelled, as though he'd been on the road a long time. His shoes had big holes in them and you could see the blistered soles of his feet, but he had an air of exhilaration now. His hair fell down over his eyes and he shoved the dark locks back. I got the impression that some days he went a long time between customers; that he didn't find cause to give away his cloth every day.

He got a fair bit unrolled. It certainly did look like prime goods, once you saw it spread out on the grass in that long expanse.

"It's so pretty!" my wife said. "Heaven help me, but I think it is *prettier* than the grass!"

"It's pretty, all right," he said. "It's a wing-dinger. Just tell me when to stop," he said. "Just shout yoo-hoo."

"Hold up a minute," she said. "I don't want to get greedy. I don't want you rolling off more than we can afford."

"You can afford it," he said.

He kept unrolling. He was up past the well house by now, whipping it off fast, though the bolt didn't appear to be getting any smaller. My wife had both hands up over her mouth. Half of her wanted to run into the house and get her purse so she could pay; the other half wanted to stay and watch this man unfurl his beautiful cloth. She whipped around to me, all agitated.

"I believe he means it," she said. "He means us to have this cloth. What do I do?"

I shook my head. This was her territory. It was the kind of adventure constant to her nature and necessary to her well-being.

"Honey," I said, "you deal with it."

The sun was bright over everything. It was whipping-hot. There wasn't much wind but I could hear the clothes flapping on the line. A woodpecker had himself a pole somewhere and I could hear him pecking. The sky was wavy blue. The trees seemed to be swaying.

He was up by the front porch now, still unrolling. It surprised us both that he could move so fast.

"Yoo-hoo," my wife said. It was no more than a peep, the sound you might make if a butterfly lands on your hand.

"Wait," he said. "One thing. One question I meant to ask. All this talk of love, your it, your those and them, it slipped my mind."

"Let's hear it," my wife said. "Ask away." It seemed to me that she spoke out of a trance. That she was as dazzled as I was.

"You two got no children," he said. "Why is that? You're out here on this nice farm, and no children to your name. Why is that?"

We hadn't expected this query from him. It did something to the light in the yard and how we saw it. It was as if some giant, dark bird had fluttered between us and the sun. Without knowing it, we sidled closer to each other. We fumbled for the other's hand. We stared off every which way. No one on our road had asked that question in a long, long time; they hadn't asked it in some years.

"We're not able," we said. Both of us spoke at the same time. It seemed to me that it was my wife's voice which carried; mine was someplace down in my chest, and dropping, as if it meant to crawl on the ground.

"We're not able," we said. That time it came out pure, without any grief to bind it. It came out the way we long ago learned how to say it.

"Oh," he said. "I see." He mumbled something else. He kicked the ground and took a little walk back and forth. He seemed angry, though not at us. "Wouldn't you know it?" he said. "Wouldn't you know it?"

He swore a time or two. He kicked the ground. He surely didn't like it.

"We're over that now," my wife said. "We're past that caring."

"I bet you are," he said. "You're past that little misfortune."

He took to unrolling his bolt again, working with his back to the sun. Down on his knees, scrambling, smoothing the material. Sweating and huffing. He was past the front porch now, and still going, getting on toward that edge where the high weeds grew.

"About here, do you think?" he asked.

He'd rolled off about fifty yards.

My wife and I slowly shook our heads, not knowing what to think.

"Say the word," he told us. "I can give you more if more is what you want."

"I'd say you were giving us too much," my wife said. "I'd say we don't need nearly that much."

"Never mind that," he said. "I'm feeling generous today."

He nudged the cloth with his fingers and rolled off a few yards more. He would have gone on unwinding his cloth had the weeds not stopped him. He stood and looked back over the great length he had unwound.

"Looks like a long white road, don't it?" he said. "You could walk that road and your feet never get dirty."

SnipSnipSnip. He began snipping. His scissors raced over the material. *SnipSnipSnip.* The cloth was sheared clear and clean of his bolt, yet it seemed to me the size of that bolt hadn't lessened any. My wife saw it too.

"He's got cloth for all eternity," she said. "He could unroll that cloth till doomsday."

The man laughed. We were whispering this, but way up by the weeds he heard us. "There's doom and there's doom," he said. "*Which* doomsday?"

I had the notion he'd gone through more than one. That he knew the picture from both sides.

"It *is* smart as grass," he said. "Smarter. It never needs watering." He chuckled at that, spinning both arms. Dancing a little. "You could make *nighties* out of this," he said. "New bedsheets. Transform your whole bedroom."

My wife made a face. She wasn't too pleased, talking *nighties* with another man.

Innocence without heartbreak, I thought. That's what we're coming to.

He nicely rolled up the cloth he'd sheared off and presented it to my wife. "I hope you like it," he said. "No complaints yet. Maybe you can make yourself a nice dress as well. Maybe two or three. Make him some shirts. I think you'll find there's plenty here."

"Goodness, it's light," she said.

"Not if you've been carrying it long as I have," he said. He pulled a blue bandanna from his pocket and wiped his face and neck. He ran his hand through his hair and slicked it back. He looked up at the sky. His dark eyes seemed to have cleared up some. They looked less broody now. "Gets hot," he said, "working in this sun. But a nice day. I'm glad I found you folks home."

"Oh, we're most always home," my wife said.

I had to laugh at that. My wife almost never *is* home. She's forever gallivanting over the countryside, checking up on this person and that, taking them her soups and jams and breads.

"We're homebodies, us two."

She kept fingering the cloth and sighing over it. She held it up against her cheek and with her eyes closed rested herself on it. The man hoisted his own bolt back on his shoulder; he seemed ready to be going. I looked at my wife's closed lids, at the soft look she had.

I got trembly, fearful of what might happen if that cloth didn't work out.

"Now look," I said to him, "what's wrong with this cloth? Is it going to rot inside a week? Tomorrow is some *other* stranger going to knock on our door saying we owe him a hundred or five hundred dollars for this cloth? Mister, I don't understand you," I said.

He hadn't bothered with me before; now he looked me dead in the eye. "I can't help being a stranger," he said. "If you never set eyes on me before, I guess that's what I would have to be. Don't you like strangers? Don't you trust them?"

My wife jumped in. Her face was fiery, like she thought I had wounded him. "We like strangers just fine," she said. "We've helped out many a-one. No, I can't say our door has ever been closed to whoever it is comes by. Strangers can sit in our kitchen just the same as our friends."

He smiled at her but kept his stern look for me. "As to your questions," he said. "You're worried about the golden goose, I can see that. Fair enough. No, your cloth will not rot. It will not shred, fade, or tear. Nor will it ever need cleaning, either. This cloth requires no upkeep whatsoever. Though a sound heart helps. A sweet disposition, too. Innocence without heartbreak, as I told you. And your wife, if it's her making the curtains or making herself a dress, she will find it to be an amazingly easy cloth to work with. It will practically do the job itself. No, I don't believe you will ever find you have any reason to complain of the qualities of that cloth."

My wife had it up to her face again. She had her face sunk in it.

"Goodness," she said, "it's *soft*! It smells so fresh. It's like someone singing a song to me."

The man laughed. "It *is* soft," he said. "But it can't sing a note, or has never been known to."

It was my wife singing. She had this little hum under her breath.

"This is the most wonderful cloth in the world," she said.

He nodded. "I can't argue with you on that score," he said. Then he turned again to me. "I believe your wife is satisfied," he said. "But if you have any doubts, if you're worried someone is going to knock on your door tomorrow asking you for a hundred or five hundred dollars, I suppose I could write you up a guarantee. I could give you a PAID IN FULL."

He was making me feel ashamed of myself. They both were. "No, no," I said, "if she's satisfied then I am. And I can see she's tickled pink. No, I beg your pardon. I meant no offence."

"No offence taken," he said.

But his eyes clouded a token. He gazed off at our road and up along the stand of trees and his eyes kept roaming until they snagged the sun. He kept his eyes there, unblinking, open, staring at the sun. I could see the red orbs reflected in his eyes.

"There is one thing," he said.

I caught my breath and felt my wife catch hers. The hitch? A hitch, after all? Coming so late?

We waited.

He shuffled his feet. He brought out his bandanna and wiped his face again. He stared at the ground.

"Should you ever stop loving," he said, "you shall lose this cloth and all else. You shall wake up one morning and it and all else will no longer be where you left it. It will all be gone and you will not know where you are. You will not know what to do with yourself. You will wish you'd never been born."

My wife's eyes went saucer-size.

He had us in some kind of spell.

Hocus-pocus, I thought. He is telling us some kind of hocus-pocus. Yet I felt my skin shudder; I felt the goose bumps rise.

"That's it?" my wife said. "That's the only catch?"

He shrugged. "That's it," he said. "Not much, is it? Not a whisper of menace for a pair such as yourselves."

My wife's eyes were gauzed over; there was a wetness in them.

"Hold on," she said. "Don't you be leaving yet. Hold this, honey."

She put the cloth in my arms. Then she hastened over to the well, pitched the bucket down, and drew it up running over with fresh water.

"Here," she said, coming back with a good dipperful. "Here's a nice drink of cool water. You need it on a day like this."

The man drank. He held the dipper in both hands, with the tips of his fingers, and drained the dipper dry, then wiped his chin with the back of a hand.

"I did indeed," he said. "That's very tasty water. I thank you."

"That's good water," she said. "That well has been here lo a hundred years. You could stay on for supper," she said. "It's getting on toward that time and I have a fine stew on the stove, with plenty to spare."

"That's kind of you," he said back, "and I'm grateful. But I'd best pass on up your road while there's still daylight left, and see who else might have need of this cloth."

My wife is not normally a demonstrative woman, not in public. Certainly not with strangers. You could have knocked me over with a feather when she up and kissed him full on the mouth, with a nice hug to boot.

"There's payment," she said, "if our money's no good."

He blushed, trying to hide his pleasure. It seemed to me she had him wrapped around her little finger ... or the other way around.

"You kiss like a woman," he said. "Like one who knows what kissing is for, and can't hardly stop herself."

It was my wife's turn to blush.

I took hold of her hand and held her down to grass, because it seemed to me another kiss or two and she'd fly right away with him.

He walked across the yard and up by the well house, leaving by the same route he had come. Heading for the road. At the turn, he spun around and waved.

"You could try the Hopkins place!" my wife called. "There's a fat woman down that road got a sea of troubles. She could surely use some of that cloth."

He smiled and again waved. Then we saw his head and his bolt of white cloth bobbing along the weeds as he took the dips and rises in the road. Then he went on out of sight.

"There's that man with some horses down the road!" my wife called. "You be careful of him!"

It seemed we heard some sound come back, but whether it was his we couldn't say.

My wife and I stood a long time in the yard, me holding the dipper and watching her, while she held her own bolt of cloth in her arms, staring off to where he'd last been.

Then she sighed dreamily and went inside.

I went on down to the barn and looked after the animals. Getting my feeding done. I talked a spell to them. Talking to animals is soothing to me, and they like it too. They pretend to stare at the walls or the floor as they're munching their feed down, but I know they listen to me. We had us an *unusual circumstance* chat. "That man with the cloth," I said. "Maybe you can tell me what you make of him."

Thirty minutes later I heard my wife excitedly calling me. She was standing out on the back doorstep, with this incredulous look.

"I've finished," she said. "I've finished the windows. *Nine* windows. It beats me how."

I started up to the house. Her voice was all shaky. Her face flushed, flinging her arms about. Then she got this new look on.

"Wait!" she said. "Stay there! Give me ten minutes!"

And she flung herself back inside, banging the door. I laughed. It always gave me a kick how she ordered me around.

I got the milk pail down under the cow. Before I'd touched and drained all four teats she was calling again.

"Come look, come look, oh come look!"

She was standing in the open doorway, with the kitchen to her back. Behind her, through the windows, I could see the streak of a red sunset and how it lit up the swing of trees. But I wasn't looking there. I was looking at her. Looking and swallowing hard and trying to remember how a body produced human speech. I had never thought of white as a color she could wear. White, it pales her some. It leaves her undefined and washes out what parts I like best. But she looked beautiful now. In her new dress she struck me down to my bootstraps. She made my chest break.

"Do you like it?" she said.

I went running up to her. I was up against her, hugging her and lifting her before she'd even had a chance to get set. I'd never held on so tightly or been so tightly held back.

Truth is, it was the strangest thing. Like we were both so innocent we hadn't yet shot up out of new ground.

"Come see the curtains," she whispered. "Come see the new sheets. Come see what else I've made. You'll see it all. You'll see how our home has been transformed."

I crept inside. There was something holy about it. About it and about us and about those rooms and the whole wide world. Something radiant. Like you had to put your foot down easy and hold it down or you'd float on up.

"That's it," she said. "That's how I feel too."

That night in bed, trying to figure it out, we wondered how Ella Mae down the road had done. How the people all along our road had made out.

"No worry," my wife said. "He'll have found a bonanza around here. There's heaps of decent people in this neck of the woods."

"Wonder where he is now?" we said.

"Wonder where he goes next?"

"Where he gets that cloth?"

"Who he *is*?"

We couldn't get to sleep, wondering about that.

Mori Yoko
Spring Storm

The small orange light on the lobby wall showed the elevator was still at the seventh floor. Natsuo's eyes were fixed on it.

From time to time her heart pounded furiously, so furiously that it seemed to begin skipping beats. For some time now she had been wild with excitement.

Intense joy is somewhat like pain, she thought. Or like a dizzy spell. Strangely, it was not unlike grief. The suffocating feeling in her chest was almost unbearable.

The elevator still had not moved from the seventh floor.

The emergency stairway was located alongside the outer walls of the building, completely exposed to the elements. Unfortunately for Natsuo, it was raining outside. There was a wind, too.

A spring storm. The words, perhaps romantic, well described the heavy, slanting rain, driven by a wind that had retained the rawness of winter. If Natsuo were to climb the stairs to the sixth floor, she would be soaked to the skin.

She took a cigarette from her handbag and lit it.

This is unusual for me, she thought. She had never smoked while waiting for the elevator. Indeed, she had not smoked anywhere while standing up.

Exhaling the smoke from the depths of her throat, she fell to thinking. I'll be experiencing all kinds of new things from now on, I've just come a big step up the ladder. No, not just one, I've jumped as many as ten steps in one leap. There were thirty-four rivals, and I beat them all.

All thirty-four people were well-experienced performers. There was a dancer with considerably more skill than she. Physically also the odds were against her: there were a sizable number of women with long, stylish legs and tight, shapely waists. One Eurasian woman had such alluring looks that everyone admired her. There were professional actresses currently active on the stage, too.

In spite of everything, Natsuo was the one selected for the role.

When the agency called to tell her the news, she at first thought she was being teased.

"You must be kidding me," she said, a little irritated. She had indeed taken it for a bad joke. "You can't trick me like this. I don't believe you."

"Let me ask you a question, then," responded the man who had been acting as her manager. In a teasing voice, he continued, "Were you just kidding when you auditioned for that musical?"

"Of course not!" she retorted. She had been quite serious and, although she would not admit it, she had wanted the role desperately. At the audition, she had done her very best.

"But I'm sure I didn't make it," she said to her manager. "At the interview, I blushed terribly."

Whenever she tried to express herself in front of other people, blood would rush to her face, turning it scarlet.

"You're a bashful person, aren't you?" one of her examiners had commented to her at the interview. His tone carried an objective observation rather than sympathetic inquiry.

"Do you think you're an introvert?" another examiner asked.

"I'm probably on the shy side," Natsuo answered, painfully aware that her earlobes had turned embarrassingly red and her palms were moist.

"The heroine of this drama," added the third examiner, "is a spirited woman with strong willpower. Do you know that?"

Natsuo had sensed the skepticism that was running through the panel of examiners. Without doubt she was going to fail the test, unless she did something right now. She looked up.

"It's true that I'm not very good at expressing myself, or speaking up for myself, in front of other people. But playing a dramatic role is something different. It's very different." She was getting desperate. "I'm very bashful about myself. But I'm perfectly all right when I play someone else."

If I am to express someone else's emotion, I have no reason to be shy, she confirmed to herself. I can calmly go about doing the job.

"Well, then, would you please play someone else?" the chief examiner said, with a nod toward the stage.

Natsuo retired to the wings of the stage and tried to calm herself. When she trotted out onto the stage and confidently faced them, she was no longer a timid, blushing woman.

It was impossible to guess, though, how the examiners appraised her performance. They showed little, if any, emotion. When the test was over there was a chorus of murmured "Thank yous." That was all.

Her manager was still speaking on the phone. "I don't know about the third-raters. But I can tell you that most good actors and actresses are introverted, naive, and always feeling nervous inside."

He then added, "If you don't believe me, why don't you go to the office of that production company and find out for yourself."

Natsuo decided to do just that.

At the end of a dimly lit hallway, a small group of men and women were looking at a large blackboard. Most of the board was powdered with half-obliterated previous scribblings, but at the top was written the cast of the new musical, with the names of the actors and actresses selected for the roles.

Natsuo's name was second from the top. It was scrawled in a large, carefree hand. The name at the top was her co-star, a well-known actor in musicals.

Natsuo stood immobile for ten seconds or so, staring at her name on the blackboard. It was her own name, but she felt as if it belonged to someone else. Her eyes still fixed on the name, she moved a few steps backwards. Then she turned around and hurried out of the building. It never occurred to her to stop by the office and thank the staff.

Sheer joy hit her a little later.

It was raining, and there was wind, too. She had an umbrella with her, but she walked without opening it. Finally realizing the fact, she stopped to unfold the umbrella.

"I did it!" she cried aloud. That was the moment. An incomparable joy began to rise up inside her, like the bubbles crowding to exit from a champagne bottle; and not just joy, pain as well, accompanied by the flow and ebb of some new irritation. That was how she experienced her moment of victory.

When she came to, she found herself standing in the lobby of her apartment building. The first person she wanted to tell the news to was, naturally, her husband, Yūsuke.

The elevator seemed to be out of order. It was not moving at all. How long had she been waiting there? Ten minutes? A couple of minutes? Natsuo had no idea. Her senses had been numbed. A round clock on the wall showed 9:25. Natsuo gave up and walked away.

The emergency stairway that zigzagged upwards was quite steep and barely wide enough for one person, so Natsuo could not open her umbrella. She climbed up the stairs at a dash.

By the time she reached the sixth floor, her hair was dripping wet and, with no raincoat on, her dress, too, was heavy with rain.

But Natsuo was smiling. Drenched and panting, she was still beaming with an excess of happiness when she pushed the intercom buzzer of their apartment.

"Why are you grinning? You make me nervous," Yūsuke said as he let her in. "You're soaking wet, too."

"The elevator never came."

"Who would have considered using the emergency stairs in this rain!"

"This apartment is no good, with a stairway like that," Natsuo said with a grin. "Let's move to a better place."

"You talk as if that were something very simple." Yūsuke laughed wryly and tossed a terry robe to her.

"But it is simple."

"Where would we find the money?"

"Just be patient. We'll get the money very soon," Natsuo said cheerfully, taking off her wet clothes.

"You passed the audition, didn't you?" Yūsuke asked, staring intently at her face. "Didn't you?"

Natsuo stared back at him. He looked nervous, holding his breath and waiting for her answer.

"Natsuo, did you pass the audition?" As he asked again, his face collapsed, his shoulders fell. He looked utterly forlorn.

"How...," she answered impulsively, "how could I have passed? I was just kidding."

Yūsuke frowned. "You failed?"

"I was competing with professionals, you know—actresses with real stage experience. How could I have beaten them?" Natsuo named several contending actresses.

"You didn't pass?" Yūsuke repeated, his frown deepening. "Answer me clearly, please. You still haven't told me whether you passed."

"What a mean person you are!" Natsuo stuttered. "You must have guessed by now, but you're forcing me to spell it out." Her eyes met his for a moment. "I didn't make it," she said, averting her eyes. "I failed with flying colors."

There was silence. Wiping her wet hair with a towel, Natsuo was aghast and mystified at her lie.

"No kidding?" said Yūsuke, starting to walk toward the kitchen. "I was in a state of shock for a minute, really."

"How come? Were you so sure I wouldn't make it?" Natsuo spoke to him from behind, her tone a test of his sincerity.

"You were competing with professionals." There was not a trace of consolation in his voice. "It couldn't be helped. You'll have another chance."

Although Yūsuke was showing sympathy, happiness hung in the air about him.

"You sound as if you were pleased to see me fail and lose my chance."

Combing her hair, Natsuo inspected her facial expression in the small mirror on the wall. You're a liar, she told her image. How are you going to unravel this mess you've got yourself into?

"How could I be happy to see you fail?" Yūsuke responded, placing a kettle on the gas range. His words carried with them the tarnish of guilt. "But, you know, it's not that great for you to get chosen for a major role all of a sudden."

"Why not?"

"Because you'd be a star. A big new star."

"You are being a bit too dramatic." Natsuo's voice sank low.

"When that happens, your husband would become like a Mr. Judy Garland. Asai Yūsuke would disappear completely, and in his place there would be just the husband of Midori Natsuo. I wouldn't like that."

"You're inventing problems for yourself," she said. "You are what you are. You are a script writer named Asai Yūsuke."

"A script writer who might soon be forced to write a musical."

"But hasn't that been your dream, to write a musical?" Natsuo's voice was tender. "Suppose, just suppose, that I make a successful debut as an actress in a musical. As soon as I become influential enough and people begin to listen to what I say, I'll let you write a script for a musical."

"Let you write, huh?" Yūsuke picked on Natsuo's phrasing. "If you talk like that even when you're making it up, I wonder how it'd be for real."

The kettle began to erupt steam. Yūsuke flicked off the flame, dropped instant coffee into two cups, and splashed in the hot water.

"Did you hear that story about Ingrid Bergman?" Yūsuke asked, his eyes looking into the distance. "Her third husband was a famous theatrical producer. A talented producer, too." Passing one of the cups to Natsuo, he continued. "One day Bergman asked her producer-husband, 'Why don't you ever try to get me a good play to act in?' He answered, 'Because you're a goose that lays golden eggs. Any play that features you is going to be a success. It will be a sellout for sure. For me, that's too easy.'" Yūsuke sipped the coffee slowly. Then, across the rising steam, he added, "I perfectly understand how he felt."

"Does this mean that I'll have to be a minor actress all my life?" Natsuo mused.

"Who knows? I may become famous one of these days," Yūsuke sighed. "Or maybe you first."

"And what would you do in the latter case?"

"Well," Yūsuke stared at the coffee. "If that happens, we'll get a divorce. That will be the best solution. Then, neither of us will be bothered by all the petty problems."

Natsuo walked toward the window. "Are you serious?" she asked.

"Yes." Yūsuke came and stood next to her. "That's the only way to handle the situation. That way, I'll be able to feel happy for you from the bottom of my heart."

"Can't a husband be happy for his wife's success?"

"Ingrid Bergman's second husband was Roberto Rosselini. Do you know the last words he said to her? He said, 'I'm tired of living as Mr. Ingrid Bergman.' Even Rosselini felt that way."

"You are not a Rosselini, nor I a Bergman."

"Our situation would be even worse."

From time to time, gusts of rain slapped at the window.

"When this spring storm is over, I expect the cherry blossoms will suddenly be bursting out," Yūsuke whispered.

"There'll be another storm in no time. The blossoms will be gone, and summer will be here." Brushing back her still-moist hair with her fingers, Natsuo turned and looked over the apartment she knew so well.

"You've been standing all this time. Aren't you getting tired?" her husband asked in a gentle voice. She shook her head.

"You're looking over the apartment as though it were for the first time," Yūsuke said, gazing at his wife's profile. "Or, is it for the last time?"

Startled by his last words, Natsuo impulsively reached into her handbag for a cigarette and put it in her mouth. Yūsuke produced a lighter from his pocket and lit it for her.

"Aren't you going to continue with your work this evening?" she asked.

"No. No more work tonight."

"What's the matter?"

"I can't concentrate when someone else is in the apartment. You know that, don't you?"

Natsuo nodded.

"Won't you sit down?" Yūsuke said.

"Why?"

"I have an uneasy feeling when you stand there and smoke like that."

Natsuo cast her eyes on the cigarette held between her fingers. "This is the second time today I've been smoking without sitting down." The words seemed to flow from her mouth at their own volition. His back towards her, Yūsuke was collecting some sheets of writing paper scattered on his desk.

"You passed the audition. Right?" he said. His voice was so low that the last word was almost inaudible.

"How did you know?"

"I knew it from the beginning."

"From the beginning?"

"From the moment you came in. You were shouting with your whole body—'I've made it, I'm the winner!' You were trembling like a drenched cat, but your face was lit up like a Christmas tree."

Natsuo did not respond.

"The clearest evidence is the way you're smoking right now."

"Did you notice it?"

"Yes."

"Me, too. It first happened when I was waiting for the elevator down in the lobby. I was so impatient, I smoked a cigarette while standing. I've got the strangest feeling about myself."

"You feel like a celebrity?"

"I feel I've outreached myself."

"But the way you look now, it's not you."

"No, it's not me."

"You'd better not smoke standing up."

"Right. I won't do it again."

There was silence.

"You don't at all feel like congratulating me?" Natsuo asked.

Yūsuke did not answer.

"Somehow I knew it might be like this," Yūsuke continued. "I knew this moment was coming."

Now she knew why her joy had felt like pain, a pain almost indistinguishable from grief. Now she knew the source of the suffocating presence in her chest.

"That Rosselini, you know ..." Yūsuke began again.

"Can't we drop the topic?"

"Please listen to me, dear. Rosselini was a jealous person and didn't want to see his wife working for any director other than himself. He would say to her, 'Don't get yourself involved in that play. It'll be a disaster.' One time, Bergman ignored the warning and took a part in a play. It was a big success. Rosselini was watching the stage from the wings. At the curtain call, Bergman glanced at him while bowing to the audience. Their eyes met. That instant, they both knew their love was over, with the thundering applause of the audience ringing in their ears ..." Yūsuke paused, and then added, "I'll go and see your musical on the opening day."

Natsuo contemplated her husband's face from the wings of the room. He looked across.

Their eyes met.

Keath Fraser
Roget's Thesaurus

I had begun my lists. Mother was always saying, "Peter, why not play outside like other boys?" Her patience with collectors was not prodigal; she didn't understand my obsession. I wanted to polish words like shells, before I let them in. Sometimes I tied on bits of string to watch them sway, bump maybe, like chestnuts. They were treasures these words. I could have eaten them had the idiom not existed, even then, to mean remorse. I loved the way they smelled, their inky scent of coal. Sniffing their penny notebook made me think of fire. (See FERVOUR.)

I fiddled with sounds and significations. No words could exist, even in their thousands, until I made them objects on paper: hairpins, lapis lazuli, teeth, fish hooks, dead bees ... Later on my study became a museum for the old weapons poets had used. Mother would have died. By then, of course, she had; pleased I had grown up to become what she approved, a doctor.

My young wife died of tumours the size of apples. That I was a practitioner of healing seemed absurd. It smothered me like fog, her dying, her breath in the end so moist. When *his* wife died my uncle took a razor to his throat. (See DESPAIR, see INSANITY, see OMEGA.) He died disbelieving in the antidote of language. Oh, my wife, I have only words to play with.

When I retired it was because of deafness. My passion for travel spent, my sense of duty to the poor used up, I remembered listening for words everywhere. At the Athenaeum, among the dying in Millbank Penitentiary, after concerts, at the Royal Society, during sermons in St. Pancras. I started to consolidate. At last I could describe—not prescribe. After fifty years I concluded synonyms were reductive, did not exist, were only analogous words. Unlike Dr. Johnson I was no poet. My book would be a philosopher's tool, my soubriquet a thesaurus.

My contribution was to relationships. I created families out of ideas like Space and Matter and Affections. I grouped words in precisely a thousand ways: reacquainted siblings, introduced cousins, befriended black sheep, mediated between enemies. I printed place names and organized a banquet.

London had never seen anything quite like it. Recalcitrant louts, my words, they scented taxonomy and grew inebrious. Mother was well out of it.

She knew me for my polite accomplishments, my papers on optics, comparative anatomy, the poor, zoology, human ageing, mathematics, the deaf and dumb. I was a Renaissance man for I chewed what I bit off. Still, I was no more satisfied with my Bridgewater Treatise on the design of all natural history than with my report for the Water Commission on pollution in the Thames. Only less pessimistic. By the time Asiatic cholera broke out, and people were vomiting and diarrhoetic, my work had been forgotten. Not until I fathered my *Thesaurus* did I dream of prinking. Who knew, perhaps crazy poets would become Roget's trollops, when they discovered his interest in truth not eloquence.

My book appeared the same year as volumes by Dickens, Hawthorne, Melville—fabulators, all of us. (See FICTION.) I too dreamed of the unity of man's existence, and offered a tool for attacking false logic, truisms, jargon, sophism. Though any fretless voice can sing if words are as precise as notes, men in power often sound discordant. Music isn't accident, nor memory history. Language (like the violin) so long to learn.

There is no language, I used to say to Mother, like our own. Look how nations that we oppress trust it. It's the bridge we use to bring back silks and spices, tobacco leaves and cinnamon. Yet all one reviewer wrote of my work was it "made eloquence too easy for the lazy and ignorant." Eloquence I have always distrusted. Maybe this is why my *Thesaurus* has gone through twenty-eight editions.

Men are odd animals. I have never felt as at home around *them* as around their words; without these they're monkeys. (See TRUISM.) The other day I was going through my book and it struck me I have more words for Disapprobation than Approbation. Why is this?

So I spend my last days at West Malvern in my ninety-first year. I no longer walk in parks. I'm pleased I fear death, it makes me feel younger. Death is a poet's idiom to take the mind off complacency. (See SWAN SONG, see CROSSING THE BAR, see THE GREAT ADVENTURE.) I have never thought of death but that it has refurbished me.

Translated by Margaret Rose

Yvette Naubert
The Pigeons in St. Louis Square

Their heads bobbing, taking mechanical little steps, they walk around the benches, the alleys, and scratch about for seeds existing only in their memory. At this early morning hour, labourers, workmen, and women factory workers rush across the square and hurry over to St. Denis Street or Sherbrooke station. The pigeons know these regular passers-by very well, all these people who ignore them and hurry along, turning their worries over in their minds instead of throwing them to the winds like useless seeds. But the pigeons don't care; it's not yet time for the old man to arrive so they peacefully go about their own business. These winged citizens, bold enough to venture out into the middle of the street, deaf to abuse and screaming tires, are not frightened by cars. Noise is so familiar to them that they would be even more fearful of a prolonged silence; perhaps the absence of human beings in St. Louis Square would turn their world upside down. They fly onto the benches, walk along the back rests, leave their droppings everywhere. They explore the alleys, sit on the edge of the silent fountain, not understanding why the bowl is empty, bathe in the bottom of the basin in the little puddles left by the rain. The history of this restless cosmopolitan place where so many races and nationalities rub elbows, where so many dispossessed persons often take up temporary residence, is transmitted from one generation to the next, from beak to feather, so to speak. At one time it had been a privileged place, with polite customs and quiet scenes filled with a harmony which had disappeared forever. The changes in the lives of men scarcely have any effect on the pigeons who like only the giver of seeds, whatever his nationality or social position.

The old gabled stone houses with their turrets, bay windows and elaborate balconies have surrounded St. Louis Square for such a long time that the pigeons have no memory of them ever being constructed. They were there when the pigeons took possession of the domain and what existed before that was lost in a night too long for a pigeon's memory. The fronts of several of these old houses have been modernised but others have been left to slide without a struggle down the slope of ravaging time.

Branches upon branches have been added to the trees; their roots have become more firmly anchored in the soil but they are still the same maples, the same elms which have sheltered for so many seasons the non-migrant birds and the others who leave as summer draws to a close, not to return for a long time afterwards. The trees are places of refuge; thanks to them we can see that spring has changed into summer or that winter, always anxious to settle in but not to leave again, is jostling autumn a little too much. Besides, winter is never completely forgotten. The memory of the struggle against the cold and the snow, the search for food, which is always scarce in winter, is conserved in a corner of the mind. But today, the sun is shining on the new leaves and the air smells like spring.

Nevertheless, the old man doesn't arrive and the pigeons are fidgeting. The dinner hour has long since passed. An old lady settles down on the bench where the old man usually sits. Out of a big black bag she brings not seeds but knitting. The wary pigeons circle around the bench, each time coming closer, but seeds do not often rain down from ladies who knit. Regular visitors as long as the weather is nice, they disappear for a long time, sometimes forever, as soon as the first frost comes. This early rising old lady is dressed in black from head to toe: a black kerchief around her head, and buttoned over a cotton dress the colour of many bereavements, a black cardigan protects her heavy shape from the cold air. Dark lines of pain are concealed in the wrinkles on her face. There is nothing white on her except for her hair and the wool hanging down from her fingers like a long worm the pigeons know is inedible. She willingly escapes from the present; in her mind's eye she sees another continent, a different country, a Portuguese village where the incessant sun of poverty shines.

Just the day before, this corner of the bench where the expatriate old lady is delving back into her past was occupied by the old man whose life had unfolded in the bosom of this country, of this city. He comes back every day to sit in front of the home where he had spent his youth and reflects upon his childhood. He doesn't have to cross the ocean to find memories; only a hundred feet separate him from them. The home where he was born and grew up is right there in front of him and his melancholy thoughts. But he had to reconstruct it in some measure to bring the past to life again because the hand of man had played havoc with it. Man is always in a hurry to change, destroy, and start over again, while the birds go on as usual. The first and second floors have been transformed into apartments; the one on the second floor is for rent. New tribes of nomads, tenants go in and out without really understanding what attracted them to this house and what made them leave it again. For the most part, they are young, they refuse stability which seems to them to be retrograde and bad and they nurture their insecurity as if it were a delicate flower. But the little balcony around which the old man's own father had put a wrought iron railing hasn't changed; perhaps it remembers a little boy with long curls and a young woman embroidering in the fresh air.

The ground floor lost its elegant entrance as did the vestibule where the coat and hat stand stood with its copper coat hooks and its mirror which often reflected women in heavy hats adorned with flowers, fruits, and birds. The walls were knocked down and the lovely oak panelling covered in grey paint in order to accommodate the offices of a real estate broker. The old man wasn't looking at the remodelled house; he was seeing the other one, the home of his memories which couldn't be drowned in a can of paint.

In the neighbouring streets echo the sounds of unofficial languages. They are the languages of a multitude of displaced men and women who have come from countries often far removed from one another and are surprised to find themselves neighbours in the same city. It seems that human beings leave their homes more willingly than the pigeons, these birds for whom distances are measured by the time it takes to return to the nest.

The horizon of these non-migratory pigeons is marked by the buildings around St. Louis Square. They are not racists, nor are they xenophobes. The language which calls them is always harmonious and the hand that throws them seeds or peanuts always pleasant. But no other voice sounds the same as the old man's, always the first to arrive, the most faithful to the daily rendezvous. The seeds he sows taste of tenderness and understanding. Only deep cooing, guttural sounds and clicks of the tongue which the birds understand perfectly are exchanged between him and the pigeons. The old man never acknowledges anyone else. The familiar faces have disappeared long ago. He haunts the square to feed the winged creatures and to contemplate from afar a certain house he hasn't been in for years but which he knows better than anyone else. Was he afraid of reviving forgotten memories? Besides, what was the use? Nothing can start over again. Time can never be turned back; nothing can resist it. In the remodelled house, the old man would no longer hear anything but the breath of ghosts, the flight of spirits, the sighs of those who are lost forever. Would he only find the room where long ago a woman cried out in childbirth? Shortly afterward the midwife presented her with a son, today an old man trying to remember. Years went by; dark days and death came into the house and stayed until the residence passed into the hands of strangers.

And yet the man didn't come to look for the bad memories but for the memory of the happy days of his childhood and his youth. It sparkled in his mind like an unchanging crystal. Perhaps he also came to try to understand and accept the present which embarrasses him like an unknown, incomprehensible language. Tossed about in the tumult of the present, he finds a precarious stability in the past.

Every morning before he arrives, the pigeons gather in a particular spot on St. Denis Street. They leave the rooftops, the trees, and their perch on the fountain and stand watch. As soon as he appears at the corner of the square near St. Denis Street, they rush up to him either taking quick little steps or flying, perch on his arms, his shoulders and his head. They eat out of his hand. The seeds rain down in large quantities. It is the best time of the day. But today the sun follows its upward course in the sky, the old man doesn't appear and the pigeons are puzzled.

The "Montreal Chinese School" stands at the corner of Clarke St. and Prince Arthur St. (On one side of the square there is one French name after the other; on the other side, English names decorate the street signs of the area developed after the conquest.) From the open windows of the school nasal voices reciting a lesson can be heard. Coming and going relatively peacefully, the pigeons find this reassuring as long as the children are inside. In the past, a very long time ago, a small boy used to amuse himself around the fountain which, at that time, had a jet of water singing in it all summer long. He used to float boats in the basin, trundle a hoop around in the alley and scare the pigeons, ancestors of those of today. The trees were not so bushy then and birds fed in the streets after the horses had passed by. On Sunday morning, distinguished people used to cross through the square, missals in hand, and in the evening after vespers, they strolled quiet-ly under the trees. In good weather, maids in their starched aprons and bonnets took the babies out for walks in their huge carriages in the afternoon.

Times had really changed; no one is more conscious of that than the nostalgic old man. Now, not only strangers, but foreigners invade the place every day. The horses had long ago disappeared. Only the pigeons remain. They come and go, flutter about and scratch for food, concerned about the absence of the old man.

The postman makes his rounds, his bag over his shoulder, a stack of letters in his hand. The stack of letters diminishes, the sack emp-ties, but it never contains even one seed. And too, the postman is not the most likeable person who comes around during the day and it's the same with the delivery men. They are all people in a hurry whose quick-moving feet have to be avoided.

A dangerous time for the pigeons is when the sun is at its zenith; the students from the "Montreal Chinese School" disperse and other school children run across the square uttering their war cries. The birds take to their nests and look after their young or seek refuge in the trees or on the silent fountain. The old lady in black sticks a long knitting needle into her knitting which disappears into the black bag. She slowly walks away, her back stooped but her legs still solid, her attention held by some memory stronger than the others. Cooking odours from continental kitchens waft through the air and children's cries, the same in any language and all latitudes, burst forth through the open windows.

The pigeons explore the alleys and the meagre grass. Sometimes under a leaf carried by the wind there is a surprise, a seed forgotten from the day before. The shadows of the trees are lost in the trees themselves; the sun illuminates everything from on high and nothing escapes its light. And too, the pigeons couldn't possibly miss seeing the old man if he were to take the notion to come at this unusual time.

Although they have heard his story many times, they don't tire of it; it's the life of a gentle man who has loved a lot. The ordinary story of an old man whose heart has never grown weary of loving, who was driven out of his paternal home by misfortune and who returns, lonesome, to reminisce about happy times in this very spot where they took place. The pigeons, who have never left this corner, understand that people come back to it and, in remembrance of the past, throw them the best possible seeds.

But, little by little, the light gives way to darkness and young mothers appear in the alleys with their beloved little children. The pigeons don't have a very great affection for them. When they are out of their carriages or push-carts, these monsters fight with the birds over the coveted peanuts. Only the arrival of the old man would reestablish the equilibrium of the day gently drawing to a close. Slow-moving men with a lost look in their eyes sit down on the unoccupied benches. Others stand around in groups, fearing the solitude of old people left to themselves. Men who are still young go from bench to bench searching for something they wouldn't dare admit. Boys and girls are stretched out on the grass and seem to take root in the soil as soon as they sit down. Motionless or slow-moving, floating in an artificial dream that only takes them to the threshold of their being, they challenge established society with their refusal which in turn engenders immobility. Sometimes they accompany the nonchalant flight of the pigeons on the guitar. Then a young man, lying down, throws a peanut or two in such a serious way, as if it's the last act he will ever perform.

On the bench where the old lady had been sitting that morning, a woman and two men using unknown words, are launched into a passionate discussion in which they express fear for this enormous country, for this crowded city which is less miraculous than they had believed. The school children with their almond eyes add the strange music of the Chinese language to the noise and the sound, and for a quarter of an hour, St. Louis Square is transformed into an oriental garden. In the fading light, more and more of the boys and girls who are coming in increasing numbers to live in the neighbourhood around the square, gather around the monument to Octave Crémazie and his Carillon soldier dying in his flag. They don't venerate him any more than do the pigeons who leave their droppings on the heads of the poet and the hero he eulogized in his forgotten verses. But the old man never went near the monument without remembering its inauguration day on June 24, 1906. In his white suit with a sailor's collar and hat, his buttoned shoes, holding his father's hand, he listened to the long boring speeches which prevented him from running about in the alleys. The speeches have long since been forgotten but not the year 1906 nor June 24 since it was the last time his father held his hand in his.

However, when nearly everything was invaded by the darkness, the tumult of a brawl breaks out among the obsessed young people. Immediately, men in black appear, brandishing long clubs. Then the young people, who had been lying in a horizontal position, assume the vertical and flee as if their legs were made only for that purpose. These nocturnal pursuits are now part of the daily existence and that's how the pigeons know that times have changed.

The street lights have been lit for a while and a few dreamers linger in the reestablished silence. Silhouettes which look like the gallows cut across St. Louis Square, permeated by the gentle night. To be sure, the lovers drifting around in the square frosted by the moonlight are experiencing the perfect love. But the pigeons don't see any of these people, not a few hours earlier did they notice a long black vehicle move along St. Louis Square on St. Denis Street and go away, carrying off the last witness to a time which has gone forever.

Tomorrow, and for a few days yet, the pigeons will wait for the old man. They will be on the lookout at the time he usually appears. But he will not come, will never come again and the pigeons will end up forgetting him completely.

Now they sleep, heads tucked under their wings.

NOTES

bereavements	grief; moods of deprivation caused by death
missals	prayer books
nocturnal	nightly
Octave Crémazie	(1827–1879) romantic poet and bookseller, known as the father of French Canadian poetry; author of "Le Drapeau de carillon" and "Le vieux soldat canadien"
St. Louis Square	famous Montréal square built in the late nineteenth century
venerate	respect deeply
vespers	church services held in late afternoon or evening

Responding to Story

When people read a story, they obviously want it to make sense for them. As readers, and as grade 12 students, you will be challenged to read stories that are mature in content and increasingly complex in the ways in which that mature content is presented. Often, writers will speak to you at multiple levels of interpretation: in images, moods, and symbols. They will demand your attention to detail, and your ability to recognize irony and to understand nuance and tone.

In other words, writers will expect you to meet them halfway. And meeting writers on their terms is what response to literature is all about: it's *you* making meaning of *their* stories.

There are a number of different approaches a reader can take in responding to literature, a number of different ways of thinking about the story. With each different type of response, you explore your understanding in a different way, from a different perspective. The way you choose to respond to a particular story will often mesh with your understanding of the story at that time.

Approaches to response include the following:

- Personal response
- Critical/Analytical response
- Creative response
- Problem-solving/Decision-making response

While each type of response has its own focus and serves its own purpose, the ways in which they all assist you to explore your total understanding of a story often overlap.

WHAT IS MEANT BY THE TERM "RESPONSE"?

Most good readers, as they are reading, subconsciously ask themselves questions about the story. Their questions are prompted by the events in the story, and by the apparent relation of those events to the idea or issue that lies at the heart of the story. Upon completing their reading of the story, they often will have discovered further questions they wish to explore. As good readers, they will have developed strategies for recognizing, asking, and answering such questions.

The questions you find in the text that follow each story selection are not exhaustive. They do, however, provide a beginning, a "way in" to making sense of the story. Good readers will always continue to ask *themselves* questions and to further their own understandings of the writers' ideas.

A useful plan is to write down your thoughts about a story before engaging in any discussion of the story in class. Your response will reflect your own interpretation of the story at that time. Thoughts come and go very quickly: by writing your thoughts down you will give them some permanence so that you can return to them later, reflect on them, and perhaps modify them if necessary. When you arrive in class ready to share, you will also be well prepared to hear your classmates' understandings of the story, and you will be able to assess their interpretations in light of your own.

PEANUTS reprinted by permission of United Feature Syndicate, Inc.

What Is "Personal Response"?

Personal response asks you to *personalize* the writer's ideas in a story by exploring the experiences of the story in relation to your *own* life. Three basic questions need to be addressed:

1. At a surface level, what does the story say?
2. At a deeper level, what does the story mean?
3. At a personal level, what does the story mean to you?

As a grade 12 student, you are expected to read a story carefully, and to arrive at a clear understanding of it. However, once you are clear about what has occurred in the story, you must then reflect upon the *significance* of the story's details. Reflections about a story's "moments" of significance—questions about plot events, observations about setting, judgements about characters—all these and more can assist you in gaining insight into the story. For example, you may decide to focus on the characters in the story. More likely, you will be drawn to one character. Examine that character's thoughts, feelings, actions, and reactions in relation to your own:

- To which character in the story are you most drawn? What draws you?
- What does this particular character say or do in the story that is of particular significance?
- What observations, questions, or concerns do you have about that character?
- What suggestions or advice could you give the character? What might you have said or done had you been in that character's position?
- In what way(s) are you like this character? Do you share any of her or his feelings? Which ones?
- What, if anything, do you admire about this character? Why?
- Would you wish to be this character? Why or why not?

Another approach to personal response is to turn to an incident from your own past. Have you ever found yourself in a similar physical, social, emotional, or psychological situation as the character? Initiate a series of private memories that take you back to that time:

- Where were you? How old were you? Who was with you?
- What initiated the incident?
- Visualize the setting: Was it day or night? Warm or cold? Do you remember the colours, the sounds, the smells that surrounded you?
- What other physical sensations come flooding back?

- How quickly or slowly did things happen?
- What emotions did you feel? Why? What caused them?
- How did everything end? Did it resolve? Were you satisfied with the outcome?
- What is the single, dominant memory that stands out?
- Why is this incident still with you? Of what significance is it to you?
- In what way does your own lived experience assist you in reaching a more complete understanding of the significance of the story situation?

In other words, use your own life experience to approach a story. In doing so, your understanding of the characters, and of the story as a whole, will be heightened. In turn, by integrating the character's experiences with your own, you allow her or his thoughts and behaviours to shed light on your own. Writers, through their characters, offer the wisdom of their own lived experiences and understandings: they can help you learn about who you are, where you have been, and who you are becoming.

What Is the Role of a Response Journal?

Many students find it effective to keep a notebook for their responses to stories. Such journals serve a number of purposes:

- They allow you as a reader to "hold" your thoughts, whether brief and fragmentary or detailed and coherent, so that your thinking can be revisited and, if need be, revised.

HERMAN® by Jim Unger

9-15 © 1983 Jim Unger

"I've seen it before. He's changing into a butterfly."

- They provide teachers with an opportunity to engage you in written discussion about your individual and shared understandings of the story.
- They provide you with a starting point for sharing your thoughts and personal stories in a group setting. At the same time, they give you space to record the thoughts of others — in a sense, to expand your thinking.
- They also allow you to compare your current thinking on an issue with your own thoughts from an earlier time. They provide you with a record of your own developing understandings.
- Finally, journals provide you with "notes" for your own writing—a poem, an essay, a story.

What Is "Critical/Analytical Response"?

Critical response asks you to probe the thoughts of the writer, but from a different perspective than that of personal response.

First of all, in critical response, you examine whether the writer has presented life issues honestly. Is the story a realistic and truthful portrayal of human thinking, feelings, actions, and reactions? Skilled writers have the ability to use their craft to manipulate readers' thoughts and emotions. Critical readers know and understand this, and through analysis and interpretation, they judge the truthfulness of the writer's ideas.

In responding critically and analytically, two basic questions are explored:

1. What does the story mean?
2. What has the writer done to convey this particular meaning to the reader?

In this textbook's introduction, "Critical Reading of Short Stories," you have been given a series of questions that help you to answer these two questions. In doing so, you are employing the strategy of *questioning* to develop comprehension, and appreciation.

In addition, critical response helps you to appreciate not only what a writer has to say, but also the *way* in which the writer says it. Critical response asks that you examine the technique of the writer. Has the writer's skill in the use of language, imagery, and form served to enhance the artistry and the presentation of the story content? In view of the writer's intent to convey a specific idea, what means—techniques, devices, choices—has the writer used, and how do they serve the story?

Any of the following story elements might be examined:

Character
- How adequately developed are the characters' emotions and motivations?
- Are characters consistent in their actions? Are they credible?
- If they change, are their changes plausible within the context of the story's action?

Plot and Conflict
- How logical and believable—rather than coincidental, arbitrary, or contrived—is the story's plot? Does each incident serve a purpose?
- How meaningful is the nature of the conflict around which the story revolves?

Setting
- In what way is the story's setting particularly suited to the idea(s) with which the story deals? Is it sufficiently detailed to serve the story's purpose?

Irony and Symbol
- Does the writer's use of irony help to engage the reader? Does it provide added insight into the story's meaning?
- Does the writer's use of allusions, motifs, and symbols effectively enhance the story's telling and reinforce its meaning?

Style
- In what way does the writer's style, or choice of language, help to create an important mood or atmosphere and to convey tone?
- How do the story's language and the characters' dialogue enhance the story's telling?
- How effective is the writer's use of sense imagery: sight, sound, smell, touch?
- What has the writer done to emphasize details and/or idea(s)? Has she or he used parallelism and contrast? Repetition and juxtaposition?

What Is "Creative Response"?

Creative response offers yet another way of deepening your understanding of a story, this time by using the story as a jumping-off point to explore and extend the ideas on your own. For example, once you understand what motivates characters, you can predict what they are *likely* to say and do in other related circumstances. If you have reached a perceptive understanding of the characters' motivations and patterns of development, you can imagine their actions in other, more unusual circumstances.

Creative response asks readers to transfer the characters—or the plot situations that give characters life—to alternative contexts or settings. Readers engage with the story and "write" new situations to extend and develop their own understandings of the ideas behind the original stories.

Creative response can take many different forms, depending on such things as the nature of the original story, the ideas the story develops, and the reader's purpose in responding. You may respond individually, or you might choose to act collaboratively, with a partner or in a small group.

Some forms of creative response that you may wish to explore include the following:

Written Response

Story sequel Add a final page to the story that acts as a denouement or "ties up" some element of the story that has gone unexplained. A sequel may also jump to a point past the end of the story, with characters reuniting or encountering new situations.

Story flashback Provide a flashback (that the writer did not) to help explain an essential quality of the story.

Phrase collage Select from the story a series of brief narrative or spoken phrases that capture the essential qualities of the story. These can be printed on separate cards or arranged on a poster. They could also be superimposed over a graphic design based on the story.

Found poem Select a series of brief phrases taken verbatim from the story and make a free verse poem that captures an essential quality of the story. Sentences/phrases may be re-ordered for the sake of coherence, repeated for emphasis, or broken into shorter lines for effect.

Newspaper front page   Report on plot incidents and characters, print interviews with characters, or provide artist's sketches that are consistent with the story and based on textual information. This activity can also be presented as a radio or television news report.

Advice column   Compose the letter a character might write in searching for help with a conflict or dilemma from the story. Then, respond as the advice columnist, sharing the advice that you believe would best serve that character.

Hidden encounters   Script the dialogue between characters that has not been reported directly by the writer, or that would inevitably take place following the conclusion of the original story.

Alternative title   Rename the story and support *your* title over the original, explaining how yours captures the essential quality of the story.

Review · Include a summary or synopsis of the story, without giving away the outcome. Make the reader curious to read the story.

Character's poem   Present one character's reflection on the events of the story, either at a key moment of crisis or at the conclusion of the story.

Character's letter
- Have a character from the story write to someone important to her or him, someone who is not present in the story.
- Provide the letter of reference written by one character on behalf of another. The letter writer's perspective should be clearly in keeping with the story details. This activity can also be presented in the form of a eulogy.

Character's diary   Prepare a series of diary entries that, taken together, describe or explain what the character was thinking as the story moved toward its conclusion. This activity is well suited to stories written from an objective narrative point of view.

Character's last will   Explain how and why the character would choose to distribute her or his possessions to other characters in the story.

Oral/Dramatic Response

Oral interpretation Present a reading of one key section of the story. Consider such elements as volume, intonation, pacing, emphasis, body language, eye contact with the audience, and setting a mood in the presentation space.

Readers' theatre Present a dramatized reading of one key section of the story. Consider elements of vocal and facial expression that are in keeping with the tone and mood of the original story. This activity might be accompanied by a slideshow of images in the background that correspond to the story's setting.

Song Present one character's "song," perhaps a lament for how things might have been. The music can be original or borrowed. If possible, present the song as a music video.

Improvisation Role-play a character in the story. Respond to fellow students' "What if?" questions. Remain true to the character's motivations and behaviours.

Interview
- Speak with a character to determine motivations for actions.
- Speak with the writer about the theme or purpose of the story.

Filming the story Present a group discussion exploring the feasibility of making a movie of the story. Points of discussion might include the story's commercial selling points, its audience, length, possible difficulties in transposing paper to film.

Radio play Present a short extract from the story reworked as a radio play. This can include appropriate sound effects and/or mood music. It should be preceded with a context-setting introduction. One version of the play might be for an adult audience. A second version might be for a younger audience.

Radio phone-in Present a simulated broadcast with calls to either some of the characters in the story, or to the story's writer. The purpose of the calls should be to develop an essential understanding of the story.

Still Visual Response

(Several of the following activities can also be presented in an electronic format.)

Mind-map   Create a purposeful grouping of several images suggested by characters, incidents, symbols, or ideas in the story. Arrange them on the page in a way that conveys one or more essential qualities of the story: theme, conflict, character development, and so on.

Visual collage   Create a photographic layout that effectively captures an essential quality of the story. Use elements of colour, placement, size, spacing, and design to achieve the intended effect.

Cover design   Design a cover for a pocketbook edition of the story that captures an essential quality of the story: the mood, a key moment, contrasting elements or characters.

Friendship manual   Design a brochure that would give direction on how one should behave in order to establish or maintain a friendship with a particular character from the story. Base your directions on actual story detail.

Strip cartoon   Select a key section of the story for representation in visual form. This can be done on paper, on a roll of overhead transparency acetate, or electronically. An introduction explaining the significance of this particular section may be useful.

Storyboard   Prepare a plan of the series of camera shots that you would use if you were to create a film version of a key incident in the story. The storyboard can also be developed into a photo essay using still photographs.

Illustration   Draw your visualization of a key scene from the story. Create two versions of the same scene: draw the scene depicting a first-person point of view from the protagonist's perspective, and then another showing the same scene from an omniscient perspective.

Videotape/Electronic Response

Video the story   Select one critical scene from the story. You may include a brief introduction that explains the significance of that scene.

Talking heads   Prepare a filmed version in which each character speaks once only, directly to the camera, offering her or his perspective regarding an issue or idea at the heart of the story. Videotape the piece using only a fixed head-and-shoulders camera shot.

Electronic slideshow/collage   Create a photo layout that effectively captures an essential quality of the story. Hyperlinked extensions can branch off into different areas of the story.

Web site   Design a character's home page, including links to several different facets of the story that capture essential qualities of that character's life: social background and preferences, emotional strengths or weaknesses, personal motivations, and so on.

What Is "Problem-Solving/Decision-Making Response"?

Literature has the power to disturb readers because it exposes truths about life. This is especially so if the truths appear in the form of issues, problems, or dilemmas that have a direct impact on readers' own lives.

Coming to terms with such real-world problems means confronting them rationally and methodically. Once you, the reader, have internalized a story's idea by relating it in some way to your own life experience, once you have critically analyzed the truthfulness of a writer's thought and expression, and once you have tested the writer's idea by creatively applying it to an alternative context, you then should be in a position to evaluate the same idea in a real-world context.

Decision-making and problem-solving response is often best carried out in a collaborative context. The following kinds of activities are appropriate:

Research   In an attempt to shed greater light on the ideas with which the story deals, search out information about either the writer or the issue that is at the heart of the story. Pool your own and others' research.

Panel discussion/Debate   Explore the differing views or perspectives of the issues at the heart of the story. For example, one side can defend the writer's "solutions" while the other side challenges them.

Trial   Put a character "on trial" for her or his actions in the story. Argue the innocence or guilt of the character in terms of that character's effect on others or on the outcome of the story.

CAN I RESPOND INDEPENDENTLY, BEYOND THE QUESTIONS?

It is important to develop confidence in your own abilities to reach an understanding of a story's controlling idea. The following three-part response format is sufficiently open-ended to assist you in consolidating your own thinking about stories. It permits you to respond both personally and critically/analytically. Each part can be a paragraph or more in length. Together, the three parts make up your response.

Part 1: Making Meaning

Identify the main idea that the story suggests, the idea at the heart of the story. Support your statement of the story's controlling idea with reference to key story details: particular passages (lines, phrases, expressions, even individual words that catch your attention); story characters, conflicts, and turning points; settings, ironies, and symbols; or any other story elements that clearly imply the story's basic theme. Do not simply retell the story. Instead, focus selectively on the three or four critical details that seem to be of most significance to the story. Why are they significant? How do they shape your understanding of the rest of the text? Explore the meaning they create for you.

Part 2: Drawing a Personal Connection

What does the idea at the heart of the story say to you *personally*? Make a brief thematic connection between the writer's controlling idea and an incident from your own past: describe the incident and demonstrate that it connects in some meaningful way to what the writer is saying. In other words, use your lived experience to interpret the experience of the text. How does what happened to *you* help you to better understand or more fully appreciate what happened in *the story*? Or, conversely, how does what happened in the story help you to better understand the significance of your lived experience?

If you are unable to connect the issue at the heart of the text with your *own* lived experience, you may instead make a connection with the lived experience of someone you know, or of someone you know about, or with the experience of someone in literature, film, art, music, or other expressions of thought or emotion.

Part 3: Expressing a Global View

Generalize beyond your own experience, and beyond the experience of the story. In what way is the idea at the heart of the story significant, not only to the writer or to you, but to all people? What makes the idea universal? How does the writer's idea shed light on the human condition? Suggest the writer's purpose in writing this story.

Consider the writer's point of view about the world as she or he describes it. Do you agree with and accept that point of view? Or do you challenge it?

HOW DO I MOVE FROM WRITING RESPONSE TO WRITING A LITERARY ANALYSIS ESSAY?

A literary analysis essay is a highly structured answer to a question of critical response. It presents a thoughtful, coherent, and perceptive argument favouring a particular critical perspective.

Sample essay question:

Much of literature deals with some aspect of the human desire to escape adverse or challenging life situations. The way in which an individual responds to a desire to escape may profoundly affect the course of that individual's life. Write an essay based on Margaret Laurence's short story "Horses of the Night," in which the writer examines the circumstances that result from an individual's desire to escape. **What ideas does the writer develop regarding the desire to escape?** Support and develop your controlling idea with reference to specific detail from the story.

1. An initial step in answering the question is to pose a brief statement (or several possible statements) that may answer the question. This theme statement will become your essay's *controlling idea*.

Sample statements:

- A sensitive individual, rather than face a world that is only functional and routine, may choose to retreat into a created world of her or his own imaginings.

- A gentle, sensitive individual will never be able to completely escape the physical restrictions and demands of the practical world. The real world is inevitably uncompromising.

- Individuals who choose escape as a way of dealing with a bleak and oppressive society may find the safety and security of their imagined world to be only temporary at best, and potentially destructive.

Choose the one statement that is most accurately, and most completely, supported by the details of the story. The statement can be revised later, if necessary, to suit your essay's thesis.

2. A subsequent step is to examine which critical elements of the story—elements of content and of form—might prove useful in answering the question.

FIGURE 1. Sample critical elements of story

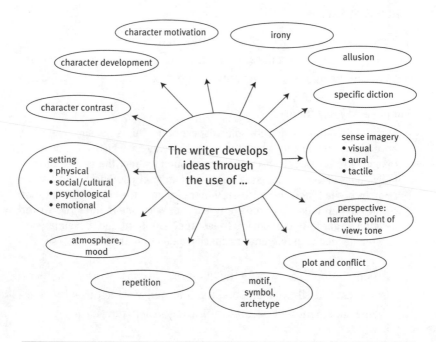

Select from this list those critical story elements that appear to have been most useful to the writer in helping to develop an idea regarding "escape." The number of elements you select for your essay will depend on several factors: the required length of the essay, the amount of detail that the essay intends to develop, and, if you are in a test situation, the amount of time available for completing the essay.

3. Next, brainstorm for story details that will support your controlling idea. Each of the following elements, if selected, would then become a separate body paragraph of the essay.

Sample brainstorming

The Story's Character Conflicts and Contrasts

Grandfather versus Chris:

> *granite, bludgeoning/[Chris] simply appeared to be elsewhere*

Vanessa's mother versus Chris:

> *"Wonderful. Only we can't afford one."/"But I figure this is really a going thing."*

Grandmother versus Chris:

> *"No. Leave [the door] open, Vanessa."/[Chris] gave no sign of feeling anything.*

Vanessa versus Chris:

> *When I had spoken ... I did not believe it./"Lots of guys work their way through university."*

Paragraph focus: While the people around Chris react with differing degrees of sensitivity to him, they nevertheless remain grounded in reality. He does not.

The Story's Narrative Point of View

The child narrator's changing perspective of Chris is made clear in the author's choice of language:

- from the ironic naïveté of childhood:
  > *"Do plain people live there?"/girls could not be travellers.*

- to early adolescence:
  > *I knew the passionate truth of his convictions/"I bet you'll sell a thousand."*

- to a maturing adolescence:
  > *at Shallow Creek: Unable to reply...comprehendingly.*

- and ending in young adulthood:
  > *Slowly, slowly.... The night must move like this for him.*

Several other elements of narrative point of view help us to understand change in the story:

- the narrator's growth/development over the course of the story
- an ironic contrast to Chris's *lack* of development: she grows while he appears to remain static, or to regress
- her arrival at a final understanding of Chris's reality

> **Paragraph focus:** Vanessa, the child, initially sees the world imaginatively through Chris's eyes. However, as she grows and matures over time, she arrives at the realization that Chris's world has remained illusory, that his unwillingness to accept the unpleasant reality of his life has never left him.

Allusion

One purpose of allusion is to create a sense of universal significance, linking the individual (motivations, goals, development, etc.) to all that has come before, thus amplifying its significance.

"Moses or God"/"Children of Israel"
   exile motif

Richard Halliburton, Hannibal
   traveller motif

> **Paragraph focus:** The reader is plagued with a sense of foreboding that Chris's fate has been determined, that he is destined never to find his "home."

Symbol
Brick House
   cool from the outside
   but the wood stove ... "going full blast"; "smelled of roasting meat"

saddle
   criss-cross brand: suggesting a movement back and forth between reality and fantasy
   miniature only, not real
   eventually "put away" by Vanessa

bridge builder
   linking two worlds
   concrete and steel
   ironically unsuited to Chris's reality

horses
   contrasting Duchess and Firefly with the "horses" of Chris's nightmares
   horses' eyes "berserk"

> **Paragraph focus:** Various objects and actions that make up Chris's world—his society, his toys, his physical being, his imagination—all are in some way symbolic of Chris's attempts to run away from the reality of his loneliness and alienation.

4. At this point, you have brainstormed several possibilities of story details. Go back to step 1: determine your essay's controlling idea. Decide which narrative elements and story details will serve the essay best. Develop the paragraphs that support your controlling idea.

WHERE DO EXAMINATIONS ABOUT STORIES FIT INTO RESPONSE?

Sometimes, fixed-response tests are administered as one way of determining your understanding of a story, and as such, they can be considered one form of "response." In writing a test that requires you to select a single correct answer, it is wise to understand the construction of such a test.

PEANUTS reprinted by permission of United Feature Syndicate, Inc.

Typically, a multiple choice examination contains a "question stem" followed by usually four possible answers. One answer either is correct or is the **most** correct. Three of the answers are "distractors": most often, two of the distractors are close to being correct or are partially correct, and one is clearly incorrect. Usually, early questions deal with more specific details and then proceed to the more general or thematic. Where possible, questions follow the order of the story.

Suggestions for answering:

1. Questions need not be answered in the order asked.
2. Pay careful attention to line references where provided. It may be helpful to read several sentences before and after these lines to remind yourself of the context for the question.
3. Pay attention to qualifying terms. Words like **best**, **most**, and **mainly** indicate that all four choices may be partially right. Only one, though, is correct.
4. With your hand or a piece of paper, cover the four answers and read only the question stem. Try to form an appropriate response before looking at the list.
5. Read all four responses carefully. Do not skim and do not leap to a conclusion.
6. If more than one item (for example, adjectives and nouns) is contained in each of the four responses, read carefully to determine that all items that make up the chosen response apply correctly to the question stem.
7. Because interpretations of the text should remain consistent, answers should be consistent. One answer should not contradict another. One answer is often the key to many other correct answers.
8. Generally, questions near the end of a test are thematic, containing keys to the interpretation of the reading. Check that your choices are consistent with previous responses.
9. Understand that distractors are designed specifically to attract the person who doesn't understand the material.
10. Do change answers upon reconsideration.

MULTIPLE CHOICE EXAMINATION: "HORSES OF THE NIGHT"

1. The **strongest** example of contrasting character foils can be seen in
   A. Chris and Grandfather Connor
   B. Chris and Vanessa's father
   C. Vanessa's mother and Grandmother Connor
   D. Vanessa and Grandmother Connor

2. The statement that **most clearly** foreshadows the terrible denouement of Chris's existence is
   A. "The way he spoke did not make me feel I had blundered." (p. 284)
   B. " 'If the boy takes after his father, it's a poor lookout for him.' " (p. 285)
   C. "He simply appeared to be absent, elsewhere." (p. 286)
   D. "His sisters ... did not exist for me, not even as photographs, because I did not want them to exist." (p. 286)

3. The connotation of the destructiveness of Grandfather Connor's inter-actions with Chris is **most vividly** indicated by the image
   A. "granite" (p. 284)
   B. "trumpeting" (p. 285)
   C. "bludgeoning" (p. 286)
   D. "black pronouncements" (p. 293)

4. " 'And the way their eyes looked when they realised they weren't going to get out.' " (p. 298) The writer's central point in Ewen's description of the horses in the mud is that
   A. war is an insult to God
   B. Chris's despair is unrelenting
   C. Ewen's influence on Chris is profound
   D. Vanessa is still too immature to comprehend

5. In the context of the whole story, the horses' eyes represent
   A. unnatural apprehension
   B. insurmountable limitation
   C. angry resignation
   D. absolute realization

6. The phrase "He had been forced to return to the alien lake of home" (p. 299) contains an example of
   A. paradox
   B. antithesis
   C. hyperbole
   D. analogy

7. The writer's **most likely** purpose in ending one paragraph with the word "passive" and beginning the next with the word "*Violent*" (p. 299) is to establish a stark contrast between
   A. Vanessa's words and Vanessa's thoughts
   B. Chris's life at Shallow Creek and his new life in the army
   C. Vanessa's understanding of Chris on the one hand and her mother's on the other
   D. the outward expression of Chris's manner and the inner turbulence of his existence

8. "I put the saddle away once more, gently and ruthlessly, back into the cardboard box." (p. 301) The effect of the final sentence of the story is heightened through the use of
   A. understatement
   B. oxymoron
   C. sarcasm
   D. metonymy

ANSWER KEY AND RATIONALE

1. **A** Grandfather Connor is as insensitive as Chris is sensitive. As well, Grandfather Connor's world is of solid things: the Brick House, the hardware business, precise time schedules. Chris's world is that of the imagination.

2. **C** The statement foreshadows Chris's ability to block out all instances of harshness and negativity directed his way; in time, even relatively ordinary real-world events will not be permitted entry into his imagined and private "elsewhere."

3. **C** "Bludgeoning" refers specifically to Grandfather Connor's words directed at Chris. The literal meaning is to beat with a blunt object. The metaphoric meaning fits with the grandfather's intent.

4. **B** Chris has reached the realization that there is no hope at all of his ever being able to adjust to the real world of other human beings. He has made the decision to accept this situation.

5. **D** "Sight" often serves writers as a symbol of understanding. "Eyes" are a means of reaching that understanding. In this nightmarish image, the eyes represent not only the ability to understand, but their "berserk"ness expresses the horror of what it is they have understood.

6. **A** The concepts of "alien" and "home" initially appear to be self-contradictory. The truth is that Shallow Creek is, for Chris, a home where he "took no part at all, none." It is a home from which he has "closed himself off."

7. **D** As with question 2, Chris is able to assume a façade, to convey a sense of casual compliance. This outward expression contrasts sharply with "the land he journeyed through ... inhabited by terrors."

8. **B** "Gently" and "ruthlessly" are relative opposites, juxtaposed into a single expression that in fact reveals a truth. Vanessa speaks both literally and metaphorically, of the object itself and of Chris.

Author Biographies

Vidyut Aklujkar

Vidyut Aklujkar writes mainly in the Marathi language and has divided her life equally so far between Canada and India. Her anthologies of essays and travelogues have been published in India, and she has had poems, TV screenplays, and academic writing published in North America and elsewhere abroad. She has been a co-editor for *Ekata*, a Marathi quarterly published in Ontario, and has taught courses in philosophy, Hindi, and Indian literature at the University of British Columbia. Aklujkar lives in Richmond, B.C., with her husband and children.

Isaac Asimov

Author of hundreds of books on a wide range of topics, including science, history, and religion, Isaac Asimov (1920–1992) was perhaps best known for his Foundation series and robot stories, which helped establish modern science fiction. Born in the Soviet Union, he came to the United States when he was eight years old. Later, he earned a Ph.D. in chemistry at Columbia University and eventually became a professor of biochemistry at Boston University. His *Intelligent Man's Guide to Science* (1960) covers all areas of science for the layman.

Ann Beattie

Born in Washington, D.C., Ann Beattie is an award-winning American short story writer and novelist. Her works include *Park City* (1998), *Picturing Will* (1990), and *Chilly Scenes of Winter* (1976). She has taught at Harvard and lately divides her time between homes in Maine and Key West, Florida.

Ambrose Bierce

Born in Ohio, Ambrose Gwinett Bierce (1842?–1914) was an American journalist and short story writer known for his cruel wit. Although he later doubted the cause he fought for, Bierce participated in the American Civil War, fighting for the Federal side, and left the army with the rank of major.

Bierce's best-known longer work was *The Devil's Dictionary* (1911). His story "An Occurrence at Owl Creek Bridge" was made into an unusual award-winning film that was shown on TV's *Twilight Zone* series. Bierce eventually disappeared into war-torn Mexico, and the details of his death remain a mystery.

Ernest Buckler

Ernest Buckler (1908–1984) was born in Dalhousie, Nova Scotia. He attended the University of Toronto, and worked in Toronto for an insurance company before returning to the family farm near Bridgeport in the Annapolis Valley. His popular fiction won many awards and was published in numerous American magazines. He is best known for his coming-of-age novel *The Mountain and the Valley* (1952) and a short story collection, *The Rebellion of Young David and Other Stories* (1975), from which "The Harness" is selected.

Anton Chekhov

Anton Chekhov (1860–1904) was one of Russia's great short story writers and dramatists. His plays include *Uncle Vanya* (1897), *Three Sisters* (1901), and *The Cherry Orchard* (1903). Chekhov stories are renowned for their mature feelings, complicated human responses, and moral issues.

Wayson Choy

 Wayson Choy was born in Vancouver in 1939 and was raised in several Chinese households. He attended the University of British Columbia and later moved to Toronto, where he now teaches English at Humber College. His memoirs and stories have been collected in *The Jade Peony* (1995; it won the Trillium Award in that year) and *Paper Shadows: A Chinatown Childhood* (1999). Choy is also an active volunteer for community literacy projects and AIDS groups.

Arthur C. Clarke

Sir Arthur Charles Clarke (b. 1917) is considered to be one of the masters of the science fiction short story. He is known for the use of accurate science facts in his writing, and many of his books' predictions (for example, the development of communication satellites) have come true. Among his more than 60 books are *Childhood's End* (1953) and *2001: A Space Odyssey* (1967), the screenplay for which he co-wrote with director Stanley Kubrick. Since 1956, Clarke has lived in Colombo, Sri Lanka.

Timothy Findley

Timothy Findley (1930-2002), one of Canada's leading fiction writers, was born in Toronto. His novel *The Wars* (1977) won the Governor General's Award for fiction and catapulted him to fame after a long apprenticeship in theatre and writing. The novel was subsequently made into a film in 1981. Findley's other major works include *The Last of the Crazy People* (1967), *Stones* (1988), *Inside Memory* (1990), and *Headhunter* (1993). The powerful "Foxes" is typical of Findley's brilliantly crafted, spare, but dramatic fiction. Findley is an Officer of the Order of Canada.

Keath Fraser

Keath Fraser (b. 1944) has published his work in many magazines. His story collections include *Taking Cover* (1982) and B.C. Book Prize winner *Foreign Affairs* (1985). He has taught at the University of Calgary and now lives in Vancouver, where he is working on a novel. Recently, he edited an anthology of travel literature, *Bad Trips* (1990), and published *As for Me and My Body* (1997), a memoir about his friend, writer Sinclair Ross.

Connie Gault

Born in Central Butte, Saskatchewan, Connie Gault (b. 1949) is a fiction writer and dramatist who has also lived in Alberta, British Columbia, Ontario, and Quebec. Her story collections include *Some of Eve's Daughters* (1987) and *Inspection of a Small Village* (1996). She is frequently published in Canadian literary magazines such as *Grain* and *NeWest Review*, and her radio dramas have been broadcast on CBC and BBC World Service.

Charlotte Perkins Gilman

Charlotte Perkins Gilman (1860–1935) lived an intense fantasy life when she was young. As an adult, she studied art and painting, and eventually became a commercial illustrator. It was through her writing, however, that she overcame a deep depression that had developed after her marriage and the birth of her first daughter. "The Yellow Wallpaper," first published in 1892 in *The New England Magazine*, was her masterpiece. One reader wrote that "Such a story ought not to be written. It was enough to drive anyone mad to read it."

Graham Greene

Graham Greene (1904–1991) was not only a popular writer, but also an editor, film critic, and member of the British Foreign Office. He wrote some 30 novels as well as essays, stories, plays, children's books, and travel books. Many popular movies have been made from his books, including *The Third Man*, *The Fallen Idol*, *The Heart of the Matter*, *Brighton Rock*, *Travels with My Aunt*, *The Comedians*, and *Our Man in Havana*. His writing is often concerned with the problems of good and evil, human choice, and characters in a state of moral or spiritual chaos.

Beverly Harris

Beverly Harris was born in Montréal, and educated at Sir George Williams University (now Concordia University) and the University of Calgary. Her short stories and poems have been widely published in literary magazines, and she has taught creative writing at the University of Calgary. "The Day They Set Out" is selected from a collection of prairie fiction entitled *Three Times Five* (1983).

Nathaniel Hawthorne

Nathaniel Hawthorne (1804–1864) was born in Salem, Massachusetts, site of the infamous witch trials. He attended college in Maine and later worked as a surveyor before returning to Concord, Massachusetts, to write for a living. Among his best-known works are *The Scarlet Letter* (1850), *The House of Seven Gables* (1851), and *Twice-Told Tales* (1837), from which "Dr. Heidegger's Experiment" has been selected for this anthology. Hawthorne's fiction is often about the supernatural, sin, and guilt.

Janette Turner Hospital

Janette Turner Hospital (b. 1942) was born in Australia and educated at the University of Queensland. After a brief stay in the United States, she settled in Kingston, Ontario, in 1971. Her short story collections include *Dislocations* (1986), *Isobars* (1990), and *Collected Stories* (1995). She has also written six novels, a novella published in French, and a crime thriller, *A Very Proper Death* (1990).

Duong Thu Huong

Duong Thu Huong (b. 1947) was born in Thai Binh, Vietnam. She served in a Communist Youth Brigade during the Vietnam War. During the 1979 war with China, Huong was a reporter at the front. She has written four novels and a story collection, *Night, Again*, from which her story "Reflections of Spring" originates.

Shirley Jackson

One of the best practitioners of the short story genre, Shirley Jackson (1919–1965) was born in San Francisco. She later moved to Bennington, Vermont, which is where she wrote her best-known works, including "The Lottery" and *The Haunting of Hill House*. Jackson's hair-raising stories are notable for their deceptively serene surfaces and dark undercurrents of human evil, fear, and horror. The mysterious Jackson is the subject of *Private Demons: The Life of Shirley Jackson*, a fascinating biography by Judy Oppenheimer.

Thomas King

Witty Native Canadian writer Thomas King (b. 1943) is a member of the Native Studies Department at the University of Lethbridge. As well, he has taught at the University of Guelph and the University of Minnesota. Widely published in Canadian and American journals, he has edited an anthology of short fiction entitled *All My Relations*. His first novel, *Medicine River*, was released in 1990, followed by a novel, *Green Grass, Running Water* (1993), and *One Good Story, That One* (1993). His work has also been adapted and broadcast on CBC Radio.

Margaret Laurence

Governor General's Award winner Margaret Laurence (1926–1987) was born in Neepawa, Manitoba, and attended what is now the University of Winnipeg. After living in Africa for several years, she moved to England and there wrote the famous Manawaka novels, including *The Stone Angel* (1964), *A Jest of God* (1966; made into the movie *Rachel, Rachel* by Paul Newman), and *The Diviners* (1974). In 1972, she settled in Lakefield, Ontario where she spent her last years writing essays about nuclear disarmament, reviews, and children's books. "Horses of the Night" is from an excellent collection of coming-of-age stories entitled *A Bird in the House* (1970).

D.H. Lawrence

David Herbert Lawrence (1885–1930) was one of the major English writers of the early twentieth century. His novels include *Sons and Lovers* (1913), *The Rainbow* (1915), *Women in Love* (1920), and the long-banned *Lady Chatterley's Lover* (1928). His personal life was as turbulent and controversial as some of his fiction. In 1912, he eloped with the wife of his tutor, and in 1929 his writings were confiscated on obscenity charges. Disgusted by English conservatism and prudishness, he spent many years travelling abroad, searching unsuccessfully for another place to call home. His fiction, such as "The Rocking-Horse Winner," is often immersed in the subconscious and employs rich symbolism.

Nancy Lord

Nancy Lord is a winner of the Alaska State Arts Council short fiction prize. Her first story collection was called *The Compass Inside Ourselves*, and "Small Potatoes" originates from another collection called *Survival* (1991). She has lived in Homer, Alaska, since 1973 and fishes commercially.

Alistair MacLeod

Born in North Battleford, Saskatchewan, Alistair MacLeod (b. 1936) eventually moved to Inverness County, Nova Scotia, and renewed his Cape Breton roots. MacLeod now resides in Windsor, Ontario, where he teaches at the University of Windsor. His celebrated story collections include *The Lost Salt Gift of Blood* (1976), *As Birds Bring Forth the Sun* (1986), and *Island* (2000). His novel *No Great Mischief* (1999) won numerous awards, including the 2001 International IMPAC Dublin Literacy Award.

Naguib Mahfouz

Born in 1911 in Ganaliyya, an old section of Cairo, Mahfouz studied philosophy at the University of Cairo. He is best known for *The Mockery of Fate* (1939), *Radobais* (1943), *The Struggle of Thebes* (1944), and *The Cairo Trilogy* (1956–1957). He is one of Egypt's leading authors and was awarded the Nobel Prize in Literature in 1988. He is widely read by Egyptians, and his work has been made into movies in his home country. In 1989, he spoke out against Ayatollah Khomeini's death sentence on author Salman Rushdie and has been threatened by Muslim fundamentalists for his stand. "Half a Day" features Mahfouz's use of allegory, symbolism, and experimental fiction methods.

Katherine Mansfield

Katherine Mansfield (1888–1923) was born in Wellington, New Zealand, and moved to London in 1908. She met and eventually became friends with several prominent literary figures, including D.H. Lawrence, and eventually married literary critic John Middleton Murry. She began to write as a journalist and later wrote short stories. Her short story collections include *In a German Pension* (1911), *Prelude* (1918), *Bliss and Other Stories* (1920), *The Garden Party and Other Stories* (1922), and *The Dove's Nest and Other Stories* (1923).

Gabriel García Márquez

Born in 1928 in Aracataca, Colombia, Márquez is his country's foremost man of letters. He is generally considered to be one of the great writers of the twentieth century. His best-known works include *One Hundred Years of Solitude* (1967) and *Love in the Time of Cholera* (1985). He won the Nobel Prize in Literature in 1982. "Tuesday Siesta" is a typically quirky Márquez story from a collection called *Big Mama's Funeral* (1962).

Charles Mungoshi

Born in 1947 and considered one of Zimbabwe's best writers, Charles Mungoshi is the author of several novels, including *Coming of the Dry Season* (1972) and *Waiting for the Rain* (1975), as well as a collection, *Stories from a Shona Childhood* (1989). Mungoshi has won numerous international awards, including the PEN and Nona awards, and his work has been published in both the Shona language and English. The story "The Setting Sun and the Rolling World" originates from a story collection bearing the same title (published in English in 1987). Mungoshi's stories have been called "brilliant," "subtle," and "sad."

Alice Munro

Alice Munro, Canada's best-known short story writer, was born in Wingham, Ontario, in 1931. She attended the University of Western Ontario, later moving to Vancouver and Victoria. Since 1972, she has lived in the southwestern Ontario town of Clinton. Munro's work has been published in eminent literary magazines such as *The New Yorker* and *The Paris Review* and is known in such faraway places as Australia, Norway, and China. Her rich, polished style often shows ordinary people in situations that always ring true. "The Shining Houses" first appeared in her debut collection *The Dance of the Happy Shades* (1968), which won a Governor General's Award.

Yvette Naubert

Yvette Naubert (1918–1982) was a French-Canadian writer who lived for a time in Paris. In 1979, she returned to Canada and served as writer-in-residence at the University of Ottawa. *Tales of Solitude* (1978), from which "The Pigeons in St. Louis Square" is taken, is her only book to be published in English; it was published originally as *Contes de la solitude* (1972) and was translated into English by Margaret Rose. Among Naubert's five novels, *L'été de la cigale* (1968) won the Prix du Cercle du Livre de France and the Prix du Concours Littéraire de Québec.

Rachel de Queiróz

Rachel de Queiróz grew up in Brazil in a household that had a library of 5000 books, and later went on to write four novels between the ages of 19 and 28 that were published in the 1930s. She is one of Brazil's best writers in a field usually dominated by male writers. Her plots are melodramatic and her heroines triumphant. She has worked more recently as a critic, a translator, and a dramatist. The building where she lives today is named after her.

Abdul Ilah Abdul Razzak

Born in Basra, Iraq, in 1939, Abdul Ilah Abdul Razzak studied Arabic literature before going on to graduate from Baghdad University in 1964. He has published two collections of stories, *Journey Inside Things* (1972) and *Ophelia Has the Earth's Body* (1976). He has also worked as a critic of modern Arabic literature.

Leon Rooke

Born in North Carolina in 1934, the witty Leon Rooke moved to Victoria in 1969, then Eden Mills, Ontario, and now lives in Winnipeg. He has written the novels *Fat Woman* (1980) and the Governor General's Award–winning *Shakespeare's Dog* (1983), as well as several story collections, including *A Bolt of White Cloth* (1984) and *Painting the Dog* (2001). Rooke has written about 300 short stories and has been published in 80 national and international anthologies.

Sinclair Ross

Born on a homestead near Prince Albert, Saskatchewan, Sinclair Ross (1908–1996) worked as a bank clerk in various small towns and was eventually transferred to Winnipeg. He lived in Spain and Greece, and eventually settled in Montréal, where he worked at the Royal Bank. An acclaimed novelist, perhaps best known for his first novel, *As for Me and My House* (1941), he published an influential story collection entitled *The Lamp at Noon and Other Stories* (1968) as well. His fiction is chiefly about the psychological effects of isolation and the Depression on the lives of rural Saskatchewan families.

Carol Shields

 Born in Chicago, Carol Shields (b. 1935) is one of Canada's top fiction writers and has lived and taught university for many years in Winnipeg. An important early witty novel *Swann* (1987) won the Arthur Ellis Fiction Writer's Award. Her recent novels include *The Republic of Love* (1992), *The Stone Diaries* (1993; both a Pulitzer Prize and a Governor General's Award winner), and *Larry's Party* (1997). Selected from one of her story collections, *Various Miracles* (1985), "Invitations" is a typical Shields story about an ordinary person faced with challenging circumstances.

Anne Tyler

Anne Tyler (b. 1941) was born in Minneapolis, Minnesota, and now lives in Baltimore. Her fiction is often set in small Southern towns and frequently deals with the subjects of isolation, suburbia, family life, and death. Her novels include *If Morning Ever Comes* (1965), *Celestial Navigation* (1974), and *The Accidental Tourist* (1985), the last of which was made into a popular feature film. Tyler has said she writes "because I want more than one life."

Jane Urquhart

Born Jane Carter in Little Long Lac, Ontario, in 1949, Jane Urquhart started her writing career as a poet with collections such as *I Am Walking in the Garden of His Imaginary Palace* (1982). In 1987, she published *Storm Glass* (1987), a collection of her stories, and solidly stepped into the genre of fiction as a major talent. Her novels since include *Changing Heaven* (1990), *Away* (1993), and the Governor General's Award–winning *The Underpainter* (1997).

W.D. Valgardson

Born in the Icelandic fishing community of Gimli, Manitoba, William Dempsey Valgardson is an award-winning author whose work has been published as far away as Russia, East Germany, and the Ukraine. The National Film Board of Canada and the CBC have produced films based on his works, including his novel *Gentle Sinners* (1980). His story collections include *Bloodflowers* (1973) and *What Can't Be Changed Shouldn't Be Mourned* (1990). His stories are strong, direct, and dramatic. Currently, he teaches creative writing at the University of Victoria, and his students have included writers such as Eden Robinson and W.P. Kinsella.

John Wickham

Born in Barbados in 1932, John Wickham worked for the World Meteorological Organization before moving to Europe. He became the editor of *The Nation*, a major Barbados newspaper, in 1979. His short stories have been widely published, and his own story collection *Discoveries* came out in 1993 and is the source of "The Light on the Sea."

Liu Xin-Wu

Born in Sichuan, Liu Xin-Wu (b. 1942) taught Chinese in a Beijing school after graduating from teacher's college in 1961. He taught until 1976 and then worked as an editor. His first writing dates back to 1958, and in 1978 his story "The Form Teacher" won a national story contest. Another story, "I Love Every Leaf in Green," won the same award a year later. In 1984, his novel *The Clock Tower* won the Mao Dun Literary Prize. "Black Walls" is a 1982 story published by the Chinese Literature Press.

Mori Yoko

Mori Yoko is a longtime admirer of Western culture and frequently alludes to Western films and personalities. Her main topic is urban men and women and their relationships with one another.

Glossary of Fiction Terms

allusion

An allusion is a brief, direct, or indirect reference to a person, place, or event from history, literature, or mythology that the author hopes or assumes the reader will recognize. Most allusions expand on or develop a significant idea, impression, or mood in the story.

At the end of "Horses of the Night," there is a quotation from the classical author Ovid. That quote refers not only to Chris's horses, but also to Chris's preference for a dreamy, romantic perspective associated with night as well as his descent into madness and, finally, death.

antagonist

The antagonist is the major character or force that opposes the *protagonist*.

In "The Shining Houses," Mary's and Mrs. Fullerton's neighbours are the antagonists who oppose Mrs. Fullerton's presence and "untidiness."

antecedent action (or **antecedent information**)

"Antecedent" means "going before," so antecedent action is the significant action that takes place before the story begins.

In "Reflections of Spring," the antecedent action refers to the relationship the adult protagonist had with a girl when he was young himself.

anticlimax

An anticlimax is a sudden shift from a relatively serious or elevated mood to one more comic or trivial.

The anticlimax of "The Destructors" occurs when the lorry driver cannot help laughing about the collapse of Old Misery's house.

antihero

An antihero is a protagonist who has none of the qualities normally expected of a hero. The term also refers to a humorous take-off on the traditional hero. The characters played by Woody Allen in his films and Mr. Bean are examples of antiheroes.

An example of an antihero is Morris Glendenning in "Foxes," a somewhat "nerdy" character who wears galoshes and acts weirdly.

atmosphere (or mood)

The atmosphere or mood is the prevailing feeling created by the story. Atmosphere usually sets up expectations in the reader about the outcome of an episode or plot. It is created by descriptive diction, imagery, and sometimes dialogue. Some teachers or critics may distinguish between the two terms by referring to the "atmosphere of a story" and the "mood created in the reader."

Much of the effectiveness of "The Pigeons in St. Louis Square" depends on the author's ability to create simultaneously a sense of change and timelessness that underlies the story.

character

The term refers to both a fictional person in a story, and the moral, dispositional, and behavioural qualities of that fictional person. The qualities of a character are generally revealed through dialogue, action, and description. Characters themselves may be classified as *flat* or *round*, *stereotyped* or *realistic*, *static* or *dynamic*. Each classification is described below. See also *foil*.

- A limited, usually minor character with only one apparent quality is a *flat character*. A *round character* is a realistic character with several dimensions. In "The Jade Peony," the grandmother, the father, and the narrator are all round characters. The characters in "Half a Day" are all flat characters.
- A *realistic character* is multidimensional and clearly has complex relationships and motivations; a *stereotyped character* is totally predictable, one-dimensional, and recognizable to the reader as "of a type" (e.g., "the jock," "the brain," "the yuppie").

   The protagonist of "Identities" is a stereotypical, well-off suburban man. In contrast, Chris in "Horses of the Night" is a realistic character described at length in that story.
- A *dynamic character*, often the protagonist, is a character who undergoes a significant, lasting change, usually in her or his outlook on life. A *static character*, on the other hand, is one who does not change in the course of the story.

   The protagonist in "Reflections of Spring" is greatly changed by recalling the girl of his past, whereas the husband in "Behind the Headlines" is a static character, a fact that leads to his wife leaving him.

characterization

Characterization is the process through which the author reveals to the reader the qualities of a character. In short stories, the author will either reveal character directly (through author comments) and/or indirectly (through the character's speech, thought, or action).

In "Identities," the protagonist is characterized through direct author description, whereas in "Frustration," the two men are characterized almost entirely by their dialogue.

character sketch

A character sketch is a short description and analysis of a character's moral, dispositional, and behavioural qualities, including adjectives, specific examples, and quotations from the story. When writing a character sketch, one does not normally describe the character's physical appearance or dress, though these, incidentally, may reflect symbolically the character's personality. The following is a sample sketch of Mrs. Fullerton in "The Shining Houses":

> *Mrs. Fullerton is a static, round character with a colourful personality. A chatty person with the wisdom of hindsight, Mrs. Fullerton delights in telling Mary anecdotes about her past. She is both eccentric and optimistic, as suggested by story details such as her pet racoon and her idea that her husband may return.*
>
> *Mrs. Fullerton is also a strong, independent character who makes a living selling eggs to the neighbourhood. Her underlying pride is suggested by her response to babysitting requests: "I tell them I got my own house to sit in and I raised my share of children." She is as set in her ways as is her house: "The place had become fixed, impregnable...." She has no desire to move despite the pressure of her sons and neighbours. It is this resolute independence that finally brings her into conflict with the neighbours in "The Shining Houses."*

climax

The climax is the highest point of emotional intensity in a story. It is the major crisis in the story and usually marks the turning point in the protagonist's fortunes.

The climax of "The Destructors" comes with the collapse of Old Misery's house.

complicating incident (or complication)

The event that initiates a conflict is the complicating incident.

The complicating incident in "An Occurrence at Owl Creek Bridge" is that Peyton is going to be hanged for war crimes.

confidant (or confidante)

The confidant(e) is the person with whom a character, usually the protagonist, shares her or his thoughts, feelings, and intentions.

Vanessa is Chris's reluctant confidante one night by the lake in "Horses of the Night."

conflict

This term refers to the struggle between opposing characters or forces (e.g., the protagonist and someone or something else). Additional conflicts, in which the protagonist is not involved, may also be found in a short story. Three common types of conflict are

- *conflict between a character and her or his environment.* The "environment" may be nature, society, or circumstance.

  In "Miss Brill," the protagonist finds herself at odds with and rejected by the society she fancies herself to be a part of.

- *conflict between two characters.* This struggle may be physical, emotional, or psychological.

  In "The Destructors," the conflicts between characters are numerous (e.g., Blackie and T., Old Misery and the boys, Old Misery and the lorry driver).

- *conflict within a character.* In this case, the character experiences conflict(s) in emotion and/or thought.

  In "Spring Storm," the protagonist later regrets not telling her partner immediately about her success at the audition.

contrast (and juxtaposition)

Contrast refers to a difference, especially a striking difference, between two things being compared. In this context, contrast may involve characters, situations, settings, moods, or points of view. Contrast is used to clarify meaning, purpose, or character, or to heighten certain moods (especially humour, horror, and suspense). Juxtapositions are contrasts in which positioning is important; for example, two contrasting characters may be placed side by side in a story.

"The Setting Sun and the Rolling World" contrasts the father's and son's perceptions of their immediate surroundings and the world at large. In "Dr. Heidegger's Experiment," a moment of illusion when the younger-looking guests are quarrelling is juxtaposed with the mirror's truthful view of old people foolishly arguing.

crisis

A crisis is a moment of intense conflict. (The major crisis of the story is called the *climax.*)

A crisis occurs in "The Harness" when David is frightened by the skeleton.

denouement (or **resolution**)

Denouement (pronounced day-NEW-mahn) is the French word for "unknotting" and refers to the "unknotting" or resolution of the plot or conflict. The denouement follows the *climax* and constitutes part or all of the falling action.

The denouement in "The Lottery" occurs after Tessie has been declared the winner and is being stoned to death by the other villagers.

dialect

Dialect is a manner of speaking or variation on a language peculiar to an individual, a people, a social class, or a geographic region. A dialect differs from the standard language of a country.

The boys in "The Destructors" speak in an English dialect and use words and idioms such as "pinched" for stolen.

dialogue

Any conversation between two or more characters in a story constitutes dialogue.

diction

Diction is the vocabulary used by a writer. For each story, the writer chooses and arranges words appropriate to her or his purpose, subject, story type, characters, and style.

The contemplative, detailed, and intensely emotional diction of "The Yellow Wallpaper" echoes the narrator's obsession with the wallpaper.

dilemma

A dilemma is a situation in which a character must make a choice between two undesirable or equally destructive alternatives. Posing a dilemma is one method an author can use to generate conflict and suspense in a story.

In "Behind the Headlines," the protagonist has to choose between a repetitive, repressed existence as a housewife and a change in life and lifestyle that will mean the end of her marriage.

dynamic character See **character.**

epiphany

Epiphany refers to a moment of significant realization and insight experienced by the protagonist, often at the end of a story. As a literary term,
it originates with James Joyce, who built each short story in his
around what he called an epiphany.

At the end of "Spring Storm," the protagonist has an epiphany about her relationship with her partner.

episode

An episode is an incident or event within the main plot of the story. Episodes can be viewed as selected portions or "scenes" developed in detail by the author.

"Holding Things Together" contains many episodes, such as the narrator's trips to the service station.

escapist fiction

This refers to stories written solely to entertain the reader, thus helping the reader to escape the daily cares and problems of reality. Even though provoking thought on the part of the reader and providing entertainment for the reader are not mutually exclusive, the term "escapist fiction" suggests an extreme. Escapist fiction has lively melodramatic plots and stereotyped or flat characters, and it requires limited involvement on the part of the reader. Many mass-market science fiction tales, westerns, thrillers, and romances fall into the category of escapist fiction.

exposition

Exposition is background information provided by the author to further the development of plot, conflict, setting, and characterization.

In "Small Potatoes," the narrator's recollection of her schooldays in Boston, her initial feelings about Alaska, and her friend's history are all considered exposition.

falling action

The falling action is the section immediately following the *climax* and lasting until the end of the story.

The section of "Dr. Heidegger's Experiment" when the old visitors age again is part of the falling action.

fantasy

A fantasy is a highly exaggerated or improbable story. As a rule, fantasy has fantastic events, characters, and/or settings not found in real life.

"The Rocking-Horse Winner," "Totem," "Half a Day," "Dr. Heidegger's Experiment," "An Occurrence at Owl Creek Bridge," "'If I Forget Thee, Oh Earth ...,'" "Frustration," and "A Bolt of White Cloth" are all examples of fantasy.

fiction

Fiction is any narrative that is imagined or invented. Fiction may be based on actual happenings, which can, in turn, make fiction seem realistic.

flashback

A flashback is a sudden switch in the plot from the present to the past. This device may be used to illustrate an important point or to aid in characterization.

"Reflections of Spring" contains a flashback to the man's youth.

flat character See **character.**

foil

A foil is a character whose behaviour, attitudes, and/or opinions contrast with those of the protagonist. The contrast of the foil helps the reader to understand better the character and motivation of the protagonist.

In "Holding Things Together," Bee and Alfred are foils to the narrator.

foreshadowing

This is a device that hints at or warns of events to happen later in the story. Foreshadowing prepares the reader for the climax, the denouement, or any changes in the protagonist.

In "The Yellow Wallpaper," the narrator's early mention of her condition and her comments about her surroundings foreshadow her later mental changes.

form

In literature, form generally means "type." It can refer to the more fundamental genres of literary work (poem, short story, novel, essay) or to the way those stories are told (myth, fairy tale, parable). In poetry especially, the term is used to describe even smaller divisions within the poetic form (elegy, epic poem, sonnet), but this is true of fiction as well (science fiction, mystery).

"An Occurrence at Owl Creek Bridge" uses nineteenth-century story breaks that move the reader around in time. The sprinkling of key words associatively throughout "Roget's Thesaurus" approximates the effect of browsing a thesaurus, which is itself another text form.

goal See **motivation.**

hero (or heroine)

This is a protagonist of a story who possesses heroic qualities, such as courage, or virtues, such as honesty. The terms "hero" and "heroine" are not interchangeable with the more general term "protagonist."

humour

Humour refers to writing that is intended to amuse the reader or provoke laughter.

"Totem" uses humour to point out relationships among and differences between North American Native and non-Native cultures and attitudes.

images (and imagery)

Images are concrete details and figures of speech that help the reader form vivid impressions of the subject of the writing. Imagery refers to the pattern of images in a single piece of writing.

The opening paragraph of "The Pigeons in St. Louis Square" consists of images (e.g., "deaf to abuse") describing the pigeons and their indifference to human beings.

indeterminate ending

A story ending in which there is no clear outcome, result, or resolved conflict is called an indeterminate ending.

"Tuesday Siesta" ends indeterminately with the mother and her daughter leaving the priest's residence.

in medias res

In medias res (pronounced in MAY-deas RAS) is a Latin term that refers to readers joining a story "in the middle of things."

One story joined *in medias res* is "The Setting Sun and the Rolling World," which opens with the son coming to say goodbye to his father.

interpretive fiction

This term refers to stories that have meaningful, usually realistic plots, conflicts, settings, and characters. Interpretive fiction is usually serious in tone and designed to be interpreted. It is instructive, unlike escapist fiction, which is designed chiefly for entertainment. All of the stories in this book are examples of interpretive fiction.

irony

Irony involves contrast between two elements and, as a literary device, provides depth of meaning and impact. When irony is used, meanings tend to become unconcealed or contradictory, an effect that we call "ironic." The following are three common types of irony:

- *Verbal irony* occurs when what a character says contrasts with what the character also or actually means.

    An example of verbal irony occurs in "The Harness" when the tired David answers, "'No,' he scoffed."

- *Dramatic irony* occurs when what a character says or believes contrasts with what the reader or other characters know to be true (for example, from information given to us by the author).

    In "The Destructors," Old Misery thinks he is helping the boys, but the readers know the boys are really playing a trick on him.

- *Situational irony* (or *irony of situation*) occurs when what finally takes place is different from what was expected or seemed appropriate.

    At the end of "Identities," the relieved man reaches for his wallet, unaware that he is about to be shot in error by the policeman.

juxtaposition See **contrast**.

local colour (and **regionalism**)
Local colour refers to the detail in a story that is specific to a geographic region or an environment. Local colour develops the setting and atmosphere; increases reader interest; adds to authenticity; and includes descriptions of locale, dress, and customs as well as dialect and ways of thinking and feeling that are characteristic of people in that setting. Regionalism refers to stories in which setting (developed with local colour) is of significance to the text and necessary to the writer's purpose.

Many local colour details suggest an impoverished South American small town in "Tuesday Siesta." The regionalism of a small, claustrophobic Depression farm during a prairie winter is used by Sinclair Ross in "The Painted Door" to heighten and underscore the characters' inner conflicts and anxiety.

mood See **atmosphere**.

moral
The stated or (more commonly) implied lesson of a story is called the moral. Viewed in isolation, a moral is a relatively unimportant part of a story and should not be confused with theme, a far more significant element of fiction.

The moral of "Invitations" is do what you really want to do, not what others want you to do.

motivation (and **goal**)

Motivation is both what causes a character to do what he or she does *and* the character's aim or goal in taking that action. The character's temperament and circumstances determine motivation. The pursuit by the protagonist of her or his goal results in the story's conflict. Characters must have sufficient and plausible motivation in order for a reader to find the story effective.

The narrator of "The Light on the Sea" is motivated to go see his former, now-aged teacher in the hope of renewing a connection with him.

narrative

Narrative is another word for "story." Narratives contain the following elements: plot, conflict, characters, setting, and point of view. Narratives may be fictional or non-fictional, and include novels, autobiographies, biographies, short stories, and anecdotes.

narrator

The narrator is the storyteller. In the case of a story told from the first-person perspective, the narrator is one of the characters; in the case of a story told from the objective, omniscient, or limited omniscient points of view, the author assumes the role of narrator.

The narrator of "The Jade Peony" is Sek-Lung.

plot

The story line or organization of events or episodes within a story is called the plot. The conventional plot has rising action, a climax, and falling action. See also *subplot*.

The plot of "Storm Glass" is about a woman trying to talk to her husband about her illness, which will change their relationship forever.

point of view

The point of view is the perspective from which a story is seen or told. Point of view establishes the relationships among author, reader, and characters. The following are the three most common points of view:

- *First-person narrative* features a character telling the story directly to the reader in the first person (i.e., using "I"). This point of view tells us what the character thinks and feels from a vantage point "inside" the story, from one character's perspective.

    "The Harness" and "The Yellow Wallpaper" are stories narrated in the first person.

- *Limited omniscient* or *third-person narrative* occurs when a story is told from "outside" the characters, but from the perspective of one character. In this point of view, the characters are referred to in the third person (as "he" or "she"), and the narrator is limited to knowing the thoughts and feelings of only that one character.

Limited omniscient narratives include "Here and Now," "The Man Who Followed His Hand," and "Tuesday Siesta."

- *Omniscient narrative*, or "all-knowing" narrative, tells the story with knowledge of the thoughts and feelings of more than one or all of the characters.

Omniscient narratives include "Dr. Heidegger's Experiment," "An Occurrence at Owl Creek Bridge," and "Metonymy, or The Husband's Revenge."

- In the least common point of view, *objective narrative*, the narrator has no special knowledge, and the story is factually presented in an unemotional way.

"The Lottery" uses the objective point of view to create suspense and a surprise ending for the reader.

predicament

A predicament is a difficult problem or unpleasant situation. Predicament should not be confused with a related term, *dilemma*.

prose

Ordinary language or literary expression not marked by obvious rhythm or rhyme is called prose. This type of language is used in short stories, essays, and modern plays. The text you are now reading is written in prose.

protagonist

The protagonist is the main character of a story from whose viewpoint the story is presented. While some protagonists may be heroes or heroines (or antiheroes and antiheroines), the term protagonist is broader and does not depend on moral judgements of the characters' actions.

The farmer-narrator, not his wife or the stranger, is the protagonist in "A Bolt of White Cloth."

purpose

Purpose refers to the main effect the author hopes to achieve: entertainment, thoughtfulness, enlightenment, action, or a demonstration of something about life or human nature. Rarely does a story have only one purpose. Purpose may include theme, but should not simply be equated with the story's main idea.

The purposes of "Janus" are to explore the significance of an object in the life of someone, and to show how it reveals the essential personality of the woman in this story.

realism

This term refers to any subject matter or techniques that create a "true-to-life" impression for the reader. Writers of realism present life "as it is" and as though the stories have simply "told themselves." In another sense, realism can also refer to stories about simple, everyday people. See also *fantasy*, *romance*, and *verisimilitude*.

"The Lost Salt Gift of Blood" uses numerous realistic details to create a sense of a people's way of life.

realistic character See **character.**

regionalism See **local colour.**

resolution See **denouement.**

rising action

Rising action in a story consists of the incidents that precede the climax. During this stage of the story, background information is given, characters and conflicts are introduced, and suspense is built up. There may even be moments of crisis. Typically, the rising action is often longer than the falling action of a story. See also *plot*.

The rising action of "The Lottery" includes all the events up to the point when Tessie is declared the "winner."

romance

Romances are entertaining stories that contain one or more of the following characteristics: fantasy, improbability, extravagance, naiveté, love, adventure, and myth.

"The Rocking-Horse Winner," "A Bolt of White Cloth," and "Half a Day" are all romances.

round character See **character.**

satire

Satire is the use of irony to ridicule an idea, a person, or a thing, often with the aim of provoking change. Satire usually targets human foibles or vices.

"Frustration" is a satire about the nature of human beings and computers, and the role of technology in preventing world-wide destruction.

science fiction

Science fiction is writing that speculates about the effects of technology or science on the future of human beings. While the purpose of some science fiction is purely escapist entertainment, science fiction can be written for a range of serious purposes, too.

"'If I Forget Thee, Oh Earth ...'" and "Frustration" are examples of science fiction.

setting

The setting is the time and place of a story. While in some stories setting may only minimally affect the plot, conflict, characters, and theme, in others it can be of great significance and be the main fictional element.

In "The Painted Door," the drab life of the Depression farm and the tumult of the winter storm are important in creating an atmosphere of anxiety and isolation.

short story

A short story is a brief fictional prose narrative, having one character, a single plot, limited setting, and one main effect. Edgar Allan Poe, one of the first significant theorists and practitioners of short story writing, said that short stories

1. can be read in one sitting, and derive their power from the fact the writer has to select details for economy and emphasis;
2. have a single effect or purpose and are constructed so that every sentence from the first to the last one supports that effect;
3. leave the reader with a feeling of satisfaction and finality, desiring no further completion or alternative ending;
4. have their basis in truth or lifelikeness.

static character See character.

stereotype

A stereotype is any fixed pattern of plot or character. Stereotyped plots usually fall into the realm of escapist fiction. Stereotyped characters are familiar figures in fiction, such as the "hard-boiled" private investigator, the "absent-minded" professor, the military officer with a "stiff upper lip." See also *character*.

The stereotype of the mysterious stranger is used in "A Bolt of White Cloth."

stream of consciousness

Stream of consciousness is a modern narrative technique that attempts to depict the uninterrupted flow of feelings and random thoughts of a character's mind. However, the author includes details relevant to plot, character, and theme in the apparently natural flow of thoughts and feelings.

In "The Pigeons in St. Louis Square," the narration occasionally shifts to the stream-of-consciousness of the birds.

style

Style is the individual manner in which an author expresses herself or himself. In fiction, style is basically determined by such grammatical and sensory aspects as diction, grammar, and images.

Because of its matter-of-fact description and folksy tone, "The Lottery" seems at first to be a simple, sentimental story about a day in the life of a rural community. Jackson's style misleads the reader's expectations in order to create a surprise ending.

subplot

A subplot is a minor story line, secondary to the main plot. Subplots may be related or unrelated to the main action, but may also be a reflection of or variation on the main plot. Compared with novels, short stories tend to have few, brief subplots (or none) because of the brevity and density required of the short story genre.

In "The Rocking-Horse Winner," the various betting episodes with Uncle Oscar are examples of a subplot.

surprise ending

The sudden twist in the direction of a story, producing a resolution that surprises the reader and often the story's characters as well, is called a surprise ending.

The last paragraph of "The Man Who Followed His Hand," in which the man's hand reveals he is still in the tree the next morning, is an example of a surprise ending.

suspense

Suspense is the feeling of anxiety and uncertainty experienced by the reader (and possibly characters) about the outcome of events or the protagonist's fate.

"Metonymy, or The Husband's Revenge" is suspenseful until the ending, when it is revealed who the jealous husband shot.

symbol

A symbol is something that stands for or represents something else. Characters, objects, events, conflicts, and settings can all be symbolic.

The paint colour in "Black Walls" symbolizes the tenant's unconventionality.

thematic statement

This is a one-sentence, general statement about life or human nature that can be derived by interpreting a story's overall message. It does not mention specifics from the story (e.g., specific names, settings, or events), but instead generalizes, accurately and comprehensively, the story's main meaning.

A theme statement for "Invitations" might be: Individuals may be better off doing what they really want to do than submitting to the will and wishes of society.

theme

The theme is the central idea of the story, usually implied rather than directly stated. It is a story's observation about life or human nature, and should never be confused with the moral.

The main idea of "Voices from Near and Far" is that parents are often emotionally devastated when their children leave home, especially in times of crisis.

universality

Universality is the quality of a story that gives it relevance beyond the narrow confines of its particular characters, subject, or setting. Stories that have universality reveal human nature or common truths of life experience. Universality in a story also implies that the story pretty much could apply to most or all people's experience.

"The Destructors" has a universality far beyond the setting of wartime London and the pranks of a gang. It suggests a fundamental male instinct to destroy and make war as well as the pleasure of destruction.

verisimilitude

Verisimilitude is a lifelike quality possessed by a story as revealed through its plot, setting, conflict, and characterization. See also *realism*.

Verisimilitude can be seen in the details of city street life described in "Foxes" as Morris walks to the museum.

vicarious experience

Vicarious experience refers to the reader sharing imaginatively in a character's feelings and experiences. Vicarious (literally, "acting or done for another") experiences can be had, for example, through reading travel literature.

"An Occurrence at Owl Creek Bridge" works because the reader vicariously experiences Peyton's hanging, escape, and eventual death.

Permission Credits

Every reasonable effort has been made to acquire permission for copyright material used in this book, and to acknowledge all such indebtedness accurately. However, all errors and omissions called to our attention will be corrected in future printings. In particular, any information regarding the copyright holders of the stories **"The Day They Set Out"** by Beverly Harris and **"Black Walls"** by Liu Xin-Wu would be greatly appreciated.

Unit One: **"Identities"** by W.D. Valgardson. From WHAT CAN'T BE CHANGED SHOULDN'T BE MOURNED. Copyright © W.D. Valgardson. Published in Canada by Douglas & McIntyre Ltd. Reprinted by permission of the publisher. **"The Shining Houses"** by Alice Munro from DANCE OF THE HAPPY SHADES. Reprinted by permission of the author's agent, Virginia Barber Literary Agency. **"Invitations"** by Carol Shields, extracted from VARIOUS MIRACLES by Carol Shields. Copyright © 1985 by Carol Shields. Reprinted by permission of Random House Canada, a division of Random House Limited. **"The Lottery"** by Shirley Jackson from THE LOTTERY AND OTHER STORIES. Reprinted by permission of Farrar, Straus & Giroux. **"Here and Now"** by Janette Turner Hospital from THE OXFORD BOOK OF STORIES BY CANADIAN WOMEN IN ENGLISH. Reprinted by permission of the author. **"On 'Miss Brill'"** by Kate Fullbrook. From KATHERINE MANSFIELD by Kate Fullbrook. Reprinted by permission of Indiana University Press. **"The Man Who Followed His Hand"** by Connie Gault. From INSPECTION OF A SMALL VILLAGE by Connie Gault. Published by Coteau Books. Reprinted with permission of the publisher. **"Foxes"** by Timothy Findley. From STONES (Viking, 1988). Copyright © 1987 Pebble Productions Inc. Reprinted with permission of the author and Westwood Creative Artists. **"The Jade Peony"** by Wayson Choy from VANCOUVER SHORT STORIES. Reprinted by permission of the author. **"Totem"** by Thomas King. From WHETSTONE (Fall 1988). Copyright © 1988 by Dead Dog Café Productions Inc. Reprinted with permission of the author and Westwood Creative Artists. **"Storm Glass"** by Jane Urquhart. From STORM GLASS by Jane Urquhart. Used by

Page 90: Ivy Images.

Page 106: Eduardo Garcia/Getty Images/FPG International.

Page 128: Daryl Benson/Masterfile.

Page 137: copyright © Susie Cushner/Graphistock.

Page 146: copyright Jonathan Bailey/Graphistock.

Page 176: copyright Ron Fehling/Masterfile.

Page 188: David H. Wells/Photonica.

Page 191: David S. Robbins/Getty Images/Stone.

Page 224: Wayne R. Bilenduke/Getty Images/Stone.

Page 250: Patrik Giardino/CORBIS/MAGMA.

Page 304: James P. Blair/National Geographic Image Collection.

Page 315: copyright © Kimbell Art Museum/CORBIS/MAGMA.

Page 323: Getty Images/Eyewire.

Page 352: Getty Images/Photodisk.

Page 384: copyright © Bruce Stromberg/Graphistock.

Page 408: Getty Images/Photodisk.

Page 410: Getty Images/Eyewire.

Page 458: PHOTOMONDO/Getty Images/FPG International.

Page 466: Jayne Hinds Bidaut/Graphistock.

Author Photos

Wayson Choy: Keith Beatty/Toronto Star/CP Picture Archive.

Timothy Findley: Dean Bicknell/Calgary Herald/CP Picture Archive.

Connie Gault: Courtesy of Connie Gault.

Thomas King: Dean Palmer/Courtesy of Thomas King.

Margaret Laurence: CP Picture Archive.

Gabriel García Márquez: CP Picture Archive.

Alice Munro: Toronto Star/CP Picture Archive.

Leon Rooke: Courtesy of Thomas Allen Publishers.

Sinclair Ross: CP Picture Archive.

Carol Shields: Courtesy of Random House of Canada.